Longman
INTRODUCTORY COURSE
FOR THE TOEFL® TEST

The Paper Test

Deborah Phillips

Longman

Longman Introductory Course for the TOEFL® Test: The Paper Test

Pearson Education, 10 Bank Street, White Plains, NY 10606

Editorial director: Pam Fishman
Project manager: Margo Grant
Development editor: Angela Castro
Vice president, director of design and production: Rhea Banker
Executive managing editor: Linda Moser
Production editors: Helen B. Ambrosio, Michael Mone
Production coordinator: Melissa Leyva
Director of manufacturing: Patrice Fraccio
Senior manufacturing buyer: Nancy Flaggman
Cover design: Ann France
CD-ROM project manager: Evelyn Fella
CD-ROM development editor: Lisa Hutchins
CD-ROM programmers: RKG Interactive Multimedia Solutions
Text design adaptation: Page Designs International, Inc.
Text composition: Page Designs International, Inc.

Library of Congress Cataloging-in-Publication Data

Phillips, Deborah
    Longman introductory course for the TOEFL test: the paper test / Deborah Phillips.
        p. cm.
    ISBN 0-13-184718-X (with answer key) — **ISBN 0-13-184719-8**
    1. English language—Textbooks for foreign speakers. 2. Test of English as a foreign language—Study guides. 3. English language—Examinations—Study guides. I. Title.

PE1128.P44 2004
428'.0076—dc22

2004040921

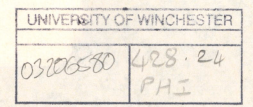

LONGMAN ON THE·WEB

Longman.com offers online resources for teachers and students. Access our Companion Websites, our online catalog, and our local offices around the world.

Visit us at **longman.com.**

Printed in the United States of America
7 8 9 10–CRK–09

CONTENTS

The Written Expression Questions   94

SECTION THREE: READING COMPREHENSION

INTRODUCTION

ABOUT THIS COURSE

PURPOSE OF THE COURSE

This course is intended to prepare students for the paper version of the TOEFL® (Test of English as a Foreign Language) test. It is based on the most up-to-date information available on the format and content of the paper TOEFL test.

Longman Introductory Course for the TOEFL Test: The Paper Test can be used in a variety of ways, depending on the needs of the reader:

1. It can be used as the primary text in a course emphasizing TOEFL test preparation.
2. It can be used as a supplementary text in a more general ESL course.
3. Along with its companion audio program, it can be used as a tool for individualized study by students preparing for the TOEFL test outside of the ESL classroom.

LEVEL OF THE BOOK

Longman Introductory Course for the TOEFL Test: The Paper Test is intended for students whose TOEFL scores are in the 380–480 range on the paper TOEFL test. This text starts *below* the level of the TOEFL test and continues up to the level of the *easier questions* on the TOEFL test. It presents and practices those language skills that appear regularly on the paper TOEFL test and are appropriate to this level.

This book is intended to be used by students who are interested in preparing for the paper TOEFL test but who are not yet ready for all of the materials found on this test. It can be used most effectively to introduce lower-level TOEFL skills and strategies prior to the study of the more advanced *Longman Preparation Course for the TOEFL Test: The Paper Test.*

WHAT IS IN THE BOOK

This book contains a variety of materials which together provide a comprehensive preparation program:

- **Diagnostic Pre-Tests** for each section of the test measure students' level of performance and allow students to determine specific areas of weakness.
- **Language Skills** for each section of the test, including the Test of Written English (TWE), provide students with a thorough understanding of the language skills that are regularly tested on the TOEFL test.
- **Test-Taking Strategies** for each section of the test provide students with clearly defined steps to maximize their performance on the test.
- **Exercises** provide practice of one or more skills in a non-TOEFL format.
- **TOEFL Exercises** provide practice of one or more skills in a TOEFL format.
- **TOEFL Review Exercises** provide practice of all of the skills taught up to that point in a TOEFL format.

- **TOEFL Post-Tests** for each section of the test measure the progress that students have made after working through the skills and strategies in the text.
- **Introductory-Level Complete Practice Tests** allow students to review all of the lower-level skills taught throughout the text in TOEFL-format tests.
- A **TOEFL-Level Complete Practice Test** provides students with the opportunity to see how the skills they have learned in this text will be incorporated into an actual TOEFL test. This test also provides students with the opportunity to determine their approximate TOEFL scores.
- **Scoring Information** allows students to determine their approximate TOEFL scores on the TOEFL-Level Complete Practice Test.
- **Diagnostic Charts** allow students to monitor their progress in specific language skills on the Pre-Tests, Post-Tests, and Complete Tests so that they can easily determine which skills have been mastered and which skills require further study.
- **Progress Charts** allow students to monitor their score improvement from the Pre-Tests to the Post-Tests and Complete Tests.
- **Recording Scripts** allow students to see the text of all the listening exercises and tests included on the audiocassettes/audio CDs.
- **Answer Sheets** allow students to practice using appropriate test forms.

WHAT IS ON THE CD-ROM

Longman Introductory CD-ROM for the TOEFL Test: The Paper Test, with over 900 questions in the format of the paper TOEFL test and 120 additional writing-practice questions, includes a variety of materials that contribute to an effective preparation program for the paper version of the TOEFL test:

- **An Overview** describes the features of the CD-ROM.
- **Skills Practice Sections** for each of the sections on the paper version of the TOEFL test, including the Test of Written English (TWE), provide students with the opportunity to review and master each of the language skills on the test.
- **Test Sections** for each section of the paper version of the TOEFL test allow students to take authentic test sections and to measure their progress. Writing tests can be printed for feedback and review.
- **Answers** and **Explanations** for all practice and test items allow students to understand their errors and learn from their mistakes.
- **Skill Reports** relate the test items on the CD-ROM to the language skills presented in the book.
- **Scoring** and **Record-Keeping** enable students to record and print out charts that keep track of their progress on all practice and test items.

The following chart describes the contents of the CD-ROM:

	SKILLS PRACTICE		SECTION TESTS	
LISTENING COMPREHENSION	**Short Dialogues**		**Listening Comprehension Tests**	
	Skill 1	10 questions	*Test 1*	50 questions
	Skill 2	10 questions	*Test 2*	50 questions
	Skill 3	10 questions	*Test 3*	50 questions
	Skill 4	10 questions		
	Skill 5	10 questions		
	Skill 6	10 questions		
	Conversations			
	Conversation 1	4 questions		
	Conversation 2	4 questions		
	Conversation 3	4 questions		
	Talks			
	Talk 1	4 questions		
	Talk 2	4 questions		
	Talk 3	4 questions		
STRUCTURE AND WRITTEN EXPRESSION	**Structure**		**Structure and Written Expression Tests**	
	Skills 1–2	20 questions	*Test 1*	40 questions
	Skills 3–4	20 questions	*Test 2*	40 questions
	Skills 5–6	20 questions	*Test 3*	40 questions
	Skills 7–8	20 questions	*Test 4*	40 questions
	Skills 9–10	20 questions	*Test 5*	40 questions
	Written Expression			
	Skills 11–13	20 questions		
	Skills 14–15	20 questions		
	Skills 16–18	20 questions		
	Skills 19–20	20 questions		
	Skills 21–23	20 questions		
	Skills 24–25	20 questions		
READING COMPREHENSION	**Main Idea Questions**		**Reading Comprehension Tests**	
	Skill 1	3 questions	*Test 1*	50 questions
	Skill 1	4 questions	*Test 2*	50 questions
	Skill 1	4 questions	*Test 3*	50 questions
	Stated Detail Questions			
	Skill 2	5 questions		
	Skill 2	7 questions		
	Skills 1–2	8 questions		

	SKILLS PRACTICE		SECTION TESTS	
READING COMPREHENSION (continued)	**Unstated Detail Questions**			
	Skill 3	6 questions		
	Skill 3	6 questions		
	Skills 1–3	7 questions		
	Implied Detail Questions			
	Skill 4	5 questions		
	Skill 4	5 questions		
	Skills 1–4	10 questions		
	Vocabulary in Context Questions			
	Skill 5	8 questions		
	Skill 5	7 questions		
	Skills 1–5	9 questions		
	"Where" Questions			
	Skill 6	6 questions		
	Skill 6	7 questions		
	Skills 1–6	11 questions		
TEST OF WRITTEN ENGLISH (TWE)	**Before and While Writing**		**TWE Tests**	
	Skills 1–5	16 questions	*Test 1*	1 question
	Skills 1–5	16 questions	*Test 2*	1 question
	Skills 1–5	16 questions	*Test 3*	1 question
			Test 4	1 question
	After Writing		*Test 5*	1 question
	Skill 6	20 questions	*Test 6*	1 question
	Skill 7A	20 questions	*Test 7*	1 question
	Skill 7B	20 questions	*Test 8*	1 question
	Skill 7C	20 questions	*Test 9*	1 question
			Test 10	1 question

This CD-ROM has been developed specifically to provide practice opportunities for the paper TOEFL test. To the extent possible, all question formats simulate those on the actual paper TOEFL test and the Test of Written English (TWE).

WHAT IS ON THE AUDIO PROGRAM

The audio program, which can be purchased to accompany this book, includes all the recorded material from the Listening Comprehension section. This program is available on either audio CDs or audiocassettes. Tracking information is included with the audio CDs.

OTHER AVAILABLE MATERIALS

Longman publishes a full suite of materials for TOEFL preparation, for both the paper and computer-based tests and for both intermediate and advanced students. Preparation materials are available for both course-based instruction and self-study. Please contact Longman's website—www.longman.com—for a complete list of these products.

ABOUT THE PAPER VERSION OF THE TOEFL TEST_____

OVERVIEW OF THE TEST

The TOEFL test is a test to measure the English proficiency of nonnative speakers of English. It is required primarily by English-language colleges and universities. Additionally, institutions such as government agencies, businesses, or scholarship programs may require this test. The TOEFL test currently exists in paper and computer formats. (The purpose of this book is to prepare students for the *paper* version of the TOEFL test. There are other Longman products to prepare students for the *computer* version of the TOEFL test.)

DESCRIPTION OF THE TEST

The paper version of the TOEFL test currently has the following sections:

- **Listening Comprehension:** To demonstrate their ability to understand spoken English, examinees must listen to various types of passages on a recording and respond to multiple-choice questions about the passages.
- **Structure and Written Expression:** To demonstrate their ability to recognize grammatically correct English, examinees must either choose the correct way to complete sentences or find errors in sentences.
- **Reading Comprehension:** To demonstrate their ability to understand written English, examinees must answer multiple-choice questions about the ideas and the meanings of words in reading passages.
- **Test of Written English (TWE):** To demonstrate their ability to produce correct, organized, and meaningful English, examinees must write an essay on a given topic in 30 minutes. The TWE is not given with every administration of the paper TOEFL test, and its score is not included in the overall TOEFL score. It is possible for you to determine whether or not the TWE will be given at a particular administration of the TOEFL test when you register for the test.

The probable format of a paper TOEFL test is outlined below. (It should be noted that on certain unannounced occasions a longer version of the paper TOEFL test is given.)

SECTION	QUESTIONS	TIME
Listening Comprehension	50 multiple-choice questions	35 minutes
Structure and Written Expression	40 multiple-choice questions	25 minutes
Reading Comprehension	50 multiple-choice questions	55 minutes
Test of Written English (TWE)	1 essay question	30 minutes

REGISTRATION FOR THE TEST

It is important to understand the following information about registration for the TOEFL test:

- The first step in the registration process is to obtain a copy of the *TOEFL Information Bulletin*. This bulletin can be obtained by ordering it or downloading it from the TOEFL website www.toefl.org, by calling 1-609-771-7100, or by mailing a request to this address:

> TOEFL Services
> Educational Testing Service
> P.O. Box 6151
> Princeton, NJ 08541-6151 USA

- From the bulletin, it is possible to determine when and where the paper version of the TOEFL test is being given.
- It is important to pay attention to registration deadlines. Registration deadlines are listed in the *TOEFL Information Bulletin;* they are generally four weeks before test dates for test centers in the United States and Canada and six weeks before test dates for test centers overseas. The registration deadlines listed in the *TOEFL Information Bulletin* are dates by which registration requests must be received by ETS; they are not dates by which registration requests must be mailed.
- Procedures for completing the registration form and submitting it are listed in the *TOEFL Information Bulletin*. These procedures must be followed exactly. Contact information for submitting registration forms from different parts of the world is listed in the *TOEFL Information Bulletin*.

HOW THE TEST IS SCORED

Students should keep the following information in mind about the scoring of the paper TOEFL test:

- The paper version of the TOEFL test is scored on a scale of 217 to 677 points.
- There is no passing score on the TOEFL test, but various institutions and organizations have their own TOEFL requirements. It is important for students to find out from each institution or organization what TOEFL score is required by that institution or organization.
- The Test of Written English (TWE) may or may not be given at a particular administration of the TOEFL test. If the TWE is given, it is scored on a scale of 1 to 6, and this score is not included in the overall TOEFL score.
- The dates when scores will be mailed out are listed in the *TOEFL Information Bulletin*. Scores are generally mailed out approximately five weeks after the test date for test centers in the United States and Canada and approximately six weeks after the test date for overseas centers.

TO THE STUDENT

HOW TO PREPARE FOR THE PAPER VERSION OF THE TOEFL TEST

The paper version of the TOEFL test is a standardized test of English. To do well on this test, you should therefore work in these areas to improve your score:

- You must work to improve your knowledge of the English *language skills* that are covered on the paper version of the TOEFL test.
- You must understand the *test-taking strategies* that are appropriate for the paper version of the TOEFL test.
- You must take *practice tests* with a focus on applying your knowledge of the appropriate language skills and test-taking strategies.

This book can familiarize you with the English language skills and test-taking strategies necessary for the paper version of the TOEFL test, and it can also provide you with a considerable amount of test practice. Additional practice of the English language skills, test-taking strategies, and tests for the paper version of the TOEFL test are found on the CD-ROM.

HOW TO USE THIS BOOK

This book provides a variety of materials to help you prepare for the paper version of the TOEFL test. Following these steps can help you to get the most out of this book:

- Take the Diagnostic Pre-Test at the beginning of each section. When you take the Pre-Test, try to reproduce the conditions and time pressure of a real TOEFL test.
  - (A) Take each section of the test without interruption.
  - (B) Work on one section at a time.
  - (C) Use the answer sheets from the back of the book.
  - (D) Use a pencil to fill in the answer oval completely.
  - (E) Erase any changes that you make carefully. If answers are not completely erased on the actual TOEFL answer sheet, they will be marked wrong.
  - (F) Time yourself for each test section. You need to experience the time pressure that exists on the actual TOEFL test.
  - (G) Play the recording one time only during the test. (You may play it more times when you are reviewing the test.)
  - (H) Mark only your answer sheet. You cannot write in a TOEFL test booklet.

- After you complete the Pre-Test, you should check your answers, diagnose your incorrect answers, and record your results.
  - (A) Check your answers using the Answer Key at the back of the book (if it is included) or according to the teacher's instructions.
  - (B) Complete the appropriate part of the Diagnostic Charts on pages 357–363 to determine which language skills you have already mastered and which need further study.
  - (C) Record your results on the Progress Chart on page 353.

- Work through the presentation and exercises for each section, paying particular attention to the skills that caused you problems in the Pre-Test. Each time that you complete a TOEFL-format exercise, try to simulate the conditions and time pressure of a real TOEFL test.
  - (A) For listening questions, play the recording one time only. Do not stop the recording between questions.
  - (B) For structure questions, allow yourself one minute for two questions. (For example, you should take five minutes for an exercise with ten questions.)
  - (C) For reading comprehension questions, allow yourself one minute for one question. (For example, if a reading passage has ten questions, you should allow yourself ten minutes to read the passage and answer the ten questions.)

- When further practice on a specific point is included in an Appendix, a note in the text directs you to this practice. Complete the Appendix exercises on a specific point when the text directs you to those exercises and it is an area that you need to improve.

- When you have completed all the skills exercises for a section, take the Post-Test for that section. Follow the directions above to reproduce the conditions and time pressure of a real TOEFL test. After you complete the Post-Test, follow the directions above to check your answers, diagnose your incorrect answers, and record your results.

- When you have completed approximately half of the course material, take the first of the Introductory-Level Complete Tests. Be sure to reproduce the conditions and time pressure of a real test. After the test, check your answers, diagnose your incorrect answers, and record your results.

- When you have completed the rest of the course material, take the second of the Introductory-Level Complete Tests. Be sure to reproduce the conditions and time pressure of a real test. After the test, check your answers, diagnose your incorrect answers, and record your results.

- When you have completed both Introductory-Level Complete Tests, take the TOEFL-Level Complete Test. Be sure to reproduce the conditions and time pressure of a real test. After the test, check your answers, diagnose your incorrect answers, determine your approximate TOEFL score, and record your results.

HOW TO USE THE CD-ROM

The CD-ROM provides additional practice of the English language skills and paper version tests to supplement the language skills and tests in the book. The material on the CD-ROM is completely different from the material in the book in order to provide the maximum amount of practice. Following these steps can help you to get the most out of the CD-ROM.

Skills Practice
- After you have completed the language skills in the book, you should complete the related skills practice exercises on the CD-ROM (see chart on next page).
- Work slowly and carefully through the skills practice exercises. The skills practice exercises are not timed but instead are designed to be done in a methodical and thoughtful way.
  - (A) Answer a question on the CD-ROM using the skills and strategies that you have learned in the book.
  - (B) Use the *Check Answer* button to determine whether the answer to that question is correct or incorrect.

	AFTER THIS IN THE BOOK:	COMPLETE THIS ON THE CD-ROM:
LISTENING COMPREHENSION	*Short Dialogues: Skill 1* *Short Dialogues: Skill 2* *Short Dialogues: Skill 3* *Short Dialogues: Skill 4* *Short Dialogues: Skill 5* *Short Dialogues: Skill 6*	*Short Dialogues: Skill 1* *Short Dialogues: Skill 2* *Short Dialogues: Skill 3* *Short Dialogues: Skill 4* *Short Dialogues: Skill 5* *Short Dialogues: Skill 6*
	Conversations: Skills 7–9	*Conversations: Conversation 1* *Conversations: Conversation 2* *Conversations: Conversation 3*
	Talks: Skills 10–12	*Talks: Talk 1* *Talks: Talk 2* *Talks: Talk 3*
STRUCTURE AND WRITTEN EXPRESSION	*Structure: Skills 1–2* *Structure: Skills 3–4* *Structure: Skills 5–6* *Structure: Skills 7–8* *Structure: Skills 9–10*	*Structure: Skills 1–2* *Structure: Skills 3–4* *Structure: Skills 5–6* *Structure: Skills 7–8* *Structure: Skills 9–10*
	Written Expression: Skills 11–13 *Written Expression: Skills 14–15* *Written Expression: Skills 16–18* *Written Expression: Skills 19–20* *Written Expression: Skills 21–23* *Written Expression: Skills 24–25*	*Written Expression: Skills 11–13* *Written Expression: Skills 14–15* *Written Expression: Skills 16–18* *Written Expression: Skills 19–20* *Written Expression: Skills 21–23* *Written Expression: Skills 24–25*
READING COMPREHENSION	*Reading Comprehension: Skill 1* *Reading Comprehension: Skill 2* *Reading Comprehension: Skill 3* *Reading Comprehension: Skill 4* *Reading Comprehension: Skill 5* *Reading Comprehension: Skill 6*	*Reading Comprehension: Skill 1* *Reading Comprehension: Skill 2* *Reading Comprehension: Skill 3* *Reading Comprehension: Skill 4* *Reading Comprehension: Skill 5* *Reading Comprehension: Skill 6*
TEST OF WRITTEN ENGLISH (TWE)	*TWE: Skills 1–5* *TWE: Skill 6* *TWE: Skill 7A* *TWE: Skill 7B* *TWE: Skill 7C*	*TWE: Skills 1–5 (Passage 1)* *TWE: Skills 1–5 (Passage 2)* *TWE: Skills 1–5 (Passage 3)* *TWE: Skill 6* *TWE: Skill 7A* *TWE: Skill 7B* *TWE: Skill 7C*

(C) If your answer is incorrect, reconsider the question and choose a different answer.

(D) Use the *Check Answer* button to check your new response. (In the Listening Comprehension section, you may listen to a passage again by using the *Listen* button.)

(E) When you are satisfied that you have figured out as much as you can on your own, use the *Explain Answer* button to see an explanation. (In the Listening Comprehension section, you may see the recording script as you listen to a passage again by using the *View Script* button.)

(F) Then move on to the next question and repeat this process.

- As you work your way through the skills practice exercises, monitor your progress on the charts included in the program.

  (A) The *Score Reports* include a list of each of the exercises that you have completed and how well you have done on each of the exercises. (If you do an exercise more than once, the results of each attempt will be listed.)

  (B) The *Skill Reports* include a list of each of the language skills in the book, how many questions related to that language skill you have answered, and what percentage of the questions you have answered correctly. In this way, you can see clearly which language skills you have mastered and which language skills require further study.

Section Tests

- Use the section tests on the CD-ROM periodically throughout the course to determine how well you have learned to apply the language skills and test-taking strategies presented in the course. The CD-ROM includes three Listening Comprehension section tests, five Structure and Written Expression section tests, three Reading Comprehension section tests, and ten Test of Written English (TWE) section tests.

- Take the tests in a manner that is as close as possible to the actual testing environment. Choose a time when you can work on a section without interruption.

- Work straight through each timed test section. The *Check Answer, Explain Answer,* and *Listen* buttons are available only in the skills practice activities. The test section is designed to be as close as possible to an actual test.

- After you complete a test section, follow the directions to go to the *Score Report* for the test that you just completed. The number correct is given in the upper right corner of the *Score Report* for the test that you just completed.

- In the *Score Report,* see which questions you answered correctly and incorrectly and see which language skills were tested in each question. Print this *Score Report* if you would like to keep your *Score Reports* together in a notebook.

- In the *Score Report* for the test that you just completed, review each question by double-clicking on a particular question. When you double-click on a question in the *Score Report,* you can see the question, the answer that you chose, the correct answer, and the *Explain Answer* button. You may click on the *Explain Answer* button to see an explanation.

- Return to the *Score Report* for a particular test whenever you would like by entering through the *Scores* button on the Main Menu. You do not need to review a test section immediately but may instead wait to review the test section.

TO THE TEACHER

HOW TO GET THE MOST OUT OF THE EXERCISES

The exercises are a vital part of the TOEFL preparation process presented in this book. Maximum benefit can be obtained from the exercises if students are properly prepared for the exercises and if the exercises are carefully reviewed after completion.

- Be sure that students have a clear idea of the appropriate skills and strategies involved in each exercise. Before beginning each exercise, review the skills and strategies that are used in that exercise. Then, when you review the exercises, reinforce the skills and strategies that can be used to determine the correct answers.
- As you review the exercises, be sure to discuss each answer, the incorrect answers as well as the correct answers. Discuss how students can determine that each correct answer is correct and each incorrect answer is incorrect.
- Two different methods are possible to review the listening exercises. One good way to review these exercises is to play back the recording, stopping after each question to discuss the skills and strategies involved in determining which answer is correct and which ones are incorrect. Another method is to have students refer to the recording script at the back of the book to discuss each question.
- The structure exercises in the correct/incorrect format present a challenge for the teacher. In exercises in which students are asked to indicate which sentences are correct and which are incorrect, it is extremely helpful for students to correct the incorrect sentences. An indication of the type of error and/or one possible correction for each incorrect sentence is included in the Answer Key. It should be noted, however, that many of the incorrect sentences can be corrected in several ways. The role of the teacher is to assist students in finding various ways that the sentences can be corrected.
- The exercises are designed to be completed in class rather than assigned as homework. The exercises are short and take very little time to complete, particularly since it is important to keep students under time pressure while they are working on the exercises. Considerably more time should be spent in reviewing the exercises than in actually doing them.

HOW TO GET THE MOST OUT OF THE TESTS

There are four different types of tests in this book: Pre-Tests, Post-Tests, Introductory-Level Complete Practice Tests, and a TOEFL-Level Complete Practice Test. When the tests are given, it is important that the test conditions be as similar to actual TOEFL test conditions as possible; each section of the test should be given without interruption and under the time pressure of the actual test. Review of the tests should emphasize the function served by each of these different types of tests:

- While reviewing the Pre-Tests, you should encourage students to determine the areas where they require further practice.
- While reviewing the Post-Tests, you should emphasize the language skills and strategies involved in determining the correct answer to each question.

- While reviewing the Introductory-Level Complete Tests, you should emphasize overall strategies for the Complete Tests and review the variety of individual language skills and strategies taught throughout the course.
- While reviewing the TOEFL-Level Complete Test, you should again emphasize overall strategies and thoroughly review those questions that test the language skills taught in this book.

HOW TO GET THE MOST OUT OF THE CD-ROM

The CD-ROM is designed to supplement the practice that is contained in the book and to provide an alternate modality for preparation for the paper version of the TOEFL test. It has a number of features that make it easy to incorporate the CD-ROM into a preparation program for the paper version of the TOEFL test. Here are some ideas to consider as you decide how to incorporate the CD-ROM into your course:

- The CD-ROM is closely coordinated with the book and is intended to provide further practice for the skills and strategies that are presented in the book. This means that the overall organization of the CD-ROM parallels the organization of the book but that the exercise material and test items on the CD-ROM are different from those found in the book. It can thus be quite effective to teach and practice the language skills and strategies in the book and then use the CD-ROM for further practice and assignments.
- The CD-ROM can be used in a computer lab during class time (if you are lucky enough to have access to a computer lab during class time), but it does not need to be used in this way. It can also be quite effective to use the book during class time and to make assignments from the CD-ROM for the students to complete outside of class, either in the school computer lab or on their personal computers. Either method works quite well.
- The CD-ROM contains both a Skills Practice section and a Test section with completely different questions in each of these sections. In the Skills Practice section, students can practice and assess their mastery of specific skills. In the Test section, students can see how well they are able to apply their knowledge of the language skills and test-taking strategies to realistic test sections.
- The CD-ROM scores the Skills Practice exercises and Test sections by showing the number correct for each section. (Equivalent TOEFL scores are not given for the section tests on the CD-ROM because all of the section tests on the CD-ROM are Introductory-Level tests.
- The CD-ROM contains printable *Skill Report* and *Score Report* forms so that you can easily and efficiently keep track of your students' progress. You may want to ask your students to print their *Score Reports* after they complete each exercise and compile the *Score Reports* in a notebook; you can then ask students to turn in their notebooks periodically so that you can easily check that the assignments have been completed and monitor the progress that students are making.
- The CD-ROM allows you to work with the Test of Written English (TWE) tests in a number of ways. In the Test section of the CD-ROM, the TWE task is to write an essay within 30 minutes. The essays can be printed when they are written so that they can be reviewed and analyzed. The essays are also automatically saved and can be accessed through the Scores Menu. It is also possible for the students to copy their essays into a word processing program so that they can make changes, corrections, and improvements to their essays.

SECTION ONE

LISTENING COMPREHENSION

1 □ 1 □ 1 □ 1 □ 1 □ 1 □ 1 □ 1

DIAGNOSTIC PRE-TEST

SECTION 1
LISTENING COMPREHENSION
Time—approximately 35 minutes
(including the reading of the directions for each part)

In this section of the test, you will have an opportunity to demonstrate your ability to understand conversations and talks in English. There are three parts to this section, with special directions for each part. Answer all the questions on the basis of what is **stated** or **implied** by the speakers you hear. Do **not** take notes or write in your test book at any time. Do **not** turn the pages until you are told to do so.

Part A

Directions: In Part A you will hear short conversations between two people. After each conversation, you will hear a question about the conversation. The conversations and questions will not be repeated. After you hear a question, read the four possible answers in your test book and choose the best answer. Then, on your answer sheet, find the number of the question and fill in the space that corresponds to the letter of the answer you have chosen.

Here is an example.

Sample Answer

Ⓐ
Ⓑ
Ⓒ
●

On the recording, you will hear:

(man)   *That exam was just awful.*
(woman)   *Oh, it could have been worse.*
(narrator) *What does the woman mean?*

In your test book, you will read: (A) The exam was really awful.
                                    (B) It was the worst exam she had ever seen.
                                    (C) It couldn't have been more difficult.
                                    (D) It wasn't that hard.

You learn from the conversation that the man thought the exam was very difficult and that the woman disagreed with the man. The best answer to the question, "What does the woman mean?" is (D), "It wasn't that hard." Therefore, the correct choice is (D).

1. (A) Her concerns were expressed.
   (B) She wonders if the concert was good.
   (C) The music was fantastic.
   (D) She wandered about during the night.

2. (A) In a bus station.
   (B) In a post office.
   (C) In an airport.
   (D) In a travel agency.

3. (A) He spends half his time with his daughter.
   (B) His daughter's under a year old.
   (C) His daughter will start school in a year and a half.
   (D) His daughter's eighteen months old.

4. (A) He's on the basketball team.
   (B) He doesn't even like to play basketball.
   (C) He's too short to make the team.
   (D) He thinks he's tall enough.

5. (A) She's thinking about her grade in the seminar.
   (B) The seminar is quite realistic.
   (C) The seminar will take a great deal of time.
   (D) She agrees with the man about the seminar.

6. (A) The location of the meeting.
   (B) The purpose of the meeting.
   (C) Who will attend the meeting.
   (D) The time the meeting starts.

7. (A) Preparing dinner later.
   (B) Going to a restaurant.
   (C) Cooking a full dinner.
   (D) Eating dinner outside in the garden.

8. (A) She is fond of Joe.
   (B) Joe is not lost anymore.
   (C) She visits Joe regularly.
   (D) The call was already made.

9. (A) He was quite fortunate.
   (B) He lacked the opportunity to play the game.
   (C) He didn't actually win the game.
   (D) He came sometime after Luke.

10. (A) It's quite clean.
    (B) It doesn't move.
    (C) It's clearly better.
    (D) It's rather dirty.

11. (A) A bus driver.
    (B) An art teacher.
    (C) A flight attendant.
    (D) A travel agent.

12. (A) His desk is made of metal.
    (B) He never meddles with his office workers.
    (C) His desk is on the right side of the office.
    (D) He works in the center of the office.

13. (A) Learning something about golf.
    (B) Taking fewer lessons than he has in the past.
    (C) Letting her play golf instead of him.
    (D) Going to play golf together.

14. (A) He does not live nearby.
    (B) They will go later.
    (C) It is not time to deliver the paper.
    (D) He does not have time to read.

15. (A) She will assign the homework tomorrow.
    (B) The man can do the homework next week.
    (C) She will return the homework next week.
    (D) The assignment must be turned in tomorrow.

GO ON TO THE NEXT PAGE ➡

16. (A) The woman is really beautiful.
    (B) The woman should repeat what she said.
    (C) He shares the woman's opinion.
    (D) He has time this year to travel.

17. (A) In a shoe store.
    (B) In a motel.
    (C) In a clothing store.
    (D) In a storage facility.

18. (A) She's going to the supermarket.
    (B) She works in a grocery store.
    (C) She's not going out.
    (D) She doesn't have enough money for groceries.

19. (A) He didn't really get the highest grade.
    (B) He's rather intelligent.
    (C) He's not done with the exam.
    (D) He's not even in the class.

20. (A) Resting for a few minutes.
    (B) Studying a bit longer.
    (C) Taking a five-hour break.
    (D) Studying for shorter periods of time.

21. (A) She needs a new suitcase.
    (B) She's putting on a suit.
    (C) She's preparing for a trip.
    (D) She just received a package.

22. (A) It was the last game.
    (B) The dream was really bad.
    (C) The man never lets her talk.
    (D) She feels the same way as the man.

23. (A) He's a bit too strong.
    (B) He's bitter about the accident.
    (C) He's still weak.
    (D) He feels the accident was not his fault.

24. (A) There seems to be a problem with the motor.
    (B) He doesn't want to be an engineer.
    (C) The music on the car stereo is good.
    (D) He likes the sound of the engine.

25. (A) An artist.
    (B) A tour guide.
    (C) A teacher.
    (D) A pilot.

26. (A) Buying some cream for coffee.
    (B) Cleaning out the garage.
    (C) Painting the apartment walls green.
    (D) Putting the apartment in order.

27. (A) He was happy to write the check.
    (B) He received a large sum of money.
    (C) He was working in a huge factory.
    (D) He found some hidden bones.

28. (A) She doesn't need to store anything.
    (B) She prefers shopping nearby.
    (C) The stores are all too far away.
    (D) She doesn't want to go shopping.

29. (A) The door was closed really hard.
    (B) Alice left because she was hungry.
    (C) The door was smoothly sanded.
    (D) Alice went out through the door on the left side.

30. (A) Take a bike ride.
    (B) Take the high road.
    (C) Go for a walk in the forest.
    (D) Look for firewood.

GO ON TO THE NEXT PAGE ➡

Part B

Directions: In this part of the test, you will hear longer conversations. After each conversation, you will hear several questions. The conversations and questions will not be repeated.

After you hear a question, read the four possible answers in your test book and choose the best answer. Then, on your answer sheet, find the number of the question and fill in the space that corresponds to the letter of the answer you have chosen.

Remember, you are **not** allowed to take notes or write in your test book.

31. (A) A new bicycle.
    (B) An inexpensive bicycle.
    (C) A fast bicycle.
    (D) A stationary bicycle.

32. (A) A half mile.
    (B) A mile.
    (C) Two miles.
    (D) Four miles.

33. (A) He doesn't like it.
    (B) It doesn't work very well.
    (C) It's broken.
    (D) He got a new one.

34. (A) Go see his friend's bicycle.
    (B) See her new apartment.
    (C) Walk to school.
    (D) Buy a new bicycle.

35. (A) Planning a trip.
    (B) Camping in the woods.
    (C) Putting up a tent.
    (D) Looking at photos.

36. (A) It looks comfortable.
    (B) It doesn't seem very big.
    (C) It looks funny.
    (D) It's full of fish.

37. (A) Standing in a river.
    (B) Putting up a tent.
    (C) Sitting in front of the tent.
    (D) Swimming in the river.

38. (A) Lots.
    (B) A few.
    (C) One.
    (D) None.

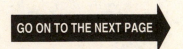

GO ON TO THE NEXT PAGE

Part C

Directions: In Part C of this section, you will hear several talks. After each talk, you will hear some questions. The talks and questions will not be repeated.

After you hear a question, you will read the four possible answers in your test book and choose the best answer. Then, on your answer sheet, find the number of the question and fill in the space that corresponds to the letter of the answer you have chosen.

Here is an example.

On the recording, you will hear:

(narrator)   *Listen to an instructor talk to his class about painting.*
(man)   *Artist Grant Wood was a guiding force in the school of painting known as American regionalist, a style reflecting the distinctive characteristics of art from rural areas of the United States. Wood began drawing animals on the family farm at the age of three, and when he was thirty-eight one of his paintings received a remarkable amount of public notice and acclaim. This painting, called American Gothic, is a starkly simple depiction of a serious couple staring directly out at the viewer.*

Now listen to a sample question.

Sample Answer
Ⓐ Ⓑ Ⓒ ⬤

(narrator)   *What style of painting is known as American regionalist?*

In your test book, you will read: (A) Art from America's inner cities.
(B) Art from the central region of the United States.
(C) Art from various urban areas in the United States.
(D) Art from rural sections of America.

The best answer to the question, "What style of painting is known as American regionalist?" is (D), "Art from rural sections of America." Therefore, the correct choice is (D).

Now listen to another sample question.

Sample Answer
Ⓐ Ⓑ ⬤ Ⓓ

(narrator)   *What is the name of Wood's most successful painting?*

In your test book, you will read: (A) *American Regionalist.*
(B) *The Family Farm in Iowa.*
(C) *American Gothic.*
(D) *A Serious Couple.*

The best answer to the question, "What is the name of Wood's most successful painting?" is (C), *American Gothic.* Therefore, the correct choice is (C).

Remember, you are **not** allowed to take notes or write in your test book.

Wait

TOEFL® test directions and format are reprinted by permission of ETS, the copyright owner. However, all examples and test questions are provided by Pearson Education, Inc.

39. (A) Only three chapters.
    (B) Three chemistry books.
    (C) Lecture notes and part of the book.
    (D) Only class notes from the lectures.

40. (A) Only multiple choice.
    (B) Short and long essays.
    (C) Three short essays.
    (D) Essays and multiple choice.

41. (A) Half an hour.
    (B) Fifty minutes.
    (C) An hour.
    (D) Ninety minutes.

42. (A) Listen to a lecture.
    (B) Study for the exam.
    (C) Read three chapters.
    (D) Take an exam.

43. (A) In a zoo.
    (B) On a boat.
    (C) In a prison.
    (D) In a lecture hall.

44. (A) A type of rock.
    (B) A Spanish explorer.
    (C) A prison in San Francisco.
    (D) A kind of bird.

45. (A) Five.
    (B) Ten.
    (C) Twenty-four.
    (D) Thirty-nine.

46. (A) It is open to visitors.
    (B) It is still in use as a prison.
    (C) It is closed to the public.
    (D) It contains few prisoners.

47. (A) Artificial plants.
    (B) Plants in plastic containers.
    (C) Plants that resemble plastic.
    (D) Plants that produce a usable substance.

48. (A) It lasts longer.
    (B) It is more artificial.
    (C) It is easy to make in a laboratory.
    (D) It is good for the environment.

49. (A) It biodegrades slowly.
    (B) It kills plants.
    (C) People never throw it away.
    (D) It is not very strong.

50. (A) Engineering.
    (B) Art.
    (C) Botany.
    (D) Geology.

**This is the end of the Listening Comprehension Diagnostic Pre-Test.
Turn off the recording.**

When you finish the test, you may do the following:

- Turn to the **Diagnostic Chart** on pages 357–363, and circle the numbers of the questions that you missed.

- Turn to the **Progress Chart** on page 353, and add your score to the chart.

LISTENING COMPREHENSION

The first section of the TOEFL test is the Listening Comprehension section. This section consists of fifty questions (some tests may be longer). You will listen to recorded materials and respond to questions about the material. You must listen carefully, because you will hear the recording one time only, and the material on the recording is not written in your test book.

There are three parts in the Listening Comprehension section of the TOEFL test:

1. **Part A** consists of thirty short conversations, each followed by a question. You must choose the best answer to each question from the four choices in your test book.

2. **Part B** consists of two longer conversations, each followed by a number of questions. You must choose the best answer to each question from the four choices in your test book.

3. **Part C** consists of three talks, each followed by a number of questions. You must choose the best answer to each question from the four choices in your test book.

GENERAL STRATEGIES

1. **Be familiar with the directions.** The directions on every TOEFL test are the same, so it is not necessary to listen carefully to them each time. You should be completely familiar with the directions before the day of the test.

2. **Listen carefully to the conversations and talks.** You should concentrate fully on what the speakers are saying on the recording because you will hear the recording one time only.

3. **Know where the easier and more difficult questions are generally found.** Within each part of the Listening Comprehension section, the questions generally progress from easy to difficult.

4. **Never leave any questions blank on your answer sheet.** Even if you are unsure of the correct response, you should answer the question. There is no penalty for guessing.

5. **Use any remaining time to look ahead at the answers to the questions that follow.** When you finish with one question, you may have time to look ahead at the answers to the next question.

THE LISTENING PART A QUESTIONS

For each of the thirty questions in Part A of the Listening Comprehension section of the TOEFL test, you will hear a short conversation between two speakers followed by a question. The conversations and questions are not written in your test book. After you listen to the conversation and question, you must choose the best answer to the question from your test book.

Example

On the recording, you hear:

　　　　(man) *I need a car to drive to Arizona, and I don't have one.*
　(woman) *Why not rent one?*
　(narrator) *What does the woman suggest?*

In your test book, you read:

(A)　Getting a red car.
(B)　Renting an apartment in Arizona.
(C)　Not driving to Arizona.
(D)　Renting a car for the trip.

Answer (D) is the best answer to the question. *Why not rent one?* is a suggestion that he rent a car for his trip to Arizona.

STRATEGIES FOR THE LISTENING PART A QUESTIONS

1. **As you listen to each short conversation, focus on the second line of the conversation.** The answer to the question is generally found in the second line of the conversation.

2. **Keep in mind that the correct answer is probably a restatement of a key word or idea in the second line of the conversation.** Think of possible restatements of the second line of the conversation.

3. **Keep in mind that certain structures and expressions are tested regularly in Listening Part A.** Listen for these structures and expressions:
   • restatements
   • negatives
   • suggestions
   • passives
   • conclusions about *who* and *where*
   • expressions of agreement

4. **Keep in mind that these questions generally progress from easy to difficult.** This means that questions 1 through 5 will be the easiest questions and questions 26 through 30 will be the hardest questions.

5. **Read the answers and choose the best answer to each question. Remember to answer each question even if you are not sure of the correct response.** Never leave any answers blank.

6. **Even if you do not understand the complete conversation, you can find the correct answer.**
   - If you only understood a few words or ideas in the second line, choose the answer that contains a restatement of those words or ideas.
   - If you did not understand anything at all in the second line of the conversation, choose the answer that sounds the most different from what you heard.
   - Never choose an answer because it *sounds like* what you heard in the conversation.

The following skills will help you to implement these strategies in Part A of the Listening Comprehension section of the TOEFL test.

Skill 1: RESTATEMENTS

Often the correct answer in Listening Part A is an answer that contains a restatement of the ideas in the second line of the conversation.

Example

On the recording, you hear:

   (woman)   *Steve, is something the matter? You don't look very good.*
   (man)   *Oh, I'm feeling a little sick today.*
(narrator)   *What does the man mean?*

In your test book, you read:

   (A) He's not very good-looking.
   (B) He's a bit ill.
   (C) He looks worse than he feels.
   (D) His feet are a little thick.

In this conversation, *sick* means *ill*, and *a little* means *a bit*. The best answer to this question is therefore answer (B) because answer (B) restates the idea in the second line of the dialogue. Please note that answer (D) is definitely *not* a correct answer because it contains *feet* instead of *feel* and *thick* instead of *sick*. These words are similar in sound but not in meaning to the words that you hear on the recording.

The following chart outlines the most important strategy in Listening Part A.

THE BEST STRATEGY: CHOOSE ANSWERS WITH RESTATEMENTS
1. As you listen to the second line of the conversation, you should focus on the key idea(s) in that line.
2. If you see a restatement of the key idea(s) in a particular answer, then you have probably found the correct answer.
3. Do not choose answers with words that sound similar to the words on the recording.

> NOTE: In Appendix A there are drills to practice distinguishing similar sounds. You may want to complete these practice drills before trying the following exercises.

EXERCISE 1: In this exercise, underline the key idea(s) in the second line of each short conversation. Then underline restatements of these key words in the answers, and choose the best answer to each question. Remember that the best answer is probably the answer that contains a restatement of the key idea(s) in the second line of the conversation.

1. (woman) *What do you like about your new house?*
    (man) *It's very close to a park.*
    (narrator) *What does the man mean?*

    (A) The house is closed up now.
    (B) He parks his car close to his house.
    (C) His home is near a park.
    (D) He doesn't really like his new house.

2. (man) *Mark said some really nice things to me.*
    (woman) *He's very grateful for what you did.*
    (narrator) *What does the woman say about Mark?*

    (A) He did a great job.
    (B) He bought a crate full of fruit.
    (C) He made a great fool of himself.
    (D) He's thankful.

3. (woman) *Sam, you've been working at the computer for hours.*
    (man) *Yes, and I need to take a break.*
    (narrator) *What does the man mean?*

    (A) The computer's broken.
    (B) He needs to relax for a while.
    (C) He should keep working.
    (D) He's broke.

TOEFL EXERCISE 1: In this exercise, listen carefully to the short conversation and question on the recording, and then choose the best answer to the question. You should look for restatements of key ideas in the second line.

 NOW BEGIN THE RECORDING AT TOEFL EXERCISE 1.

1. (A) The dance was fun.
   (B) It was a good time to dance.
   (C) She thinks the man is such a good dancer.
   (D) Tonight is the last time to dance.

2. (A) She's quite thirsty.
   (B) She'll be ready in a half hour.
   (C) She needs to leave now.
   (D) She was ready thirty minutes ago.

3. (A) The woman should teach the class herself.
   (B) The woman should see a psychiatrist.
   (C) It's a good idea to speak with the instructor.
   (D) He would like to discuss psychology with the woman.

4. (A) She has a starring role.
   (B) She has not found a job yet.
   (C) She found the lost dog.
   (D) She just began working.

5. (A) He shares everything he has.
   (B) He has to find his lost shirt.
   (C) He is climbing the stairs to the apartment.
   (D) He has to get a roommate.

6. (A) His vacation is full of activities.
   (B) In autumn he'll have a vacation.
   (C) He can't have a vacation because he suffered a fall.
   (D) He's foolish to take a vacation now.

7. (A) The book was very enjoyable.
   (B) It was unpleasant to get rid of the bugs.
   (C) She only reads when it is quiet.
   (D) It is pleasant to ride a bike.

8. (A) He hasn't traveled much lately.
   (B) There were a lot of cars on the road.
   (C) He needs to lose weight.
   (D) The tray was thick and heavy.

9. (A) He doesn't know how to play the game.
   (B) He has to write a story for class.
   (C) He needs to complete an assignment.
   (D) He has already finished the report.

10. (A) He always minds his own business.
    (B) He manages to avoid working.
    (C) He is the manager of the department.
    (D) He is the boss of his own company.

Skill 2: NEGATIVES

Negative expressions are very common in Listening Part A. The most common kind of correct response to a negative statement is a positive statement containing a word with an opposite meaning.

Example

On the recording, you hear:

    (woman) *Did you get a lot of work done at the library today?*
       (man) *I couldn't. It wasn't very quiet there.*
    (narrator) *What does the man mean?*

In your test book, you read:

  (A) The library was noisy.
  (B) He got a lot done.
  (C) He couldn't quite get to the library today.
  (D) The library's a good place to work because it's quiet.

The correct answer is answer (A). If it was *not quiet* in the library, this means that it was *noisy*. Notice that the correct answer uses *noisy*, the opposite of *quiet*.

The following chart shows how negatives can be tested on the TOEFL test.

NEGATIVE SENTENCES		
EXAMPLE	**CORRECT ANSWER**	**NEGATIVE EXPRESSION**
Tom is *not sad* about the results.	Tom is *happy* about the results.	*not sad = happy*
The door isn't *open.*	The door is *closed.*	*not open = closed*
Steve *did not pass* the class.	Steve *failed* the class.	*did not pass = failed*

EXERCISE 2: In this exercise, underline the negative expression in the second line of each short conversation. Then read the question, and choose the best answer to that question. Remember that the best answer is one that uses an opposite meaning.

1. (woman) *You made so many mistakes*
           in this homework.
      (man) *I wasn't very careful.*
  (narrator) *What does the man mean?*

  (A) He was rather careless.
  (B) He does not care about mistakes.
  (C) He took care of the work at home.
  (D) He did not carry the work home.

2.   (man) *Is there a lot of soup? I'm kind of hungry.*
  (woman) *Sorry, there's not a lot.*
(narrator) *What does the woman mean?*

(A) There's not very much soap.
(B) She doesn't like soup.
(C) There's only a little soup.
(D) The man should not be hungry.

3.   (woman) *How was the weather on your trip?*
  (man) *There wasn't a cloud in the sky.*
(narrator) *What does the man mean?*

(A) It was cloudy.
(B) He couldn't see the sky.
(C) It wasn't very crowded.
(D) There was a lot of sunshine.

TOEFL EXERCISE 2: In this exercise, listen carefully to the short conversation and question on the recording, and then choose the best answer to the question. You should pay particular attention to negative expressions.

 NOW BEGIN THE RECORDING AT **TOEFL EXERCISE 2.**

1. (A) He was on time.
   (B) He's sorry he was late.
   (C) He doesn't know why he was late.
   (D) He hasn't come there lately.

2. (A) She's sorry she brought the book.
   (B) She remembered to say she was sorry.
   (C) She forgot the book.
   (D) She didn't remember the ring.

3. (A) The baby's nodding off.
   (B) The baby's asleep.
   (C) The baby's on the way home.
   (D) The baby's just waking up.

4. (A) He wants to go by himself.
   (B) He isn't going on the trip.
   (C) He has a large number of friends.
   (D) He isn't traveling alone.

5. (A) She does not have time to park the car.
   (B) She has some free time.
   (C) She has not been to the park in a while.
   (D) The park is too wild.

6. (A) He closed the windows.
   (B) It didn't rain.
   (C) The windows were open during the storm.
   (D) He saw the rain through the windows.

7. (A) She's certain the plant's alive.
   (B) She's not sure what happened to the plant.
   (C) She planned to throw it out.
   (D) She's sure the plant should be thrown out.

8. (A) The apple is good because it's sweet.
   (B) There is an apple in each suite.
   (C) The apple doesn't look good.
   (D) The apple is sour.

9. (A) It's cheap.
   (B) It costs a lot.
   (C) It has a few problems.
   (D) It's hard to find.

10. (A) She must leave the rock there.
    (B) She needs a big rock.
    (C) She should take the rock with her.
    (D) She should take a bigger rock.

TOEFL REVIEW EXERCISE (Skills 1–2): In this exercise, listen carefully to the short conversation and question on the recording, and then choose the best answer to the question.

 NOW BEGIN THE RECORDING AT TOEFL REVIEW EXERCISE (SKILLS 1–2).

1. (A) She couldn't think of a single answer.
   (B) The test was easy.
   (C) It was impossible to think during the exam.
   (D) It was too quiet.

2. (A) He will finish quickly.
   (B) He works slowly.
   (C) He isn't worried.
   (D) He doesn't like to work.

3. (A) Her mother and father were hungry.
   (B) She was angry at her parents.
   (C) Her mother and father got home too late.
   (D) Her parents were mad.

4. (A) He didn't get a car.
   (B) The car he got wasn't real; it was a toy.
   (C) He really wanted a car but couldn't get one.
   (D) The car that he just bought is old.

5. (A) Take some seeds.
   (B) Sit down.
   (C) Make an appointment.
   (D) Take some time.

6. (A) It was difficult to play because of the wind.
   (B) He's unhappy because they lost.
   (C) He doesn't like playing football in the winter.
   (D) He's not very happy about the way they won.

7. (A) He paid the rent two days ago.
   (B) The rent wasn't due the day before yesterday.
   (C) One day earlier he'd rented an apartment.
   (D) Yesterday he spent the whole day ranting.

8. (A) Barry's too old to enjoy camping.
   (B) Not enough people are going camping.
   (C) This weekend is not a good time for camping.
   (D) Barry's too young to go camping.

9. (A) He has to water the lawn.
   (B) He's sorry about having to move.
   (C) He's washing his clothes.
   (D) He can't move right now.

10. (A) He thinks the weather there is great.
    (B) He prefers dry weather.
    (C) The weather there is good for humans.
    (D) He likes wet weather.

SKILL 3: SUGGESTIONS

Suggestions are common in Listening Part A, so you should become familiar with them. The following example shows an expression of a suggestion.

> **Example**
>
> On the recording, you hear:
>
> >   (man) *I haven't talked with my parents in a while.*
> > (woman) *Why don't you call them now?*
> > (narrator) *What does the woman suggest?*
>
> In your test book, you read:
>
> (A) Calling off his visit.
> (B) Talking about his parents.
> (C) Calling his parents in a while.
> (D) Phoning his family.

In this example, the expression *why don't* is an expression of suggestion, so the woman's suggestion is to *call* them. This means that the woman suggests *phoning* his family. The best answer is therefore answer (D).

The following chart lists common expressions that show suggestion.

EXPRESSIONS OF SUGGESTION		
Why ... not ...?	*Why not ...?*	*Let's ...*

EXERCISE 3: In this exercise, underline the expression of suggestion in each short conversation. Then read the question, and choose the best answer to that question. Remember that the best answer is one that gives a suggestion.

1.   (man) *The weather's so beautiful today.*
   (woman) *Let's walk to school instead of driving.*
   (narrator) *What does the woman suggest?*

   (A) Taking the car to school.
   (B) Taking a walk instead of going to school.
   (C) Going for a drive in the beautiful weather.
   (D) Walking to class.

2. (woman) *I never have enough spending money.*
       (man) *Why not get a part-time job?*
   (narrator) *What does the man suggest?*

   (A) Spending less money.
   (B) Doing a better job at work.
   (C) Earning some money.
   (D) Spending less time at her job.

3.   (man) *We don't have any plans tonight, do we?*
   (woman) *No, so why don't we invite some friends over to dinner?*
   (narrator) *What does the woman suggest?*

   (A) Having a dinner party.
   (B) Stopping the fight with their friends.
   (C) Planning a trip.
   (D) Making some new friends.

TOEFL EXERCISE 3: In this exercise, listen carefully to the short conversation and question on the recording, and then choose the best answer to the question. You should pay particular attention to expressions of suggestion.

 NOW BEGIN THE RECORDING AT TOEFL EXERCISE 3.

1. (A) Going to work.
   (B) Getting some exercise.
   (C) Relaxing for a while.
   (D) Visiting her friend Jim.

2. (A) Completing the work later.
   (B) Finishing more of the work now.
   (C) Trying to do the work today.
   (D) Resting tomorrow.

3. (A) Cooling off the house.
   (B) Turning down the heat.
   (C) Raising the temperature.
   (D) Finding something to eat.

4. (A) Fixing the car.
   (B) Breaking the news to the others.
   (C) Buying another automobile.
   (D) Going down the hill in the car.

5. (A) Putting up shelves.
   (B) Selling the books.
   (C) Looking for the lost books.
   (D) Rearranging the books.

6. (A) Visiting her sister.
   (B) Getting a baby-sitter.
   (C) Letting her sister see the clothes.
   (D) Giving the clothes away.

7. (A) Postponing the trip.
   (B) Leaving immediately.
   (C) Putting on a play tomorrow.
   (D) Going later tonight.

8. (A) Working on the term paper the whole day.
   (B) Spending a little money on paper.
   (C) Doing a better job of planning her term paper.
   (D) Spending the whole term on the paper.

9. (A) Getting a new television.
   (B) Checking which programs are coming on.
   (C) Checking their watches.
   (D) Seeing a comedy on television.

10. (A) Making some extra money.
    (B) Depositing the money in his account.
    (C) Buying something with the money.
    (D) Checking out several banks.

TOEFL REVIEW EXERCISE (Skills 1–3): In this exercise, listen carefully to the short conversation and question on the recording, and then choose the best answer to the question.

 NOW BEGIN THE RECORDING AT TOEFL REVIEW EXERCISE (SKILLS 1–3).

1. (A) He prefers to stay home.
   (B) He has to take many trips.
   (C) He has a lot of tasks to do.
   (D) He works well at home.

2. (A) There's nothing in the car.
   (B) He has enough time now.
   (C) He doesn't want a car now.
   (D) He prefers to do it later.

3. (A) Making less noise.
   (B) Spending more time away from the apartment.
   (C) Moving the furniture around the apartment.
   (D) Changing apartments.

4. (A) He overstepped his authority.
   (B) He worked too much in the morning.
   (C) He stayed in bed too long.
   (D) He was late getting home in the morning.

5. (A) She's rather quiet.
   (B) He doesn't really know her.
   (C) She's had many difficulties.
   (D) He's never talked to her.

6. (A) Fixing something to drink.
   (B) Adding lemon to the cake.
   (C) Paying thirty dollars.
   (D) Picking lemons from the tree.

7. (A) Write a letter.
   (B) Complete the assignment for him.
   (C) Tell him the time.
   (D) Phone him in a while.

8. (A) Getting up in the afternoon.
   (B) Having his hair cut.
   (C) Cutting the flowers in the garden.
   (D) Growing his hair long.

9. (A) She's sure she saw him.
   (B) She doubts what he said.
   (C) She isn't sure she told him her name.
   (D) She shares his beliefs.

10. (A) The break regularly lasts an hour.
    (B) No dishes were broken.
    (C) The break comes at its usual time.
    (D) It regularly takes an hour to rake the lawn.

SKILL 4: PASSIVES

It is sometimes difficult to understand *who* or *what* is doing the action in a passive sentence. This problem is often tested in Listening Part A.

Example

On the recording, you hear:

    (man) *Is that a new chair?*
 (woman) *Yes, we just bought it last week.*
(narrator) *What does the woman mean?*

In your test book, you read:

  (A) She brought the chair with her.
  (B) The chair was lost for a week.
  (C) The chair was purchased recently.
  (D) She bought the last chair from the store.

In this conversation, the woman uses an active idea, *we . . . bought it [the chair]*. The correct answer uses the passive idea *the chair was purchased*. Therefore, the best answer to the question above is answer (C).

You should note the following about passive sentences in Listening Part A.

PASSIVE STATEMENTS
1. If the conversation contains a *passive* statement, the answer to the question is often an *active* statement.
2. If the conversation contains an *active* statement, the answer to the question is often a *passive* statement.
NOTE: Check carefully *who* or *what* is doing the action in these questions.

EXERCISE 4: In this exercise, each of the correct answers is either a passive restatement of an active sentence or an active restatement of a passive sentence. Read the short conversation, and underline the key active or passive statement. Then read the question, and choose the best answer to the question. Make sure you understand *who* or *what* is doing the action in these passive sentences.

1. (man) *What happened to your notebook?*
    (woman) *I left it in the cafeteria.*
    (narrator) *What does the woman imply?*

    (A) The cafeteria is to the left.
    (B) She left a note on the cafeteria door.
    (C) She took some notes in the cafeteria.
    (D) The notebook was left in the cafeteria.

2. (man) *When are we going to talk about the problem with the copy machine?*
    (woman) *It will be discussed at the meeting tomorrow.*
    (narrator) *What does the woman mean?*

    (A) She needs to make copies before the meeting.
    (B) They will talk about the problem tomorrow.
    (C) It is a problem to have a meeting.
    (D) They must discuss whether or not to have a meeting.

3. (woman) *Did you correct the paper?*
    (man) *I checked every single line again and again.*
    (narrator) *What does the man mean?*

    (A) The paper has been thoroughly corrected.
    (B) He wrote many of the lines over and over.
    (C) The checkmarks were on every line of the paper.
    (D) He wrote a check for the paper.

TOEFL EXERCISE 4: In this exercise, listen carefully to the short conversation and question on the recording, and then choose the best answer to the question. You should pay particular attention to passives.

 NOW BEGIN THE RECORDING AT TOEFL EXERCISE 4.

1. (A) Her family just arrived.
   (B) She must pack to go visit her family.
   (C) She opened the door to greet her family.
   (D) The box from her family was opened.

2. (A) He completed the report.
   (B) He's coming to work on the report.
   (C) The report is due tomorrow morning.
   (D) The report still needs an infinite amount of work.

3. (A) The parents are in bed now.
   (B) The children were allowed to stay up.
   (C) The parents stayed away from the children.
   (D) The children have gone to bed.

4. (A) He got lost.
   (B) The door was not in front of the house.
   (C) He did not need a key to the door.
   (D) The key was lost.

5. (A) He picked out some flowered wallpaper for the dining room.
   (B) The dining room table has flowers painted on it.
   (C) The flowers were placed on the table.
   (D) The flowers were grown in the dining room.

6. (A) Nothing is really the matter.
   (B) She stole some money.
   (C) She left her purse in the store.
   (D) Someone took her purse.

7. (A) He's quite scared.
   (B) He likes her pets.
   (C) He would like to pick up a little snake.
   (D) He frightens the snakes.

8. (A) She wrote directions in a letter.
   (B) Instructions were followed exactly.
   (C) A new director has been appointed.
   (D) She would follow the man to the housing project.

9. (A) They can cook supper in no time.
   (B) He doesn't know how to play tennis.
   (C) He's a super cook.
   (D) Dinner needs to be prepared.

10. (A) The exam really is tomorrow.
    (B) There was a change in the content of the exam.
    (C) The professor moved the exam to another day.
    (D) They have to change their plans for tomorrow.

TOEFL REVIEW EXERCISE (Skills 1–4): In this exercise, listen carefully to the short conversation and question on the recording, and then choose the best answer to the question.

 Now begin the recording at TOEFL Review Exercise (skills 1–4).

1. (A) It's the middle of the winter.
   (B) The weather is not very calm.
   (C) The boat needs wind to go.
   (D) They need to unwind the sails.

2. (A) Taking two hats with him.
   (B) Aspiring to greater achievements.
   (C) Taking some medication.
   (D) Moving his head.

3. (A) He gets up every day at sunrise.
   (B) The door is open to let the sunshine in.
   (C) He parks his car out of the sunlight.
   (D) The park is open all day long.

4. (A) She ate part of Steve's meal.
   (B) Steve didn't pay for his meal.
   (C) Steve had five courses for dinner.
   (D) She was given some money.

5. (A) He did the problem completely.
   (B) He corrected the homework.
   (C) He was totally wrong.
   (D) He did well on the math exam.

6. (A) The washing machine was repaired.
   (B) He washed some clothes this morning.
   (C) He broke some dishes while he was washing them.
   (D) The washing machine needs to be fixed.

7. (A) Registering in algebra immediately.
   (B) Finding another school.
   (C) Enrolling in the course later.
   (D) Repeating the course next semester.

8. (A) It's red.
   (B) It's not dry.
   (C) It needs to be watched.
   (D) He's going to wash it.

9. (A) Everyone feels relaxed at the party.
   (B) There are enough people to have a party.
   (C) The amount of food is adequate.
   (D) Part of the food is on the table.

10. (A) The meeting was at four o'clock.
    (B) Everyone came to the meeting in uniforms.
    (C) The information was given at the meeting.
    (D) No one was uninformed about the meeting.

SKILL 5: *WHO AND WHERE*

It is common in Listening Part A to ask you to draw some kind of conclusion. In this type of question the answer is not clearly stated; instead you must draw a conclusion based on clues given in the conversation. One kind of conclusion that is common in this part of the test is to ask you to determine *who* the speaker is, based on clues given in the conversation.

Example

On the recording, you hear:

       (man) *What do you do during your <u>performances</u>?*
  (woman) *I play the <u>piano</u> and <u>sing</u>.*
(narrator) <u>Who</u> *is the woman most likely to be?*

In your test book, you read:

(A) An athlete.
(B) A member of the audience.
(C) A clerk in a music store.
(D) A <u>musician</u>.

The clues *performances*, *piano*, and *sing* in the conversation tell you that the woman is probably a *musician*. Answer (D) is therefore the correct answer.

    Another type of conclusion that is common in Listening Part A is to determine *where* the conversation probably takes place, based on clues given in the conversation.

Example

On the recording, you hear:

       (man) *I'd like to open an account, please.*
  (woman) *What type of account would you like, a <u>checking</u> or*
                     <u>savings account</u>?
(narrator) <u>Where</u> *does this conversation probably take place?*

In your test book, you read:

(A) In an accounting class.
(B) In a <u>bank</u>.
(C) At a service station.
(D) In a market.

The clue *checking or savings account* in the conversation tells you that this conversation probably takes place in a *bank*. Answer (B) is therefore the correct answer.

The following chart outlines the key point that you should remember about this type of question.

CONCLUSIONS ABOUT *WHO* AND *WHERE*
It is common for you to be asked to draw the following conclusions in Listening Part A:
1. *Who* is probably talking?
2. *Where* does the conversation probably take place?

EXERCISE 5: In this exercise, read the short conversation and question, underline the clues that help you answer the question, and then choose the best answer. You will have to draw conclusions about *who* and *where*.

1.   (man) *I'd like to mail this package, please.*
    (woman) *First or second class?*
    (narrator) *Who is the woman most likely to be?*

    (A) A school administrator.
    (B) A postal worker.
    (C) A banker.
    (D) A teacher.

2.   (woman) *How much are the flowers?*
    (man) *Ten dollars a bouquet.*
    (narrator) *Where does this conversation probably take place?*

    (A) In a bakery.
    (B) In a grocery store.
    (C) In a florist shop.
    (D) In a garden.

3.   (man) *I need to get this prescription filled.*
    (woman) *If you'll take a seat, I'll have your medicine ready for you in a moment.*
    (narrator) *Who is the woman most likely to be?*

    (A) A pharmacist.
    (B) A baby-sitter.
    (C) A flight attendant.
    (D) A doctor.

TOEFL EXERCISE 5: In this exercise, listen carefully to the short conversation and question on the recording, and then choose the best answer to the question. You will have to draw conclusions about *who* and *where*.

 Now begin the recording at TOEFL Exercise 5.

1. (A) In a hotel room.
  (B) At a restaurant.
  (C) At the beach.
  (D) In a desert.

2. (A) A manager.
  (B) A teacher.
  (C) A lawyer.
  (D) A librarian.

3. (A) In a library.
   (B) In a doctor's office.
   (C) In a bookstore.
   (D) In a grocery store.

4. (A) A beautician.
   (B) A secretary.
   (C) A dentist.
   (D) A gas station attendant.

5. (A) In a plane.
   (B) In a car.
   (C) On a bus.
   (D) On a boat.

6. (A) A weather forecaster.
   (B) A minister.
   (C) A marriage counselor.
   (D) A bride.

7. (A) In an airport.
   (B) At a gas station.
   (C) At a supermarket.
   (D) In a bike shop.

8. (A) A musician.
   (B) An office worker.
   (C) A professor.
   (D) An athlete.

9. (A) In a clothing store.
   (B) At a car wash.
   (C) In a laundry.
   (D) At a grocery store.

10. (A) A bank teller.
    (B) A travel agent.
    (C) A police officer.
    (D) A bus driver.

TOEFL REVIEW EXERCISE (Skills 1–5): In this exercise, listen carefully to the short conversation and question on the recording, and then choose the best answer to the question.

 NOW BEGIN THE RECORDING AT TOEFL REVIEW EXERCISE (SKILLS 1–5).

1. (A) Shutting the window.
   (B) Moving closer to the window.
   (C) Closing down the building.
   (D) Cooling the room off.

2. (A) The plane came in at night.
   (B) The flight was scheduled to last two hours.
   (C) The fight started at two o'clock.
   (D) The plane landed on time.

3. (A) In a clothing store.
   (B) At a pool.
   (C) At a racetrack.
   (D) In a restaurant.

4. (A) He's unhappy with the sofa.
   (B) He likes the news.
   (C) He's heard the unpleasant news.
   (D) He always tries to please everyone.

5. (A) He missed the bus he wanted to take.
   (B) He's sorry he bought the yellow shirt.
   (C) He made a huge error.
   (D) What happened was a mystery.

6. (A) Tuition is due soon.
   (B) She has a free day tomorrow.
   (C) The school is free.
   (D) The room will be painted tomorrow.

7. (A) He plays football regularly.
   (B) He heard some people playing football.
   (C) He was injured during a game.
   (D) He hurt someone during a game.

(continued on next page)

8. (A) Some of the seats were empty.
   (B) All the chairs were full.
   (C) The lecturer was standing the whole time.
   (D) He was seated at the back of the lecture hall.

9. (A) Putting on a new suit.
   (B) Tasting the soup again.
   (C) Putting some soup in the bowls.
   (D) Adding flavorings to the soup.

10. (A) A student.
    (B) A receptionist.
    (C) A salesclerk.
    (D) A dean.

Skill 6: AGREEMENT

Expressions of agreement are common in Listening Part A, so you should become familiar with them. The following example shows agreement with a positive statement.

Example

On the recording, you hear:

      (man) *I thought that the meal was overpriced.*
   (woman) <u>*Me, too.*</u>
 (narrator) *What does the woman mean?*

In your test book, you read:

  (A) There were too many spices in the meat.
  (B) She has the <u>same opinion</u> of the meal as the man.
  (C) She wants to share the man's meal.
  (D) The price of the meal was great.

The expression *me, too* shows agreement with a positive statement, so the woman means that she has the *same opinion* as the man. The best answer is therefore answer (B).

The following chart lists common expressions that show agreement. You should become familiar with these expressions.

EXPRESSIONS OF AGREEMENT			
So do I.	*I'll say.*	*Me, too.*	*You can say that again.*

EXERCISE 6: In this exercise, underline the expression of agreement in each short conversation. Then read the question, and choose the best answer to that question. Remember that the best answer is one that shows agreement.

1. (woman) *This homework is going to take forever.*
    (man) *I'll say!*
    (narrator) *What does the man mean?*

    (A) It's going to take forever to get home.
    (B) It takes a long time to get from home to work.
    (C) He and the woman have the same opinion about the homework.
    (D) He needs to take the homework to class.

2. (woman) *A trip to the park might be nice.*
    (man) *You can say that again!*
    (narrator) *What does the man mean?*

    (A) The woman should repeat what she said.
    (B) It's nice in the park at night.
    (C) The woman should tell him about part of the trip.
    (D) He agrees about the trip to the park.

3. (man) *I think it's time to go home.*
    (woman) *So do I.*
    (narrator) *What does the woman mean?*

    (A) They don't have time to do it.
    (B) She also thinks it's a good idea to leave.
    (C) She thinks they are at home.
    (D) They are unsure about the time.

TOEFL EXERCISE 6: In this exercise, listen carefully to the short conversation and question on the recording, and then choose the best answer to the question. You should pay particular attention to expressions of agreement.

 NOW BEGIN THE RECORDING AT TOEFL EXERCISE 6.

1. (A) She needs to check into the hospital.
    (B) She thinks the man should visit her.
    (C) She doesn't want to go to the hospital.
    (D) She shares the man's opinion.

2. (A) The man should repeat himself.
    (B) The prize was quite new.
    (C) She was also surprised.
    (D) The new surface was praised.

3. (A) The woman has a nice pet.
    (B) He agrees with the woman.
    (C) A bit of luck would be nice.
    (D) He should put the drinks on ice.

4. (A) They moved just after the baby was born.
    (B) He saw that the woman was moving.
    (C) The movie was really good.
    (D) He shares the woman's opinion.

(continued on next page)

5. (A) She has over three classes.
   (B) She's glad to talk about the classes.
   (C) She'd like him to tell her about the classes.
   (D) She's also happy that the classes are finished.

6. (A) His ideas about sports are similar to the woman's.
   (B) They should watch a game on television together.
   (C) He thinks he's better at sports than the woman.
   (D) He doesn't like sports at all.

7. (A) She needs a straw for the coffee.
   (B) She agrees with the man.
   (C) She has been coughing strongly.
   (D) She is feeling strong today.

8. (A) It was possible to take a math class.
   (B) The matter could not possibly be discussed.
   (C) It was impossible to attend the math exam.
   (D) He has the same opinion as the woman.

9. (A) They always go out for dinner.
   (B) They should cook dinner outside.
   (C) She thinks they should go out, too.
   (D) She would like the man to prepare dinner tonight.

10. (A) He is in agreement about the teacher.
    (B) Her story was quite interesting.
    (C) He would like the woman to respect what he said.
    (D) The history teacher will give the same lecture again.

TOEFL REVIEW EXERCISE (Skills 1–6): In this exercise, listen carefully to the short conversation and question on the recording, and then choose the best answer to the question.

 NOW BEGIN THE RECORDING AT TOEFL REVIEW EXERCISE (SKILLS 1–6).

1. (A) Baking some pies.
   (B) Climbing some trees.
   (C) Having some dessert.
   (D) Picking some apples.

2. (A) There are thirty questions on the test.
   (B) About a half hour remains.
   (C) The test will begin soon.
   (D) Thirty students are taking the test.

3. (A) She agrees with the man.
   (B) They should visit their friend Bill.
   (C) It would be a good idea to play billiards.
   (D) The bills have already been paid.

4. (A) A florist.
   (B) A barber.
   (C) A chef.
   (D) A gardener.

5. (A) She failed the test.
   (B) She's not exactly sure about the exam.
   (C) Her statistics were quite exact.
   (D) She received a passing grade.

6. (A) In a fast-food restaurant.
   (B) In a grocery store.
   (C) In an airport.
   (D) In a service station.

7. (A) Going down to the bottom of the lake.
   (B) Swimming in the lake.
   (C) Riding a boat across the lake.
   (D) Taking a picture of the beautiful lake.

8. (A) He asked a number of questions.
   (B) He expressed his doubts about the situation.
   (C) He is an honorable man.
   (D) He said what he really felt.

9. (A) He would like a cold drink, too.
   (B) The woman should repeat what she said.
   (C) He doesn't like the taste of the drink.
   (D) It's too cold to stop for a drink.

10. (A) He wants to have some water.
    (B) The grass is quite dry.
    (C) He's waiting for the loan to be approved.
    (D) He's going to mow the lawn this week.

THE LISTENING PART B QUESTIONS

Part B of the Listening Comprehension section of the TOEFL test consists of two long conversations, each followed by a number of questions. You will hear the conversations and the questions on a recording; they are not written in your test book. You must choose the best answer to each question from the four choices that are written in your test book.

The conversations are often about some aspect of school (how difficult a class is, how to write a research paper, how to register for a course) or about general living (renting an apartment, playing sports, going to the bank). The conversations can also be about topics currently in the news in the United States (desalination of the water supply, recycling of used products, damage from a storm or some other type of natural phenomenon).

Example

On the recording, you hear:

(narrator) *Questions 1 through 4. Listen to a conversation between two people who are decorating an apartment.*

(woman) *Hey, Walt. Do you think you could help me hang these pictures on the wall? There are only two of them.*

(man) *Sure, Monica. Where do you want them to go?*

(woman) *I'd like the picture of the mountains over the fireplace, and I'd like the picture of my family over the sofa. What do you think?*

(man) *I think they'll look fine there. How about if you hold the pictures while I hammer the nails into the wall?*

(woman) *Okay. Let's start with the picture of my family.*

Questions:

1. On the recording, you hear:

   (narrator) *What are the man and woman discussing?*

   In your test book, you read:

   (A) Taking some pictures.
   (B) Hanging some plants.
   (C) Taking a trip to the mountains.
   (D) Putting some pictures on the wall.

2. On the recording, you hear:

   (narrator) *How many pictures are there?*

   In your test book, you read:

   (A) One.
   (B) Two.
   (C) Three.
   (D) Four.

3. On the recording, you hear:

(narrator) *Where is the picture of the woman's family going?*

In your test book, you read:

(A) In the fireplace.
(B) Above the sofa.
(C) Home with Walt.
(D) To the top of the mountain.

4. On the recording, you hear:

(narrator) *What is Walt probably going to do next?*

In your test book, you read:

(A) Sit on the sofa.
(B) Photograph Monica's family.
(C) Hammer the nails into the wall.
(D) Climb the walls.

The first question asks what the man and woman are discussing. Since the woman asks the man to help *hang these pictures on the wall*, the best answer to this question is answer (D), *putting some pictures on the wall*. The second question asks how many pictures there are, and the woman clearly says that there are *two*, so the best answer is answer (B). The third question asks where the family picture is going. The woman says that she would like the family picture *over the sofa*, so the best answer to this question is answer (B), *above the sofa*. The last question asks what Walt is probably going to do. Walt has suggested that he should *hammer the nails into the wall*, so the best answer is answer (C).

STRATEGIES FOR THE LISTENING PART B QUESTIONS

1. **If you have the time, preview the answers to the Listening Part B questions.** While you are looking at the answers, you should try to anticipate the questions for each of the groups of answers.

2. **Listen carefully to the first line of the conversation.** The first line of the conversation often contains the main idea, subject, or topic of the conversation, and you will often be asked to answer such questions.

3. **As you listen to the conversation, follow along with the answers in your test book, and try to determine the correct answers.** Detail questions are generally answered in order in the conversation, and the answers often sound the same as what is said on the recording.

4. **You should guess even if you are not sure.** Never leave any answers blank.

5. **Use any remaining time to look ahead at the answers to the questions that follow.**

The following skills will help you to implement these strategies in Part B of the Listening Comprehension section of the TOEFL test.

Skill 7: THE QUESTIONS

It is very helpful to your ability to answer individual questions in Listening Part B if you can anticipate what the questions will be and listen specifically for the answers to those questions.

Example

In your test book, you read:

    (A) On Monday.
    (B) Next week.
    (C) Tomorrow.
    (D) After class.

You try to anticipate the question:

When will something happen?

In this example, you can be quite certain that one of the questions will be about when something will happen. Since you are sure that this is one of the questions, you can listen carefully for clues that will give you the answer. This example shows that a helpful strategy therefore is to look briefly at the answers in the test book, before you actually hear the conversations on the recording, and try to determine the questions that you will be asked to answer.

EXERCISE 7: Study the following answers and try to determine what the questions will be. (You should note that perhaps you will only be able to predict part of a question, rather than the complete question.) If you cannot predict the question in a short period of time, then move on to the next group of answers. Question 1 has been answered for you.

1. Question: <u>What . . . ?</u>
    (A) What the assignment is.
    (B) How good the professor is.
    (C) The information in Chapter Six.
    (D) What questions they should ask the professor.

2. Question: _____
    (A) Six pages.
    (B) Six chapters.
    (C) Sixty pages.
    (D) The sixth chapter.

3. Question: _____
    (A) Whether or not they should read the chapters.
    (B) Whether or not they should answer the questions.
    (C) Which chapters they should read.
    (D) When the professor gave the assignment.

4. Question: _____
    (A) Turn in the assignment.
    (B) See the professor.
    (C) Go to class.
    (D) Talk to a classmate.

5. Question: _____
    (A) A bee stung him.
    (B) He saw some bees and hornets.
    (C) He was stung by a hornet.
    (D) He took some eggs from a nest.

6. Question: _____
    (A) To liberate bees.
    (B) To protect their nests.
    (C) To hatch their eggs.
    (D) To defend the park.

7. Question: _____
    (A) A hornet's nest.
    (B) Some bee's eggs.
    (C) A parked car.
    (D) A swarm of bees.

8. Question: _____
    (A) To stay indoors.
    (B) To see where the hornet's nest is located.
    (C) Not to walk in the same location as Greg.
    (D) To keep away from Greg.

9. Question: _____
    (A) The size of the campus.
    (B) The city bus system.
    (C) The length of time for each class.
    (D) The university bus system.

10. Question: _____
    (A) The entire campus.
    (B) Part of the campus.
    (C) The campus and the city.
    (D) Only the off-campus areas.

(continued on next page)

11. Question: _____
    (A) Nothing.
    (B) Three dollars.
    (C) A few cents.
    (D) Fifty cents.

12. Question: _____
    (A) Red.
    (B) Green.
    (C) Yellow.
    (D) Blue.

Skill 8: THE TOPIC

As you listen to each conversation in Listening Part B, you should be thinking about the topic (subject) or main idea for each conversation. Since the first one or two sentences generally give the topic, you should be asking yourself what the topic is while you are listening carefully to the first part of the conversation.

Example

On the recording, you hear:

    (narrator) *Listen to the conversation between two students.*
        (man) *What did you think of that <u>history exam</u>?*
    (woman) *That was the <u>hardest exam</u> I've ever seen.*
        (man) *And it wasn't just hard! It was <u>long</u>, too.*

You think:

    The topic of conversation is a very long and difficult history exam.

EXERCISE 8: Listen to the first part of each of the conversations, and decide on the topic of each conversation.

 Now begin the recording at Exercise 8.

1. What is the topic of Conversation 1?

   _____

2. What is the topic of Conversation 2?

   _____

3. What is the topic of Conversation 3?

   _____

SKILL 9: THE ORDER OF THE ANSWERS

The answers in Listening Part B are generally found in order in the conversation. This means that as you listen to the conversation, you should be thinking about the answers to the questions in the order that they are listed in the test book.

Example

On the recording, you hear:

(narrator) *Questions 1 and 2. Listen to two students on a university campus.*

(man) *Can you help me? I'm lost.*

(woman) *Sure. Where are you trying to go?*

(man) *I have a class in Stanfield Hall at 3:00. I thought I knew where I was going, but I guess I was wrong.*

(woman) *You certainly are lost. Stanfield Hall is on the other side of the university. I'm heading in that direction. Come on with me and I'll show you the way.*

(man) *Thanks. You're a lifesaver.*

On the recording, you hear:

(narrator) 1. *What problem does the man have?*
2. *Where is Stanfield Hall?*

In your test book, you read (same time):

1. (A) He's sick.
   (B) He's lost.
   (C) He's tired.
   (D) He's broke.

2. (A) Directly in front of them.
   (B) To the left.
   (C) Quite nearby.
   (D) On the other side of campus.

When you read the answers to the first question, you can anticipate that the first question is about a man and some type of problem he has. As you listen, you hear the man say that *he is lost*. Therefore, you can anticipate that the best answer to the first question will be answer (B).

When you read the answers to the second question, you can anticipate that the second question is going to ask where something is. In the conversation, the woman explains that Stanfield Hall is *on the other side of the university*. Therefore, as you are listening you can anticipate that the correct answer to the second question is answer (D).

EXERCISE 9: Listen to each complete conversation, and answer the questions that follow.

 NOW BEGIN THE RECORDING AT EXERCISE 9.

1. (A) What the assignment is.
   (B) How good the professor is.
   (C) The information in Chapter Six.
   (D) What questions they should ask
       the professor.

2. (A) Six pages.
   (B) Six chapters.
   (C) Sixty pages.
   (D) The sixth chapter.

3. (A) Whether or not they should read
       the chapters.
   (B) Whether or not they should
       answer the questions.
   (C) Which chapters they should read.
   (D) When the professor gave the
       assignment.

4. (A) Turn in the assignment.
   (B) See the professor.
   (C) Go to class.
   (D) Talk to a classmate.

5. (A) A bee stung him.
   (B) He saw some bees and hornets.
   (C) He was stung by a hornet.
   (D) He took some eggs from a nest.

6. (A) To liberate bees.
   (B) To protect their nests.
   (C) To hatch eggs.
   (D) To defend the park.

7. (A) A hornet's nest.
   (B) Some bee's eggs.
   (C) A parked car.
   (D) A swarm of bees.

8. (A) To stay indoors.
   (B) To see where the hornet's nest is
       located.
   (C) Not to walk in the same location
       as Greg.
   (D) To keep away from Greg.

9. (A) The size of the campus.
   (B) The city bus system.
   (C) The length of time for each class.
   (D) The university bus system.

10. (A) The entire campus.
    (B) Part of the campus.
    (C) The campus and the city.
    (D) Only the off-campus areas.

11. (A) Nothing.
    (B) Three dollars.
    (C) A few cents.
    (D) Fifty cents.

12. (A) Red.
    (B) Green.
    (C) Yellow.
    (D) Blue.

TOEFL EXERCISE (Skills 7–9): In this exercise, you will use all of the information that you learned in Skills 7 through 9.

 NOW BEGIN THE RECORDING AT TOEFL EXERCISE (SKILLS 7–9).

1. (A) Where the woman lives.
   (B) Where the man can find out the time.
   (C) Where the school is located.
   (D) Where the man can mail something.

2. (A) Several streets away.
   (B) Just over one block away.
   (C) Four miles away.
   (D) A great distance.

3. (A) For one hour.
   (B) For two hours.
   (C) For four hours.
   (D) For five hours.

4. (A) Go buy a package.
   (B) Go pick up his mail.
   (C) Go mail a package.
   (D) Get into his car.

5. (A) From a textbook.
   (B) From the television.
   (C) From a magazine.
   (D) From a lecture.

6. (A) How trees are grown in America.
   (B) How paper is made from trees.
   (C) Why paper is used so much.
   (D) The amount of paper that Americans use.

7. (A) 50 tons.
   (B) 50 million tons.
   (C) 85 million tons.
   (D) 850 million tons.

8. (A) Cut down more trees.
   (B) Use less paper.
   (C) Produce more paper.
   (D) Read more about the problem.

9. (A) The difficulty in finding some books.
   (B) How far it is to the library.
   (C) The amount of reading they must do.
   (D) How much they don't like the books.

10. (A) A speed-reading class.
    (B) An American novels class.
    (C) A library skills class.
    (D) A class in literary criticism.

11. (A) Some novels.
    (B) Some short stories.
    (C) A textbook.
    (D) Some journal articles.

12. (A) Go to the library.
    (B) Head for class.
    (C) Return to the dorms.
    (D) Start reading.

THE LISTENING PART C QUESTIONS

Part C of the Listening Comprehension section of the TOEFL test consists of three talks, each followed by a number of questions. You will hear the talks and the questions on a recording; they are not written in your test book. You must choose the best answer to each question from the four choices that are written in your test book. Like the conversations in Listening Part B, the talks are often about some aspect of school life or topics currently in the news. It is also very common for the talks to be shortened versions of lectures from courses taught in American colleges and universities.

Example

On the recording, you hear:

(narrator) *Questions 1 through 4. Listen to a lecture in a history class.*

(woman) *Salt, which today seems so plentiful to us, in the past used to be a valuable commodity. In the ancient past in China, salt was used to make coins, and in parts of Africa it was traded in place of money. In the Roman Empire, soldiers were not paid in money but were instead paid in salt. In fact, the English word "salary," which means the amount of money that one earns, comes from the Latin root for "salt."*

Questions:

1. On the recording, you hear:

    (narrator) *What is the topic of the talk?*

    In your test book, you read:

    (A) Valuable commodities.
    (B) Salt.
    (C) Ancient China.
    (D) Money.

2. On the recording, you hear:

    (narrator) *What was salt used for in China?*

    In your test book, you read:

    (A) To spice food.
    (B) To build houses.
    (C) To make coins.
    (D) To locate Africa.

3. On the recording, you hear:

   (narrator) *What does "salary" mean in English?*

   In your test book, you read:

   (A) Coins.
   (B) <u>Earnings.</u>
   (C) Soldiers.
   (D) Commodities.

4. On the recording, you hear:

   (narrator) *What is the meaning of the root "sal" in Latin?*

   In your test book, you read:

   (A) <u>Salt.</u>
   (B) Rome.
   (C) Money.
   (D) Trade.

The first question asks about the topic of the talk. The speaker begins with *salt* and continues to talk about it throughout the passage, so the best answer is answer (B). The second question asks about the use of salt in China. The speaker says that *in China, salt was used to make coins,* so the best answer is answer (C). The third question asks the meaning of *salary.* The speaker says that *salary* means *the amount of money that one earns,* so the best answer is answer (B). The last question asks about the meaning of the root *sal.* The speaker says that *"salary"* . . . *comes from the Latin root for "salt,"* so the best answer is answer (A).

STRATEGIES FOR THE LISTENING PART C QUESTIONS

1. **If you have time, preview the answers to the Listening Part C questions.** While you are looking at the answers, you should try to anticipate the questions for each of the groups of answers.

2. **Listen carefully to the first line of the talk.** The first line of the talk often contains the main idea, subject, or topic of the talk, and you will often be asked this type of question.

3. **As you listen to the talk, follow along with the answers in your test book and try to determine the correct answers.** Detail questions are generally answered in order in the talk, and the answers often sound the same as what is said on the recording.

4. **You should guess even if you are not sure.** Never leave any answers blank.

5. **Use any remaining time to look ahead at the answers to the questions that follow.**

The following skills will help you to implement these strategies in Part C of the Listening Comprehension section of the TOEFL test.

SKILL 10: THE QUESTIONS

It is very helpful to your ability to answer individual questions in Listening Part C if you can anticipate what the questions will be and listen specifically for the answers to those questions (as you did in Listening Part B).

Example

In your test book, you read:

    (A) For a week.
    (B) Since yesterday.
    (C) For two days.
    (D) Since 10:00 this morning.

You try to anticipate the question:

How long has (something) been going on?

In this example, you can be quite certain that one of the questions will be about how long something has been going on. Since you are sure that this is one of the questions, you can listen carefully for clues that will give you the answer. This example shows that a helpful strategy in Listening Part C (just as in Listening Part B) therefore is to look briefly at the answers in the test book, before you actually hear the talks on the recording, and try to determine the questions that you will be asked to answer.

EXERCISE 10: Study the following answers and try to determine what the questions will be. (You should note that perhaps you will only be able to predict part of a question, rather than the complete question.) If you cannot predict the question in a short period of time, then move on to the next group of answers. Question 1 has been answered for you.

1. Question: <u>What type of plant is this?</u>
    (A) A beautiful plant.
    (B) A poisonous plant.
    (C) A delicious plant.
    (D) A fast-growing plant.

2. Question: _____
    (A) In vegetable gardens.
    (B) Only in the United States.
    (C) In supermarkets.
    (D) In many different places.

3. Question: _____
    (A) Its leaves resemble parsley.
    (B) It grows next to carrots.
    (C) Its leaves are shaped like carrots.
    (D) It does not have roots.

4. Question: _____
   (A) The person may die.
   (B) The person may get lots of healthful nutrients.
   (C) The person may enjoy it and want more.
   (D) The person may become dangerous.

5. Question: _____
   (A) A story-writing contest.
   (B) A frog-catching contest.
   (C) A singing contest.
   (D) A frog-jumping contest.

6. Question: _____
   (A) Sixty-three.
   (B) Two hundred.
   (C) Two thousand.
   (D) Forty thousand.

7. Question: _____
   (A) One.
   (B) Two.
   (C) Three.
   (D) Four.

8. Question: _____
   (A) The contest took place for years before Twain wrote about it.
   (B) Twain wrote about the contest while he was watching it for the first time.
   (C) Twain went to see the contest many times during his lifetime.
   (D) Twain wrote about the contest before it actually took place.

9. Question: _____
   (A) A student.
   (B) A professor.
   (C) A bookstore clerk.
   (D) A librarian.

10. Question: _____
    (A) The place where students get ID cards.
    (B) The place where students can use computers.
    (C) The place where students check books out.
    (D) The place where students find books in the library.

11. Question: _____
    (A) A fee.
    (B) A student ID card.
    (C) Permission from the instructor.
    (D) A computer.

(continued on next page)

12 Question: _____
   (A) A few hours.
   (B) Two days.
   (C) Fourteen days.
   (D) Two months.

SKILL 11: THE TOPIC

As you listen to each talk in Listening Part C, you should be thinking about the topic (subject) or main idea for each talk (as you did in Listening Part B). Since the first sentence is generally a topic sentence, you should be asking yourself what the topic is while you are listening carefully to the first part of the talk.

Example

On the recording, you hear:

   (narrator)   *Listen to a talk at the start of a meeting.*
   (woman)   *I'd like to call this <u>meeting</u> to order now. This is the third monthly <u>meeting of the science club</u> this semester, and today we need to discuss the upcoming <u>science fair</u>.*

You think:

   The topic of the talk is a meeting of the science club to discuss the science fair.

EXERCISE 11: Listen to the first part of each of the talks, and decide on the topic of each talk.

 NOW BEGIN THE RECORDING AT EXERCISE 11.

1. What is the topic of Talk 1?

   _____

2. What is the topic of Talk 2?

   _____

3. What is the topic of Talk 3?

   _____

SKILL 12: THE ORDER OF THE ANSWERS

The answers in Listening Part C are generally found in order in the talk (as they were in Listening Part B). This means that as you listen to the talk, you should be thinking about the answers to the questions in the order that they are listed in the test book.

Example

On the recording, you hear:

(narrator) *Questions 1 through 3.*
Listen to a talk about cats.

(woman) *Many people are allergic to cats. If they come in contact with cats, they sneeze, their skin turns red, and their eyes begin to burn. However, it is not only people who suffer from allergies. Cats may also be allergic to pollen, dust, and perfumes, many of the same agents that cause allergies in people. Perhaps your cat is sneezing and has watery eyes. If you think that your cat has some allergies, a veterinarian can prescribe medication to help solve the problem.*

In your test book, you read (same time):

1. (A) They shout.
   (B) They drive red cars.
   (C) They sneeze.
   (D) They close their eyes.

2. (A) They often wear perfume.
   (B) They can have allergies.
   (C) They don't ever suffer.
   (D) They like dust and pollen.

3. (A) Nothing.
   (B) Bathe it frequently.
   (C) Put it outside.
   (D) Give it medicine.

On the recording, you hear:

(narrator) 1. *What happens to people who suffer from allergies?*
2. *What is mentioned about cats?*
3. *What can someone do with a cat that has allergies?*

The first question asks what happens to people who suffer from allergies. The speaker says that *they sneeze,* so the best answer is answer (C). The second question asks what is mentioned about cats. The speaker says that *cats may also be allergic,* so the best answer is answer (B), *they can have allergies.* The third question asks what to do with a cat that has allergies. The speaker says that a *veterinarian can prescribe medication,* so the best answer is answer (D), *give it medicine.*

EXERCISE 12: Listen to each complete talk, and answer the questions that follow.

 NOW BEGIN THE RECORDING AT EXERCISE 12.

1. (A) A beautiful plant.
   (B) A poisonous plant.
   (C) A delicious plant.
   (D) A fast-growing plant.

2. (A) In vegetable gardens.
   (B) Only in the United States.
   (C) In supermarkets.
   (D) In many different places.

3. (A) Its leaves resemble parsley.
   (B) It grows next to carrots.
   (C) Its leaves are shaped like carrots.
   (D) It does not have roots.

4. (A) The person may die.
   (B) The person may get lots of healthful nutrients.
   (C) The person may enjoy it and want more.
   (D) The person may become dangerous.

5. (A) A story-writing contest.
   (B) A frog-catching contest.
   (C) A singing contest.
   (D) A frog-jumping contest.

6. (A) Sixty-three.
   (B) Two hundred.
   (C) Two thousand.
   (D) Forty thousand.

7. (A) One.
   (B) Two.
   (C) Three.
   (D) Four.

8. (A) The contest took place for years before Twain wrote about it.
   (B) Twain wrote about the contest while he was watching it for the first time.
   (C) Twain went to see the contest many times during his lifetime.
   (D) Twain wrote about the contest before it actually took place.

9. (A) A student.
   (B) A professor.
   (C) A bookstore clerk.
   (D) A librarian.

10. (A) The place where students get ID cards.
    (B) The place where students can use computers.
    (C) The place where students check books out.
    (D) The place where students find books in the library.

11. (A) A fee.
    (B) A student identification card.
    (C) Permission from the instructor.
    (D) A computer.

12. (A) A few hours.
    (B) Two days.
    (C) Fourteen days.
    (D) Two months.

TOEFL EXERCISE (Skills 10–12): In this exercise, you will use all of the information that you learned in Skills 10 through 12.

 NOW BEGIN THE RECORDING AT TOEFL EXERCISE (SKILLS 10–12).

1. (A) An artist.
   (B) A circus performer.
   (C) John Ringling.
   (D) A tour guide.

2. (A) Because he was from Sarasota, Florida.
   (B) Because he knew Rubens.
   (C) Because he started a circus.
   (D) Because he painted baroque-style paintings.

3. (A) Modern circus equipment.
   (B) Paintings by Rubens.
   (C) A parade wagon.
   (D) A famous portrait of the Ringling brothers.

4. (A) Enter the museum.
   (B) Go to the circus.
   (C) Return to the bus.
   (D) Meet the Ringlings.

5. (A) An assembly line.
   (B) A car.
   (C) A company.
   (D) An inventor.

6. (A) In 1908.
   (B) In 1914.
   (C) In 1918.
   (D) In 1924.

7. (A) It was faster.
   (B) It was more efficient.
   (C) It was more individualized.
   (D) It was cheaper.

8. (A) It increased slowly.
   (B) It increased quickly.
   (C) It remained about the same.
   (D) It decreased.

9. (A) Students who will soon graduate from the Psychology Department.
   (B) Professors in the Psychology Department.
   (C) Graduate students in the Psychology Department.
   (D) Graduate advisors.

10. (A) Whether to write a thesis or take an exam.
    (B) Whether to be graduate or undergraduate students.
    (C) Whether to graduate this year or next.
    (D) Whether or not to study psychology.

11. (A) Exams covering one or two hundred pages.
    (B) Exams about research.
    (C) Exams covering all material in the program.
    (D) Exams about recent developments in psychology.

12. (A) Today.
    (B) Soon.
    (C) Within six weeks.
    (D) Within half a year.

TOEFL POST-TEST

SECTION 1
LISTENING COMPREHENSION
Time—approximately 35 minutes
(including the reading of the directions for each part)

In this section of the test, you will have an opportunity to demonstrate your ability to understand conversations and talks in English. There are three parts to this section, with special directions for each part. Answer all the questions on the basis of what is **stated** or **implied** by the speakers you hear. Do **not** take notes or write in your test book at any time. Do **not** turn the pages until you are told to do so.

Part A

Directions: In Part A you will hear short conversations between two people. After each conversation, you will hear a question about the conversation. The conversations and questions will not be repeated. After you hear a question, read the four possible answers in your test book and choose the best answer. Then, on your answer sheet, find the number of the question and fill in the space that corresponds to the letter of the answer you have chosen.

Here is an example.

On the recording, you will hear:

Sample Answer

(man)   *That exam was just awful.*
(woman)   *Oh, it could have been worse.*
(narrator) *What does the woman mean?*

In your test book, you will read: (A) The exam was really awful.
                                   (B) It was the worst exam she had ever seen.
                                   (C) It couldn't have been more difficult.
                                   (D) It wasn't that hard.

You learn from the conversation that the man thought the exam was very difficult and that the woman disagreed with the man. The best answer to the question, "What does the woman mean?" is (D), "It wasn't that hard." Therefore, the correct choice is (D).

Wait

1. (A) She doesn't want to go to class.
    (B) Art has her glasses.
    (C) The artist will begin the portrait tonight.
    (D) The course starts this evening.

2. (A) A waiter.
    (B) A baker.
    (C) A neighbor.
    (D) A tour guide.

3. (A) She's in the center of the shop.
    (B) She went shopping for a new car.
    (C) She took her car to the store.
    (D) She was driving him crazy.

4. (A) He lied.
    (B) He's upset.
    (C) He did not tell her his name.
    (D) He's always truthful.

5. (A) He believes that the woman has found some good pieces.
    (B) He agrees that the prices are low.
    (C) He would like to have a chance to say something.
    (D) He thinks that the woman is wrong about the prices.

6. (A) Listen to him.
    (B) Pay the check.
    (C) Attend the meeting.
    (D) Speak more clearly.

7. (A) Not moving inside.
    (B) Playing in the rain.
    (C) Not going out.
    (D) Running hard.

8. (A) The courts have decided on a new judge.
    (B) The judge made himself available for questions.
    (C) The judge decided on the issue.
    (D) The decision about the judge was finally made.

9. (A) She was unable to attend the chemistry class.
    (B) She couldn't find the answer to the problem.
    (C) Chemistry class just finished.
    (D) She has a problem with her chemistry teacher.

10. (A) Stay home.
    (B) Watch television.
    (C) Buy a new house.
    (D) Go out.

11. (A) In a business office.
    (B) In an airplane.
    (C) In a gymnasium.
    (D) In a classroom.

12. (A) He is probably swimming.
    (B) He is poor.
    (C) Nobody knows where he is.
    (D) He should not be in the pool.

13. (A) Taking naps during the day.
    (B) Sleeping longer during the night.
    (C) Getting him tired out before sleeping.
    (D) Only sleeping a little at night.

14. (A) The chapter was difficult to read.
    (B) She didn't even try to read the chapter.
    (C) She got through the chapter rather easily.
    (D) She will try to read the chapter later today.

15. (A) He's working as a security guard.
    (B) His garden is successful.
    (C) There are a lot of stones in the garden.
    (D) He enjoys the rocking chair.

16. (A) Beautiful weather is impossible.
    (B) She thinks the wedding is beautiful.
    (C) She shares the man's opinion.
    (D) The red dress is incredible.

GO ON TO THE NEXT PAGE ➡

17. (A) A railroad conductor.
    (B) A bus driver.
    (C) A math teacher.
    (D) A mechanic.

18. (A) The sandwich needed some spices.
    (B) The lunch did not taste very good.
    (C) She had a delicious meal.
    (D) She hardly tasted the sandwich.

19. (A) She's no longer sick.
    (B) She has no feelings.
    (C) Her health is always good.
    (D) He feels better than she does.

20. (A) Watching the professor closely in class.
    (B) Spending more time working in his office.
    (C) Studying psychology more often.
    (D) Talking to his professor.

21. (A) It's difficult for him to save money.
    (B) He wants to purchase a home near the ocean.
    (C) He goes to the beach often.
    (D) Buying a house is out of reach for him.

22. (A) Sally has many friends.
    (B) He doesn't understand anything about Sally.
    (C) He also thinks that Sally was not nice.
    (D) Sally said many different things.

23. (A) The stereo is not loud enough.
    (B) He is going to turn the stereo off.
    (C) The woman should turn and face the stereo.
    (D) The woman doesn't want to hear the music.

24. (A) He was not present during the overture.
    (B) He was in over his head.
    (C) He repeatedly expressed his appreciation.
    (D) He thinks the present is overpriced.

25. (A) In a bank.
    (B) In an airport.
    (C) In a store.
    (D) In a hotel.

26. (A) Hanging the pictures on the wall.
    (B) Taking some photographs.
    (C) Sitting closer to the wall.
    (D) Visiting his hometown.

27. (A) She doesn't know who Carl is.
    (B) She already had a meeting with Carl.
    (C) She needs to tell Carl about the meeting.
    (D) She knows where Carl lives.

28. (A) His book was not really cheap.
    (B) He bought a used text.
    (C) His book does not include the latest news.
    (D) He did not know anything about the textbooks.

29. (A) It was announced that there would be a new teacher.
    (B) He wanted to give something to the teacher.
    (C) The instructor said that a test would be given.
    (D) The teacher returned the exams.

30. (A) There has been a lot of decay.
    (B) The government is decadent.
    (C) The government has decided to conduct a new survey.
    (D) The population is counted every ten years.

GO ON TO THE NEXT PAGE ➤

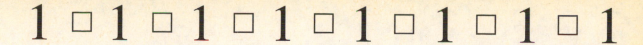
Part B

Directions: In this part of the test, you will hear longer conversations. After each conversation, you will hear several questions. The conversations and questions will not be repeated.

After you hear a question, read the four possible answers in your test book and choose the best answer. Then, on your answer sheet, find the number of the question and fill in the space that corresponds to the letter of the answer you have chosen.

Remember, you are **not** allowed to take notes or write in your test book.

31. (A) At one o'clock.
    (B) At two o'clock.
    (C) At three o'clock.
    (D) At four o'clock.

32. (A) Ski.
    (B) Read books on skiing.
    (C) Buy skiing equipment.
    (D) Plan ski trips.

33. (A) He doesn't know how to ski.
    (B) He doesn't know where the meeting is.
    (C) He doesn't know what time the meeting starts.
    (D) He is afraid of skiing.

34. (A) Leave on a skiing trip.
    (B) Go with the woman to the meeting.
    (C) Try on some skis.
    (D) Give a lecture to the ski club.

35. (A) From the radio.
    (B) From a book.
    (C) From the newspaper.
    (D) From a lecture.

36. (A) You can eat it.
    (B) It tastes like fast food.
    (C) It is inexpensive.
    (D) You cannot see it.

37. (A) Paper.
    (B) Fries.
    (C) Corn.
    (D) Burgers.

38. (A) It is not as good as paper.
    (B) It should not be used for fast food.
    (C) It should be faster than paper.
    (D) It might be healthier than the food.

GO ON TO THE NEXT PAGE →

Part C

Directions: In Part C of this section, you will hear several talks. After each talk, you will hear some questions. The talks and questions will not be repeated.

After you hear a question, you will read the four possible answers in your test book and choose the best answer. Then, on your answer sheet, find the number of the question and fill in the space that corresponds to the letter of the answer you have chosen.

Here is an example.

On the recording, you will hear:

(narrator) *Listen to an instructor talk to his class about painting.*
(man) *Artist Grant Wood was a guiding force in the school of painting known as American regionalist, a style reflecting the distinctive characteristics of art from rural areas of the United States. Wood began drawing animals on the family farm at the age of three, and when he was thirty-eight one of his paintings received a remarkable amount of public notice and acclaim. This painting, called* American Gothic, *is a starkly simple depiction of a serious couple staring directly out at the viewer.*

Now listen to a sample question.   **Sample Answer**
                                                     (A)
(narrator) *What style of painting is known as American regionalist?*   (B)
                                                     (C)
In your test book, you will read: (A) Art from America's inner cities.   ●
                                   (B) Art from the central region of the
                                       United States.
                                   (C) Art from various urban areas in the
                                       United States.
                                   (D) Art from rural sections of America.

The best answer to the question, "What style of painting is known as American regionalist?" is (D), "Art from rural sections of America." Therefore, the correct choice is (D).

Now listen to another sample question.   **Sample Answer**
                                                     (A)
(narrator) *What is the name of Wood's most successful painting?*   (B)
                                                     ●
In your test book, you will read: (A) *American Regionalist.*   (D)
                                   (B) *The Family Farm in Iowa.*
                                   (C) *American Gothic.*
                                   (D) *A Serious Couple.*

The best answer to the question, "What is the name of Wood's most successful painting?" is (C), *American Gothic.* Therefore, the correct choice is (C).

Remember, you are **not** allowed to take notes or write in your test book.

39. (A) To the Grand Canyon.
    (B) To a jewelry show.
    (C) To a deserted stone building.
    (D) To the Petrified Forest.

40. (A) To the Grand Canyon.
    (B) To the Colorado River.
    (C) To a tree house.
    (D) To the Petrified Forest.

41. (A) It has fallen in the river.
    (B) It has turned to stone.
    (C) It has grown larger.
    (D) It has gotten softer.

42. (A) Swim in the river.
    (B) Walk through the trees.
    (C) Stay at a distance.
    (D) Take any petrified wood.

43. (A) Graduation requirements.
    (B) School clothing.
    (C) The date of the December graduation ceremony.
    (D) Which students will be seniors.

44. (A) Read it.
    (B) File it in their personal files.
    (C) Study it.
    (D) Give it to an advisor.

45. (A) A university class schedule.
    (B) A cap and gown.
    (C) A blue and gold flag.
    (D) A graduate school catalogue.

46. (A) Any time before graduation.
    (B) At the beginning of the senior year.
    (C) Before the end of December.
    (D) In the springtime.

47. (A) Training dogs to use smell.
    (B) Techniques of dog trainers.
    (C) The smells of various types of food.
    (D) How dog breeds are different.

48. (A) Most have no sense of smell.
    (B) They are all unable to smell drugs.
    (C) They have equally good senses of smell.
    (D) Most are quite untrainable.

49. (A) They are small.
    (B) They are friendly.
    (C) They react quickly.
    (D) They work well in the cold.

50. (A) Airports.
    (B) People.
    (C) Luggage.
    (D) Snow.

**This is the end of Section 1. Stop work on Section 1.
Turn off the recording.**

When you finish the test, you may do the following:

- Turn to the **Diagnostic Chart** on pages 357–363, and circle the numbers of the questions that you missed.

- Turn to the **Progress Chart** on page 353, and add your score to the chart.

SECTION TWO

STRUCTURE AND WRITTEN EXPRESSION

DIAGNOSTIC PRE-TEST

SECTION 2
STRUCTURE AND WRITTEN EXPRESSION
Time—25 minutes
(including the reading of the directions)
Now set your clock for 25 minutes.

This section is designed to measure your ability to recognize language that is appropriate for standard written English. There are two types of questions in this section, with special directions for each type.

Structure

Directions: These questions are incomplete sentences. Beneath each sentence you will see four words or phrases, marked (A), (B), (C), and (D). Choose the **one** word or phrase that best completes the sentence. Then, on your answer sheet, find the number of the question and fill in the space that corresponds to the letter of the answer you have chosen.

Look at the following examples.

Example I   **Sample Answer**

The president _____ the election by a landslide.

(A) won
(B) he won
(C) yesterday
(D) fortunately

The sentence should read, "The president won the election by a landslide." Therefore, you should choose answer (A).

Example II   **Sample Answer**

When _____ the conference?

(A) the doctor attended
(B) did the doctor attend
(C) the doctor will attend
(D) the doctor's attendance

The sentence should read, "When did the doctor attend the conference?" Therefore, you should choose answer (B).

GO ON TO THE NEXT PAGE ➡

1. In the early 1900s, Eastman _____ inexpensive Brownie box cameras.

   (A) it developed
   (B) it was developed
   (C) developed
   (D) developing

2. _____ the discovery of the fossilized remnants of tides in one-billion-year-old rocks.

   (A) Geological reports
   (B) Geologists report
   (C) The reports of geologists
   (D) Geologists' reports

3. The Brooklyn Bridge _____ took thirteen years to complete.

   (A) in New York
   (B) is in New York
   (C) it is in New York
   (D) which New York

4. Genes control all of the physical _____ we inherit.

   (A) that traits
   (B) that are traits
   (C) traits that
   (D) traits are that

5. Indigo can be extracted from a plant, and then _____ to dye cloth blue.

   (A) it
   (B) using
   (C) using it
   (D) it can be used

6. _____ in the United States spends 900 hours per year in class and 1,170 hours in front of the television.

   (A) The average third-grader
   (B) The third grade is average
   (C) There are three grades
   (D) Three average grades

7. Researchers have begun studying what _____ is on human circadian rhythms.

   (A) it is the effect of light
   (B) the light affects
   (C) is affecting the light
   (D) the effect of light

8. If calcium oxide remains exposed to air, _____ to calcium carbonate.

   (A) turning
   (B) turns
   (C) it turns
   (D) the turn

9. Some early batteries used concentrated nitric acid, _____ gave off poisonous fumes.

   (A) they
   (B) then they
   (C) but they
   (D) but they had

10. The sound produced by an object _____ in a periodic way involves more than the simple sine wave.

    (A) it vibrates
    (B) vibrating
    (C) is vibrating
    (D) vibrates

11. Prior to the discovery of anesthetics in 1846, surgery was done _____ was still conscious.

    (A) while the patient
    (B) the patient felt
    (C) during the patient's
    (D) while patiently

GO ON TO THE NEXT PAGE

12. The drastic decline of the beaver helps to illustrate what _____ to the ecosystems of the North American continent.

    (A) happening
    (B) the happening
    (C) has happened
    (D) about happening

13. The use of shorthand died out in the Middle Ages because of _____ with witchcraft.

    (A) the association was imagined
    (B) associate the imagination
    (C) imagine the association
    (D) the imagined association

14. A yacht is steered with a rudder, _____ the flow of water that passes the hull.

    (A) which deflecting
    (B) deflects
    (C) it deflects
    (D) which deflects

15. For top speed and sudden acceleration, the accelerator pump feeds additional gasoline from the float chamber into _____ above the venturi tube.

    (A) the air flows
    (B) the air flow
    (C) the air is flowing
    (D) flows the air

GO ON TO THE NEXT PAGE

Written Expression

Directions: In these questions, each sentence has four underlined words or phrases. The four underlined parts of the sentence are marked (A), (B), (C), and (D). Identify the **one** underlined word or phrase that must be changed in order for the sentence to be correct. Then, on your answer sheet, find the number of the question and fill in the space that corresponds to the letter of the answer you have chosen.

Look at the following examples.

Example I

The four string on a violin are tuned
  A   B   C   D

in fifths.

Sample Answer

Ⓐ ● Ⓒ Ⓓ

The sentence should read, "The four strings on a violin are tuned in fifths." Therefore, you should choose answer (B).

Example II

The research for the book *Roots* taking
    A   B   C

Alex Haley twelve years.
           D

Sample Answer

Ⓐ Ⓑ ● Ⓓ

The sentence should read, "The research for the book *Roots* took Alex Haley twelve years." Therefore, you should choose answer (C).

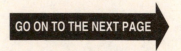

16. In 1732, coach <u>travelers</u> could <u>got</u> from New York <u>to</u> Philadelphia in about two <u>days</u>.
    <u> </u>A <u> </u>B <u> </u>C <u> </u>D

17. Some <u>of the</u> District of Columbia <u>are</u> on low-lying, <u>marshy</u> ground.
    <u> </u>A <u> </u>B <u> </u>C <u> </u>D

18. <u>Georgia's</u> economy is <u>based</u> <u>main</u> on <u>agriculture</u>.
    <u> </u>A <u> </u>B <u> </u>C <u> </u>D

19. The Paul Revere House was <u>built</u> in 1676, and today <u>its</u> the <u>oldest</u> <u>wooden</u> building in Boston.
    <u> </u>A <u> </u>B <u> </u>C <u> </u>D

20. Conifers <u>such as</u> cedars, firs, and pines <u>bear</u> <u>its</u> seeds in <u>cones</u>.
    <u> </u>A <u> </u>B <u> </u>C <u> </u>D

21. A dome is a <u>semispherical</u> <u>structures</u> on <u>top of</u> a <u>building</u>.
    <u> </u>A <u> </u>B <u> </u>C <u> </u>D

22. Succulents <u>suck up</u> water in just a few <u>hour</u>, but they can <u>store</u> it in <u>their stems</u> for months.
    <u> </u>A <u> </u>B <u> </u>C <u> </u>D

23. Flying buttresses <u>enabled</u> builders to <u>put</u> up tall but <u>thinnest</u> stone <u>walls</u>.
    <u> </u>A <u> </u>B <u> </u>C <u> </u>D

24. Weather forecasters <u>monitor</u> barometric <u>pressures</u> and record <u>they</u> on charts as <u>isobars</u>.
    <u> </u>A <u> </u>B <u> </u>C <u> </u>D

25. In <u>many languages</u>, the forms of a word <u>varies</u> to express <u>such</u> contrasts as number, gender,
    <u> </u>A <u> </u>B <u> </u>C
    and <u>tense</u>.
    <u> </u>D

26. A Milky Way object <u>that</u> erupted in the constellation Scorpius has <u>provides</u> information to
    <u> </u>A <u> </u>B
    <u>astronomers</u> <u>since</u> July.
    <u> </u>C <u> </u>D

27. <u>Much</u> fossils are <u>found</u> in <u>coal-bearing</u> <u>rocks</u>.
    <u> </u>A <u> </u>B <u> </u>C <u> </u>D

28. When salt is <u>added</u> to ice, <u>this</u> mixture becomes <u>coldly</u> enough to <u>freeze</u> ice cream.
    <u> </u>A <u> </u>B <u> </u>C <u> </u>D

29. During the eighteenth and nineteenth <u>centuries</u>, Long Island was <u>chiefly</u> an <u>agricultural</u> region
    <u> </u>A <u> </u>B <u> </u>C
    with fishing, whaling, and <u>build ships</u> as the important industries.
    <u> </u>D

30. No one <u>who</u> has studied the Battle of Little Bighorn <u>know</u> the exact route that Custer and <u>his</u>
    <u> </u>A <u> </u>B <u> </u>C
    detachment <u>took</u>.
    <u> </u>D

GO ON TO THE NEXT PAGE ➡

31. The folktales <u>which</u> the brothers Grimm had <u>collecting</u> were <u>translated</u> into English <u>in</u> 1823.
           A   B   C   D

32. In <u>our</u> solar system, nine planets, fifty-seven moons, <u>several dozen</u> comets, several million
      A   B

    asteroids, and billions of meteorites have <u>so far</u> been <u>discover</u>.
                                              C   D

33. From the 1850s until after the turn of the century, <u>many</u> of America's super-rich <u>families</u> <u>made</u>
                                                        A   B   C

    Newport <u>his</u> favorite summer resort.
             D

34. Mars may <u>looks</u> red because <u>it is</u> <u>covered</u> with <u>a layer</u> of soft red iron oxide.
                A   B   C   D

35. The radioactive substances <u>that pose</u> the greatest harm to humanity have neither <u>very short</u> <u>or</u>
                                     A   B   C

    very long half <u>lives</u>.
                  D

36. A robin cocks <u>its</u> head to peer at <u>a worm</u> with one <u>eyes</u> and not to hear it, as was <u>once</u> thought.
                A   B   C   D

37. Film <u>sound</u> is often <u>record</u> by an analog system <u>which</u>, like the compact disc, <u>uses</u> light.
                A   B   C   D

38. The scribes of the Middle Ages <u>used</u> quill pens <u>to produce</u> <u>their</u> <u>high</u> decorated manuscripts.
                                       A   B   C D

39. The principles of physics <u>described</u> by Christian Doppler in 1842 for the movement of stars <u>has</u>
                                         A   B

    been <u>adapted</u> to evaluate the movement of <u>blood</u> within the heart.
             C   D

40. The *Pioneer 10* and *11* spacecraft <u>were</u> the <u>first</u> vehicles of humankind to venture beyond the
                                                A   B

    limits of <u>ours</u> solar system.
        C   D

This is the end of the Structure and Written Expression Diagnostic Pre-Test.

When you finish the test, you may do the following:

- Turn to the **Diagnostic Chart** on pages 357–363, and circle the numbers of the questions that you missed.

- Turn to the **Progress Chart** on page 353, and add your score to the chart.

STRUCTURE AND WRITTEN EXPRESSION

The second section of the TOEFL test is the Structure and Written Expression section. This section consists of forty questions (some tests may be longer). You have twenty-five minutes to complete the forty questions in this section.

There are two types of questions in the Structure and Written Expression section of the TOEFL test:

1. **Structure** (questions 1–15) consists of fifteen sentences in which part of the sentence has been replaced with a blank. Each sentence is followed by four answer choices. You must choose the answer that completes the sentence in a grammatically correct way.

2. **Written Expression** (questions 16–40) consists of twenty-five sentences in which four words or groups of words have been underlined. You must choose the underlined word or group of words that is *not* correct.

GENERAL STRATEGIES

1. **Be familiar with the directions.** The directions on every TOEFL test are the same, so it is not necessary to spend time reading the directions carefully when you take the test. You should be completely familiar with the directions before the day of the test.

2. **Begin with questions 1 through 15.** Anticipate that questions 1 through 5 will be the easiest. Anticipate that questions 11 through 15 will be the most difficult. Do not spend too much time on questions 11 through 15. There will be easier questions that come later.

3. **Continue with questions 16 through 40.** Anticipate that questions 16 through 20 will be the easiest. Anticipate that questions 36 through 40 will be the most difficult. Do not spend too much time on questions 36 through 40.

4. **If you have time, return to questions 11 through 15.** You should spend extra time on questions 11 through 15 only after you spend all the time that you want on the easier questions.

5. **Never leave any questions blank on your answer sheet.** Even if you are not sure of the correct response, you should answer the question. There is no penalty for guessing.

THE STRUCTURE QUESTIONS

Questions 1 through 15 in the Structure and Written Expression section of the TOEFL test measure your knowledge of the correct structure of English sentences. The questions in this section are multiple-choice questions in which you must choose the letter of the answer that best completes the sentence.

Example

_____ greeted me enthusiastically at the front door.

(A) Parental
(B) If
(C) My friends
(D) Them

In this example, you should notice immediately that the sentence has a verb, *greeted*, and that the verb needs a subject. Answers (A), (B), and (D) are incorrect because *parental*, *if*, and *them* are not subjects. The correct answer is answer (C).

STRATEGIES FOR THE STRUCTURE QUESTIONS

1. **First study the sentence.** Your purpose is to determine what is needed to complete the sentence correctly.

2. **Then study each answer based on how well it completes the sentence.** Eliminate answers that do not complete the sentence correctly.

3. **Do not try to eliminate incorrect answers by looking only at the answers.** The incorrect answers are generally correct by themselves. The incorrect answers are generally incorrect only when used to complete the sentence.

4. **Never leave any answers blank.** Be sure to answer each question even if you are unsure of the correct response.

5. **Do not spend too much time on the Structure questions.** Be sure to leave adequate time for the Written Expression questions.

The following skills will help you to implement these strategies in the Structure section of the TOEFL test.

Skill 1: SUBJECTS AND VERBS

You know that a sentence in English should have a subject and a verb. The most common types of problems that you will encounter in the Structure section of the TOEFL test are related to subjects and verbs; perhaps the sentence is missing either the subject, or the verb, or both; perhaps the sentence has an extra subject or verb.

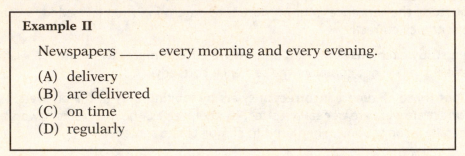

In this example, you should notice immediately that there is a verb, *was ringing*, but there is no subject. Answer (C) is the best answer because it is a singular subject that agrees with the singular verb *was ringing*. Answer (A), *loudly*, and answer (B), *in the morning*, are not subjects, so they are not correct. Although answer (D), *bells*, could be a subject, it is not correct because *bells* is plural and it does not agree with the singular verb *was ringing*.

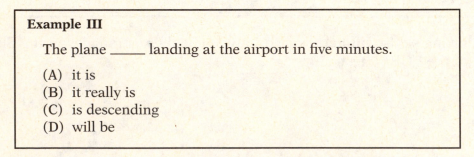

In this example, you should notice immediately that the sentence has a subject, *newspapers*, but that there is no verb. Because answer (B), *are delivered*, is a verb, it is the best answer. Answers (A), (C), and (D) are not verbs, so they are not correct.

> **Example III**
>
> The plane _____ landing at the airport in five minutes.
>
> (A) it is
> (B) it really is
> (C) is descending
> (D) will be

This sentence has a subject, *plane*, and has part of a verb, *landing*; to be correct, some form of the verb *be* is needed to make the verb complete. Answers (A) and

(B) are incorrect because the sentence already has a subject, *plane,* and does not need the extra subject *it.* Answer (C) is incorrect because *descending* is an extra part of a verb that is unnecessary because of *landing.* Answer (D) is the best answer; *will be* together with *landing* is a complete verb.

The following chart outlines the key information that you should remember about subjects and verbs.

SUBJECTS AND VERBS
A *sentence* in English must have at least one *subject* and one *verb.* **The first thing you should do as you read a sentence in the Structure section of the TOEFL test is to find the *subject* and the *verb.***

EXERCISE 1: Underline the subjects once and the verbs twice in each of the following sentences. Then indicate if the sentences are correct (C) or incorrect (I).

__I__   1. My best <u>friend</u> always helpful with problems.

__C__   2. The bus <u>schedule</u> <u><u>has changed</u></u> since last week.

_____   3. Accidentally dropped the glass on the floor.

_____   4. The customer paying the clerk for the clothes.

_____   5. The professor handed the syllabus to the students.

_____   6. Each day practiced the piano for hours.

_____   7. The basketball player tossed the ball into the hoop.

_____   8. The new student in the class very talkative and friendly.

_____   9. Walking with the children to school.

_____ 10. The whales headed south for the winter.

SKILL 2: OBJECTS OF PREPOSITIONS _____

An object of a preposition is a noun or a pronoun that comes after a preposition such as *in, at, of, to, by, behind,* and *on* to form a prepositional phrase.

The trip (to the *island*) (on *Saturday*) will last (for three *hours*).

This sentence contains three objects of prepositions. *Island* is the object of the preposition *to*; *Saturday* is the object of the preposition *on*; *hours* is the object of the preposition *for*.

An object of a preposition can cause confusion in the Structure section of the TOEFL test because it can be mistaken for the subject of a sentence.

Example

To Mike _____ was a big surprise.

(A) really
(B) the party
(C) funny
(D) when

In this example, you should look first for the subject and the verb. You should notice the verb *was* and should also notice that there is no subject. Do not think that *Mike* is the subject; *Mike* is the object of the preposition *to*, and one noun cannot be both a subject and an object at the same time. Because a subject is needed in this sentence, answer (B), *the party,* is the best answer. Answers (A), (C), and (D) are not correct because they cannot be subjects.

The following chart outlines the key information that you should remember about objects of prepositions.

OBJECTS OF PREPOSITIONS

A *preposition* is followed by a noun or pronoun that is called an *object of the preposition.* **If a word is an *object of a preposition,* it is <u>not</u> the *subject.***

NOTE: A list of prepositions and exercises to practice recognizing these prepositions can be found in Appendix B at the back of the text. You may want to complete these exercises before continuing with Exercise 2.

EXERCISE 2: Each of the following sentences contains one or more prepositional phrases. Underline the subjects once and the verbs twice. Circle the prepositional phrases that come before the verb. Then indicate if the sentences are correct (C) or incorrect (I).

_C_   1. The name (of the baby) (in the crib) is Jack.

_I_   2. (By the next meeting) (of the class) need to turn in the papers.

_____   3. The directions to the exercise on page 20 unclear.

_____   4. Because of the heavy rain throughout the night, the walkways are muddy.

_____   5. During the week eat lunch in the school cafeteria.

_____   6. In the morning after the concert was tired.

_____   7. In the summer the trip to the mountains is our favorite trip.

_____   8. In a box on the top shelf of the cabinet in the hallway of the house.

_____   9. With her purse in her hand ran through the door.

_____   10. At 1:00 in the morning the alarm clock on the table beside the bed rang.

EXERCISE (Skills 1–2): Underline the subjects once and the verbs twice. Circle the prepositional phrases that come before the verb. Then indicate if the sentences are correct (C) or incorrect (I).

_____   1. During the meeting in the office discussed the schedule.

_____   2. The doctor gave the patient a prescription.

_____   3. The tall evergreen trees along the road.

_____   4. The watch in the jewelry box needs a new battery.

_____   5. Pleasantly greets everyone in all the offices every morning.

_____   6. In the office of the building across the street from the park on the corner.

_____   7. The dishes in the sink really need to be washed as soon as possible.

_____   8. In a moment of worry about the problem with the cash in the account.

_____ 9. The plane from New York circling the airport.

_____ 10. On a regular basis the plants in the boxes under the window in the kitchen are watered and fed.

TOEFL EXERCISE (Skills 1–2): Choose the letter of the word or group of words that best completes the sentence.

1. Mark Twain _____ the years after the Civil War the "Gilded Age."

    (A) called
    (B) calling
    (C) he called
    (D) his calls

2. Early _____ toes instead of hooves on their feet.

    (A) horses
    (B) had horses
    (C) horses had
    (D) horses having

3. _____ grow close to the ground in the short Arctic summer.

    (A) Above tundra plants
    (B) Tundra plants
    (C) Tundra plants are found
    (D) For tundra plants

4. In 1867, _____ Alaska from the Russians for $7.2 million.

    (A) purchased the United States
    (B) to purchase the United States
    (C) the United States' purchase of
    (D) the United States purchased

5. Between 1725 and 1750, New England witnessed an increase in the specialization of _____.

    (A) occupations
    (B) occupies
    (C) they occupied
    (D) it occupied them

6. The large carotid artery _____ to the main parts of the brain.

    (A) carrying blood
    (B) blood is carried
    (C) carries blood
    (D) blood carries

7. _____ radio as the first practical system of wireless telegraphy.

    (A) Marconi's development
    (B) The development by Marconi
    (C) Developing Marconi
    (D) Marconi developed

8. In 1975, the first successful space probe to _____ beginning to send information back to Earth.

    (A) Venus
    (B) Venus the
    (C) Venus was
    (D) Venus it was

9. The two biggest resort _____ Arkansas are Hot Springs and Eureka Springs.

    (A) in
    (B) towns in
    (C) towns are
    (D) towns are in

10. NASA's Lyndon B. Johnson Space Center _____ control center for the Mercury, Gemini, and Apollo space flights.

    (A) it was at the
    (B) it was the
    (C) was the
    (D) the

SKILL 3: PRESENT PARTICIPLES

Present participles can cause confusion in the Structure section of the TOEFL test because a present participle can be either an adjective or a part of the verb. A present participle is the *-ing* form of the verb. It is part of the verb when it is preceded by some form of the verb *be*.

> The train *is arriving* at the station now.
> VERB

In this sentence, *arriving* is part of the verb because it is accompanied by *is*.

A present participle is an adjective when it is not accompanied by some form of the verb *be*.

> The train *arriving* at the station now is an hour late.
> ADJECTIVE

In this sentence, *arriving* is an adjective and not part of the verb because it is not accompanied by some form of *be*. The verb in this sentence is *is*.

The following example shows how a present participle can be confused with the verb in the Structure section of the TOEFL test.

Example

The film _____ appearing at the local theater is my favorite.

(A) now
(B) is
(C) it
(D) was

In this example, if you look at only the first words of the sentence, it appears that *film* is the subject and *appearing* is part of the verb. If you think that *appearing* is part of the verb, you might choose answer (B), *is*, or answer (D), *was*, to complete the verb. However, these two answers are incorrect because *appearing* is not part of the verb. You should recognize that *appearing* is a participial adjective rather than a verb because there is another verb in the sentence, *is*. In this sentence, there is a complete subject, *film*, and a complete verb, *is*, so this sentence does not need another subject or verb. The best answer to this question is answer (A).

The following chart outlines the key information you should remember about present participles.

PRESENT PARTICIPLES
A *present participle* is the *-ing* form of the verb. **The *present participle* can be (1) part of the *verb* or (2) an *adjective*.** It is part of the *verb* when it is accompanied by some form of the verb *be*. It is an *adjective* when it is not accompanied by some form of the verb *be*.

EXERCISE 3: Each of the following sentences contains one or more present participles. Underline the subjects once and the verbs twice. Circle the present participles, and label them as adjectives or verbs. Then indicate if the sentences are correct (C) or incorrect (I).

_C_   1. The (crying) baby needs to be picked up.
           ADJ.

_I_   2. The clothes are (lying) on the floor should go into the washing machine.
                        VERB

_____   3. The waitress bringing the steaming soup to the waiting diners.

_____   4. Most of the striking workers are walking the picket line.

_____   5. For her birthday, the child is getting a talking doll.

_____   6. The setting sun creating a rainbow of colors in the sky.

_____   7. The ship is sailing to Mexico is leaving tonight.

_____   8. The letters needing immediate answers are on the desk.

_____   9. The boring class just ending a few minutes ago.

_____   10. The fast-moving clouds are bringing freezing rain to the area.

SKILL 4: PAST PARTICIPLES _____

Past participles can cause confusion in the Structure section of the TOEFL test because a past participle can be either an adjective or a part of the verb. The past participle is the form of the verb that appears with *have* or *be*. It often ends in *-ed*, but there are also many irregular past participles in English.

> The mailman *has left* a letter in the mailbox.
>   VERB

> The classes *were taught* by Professor Smith.
>   VERB

In the first sentence, the past participle *left* is part of the verb because it is accompanied by *has*. In the second sentence, the past participle *taught* is part of the verb because it is accompanied by *were*.

A past participle is an adjective when it is not accompanied by some form of *be* or *have*.

> The letter *left* in the mailbox was for me.
>   ADJECTIVE

> The classes *taught* by Professor Smith were very interesting.
>   ADJECTIVE

In the first sentence, *left* is an adjective rather than a verb because it is not accompanied by a form of *be* or *have* (and there is a verb, *was*, later in the sentence). In the second sentence, *taught* is an adjective rather than a verb because it is not accompanied by a form of *be* or *have* (and there is a verb, *were*, later in the sentence).

The following example shows how a past participle can be confused with the verb in the Structure section of the TOEFL test.

Example

The bread _____ baked this morning smelled delicious.

(A) has
(B) was
(C) it
(D) just

In this example, if you look only at the first few words of the sentence, it appears that *bread* is the subject and *baked* is either a complete verb or a past participle that needs a helping verb. But if you look further in the sentence, you will see the verb *smelled*. You will then recognize that *baked* is a participial adjective and is therefore not part of the verb. Answers (A) and (B) are incorrect because *baked* is an adjective and does not need a helping verb such as *has* or *was*. Answer (C) is incorrect because there is no need for the subject *it*. Answer (D) is the best answer to this question.

The following chart outlines the key information that you should remember about past participles.

PAST PARTICIPLES

A *past participle* often ends in *-ed,* but there are also many irregular past participles. For many verbs, including *-ed* verbs, the *simple past* and the *past participle* are the same and can be easily confused. **The *-ed* form of the verb can be (1) the *simple past,* (2) the *past participle* of a verb, or (3) an *adjective.***

EXERCISE 4: Each of the following sentences contains one or more past participles. Underline the subjects once and the verbs twice. Circle the past participles, and label them as adjectives or verbs. Then indicate if the sentences are correct (C) or incorrect (I).

__I__ 1. The food is (served) in this restaurant is delicious.
           VERB

__C__ 2. The plane landed on the (deserted) runway.
                                    ADJ.

_____ 3. The unexpected guests arrived just at dinnertime.

_____ 4. The courses are listed in the catalogue are required courses.

_____ 5. The teacher found the lost exam.

_____ 6. The small apartment very crowded and disorganized.

_____ 7. The photographs developed yesterday showed Sam and his friends.

_____ 8. The locked drawer contained the unworn jewels.

_____ 9. The tree was blown over in the storm was cut into logs.

_____ 10. The students registered in this course are listed on that sheet of paper.

EXERCISE (Skills 3–4): Each of the following sentences contains one or more participles. Underline the subjects once and the verbs twice. Circle the participles, and label them as adjectives or verbs. Then indicate if the sentences are correct (C) or incorrect (I).

_____ 1. Our hosts are serving drinks on the tiled patio.

_____ 2. The tired woman taking a much needed nap.

_____ 3. The letters were sent on Monday arrived on Wednesday.

_____ 4. The winners deserved the big prize.

_____ 5. The plants are growing in the garden need a lot of water.

_____ 6. The shining stars lit up the darkened sky.

_____ 7. The driver rapidly increased the speed of the racing car.

_____ 8. The excited children trying to build a snowman in the falling snow.

____ 9. The students are completing the course will graduate in June.

____ 10. The dissatisfied customer is returning the broken toaster to the store.

TOEFL EXERCISE (Skills 3–4): Choose the letter of the word or group of words that best completes the sentence.

1. The first _____ appeared during the last period of the dinosaurs' reign.

   (A) flowers are plants
   (B) plants have flowers
   (C) plants flowers
   (D) flowering plants

2. The earliest medicines _____ from plants of various sorts.

   (A) obtaining
   (B) they obtained
   (C) were obtained
   (D) they were obtained

3. Simple sails were made from canvas _____ over a frame.

   (A) a stretch
   (B) stretched
   (C) was stretched
   (D) it was stretched

4. Pluto's moon, Charon, _____ in a slightly elliptical path around the planet.

   (A) moving
   (B) is moving
   (C) it was moving
   (D) in its movement

5. Techniques of breath control form an essential part of any _____ program to improve the voice.

   (A) it trains
   (B) train
   (C) trains
   (D) training

6. Robert E. Lee _____ the Confederate army to General Grant in 1865 at the Appomattox Courthouse.

   (A) surrendered
   (B) he surrendered
   (C) surrendering
   (D) surrender

7. The pituitary gland, _____ the brain, releases hormones to control other glands.

   (A) found below
   (B) it is found below
   (C) its foundation below
   (D) finds itself below

8. At around two years of age, many children regularly produce sentences _____ three or four words.

   (A) are containing
   (B) containing
   (C) contain
   (D) contains

9. Multinational companies _____ it increasingly important to employ internationally acceptable brand names.

   (A) finding
   (B) are finding
   (C) they find
   (D) they are finding

10. The cornea is located under the conjunctiva, on _____ of the eye.

   (A) the part is exposed
   (B) exposed the part
   (C) the exposed part
   (D) exposes the part

TOEFL REVIEW EXERCISE (Skills 1–4): Choose the letter of the word or group of words that best completes the sentence.

1. _____ first settled the Hawaiian Islands between A.D. 300 and 750.

   (A) The Polynesians
   (B) The Polynesians arrived
   (C) Because of the Polynesians
   (D) It was the Polynesians

2. In 1066, a bright comet _____ in the sky attracted much attention.

   (A) was appearing
   (B) appears
   (C) it appeared
   (D) appearing

3. In some daguerreotype cameras, _____ through a hole in the back of the box.

   (A) the object's view
   (B) the object was viewed
   (C) from the view of the object
   (D) viewed the object

4. In the Stone Age, stone tools _____ with other rock materials.

   (A) polishing
   (B) they polished
   (C) for polish
   (D) were polished

5. The first steamship to cross the Atlantic _____ Savannah, in 1819.

   (A) was the
   (B) it was the
   (C) the
   (D) in it the

6. The Earth's plates meet each other at cracks in the Earth _____ faults.

   (A) were called
   (B) calls
   (C) called
   (D) it was called

7. The first plant-like organisms probably _____ in the sea, perhaps 3 billion years ago.

   (A) life
   (B) living
   (C) lived
   (D) it was living

8. In male pattern baldness, _____ strongly influences the degree of hair loss.

   (A) heredity
   (B) inherited
   (C) inherits
   (D) heredity has

9. In *Watch the Skies,* Curtis Peebles _____ attempt to explain America's belief in flying saucers.

   (A) makes a fascinating
   (B) making a fascinating
   (C) fascination with making
   (D) fascination made a

10. The irregular coastline of _____ a succession of bays and inlets, with the hook of the Cape Cod peninsula in the southeast.

   (A) Massachusetts
   (B) Massachusetts is
   (C) Massachusetts it is
   (D) Massachusetts on

SKILL 5: COORDINATE CONNECTORS

Many sentences in English have more than one clause. (A clause is a group of words containing a subject and a verb.) When you have two clauses in an English sentence, you must connect the two clauses correctly. One way to connect two clauses is to use *and, but, or,* or *so* between the clauses.

> The sun was shining, *and* the sky was blue.

> The sky was blue, *but* it was very cold.

> It may rain tonight, *or* it may be clear.

> It was raining outside, *so* I took my umbrella.

In each of these examples, there are two clauses that are correctly joined with a coordinate connector—*and, but, or,* or *so*—and a comma (,).

The following example shows how this sentence pattern could be tested in the Structure section of the TOEFL test.

Example

I forgot my coat, _____ I got very cold.

(A) then
(B) so
(C) later
(D) as a result

In this example, you should notice quickly that there are two clauses, *I forgot my coat* and *I got very cold*. This sentence needs a connector to join the two clauses. *Then, later,* and *as a result* are not connectors, so answers (A), (C), and (D) are not correct. The best answer is answer (B) because *so* can connect two clauses in this manner.

The following chart lists the coordinate connectors and the sentence pattern used with them.

COORDINATE CONNECTORS			
and	*but*	*or*	*so*
S V ,	coordinate connector	S V	
It was raining ,	but	Bill went out to play.	

EXERCISE 5: Each of the following sentences contains more than one clause. Underline the subjects once and the verbs twice. Circle the connectors. Then indicate if the sentences are correct (C) or incorrect (I).

__C__   1. The lawn needs water every day, (or) it will turn brown.

__I__   2. The book was not long, (but) it difficult to read.

_____   3. It was raining, so decided not to go camping.

_____   4. The material has been cut, and the pieces have been sewn together.

_____   5. The patient took all the medicine, he did not feel much better.

_____   6. The bill must be paid immediately, or the electricity will be turned off.

_____   7. The furnace broke so the house got quite cold.

_____   8. The dress did not cost too much, but the quality it seemed excellent.

_____   9. The leaves kept falling off the trees, and the boys kept raking them up, but the yard was still covered.

_____   10. The mail carrier has already delivered the mail, so the letter is not going to arrive today, it probably will arrive tomorrow.

SKILL 6: ADVERB CLAUSE CONNECTORS _____

Sentences with *adverb clauses* have two basic patterns in English. Study the clauses and connectors in the following sentences:

He is tired because he has been working so hard.

Because he has been working so hard, he is tired.

In each of these examples, there are two clauses: *he is tired* and *he has been working so hard*. The clause *he has been working so hard* is an adverb clause that is introduced with the connector *because*. In the first example, the connector *because* comes in the middle of the sentence, and no comma (,) is used. In the second example, the connector *because* comes at the beginning of the sentence. In this pattern, when the connector comes at the beginning of the sentence, a comma (,) is required in the middle of the sentence.

The following example shows how this sentence pattern could be tested in the Structure section of the TOEFL test.

> **Example**
>
> _____ arrived at the library, he started to work immediately.
>
> (A) The student
> (B) When
> (C) He
> (D) After the student

In this example, you should recognize easily that the verb *arrived* needs a subject. There is also another clause, *he started to work immediately.* If you choose answer (A) or answer (C), you will have a subject for the verb *arrived,* but you will not have a connector to join the two clauses. Because you need a connector to join two clauses, answers (A) and (C) are incorrect. Answer (B) is incorrect because there is no subject for the verb *arrived.* Answer (D) is the best answer because there is a subject, *student,* for the verb, *arrived,* and there is a connector, *after,* to join the two clauses.

The following chart lists common adverb connectors and the sentence patterns used with them.

ADVERB CLAUSE CONNECTORS			
TIME	**CAUSE**	**CONDITION**	**CONTRAST**
after until as when before while since	because since	if whether	although even though though while
S V *Matt felt good* (adverb connector) *because* S V *he passed.*			
(adverb connector) *Because* S V , *Matt passed ,* S V *he felt good.*			

EXERCISE 6: Each of the following sentences contains more than one clause. Underline the subjects once and the verbs twice. Circle the connectors. Then indicate if the sentences are correct (C) or incorrect (I).

__C__   1. (After) the plane circled the airport, it landed on the main runway.

__I__   2. The registration process took many hours (since) the lines so long.

_____   3. This type of medicine can be helpful, it can also have some bad side effects.

_____   4. The waves were amazingly high when the storm hit the coastal town.

_____   5. We need to get a new car whether is on sale or not.

_____   6. Just as the bread came out of the oven, while a wonderful aroma filled the kitchen.

_____   7. Everyone has spent time unpacking boxes since the family moved into the new house.

_____   8. Although the area is a desert many plants bloom there in the springtime.

_____   9. The drivers on the freeway drove slowly and carefully while the rain was falling heavily because they did not want to have an accident.

_____ 10. If you plan carefully before you take a trip, will have a much better time because the small details will not cause problems.

EXERCISE (Skills 5–6): Each of the following sentences contains more than one clause. Underline the subjects once and the verbs twice. Circle the connectors. Then indicate if the sentences are correct (C) or incorrect (I).

_____   1. The lawyer presented a strong case, but the client was still found guilty.

_____   2. After the children read some stories before they went to bed.

_____   3. The report needed to be completed, the workers stayed late every night for a week.

_____   4. If you do not turn on the lights, you will trip in the dark.

_____   5. A thick fog came rolling in, so planes unable to land.

_____   6. All of the shoes are on sale until the current stock is gone.

_____   7. The ship leaving the dock even though some passengers were not on board.

_____   8. The outline must be turned in to the teacher a week before the paper is due, and must approve it.

_____   9. Because the food was cold when it was served the diners sent it back to the kitchen.

_____ 10. You should slow down while you are driving, or the police will pull your car over.

TOEFL EXERCISE (Skills 5–6): Choose the letter of the word or group of words that best completes the sentence.

1. A spacecraft is freed from friction _____ launched into space.

   (A) it
   (B) it is
   (C) after is
   (D) after it is

2. _____ with their surroundings, or they hide in crevices for protection.

   (A) Lobsters
   (B) Lobsters blend
   (C) Lobsters blending
   (D) Because lobsters blend

3. _____ a ball-and-socket joint, the elbow is a simple hinge joint.

   (A) While the shoulder
   (B) While the shoulder is
   (C) The shoulder is
   (D) The shoulder

4. A car has several sections with moving parts, _____ of those parts is essential.

   (A) good lubrication
   (B) well lubricated
   (C) and good lubrication
   (D) and well lubricated

5. Bears cannot see well _____ small eyes.

   (A) bears have
   (B) because having
   (C) because they have
   (D) because of bears

6. _____ at the Isthmus of Panama, so animals were able to migrate between North and South America.

   (A) A land bridge existed
   (B) When a land bridge existed
   (C) A land bridge
   (D) With a land bridge

7. _____ mostly made of granite, it also contains some human-made materials.

   (A) The Empire State Building
   (B) The Empire State Building is
   (C) Although the Empire State Building is
   (D) Although the Empire State Building is built

8. Pressure differences make the eardrum vibrate _____ the ear.

   (A) enters the sound waves
   (B) as sound waves
   (C) sound waves enter
   (D) as sound waves enter

9. An optical microscope magnifies as much as 2,000 times, but an electron microscope _____ as much as a million times.

   (A) magnifying
   (B) it magnifies
   (C) can magnify
   (D) magnify it

10. If scientific estimates are accurate, _____ with the Earth about 20,000 years ago.

   (A) the Cañon Diablo meteorite collided
   (B) the collision of the Cañon Diablo meteorite
   (C) the Cañon Diablo meteorite colliding
   (D) colliding the Cañon Diablo meteorite

TOEFL REVIEW EXERCISE (Skills 1–6): Choose the letter of the word or group of words that best completes the sentence.

1. _____ of the Pueblo Indians centered on intensive agriculture.

   (A) The economic activity
   (B) Because the economic activity
   (C) The economy was active
   (D) When the economic activity

2. In popular terminology, any long snowstorm with _____ is called a blizzard.

   (A) the amount of wind is large
   (B) a large amount of wind
   (C) it is very windy
   (D) very windy

3. Nuclear power can be produced by fusion, _____ produced by fission.

   (A) it can also be
   (B) it can also
   (C) and it can also be
   (D) and it can also

4. _____, igneous rocks may be changed into gneisses.

   (A) The temperature is high
   (B) If the temperature is high
   (C) High temperatures
   (D) If high temperature

5. In 1905, Henry Flagler _____ his plans to extend his Florida East Coast Railway out across the sea to Key West.

   (A) it was announced
   (B) announcement
   (C) the announcement of
   (D) announced

6. The sound _____ from a vibrating object will be high or low depending on the number of vibrations.

   (A) comes
   (B) it is coming
   (C) is coming
   (D) coming

7. During the late 1880s, urban streetcars were electrified through _____ large motors.

   (A) they used
   (B) used
   (C) the use of
   (D) when they used

8. _____ almost 274 square miles, but 96 percent of the park is under water.

   (A) Although Biscayne National Park encompasses
   (B) Biscayne National Park encompasses
   (C) Biscayne National Park encompassing
   (D) Biscayne National Park

9. Legislation _____ in 1916 and 1917 gave the Wilson administration authority to intervene in the national economy if it proved necessary.

   (A) it was passed
   (B) was passed
   (C) passed
   (D) passes

10. Because a family of birds set up housekeeping in Joel Chandler Harris's mailbox when the birds were in need of a place to stay, _____ the Wren's Nest.

   (A) the home is named
   (B) so the home is named
   (C) naming the home
   (D) the home's name

SKILL 7: NOUN CLAUSE CONNECTORS _____

A noun clause is a clause that functions as a noun; because the noun clause functions as a noun, it can be used in a sentence as an object of a verb (if it follows a verb) or an object of a preposition (if it follows a preposition). Study the clauses and connectors in the following sentences.

I don't know | *why* he said such things. |
NOUN CLAUSE AS OBJECT OF VERB

I am thinking about | *why* he said such things. |
NOUN CLAUSE AS OBJECT OF PREPOSITION

In the first example, there are two clauses, *I don't know* and *he said such things.* These two clauses are joined with the connector *why.* *Why* changes the clause *he said such things* into a noun clause which functions as the object of the verb *don't know.*

In the second example, the two clauses *I am thinking* and *he said such things* are also joined by the connector *why.* *Why* changes the clause *he said such things* into a noun clause which functions as the object of the preposition *about.*

The following example shows how these sentence patterns could be tested in the Structure section of the TOEFL test.

Example

The citizens worry about _____ is doing.

(A) what the government
(B) the government
(C) what
(D) what the government it

In this example, the sentence contains the main subject and verb, *the citizens worry,* and it also contains an additional verb, *is doing.* The sentence needs a subject for the verb *is doing* and a connector to join the two clauses. The best answer is answer (A) because it has the connector *what* and the subject *government.* Answer (B) is incorrect because it does not have a connector. Answer (C) is incorrect because it does not have a subject for *is doing.* Answer (D) is incorrect because it has two subjects for *is doing.*

The following chart lists the noun clause connectors and the sentence patterns used with them.

NOUN CLAUSE CONNECTORS
• *what, when, where, why, how* • *whether, if* • *that*

S	V	noun clause connector		S	V	
Sally	*explained*	*why*		*she*	*did*	*it.*

EXERCISE 7: Each of the following sentences contains more than one clause. Underline the subjects once and the verbs twice. Circle the connectors. Then indicate if the sentences are correct (C) or incorrect (I).

__C__   1. It is unfortunate (that) the meal is not ready yet.

__I__   2. She told me (when) should pick up the children.

_____   3. The instructor explained where was the computer lab located.

_____   4. We could not believe what he did to us.

_____   5. Do you want to know if it going to rain tomorrow?

_____   6. We never know whether we will get paid or not.

_____   7. This evening you can decide what do you want to do.

_____   8. The manager explained how wanted the work done.

_____   9. The map showed where the party would be held.

_____ 10. Can you tell me why was the mail not delivered today?

Skill 8: NOUN CLAUSE CONNECTOR/SUBJECTS _____

In Skill 7 we saw that noun clause connectors can be used to introduce noun clauses. In Skill 8 we will see that in some cases a noun clause connector is not just a connector; a noun clause connector can also be the subject of the clause at the same time. Study the clauses and connectors in the following sentences.

> I know *what* happened yesterday.
> NOUN CLAUSE AS OBJECT OF VERB

> We are thinking about *what* happened yesterday.
> NOUN CLAUSE AS OBJECT OF PREPOSITION

In the first example, there are two clauses: *I know* and *what happened yesterday.* These two clauses are joined by the connector *what.* It is important to understand that in this sentence the word *what* serves two functions. It is both the subject of the verb *happened* and the connector that joins the two clauses.

In the second example, there are two clauses. In the first clause *we* is the subject of *are thinking.* In the second clause *what* is the subject of *happened. What* also serves as the connector that joins the two clauses. The noun clause *what happened yesterday* functions as the object of the preposition *about.*

The following example shows how this sentence pattern could be tested in the Structure section of the TOEFL test.

Example

The company was prepared for _____ happened with the economy.

(A) it
(B) the problem
(C) what
(D) when

In this example, the sentence contains the main clause *the company was prepared* and another verb, *happened.* The sentence needs a subject for the verb *happened* and a connector to join the two clauses. Answer (C) is the best answer because *what* is both a connector and a subject. Answer (A) is incorrect because *it* is a subject, but there is no connector. Answer (B) is incorrect because *the problem* is a subject, but there is no connector. Answer (D) is incorrect because *why* is a connector, but it is not a subject.

The following chart lists the noun clause connector/subjects and the sentence pattern used with them.

NOUN CLAUSE CONNECTOR/SUBJECTS		
who	*what*	*which*
S V	**noun clause connector/ subject**	**V**
Al told me	*what*	*happened.*

EXERCISE 8: Each of the following sentences contains more than one clause. Underline the subjects once and the verbs twice. Circle the connectors. Then indicate if the sentences are correct (C) or incorrect (I).

_C_   1. The teacher heard (who) answered the question.

_I_   2. I do not understand (what) it went wrong.

_____   3. Of the three movies, I can't decide which is the best.

_____   4. She did not remember who in her class.

_____   5. No one is sure what did it happen in front of the building.

_____   6. We found out which was her favorite type of candy.

_____   7. Do you know what caused the plants to die?

_____   8. I am not sure which it is the most important course in the program.

_____   9. We thought about who would be the best vice president.

_____   10. She saw what in the box in the closet.

EXERCISE (Skills 7–8): Each of the following sentences contains more than one clause. Underline the subjects once and the verbs twice. Circle the connectors. Then indicate if the sentences are correct (C) or incorrect (I).

_____   1. It doubtful whether he will pass the test or not.

_____   2. The group discussed who he should receive the prize.

_____   3. It is not certain why the class was cancelled.

_____   4. I will do what does it need to be done.

_____   5. We forgot when did the movie start.

_____   6. I would like to ask if you could come over for dinner this weekend.

_____   7. The children knew which the best game to play.

_____   8. The advisor informed her that needed to add another class.

_____   9. He saw who took the money.

_____   10. It is unclear how the window got broken.

TOEFL EXERCISE (Skills 7–8): Choose the letter of the word or group of words that best completes the sentence.

1. Today, the true story of _____ at Little Bighorn remains a mystery.

   (A) happened
   (B) it happened
   (C) what happened
   (D) what happening

2. For more than a decade, _____ that certain species are becoming scarce.

   (A) the warnings of bird-watchers
   (B) warn the bird-watchers
   (C) bird-watchers have warned
   (D) a warning for bird-watchers

3. Early in the eighteenth century, Halley accurately predicted when _____ of 1682 would return.

   (A) the comet
   (B) was the comet
   (C) the comet was
   (D) had the comet

4. No single factor explains why _____ vary so greatly among individuals.

   (A) aging affects
   (B) the effects of aging
   (C) aging has an effect
   (D) the aging effect

5. Lack of clarity about _____ the party in the coming year will be removed at the party's convention.

   (A) will lead
   (B) lead
   (C) they will lead
   (D) who will lead

6. We do not _____ the bow drill was first developed for woodworking or fire making.

   (A) whether it
   (B) know whether it
   (C) know whether
   (D) sure whether

7. Minute Man National Historical Park is a monument to where _____.

   (A) the beginning of the Revolutionary War
   (B) in the beginning of the Revolutionary War
   (C) the Revolutionary War to begin
   (D) the Revolutionary War began

8. Tests on the colors of cars were conducted at the University of California to determine _____ the safest colors for cars.

   (A) which
   (B) which were
   (C) if
   (D) how were

9. The National Institute of Dental Research estimates _____ in fluoridated areas have about 25 percent less tooth decay than children elsewhere.

   (A) for school children
   (B) school children's
   (C) that school children
   (D) that for school children

10. The process of photosynthesis explains how _____ able to use the energy in sunlight to manufacture foods from the simple chemicals in air and water.

   (A) green plants
   (B) green plants are
   (C) planting greens
   (D) with green plants are

TOEFL REVIEW EXERCISE (Skills 1–8): Choose the letter of the word or group of words that best completes the sentence.

1. Air near the equator _____ a faster west-to-east motion than air farther from the equator.

   (A) to have
   (B) it has
   (C) has
   (D) having

2. About 4000 B.C., humans discovered that _____ obtained from special rocks called ores.

   (A) metals could be
   (B) the ability of metallic
   (C) possibly metallic
   (D) could metals be

3. _____ quickly after an animal dies.

   (A) In the degradation of DNA
   (B) Degrading DNA
   (C) DNA degrades
   (D) For DNA to degrade

4. _____ aerodynamic design has contributed greatly to reducing resistance to motion.

   (A) Improved
   (B) It improves
   (C) Improvement
   (D) They improve

5. The southern part of Florida is much warmer in the winter than the northern part, so more _____ to the south.

   (A) flocking tourists
   (B) touring flocks
   (C) flocks of tourists
   (D) tourists flock

6. The Moon's gravity pulls water on the near side of the Earth toward the Moon, and this is what _____ tides to occur.

   (A) the cause
   (B) causes
   (C) causing
   (D) the cause of

7. _____, they pick up fragments of rock which become frozen into the base of the ice.

   (A) Glaciers move
   (B) Glaciers moving
   (C) They were glaciers
   (D) As glaciers move

8. The tape measure first evolved from _____ used by the Egyptians.

   (A) the chains measure
   (B) the chains are measured
   (C) the chains are measuring
   (D) the measuring chains

9. A typical Atlantic hurricane starts as a low pressure system near _____.

   (A) Africa coasts
   (B) coast to Africa
   (C) the African coast
   (D) Africa has a coast

10. It is not clear whether the subdivisions of the neocortex _____ units.

    (A) individual
    (B) are individual
    (C) they are individual
    (D) individually

SKILL 9: ADJECTIVE CLAUSE CONNECTORS

An adjective clause describes a noun. Because the clause is an adjective, it is positioned directly after the noun that it describes.

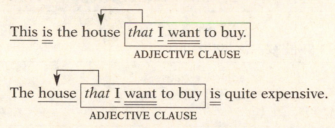

This is the house *that* I want to buy.
ADJECTIVE CLAUSE

The house *that* I want to buy is quite expensive.
ADJECTIVE CLAUSE

In the first example, there are two clauses: *this* is the subject of the verb *is*, and *I* is the subject of the verb *want*. *That* is the adjective clause connector that joins these two clauses, and the adjective clause *that I want to buy* describes the noun *house*.

In the second example, there are also two clauses: *house* is the subject of the verb *is*, and *I* is the subject of the verb *want*. In this sentence also, *that* is the adjective clause connector that joins these two clauses, and the adjective clause *that I want to buy* describes the noun *house*.

The following example shows how these sentence patterns could be tested in the Structure section of the TOEFL test.

Example

The job _____ started yesterday was rather difficult.

(A) when
(B) was
(C) after
(D) that he

In this example, you should notice quickly that there are two clauses: *job* is the subject of the verb *was*, and the verb *started* needs a subject. Because there are two clauses, a connector is also needed. Answers (A) and (C) have connectors, but there are no subjects, so these answers are not correct. Answer (B) changes *started* into a passive verb; in this case the sentence would have one subject and two verbs, so answer (B) is not correct. The best answer to this question is answer (D). The correct sentence should say: *The job that he started yesterday was rather difficult*. In this sentence *job* is the subject of the verb *was*, *he* is the subject of the verb *started*, and the connector *that* joins these two clauses.

The following chart lists the adjective clause connectors and the sentence patterns used with them.

ADJECTIVE CLAUSE CONNECTORS		
whom (for people)	*which* (for things)	*that* (for people or things)

S **V**	adjective clause connector	**S** **V**
I *like* *the dress*	*that*	*you* *are wearing.*

S	adjective clause connector	**S** **V** **V**	
The dress	*that*	*you* *are wearing* *is* *beautiful.*	

NOTE: The adjective connectors can be omitted. This omission is very common in spoken English or in casual written English. It is not as common in formal English or in the Structure section of the TOEFL test.

EXERCISE 9: Each of the following sentences contains more than one clause. Underline the subjects once and the verbs twice. Circle the connectors. Then indicate if the sentences are correct (C) or incorrect (I).

_C_ 1. I did not believe the story (that) he told me.

_I_ 2. Ms. Brown, (whom) did you recommend for the job, will start work tomorrow.

_____ 3. The lecture notes which lent me were not clearly written.

_____ 4. Sally has an appointment with the hairdresser whom you recommended.

_____ 5. The phone number that you gave me.

_____ 6. She is able to solve all the problems which did she cause.

_____ 7. The day that she spent on the beach left her sunburned.

_____ 8. Next week I am going to visit my cousins, whom have not seen in several years.

_____ 9. Did you forget the promise whom you made?

_____ 10. The teacher whom the students like the most is their history teacher.

SKILL 10: ADJECTIVE CLAUSE CONNECTOR/SUBJECTS

In Skill 9 we saw that adjective clause connectors can be used to introduce clauses that describe nouns. In Skill 10 we will see that in some cases an adjective clause connector is not just a connector; an adjective clause connector can also be the subject of the clause at the same time.

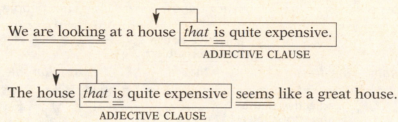

In the first example, there are two clauses: *we* is the subject of the verb *are looking*, and *that* is the subject of the verb *is*. These two clauses are joined with the connector *that*. Notice that in this example the word *that* serves two functions at the same time: it is the subject of the verb *is*, and it is the connector that joins the two clauses. The adjective clause *that is quite expensive* describes the noun *house*.

In the second example, there are also two clauses: *house* is the subject of the verb *seems*, and *that* is the subject of the verb *is*. In this example, *that* also serves two functions: it is the subject of the verb *is*, and it is the connector that joins the two clauses. Because *that is quite expensive* is an adjective clause describing the noun *house*, it directly follows *house*.

The following example shows how these sentence patterns could be tested in the Structure section of the TOEFL test.

Example

_____ just dropped off a package for you is my sister.

(A) The woman
(B) The woman who
(C) Because the woman
(D) With the woman

In this example, you should notice immediately that the sentence has two verbs, *dropped* and *is*, and each of them needs a subject. The only answer that has two subjects is answer (B), so answer (B) is the correct answer. The correct sentence should say: *The woman who just dropped off a package for you is my sister.* In this sentence *woman* is the subject of the verb *is*, and *who* is the subject of the verb *dropped*. *Who* is also the connector that joins the two clauses.

The following chart lists the adjective clause connector/subjects and the sentence patterns used with them.

ADJECTIVE CLAUSE CONNECTOR/SUBJECTS		
who (for people)	*which* (for things)	*that* (for people or things)
S **V** adjective clause connector/subject **V** *I* *bought* *the dress* *that* *was* *on sale.*		
S adjective clause connector/subject **V** **V** *The dress* *that* *was* *on sale* *was* *beautiful.*		
NOTE: Although adjective clause connectors (Skill 9) can be omitted in informal English, adjective clause connector/subjects (Skill 10) can never be omitted.		

EXERCISE 10: Each of the following sentences contains more than one clause. Underline the subjects once and the verbs twice. Circle the connectors. Then indicate if the sentences are correct (C) or incorrect (I).

__C__   1. The children (that) were vaccinated did not get sick.

__I__   2. I did not vote for the politician (who) he just won the election.

_____   3. The dog that barking belongs to my neighbor.

_____   4. I took two of the blue pills, which were very effective.

_____   5. We rented an apartment from the landlord who does he own the buildings on Maple Street.

_____   6. She forgot to attend the meeting which it began at 11:00.

_____   7. Any student who does not turn in the paper by Friday will fail the class.

_____   8. The people which came in late had to sit at the back.

_____   9. The courses that satisfy the graduation requirements they are difficult.

_____   10. After dinner she went to visit her parents, who were living down the street.

EXERCISE (Skills 9–10): Each of the following sentences contains more than one clause. Underline the subjects once and the verbs twice. Circle the connectors. Then indicate if the sentences are correct (C) or incorrect (I).

_____ 1. My sisters prefer to eat food that have cooked themselves.

_____ 2. The boat that hit the underwater rock sank.

_____ 3. The car which he was driving could not possibly be his.

_____ 4. The children built a house in the tree that in the backyard.

_____ 5. The cost of the trip which we wanted to take.

_____ 6. The children are playing with the toys which their mother told them to put away.

_____ 7. The guests who were seated around the dinner table.

_____ 8. The students have to read all the chapters which are on the test.

_____ 9. I really do not like the artists which you like.

_____ 10. The stones that they were set in the ring were quite valuable.

TOEFL EXERCISE (Skills 9–10): Choose the letter of the word or group of words that best completes the sentence.

1. Modern humans, who first appeared about 600,000 years ago, _____ _Homo sapiens._

   (A) calling
   (B) were called
   (C) they called
   (D) they were called

2. The first writing _____ evidence of is on Mesopotamian clay tablets.

   (A) we
   (B) that we
   (C) has
   (D) that we have

3. _____ drought-resistant plants which store water in fleshy tissue.

   (A) Succulents are
   (B) Succulents
   (C) They are succulents
   (D) Succulents which are

4. Benjamin Kabelsky, whom _____ as Jack Benny, was a famous comedian in vaudeville and on radio and television.

   (A) most people's knowledge
   (B) most people know
   (C) knowing most people
   (D) the knowledge of most people

5. _____ that hunted other animals tended to have very narrow, sharp, curved claws.

   (A) For dinosaurs
   (B) Dinosaurs are known
   (C) Dinosaurs
   (D) Like dinosaurs

6. The first eyeglasses had convex lenses for the aged who _____ farsighted.

   (A) had become
   (B) they had become
   (C) becoming
   (D) it became

7. Chimney Rock, _____ 500 feet above the North Platte River, has eroded considerably in the last two centuries.

   (A) stands
   (B) is standing
   (C) it stands
   (D) which stands

8. _____ that accompany recurring bouts of severe depression reduce bone density.

   (A) It changes hormones
   (B) Hormonal changes
   (C) The hormones change
   (D) The change in hormones is

9. Willa Cather is an author _____ for her evocative and memorable vision of frontier prairie life.

   (A) whom readers
   (B) the praise of readers
   (C) whom praisings
   (D) whom readers praise

10. Mars's tiny moon Phobos is a small mountain of rock that _____ from the asteroid belt by Mars's gravitational pull.

    (A) was probably captured
    (B) it probably
    (C) the probable capture
    (D) probably the capture

TOEFL REVIEW EXERCISE (Skills 1–10): Choose the letter of the word or group of words that best completes the sentence.

1. _____ is famous as the home of the U.S. Naval Academy.

   (A) Annapolis
   (B) Because of Annapolis
   (C) Why Annapolis
   (D) Because Annapolis

2. Some scientists think _____ be a planet but a moon of Neptune.

   (A) that Pluto does not seem
   (B) not Pluto
   (C) Pluto that might not
   (D) that Pluto might not

3. With _____ of sophisticated oil lamps, elaborate tools were made to cut the wicks.

   (A) appeared
   (B) the appearance
   (C) the appearance was
   (D) it appeared

4. Fort Union was the site of what _____ principal fur-trading post on the upper Missouri River.

   (A) the
   (B) being the
   (C) was the
   (D) it was the

5. Since _____ commercial risk, it has to appeal to a large audience to justify its cost.

   (A) the face of the movie
   (B) moving faces
   (C) a movie faces
   (D) to face a movie

6. A current of water known as the Gulf Stream comes up from the Gulf of Mexico, and then _____ the North Atlantic toward Europe.

   (A) it crosses
   (B) crossing
   (C) with its crosses
   (D) crosses it

7. Systems _____ the two symbols 0 and 1 are called binary number systems.

   (A) use
   (B) they use
   (C) uses
   (D) using

8. Genes, _____ the blueprints for cell construction, exist in tightly organized packages called chromosomes.

   (A) are
   (B) they are
   (C) which
   (D) which are

9. The Earth's atmosphere consists of gases _____ in place around the Earth by the gravitational pull of the planet.

   (A) held
   (B) hold
   (C) it holds
   (D) the hold

10. Oscar Hammerstein II collaborated with a number of composers including Jerome Kern, whom _____ in writing the musical *Show Boat*.

    (A) joined
    (B) was joined
    (C) he joined
    (D) joining

THE WRITTEN EXPRESSION QUESTIONS

Questions 16 through 40 in the Structure and Written Expression section of the TOEFL test measure your knowledge of the correct way to express yourself in English writing. Each question in this section consists of one sentence in which four words or groups of words have been underlined. You must choose the letter of the word or group of words that is *not* correct.

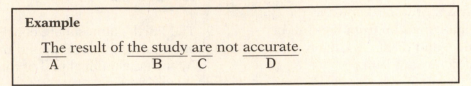

If you look at the underlined words in this example, you should see that the verb *are* is not correct. The verb should be the singular *is* because the subject *result* is singular. Therefore, you should choose answer (C) because (C) is not correct.

STRATEGIES FOR THE WRITTEN EXPRESSION QUESTIONS

1. **First look at the underlined word or groups of words.** You want to see if you can spot which of the four answer choices is *not* correct.

2. **If you have been unable to find the error by looking only at the four underlined expressions, then read the complete sentence.** Often an underlined expression is incorrect because of something in another part of the sentence.

3. **Never leave any answers blank.** Be sure to answer each question even if you are unsure of the correct response.

The following skills will help you to implement these strategies in the Written Expression questions.

SKILL 11: AGREEMENT AFTER PREPOSITIONAL PHRASES ____

Subject/verb agreement is simple: if the subject of a sentence is singular, then the verb must be singular; if the subject of the sentence is plural, then the verb must be plural. An *s* on a verb usually indicates that a verb is singular, while an *s* on a noun usually indicates that the noun is plural. (Do not forget irregular plurals of nouns such as *women, children,* and *people.*)

> The <u>dog</u> <u>barks</u> at night.

> The <u>dogs</u> <u>bark</u> at night.

In the first example, the singular subject *dog* requires a singular verb, *barks*. In the second example, the plural subject *dogs* requires a plural verb, *bark*.

Sometimes prepositional phrases can come between the subject and the verb on the TOEFL test, and this can cause confusion. If the object of the preposition is singular and the subject is plural, or if the object of the preposition is plural and the subject is singular, there can be a problem in making the subject and verb agree.

> The <u>door</u> (to the rooms) <u>are</u>* locked.
>   SINGULAR   PLURAL

> The <u>doors</u> (to the room) <u>is</u>* locked.
>   PLURAL   SINGULAR

(* indicates an error)

In the first example, you might think that *rooms* is the subject because it comes directly in front of the verb *are*. However, *rooms* is not the subject because it is the object of the preposition *to*. The subject of the sentence is *door*, so the verb should be *is*. In the second example, you might think that *room* is the subject because it comes directly in front of the verb *is*. You should recognize in this example that *room* is not the subject because it is the object of the preposition *to*. Because the subject of the sentence is *doors*, the verb should be *are*.

The following chart outlines the key information that you should understand about subject/verb agreement with prepositional phrases.

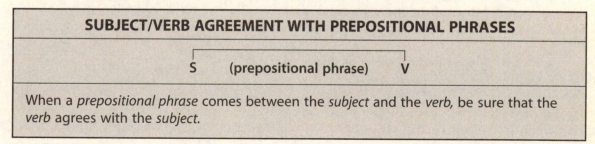

SUBJECT/VERB AGREEMENT WITH PREPOSITIONAL PHRASES
S   (prepositional phrase)   V
When a *prepositional phrase* comes between the *subject* and the *verb*, be sure that the *verb* agrees with the *subject*.

EXERCISE 11: Each of the following sentences has one or more prepositional phrases between the subject and verb. Put parentheses around the prepositional phrases. Underline the subjects once and the verbs twice. Then indicate if the sentences are correct (C) or incorrect (I).

__C__   1. The <u>subject</u> (of the lectures) <u><u>was</u></u> quite interesting.

__I__   2. The <u>supplies</u> (for the camping trip) <u><u>needs</u></u> to be packed.

_____   3. The chairs under the table in the dining room is quite comfortable.

_____   4. The players on the winning team in the competition were very talented.

_____   5. The food for the guests at the party are on the long tables.

_____   6. The cost of the clothes was higher than I had expected.

_____   7. The rugs in the front rooms of the house are going to be washed today.

_____   8. The servers in this restaurant always does their job efficiently.

_____   9. The lights in the corner of the room need to be kept on all night.

_____   10. The meeting of the members of the council begins at 3:00 in the afternoon.

SKILL 12: AGREEMENT AFTER EXPRESSIONS OF QUANTITY

A particular agreement problem occurs when the subject is an expression of quantity such as *all, most,* or *some* followed by the preposition *of.* In this situation, the subject (*all, most,* or *some*) can be singular or plural, depending on what follows the preposition *of.*

> <u>Most</u> (of the *meal*) <u><u>was</u></u> delicious.
> SINGULAR

> <u>Most</u> (of the *meals*) <u><u>were</u></u> delicious.
> PLURAL

> <u>Most</u> (of the *food*) <u><u>was</u></u> delicious.
> UNCOUNTABLE

In the first example, the subject *most* refers to the singular noun *meal,* so the correct verb is therefore the singular verb *was.* In the second example, the subject *most* refers to the plural noun *meals,* so the correct verb is the plural verb *were.* In the third example, the subject *most* refers to the uncountable noun *food,* so the correct verb is therefore the singular verb *was.*

These sentences contain examples of the types of problems that are common on the TOEFL test.

<u>All</u> (of the book) <u>were</u>* interesting.

<u>Half</u> (of the students) <u>is</u>* late to class.

In the first example, the plural verb *were* should be the singular verb *was* because the subject *all* refers to the singular noun *book*. In the second example, the singular verb *is* should be the plural verb *are* because the subject *half* refers to the plural noun *students*.

The following chart outlines the key information that you should understand about subject/verb agreement after expressions of quantity.

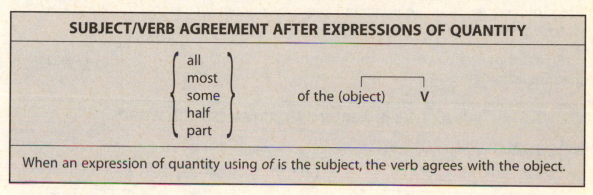

SUBJECT/VERB AGREEMENT AFTER EXPRESSIONS OF QUANTITY

all
most
some
half
part

of the (object)   V

When an expression of quantity using *of* is the subject, the verb agrees with the object.

EXERCISE 12: Each of the following sentences has a quantity expression as the subject. Underline the subjects once and the verbs twice. Circle the objects that the verbs agree with. Then indicate if the sentences are correct (C) or incorrect (I).

_C_   1. <u>Half</u> of the (students) in the class <u>arrive</u> early.

_I_   2. <u>Some</u> of the (fruit) <u>are</u> rotten.

_____   3. All of the next chapter contains very important information.

_____   4. Most of the people in the room is paying attention.

_____   5. Part of the soup is left on the stove.

_____   6. Some of the movie were just too violent for me.

_____   7. All of the details in the report needs to be checked.

_____   8. Most of the money is needed to pay the bills.

_____ 9. The first half of the class consists of lecture and note taking.

_____ 10. Some of the questions on the test was impossible to answer.

SKILL 13: AGREEMENT AFTER CERTAIN WORDS _____

Certain words in English are always grammatically singular, even though they might have plural meanings.

Everybody in the theater <u>are watching</u>* the film attentively.

Even though we understand from this example that a lot of people are watching the film, *everybody* is singular and requires a singular verb. The plural verb *are watching* should be changed to the singular verb *is watching*.

The following chart lists the grammatically singular words that have plural meanings.

SUBJECT/VERB AGREEMENT AFTER CERTAIN WORDS
These words or expressions are grammatically singular, so they take singular verbs:

anybody	*everybody*	*nobody*	*somebody*	*each* (+ noun)
anyone	*everyone*	*no one*	*someone*	*every* (+ noun)
anything	*everything*	*nothing*	*something*	

EXERCISE 13: Each of the following sentences contains one of the words that is grammatically singular but has a plural meaning. Underline these words once and underline the verbs twice. Then indicate if the sentences are correct (C) or incorrect (I).

__I__ 1. <u>Anybody</u> <u>are</u> welcome at the party.

__C__ 2. <u>No one</u> here <u>is</u> afraid of skydiving.

_____ 3. Everyone in the world needs love and respect.

_____ 4. Someone have to clean up the house.

_____ 5. Each plant in the garden appear healthy and strong.

_____ 6. You should understand that anything is possible.

_____ 7. Everything in the salad are good for you.

_____ 8. Nobody in the class have completed the assignment on time.

_____ 9. I am sure that every detail have been considered.

_____ 10. Everybody know the rules, but somebody is not following them.

EXERCISE (Skills 11–13): Each of the following sentences may have a problem with subject/verb agreement. Underline the subjects once and the verbs twice. Then indicate if the sentences are correct (C) or incorrect (I).

_____ 1. The receptionist in the entryway to the offices is able to answer your questions.

_____ 2. All of the information in the documents are important.

_____ 3. Anyone in one of the classes has to take the final exam.

_____ 4. The coordinator of community services are arranging the program.

_____ 5. Most of the car are covered with mud.

_____ 6. Nothing more is going to be completed today.

_____ 7. The drinks in the pitchers on the table in the ballroom is for everyone.

_____ 8. Everybody were told to be here at 8:00, but somebody is not here.

_____ 9. Some of the meetings at the conference are limited to ten participants.

_____ 10. The sauce on the vegetables in the yellow bowl taste really delicious.

TOEFL EXERCISE (Skills 11–13): Choose the letter of the underlined word or group of words that is not correct.

_____ 1. Nobody <u>know</u> when the <u>process</u> of glass-making <u>was</u> <u>invented</u>.
                A   B   C   D

_____ 2. Sugars <u>like</u> glucose <u>is</u> <u>made</u> <u>up</u> of carbon, hydrogen, and oxygen atoms.
                  A   B C   D

_____ 3. Part of the electricity <u>used</u> in the United States <u>today</u> <u>come</u> from
                                 A   B   C
         hydroelectric <u>sources</u>.
                       D

_____ 4. The languages of the world <u>presents</u> a vast <u>array</u> of structural <u>similarities</u> and
                                      A   B   C
         <u>differences</u>.
            D

_____ 5. The rise of multinationals <u>have</u> <u>resulted</u> in a great deal of legal ambiguity
                                   A   B
         because multinationals <u>can</u> <u>operate</u> in so many jurisdictions.
                                 C   D

_____ 6. All of the east–west interstate highways in the United States <u>has</u> even
                                                           A
         <u>numbers</u>, while north–south interstate highways <u>are</u> <u>odd-numbered</u>.
          B   C   D

_____ 7. <u>When</u> a massive star in the large Magellanic Cloud <u>exploded</u> in 1987, a wave
         A   B
         of neutrinos <u>were</u> <u>detected</u> on Earth.
                     C   D

_____ 8. Some of the agricultural <u>practices</u> <u>used</u> today <u>is</u> responsible for <u>fostering</u>
                                    A   B   C   D
         desertification.

_____ 9. Every open space in the <u>targeted</u> area that <u>has</u> grass and a few bushes <u>are</u>
                            A   B   C
         <u>occupied</u> by the white-crowned sparrow.
          D

_____ 10. Krakatoa <u>is remembered</u> as the volcano that <u>put</u> so much ash into the air that
                           A   B
         sunsets around the world <u>was affected</u> for two years <u>afterward</u>.
                                C   D

TOEFL REVIEW EXERCISE (Skills 1–13): Choose the letter of the word or group of words that best completes the sentence.

1. _____ the earliest system of writing.

   (A) The constitution of pictograms
   (B) Pictograms in the constitution
   (C) Constitute the pictograms
   (D) Pictograms constitute

2. At temperatures _____ absolute zero, substances possess minimal energy.

   (A) approach
   (B) approaches
   (C) approaching
   (D) they approach

3. The Earth's one-year revolution around the Sun changes how _____ on one hemisphere or the other.

   (A) falling sunlight
   (B) the fall of sunlight
   (C) sunlight in the fall
   (D) sunlight falls

4. Though sporadic interest in regional dialects _____ for centuries, the first large-scale systematic studies did not take place until the nineteenth century.

   (A) has existed
   (B) it existed
   (C) has it existed
   (D) existing with it

Choose the letter of the underlined word or group of words that is not correct.

_____ 5. The waters of the Chattahoochee River fills Lake Lanier.
           A   B   C D

_____ 6. The first set of false teeth similar to those in use today it was made in France
                      A   B C D
        in the 1780s.

_____ 7. The term "Yankee" was originally a nickname for people from New England,
                      A
        but now anyone from the United States are referred to as a Yankee.
                                    B   C   D

_____ 8. A network of small arteries, mostly sandwiched between the skin and the
                                      A
        underlying muscles, supply blood to the face and scalp.
          B   C   D

_____ 9. Mesquite is a small tree in the Southwest who can withstand the severest
               A   B   C   D
        drought.

_____ 10. At the end of the Revolution, most of the army units of the young nation was
              A   B
        almost entirely disbanded, leaving a total national military force of 80 men
                      C   D
        in 1784.

Skill 14: PARALLEL STRUCTURE WITH COORDINATE CONJUNCTIONS

The job of the coordinate conjunctions (*and, but, or*) is to join together equal expressions. In other words, what is on one side of these words must be parallel to what is on the other side. These conjunctions can join nouns, or verbs, or adjectives, or phrases, or clauses; they just must join together the same structures. Here are examples of equal structures correctly joined by coordinate conjunctions:

He discussed the problem with the nurse *and* the doctor.

The professor was knowledgeable *but* boring.

She hikes, jogs, *or* rides her bicycle whenever she can.

There are meetings in the morning, in the afternoon, *and* in the evening.

You can do the work because you want to do it *or* because you have to do it.

In the first example, two nouns are joined by the coordinate conjunction *and*. In the second example, two adjectives are joined by the coordinate conjunction *but*. In the third example, three verbs are joined by the coordinate conjunction *or*. In the fourth example, three phrases are joined by the coordinate conjunction *and*. In the last example, two clauses are joined by the coordinate conjunction *or*.

The sentences that follow show the types of errors in parallel structure that are common on the TOEFL test.

The evening dress was beauty* but expensive.

The student reads each chapter, takes a lot of notes, and memories* the material.

In the first example, the coordinate conjunction *but* joins the noun *beauty* and the adjective *expensive*. The adjective *beautiful* is needed in place of *beauty*. In the second example, the coordinate conjunction *and* joins the verb *reads*, the verb *takes*, and the plural noun *memories*. The verb *memorizes* is needed in place of *memories*.

The following chart outlines the use of parallel structures with coordinate conjunctions.

PARALLEL STRUCTURE WITH COORDINATE CONJUNCTIONS		
(same structure)	and but or	(same structure)
(same structure), (same structure),	and but or	(same structure)

NOTE: A list of common word endings and exercises to practice their use are included at the back of the text in Appendix C. You may want to complete these exercises before you continue with Skills 14 through 15.

EXERCISE 14: Each of the following sentences contains words or groups of words that should be parallel. Circle the word that indicates that the sentence should have parallel parts. Underline the parts that should be parallel. Then indicate if the sentences are correct (C) or incorrect (I).

__I__   1. The pastries in that shop are <u>very expensive</u> (but) <u>quite deliciously</u>.

__C__   2. You can find some change to buy a paper <u>in the drawer</u>, <u>on top of the dresser</u>, (or) <u>in the jar</u>.

_____   3. The living room was decorated with expensive paintings and elegance lamps.

_____   4. He knew that the financial problems were serious, that the situation was not going to improve, and that he needed to get a job.

_____   5. All day long during the trip to the mountains, they were skiing, sledding, or played in the snow.

_____   6. The car needs new tires but not a new engine.

_____   7. He stops working when he gets too tired to continue or when he has finished.

_____   8. To get to the office, you should go through this door, turn to the left, and continuation down the hall.

_____   9. For dessert we could serve lemon pie, fruit tarts, chocolate cake, or butter cookies.

_____   10. The sick child needs some medicine, some juice, and to rest.

Skill 15: PARALLEL STRUCTURE WITH PAIRED CONJUNCTIONS

The paired conjunctions *both . . . and, either . . . or, neither . . . nor,* and *not only . . . but also* require parallel structures.

> The lecture was *both* <u>informative</u> *and* <u>enjoyable</u>.
>
> *Either* <u>the history exam</u> *or* <u>the physics exam</u> is on Tuesday.
>
> The missing papers are *neither* <u>on his desk</u> *nor* <u>in the file</u>.
>
> He visited *not only* <u>his cousin</u> *but also* <u>his grandmother</u>.

The following is not parallel and must be corrected:

> They want *either* <u>to play tennis</u> *or* <u>golf</u>*.

It is not correct because *to play tennis* is not parallel to *golf*. It can be corrected in different ways.

> They want *either* <u>to play tennis</u> *or* <u>to play golf</u>.
>
> They want to play *either* <u>tennis</u> *or* <u>golf</u>.

When you are using these paired conjunctions, be sure that the correct parts are used together. The following are incorrect:

> He lent me *both* <u>some paper</u> *or** <u>a pencil</u>.
>
> *Either* <u>breakfast</u> *nor** <u>lunch</u> is included in the price.

These sentences are incorrect because the wrong parts of the paired conjunctions are used together. In the first example, *and* should be used with *both*. In the second example, *or* should be used with *either*.

The following chart outlines the use of parallel structure with paired conjunctions.

PARALLEL STRUCTURE WITH PAIRED CONJUNCTIONS			
both *either* *neither* *not only*	(same structure)	*and* *or* *nor* *but also*	(same structure)

EXERCISE 15: Each of the following sentences contains words or groups of words that should be parallel. Circle the word or words that indicate that the sentence should have parallel parts. Underline the parts that should be parallel. Then indicate if the sentences are correct (C) or incorrect (I).

__I__   1. He (either) lied (or) telling an unbelievable story.

__C__   2. The music at the concert was (neither) well played (nor) well liked.

_____   3. He regularly studies both in the morning or in the evening.

_____   4. The play that we saw last night was not only rather delightful but also quite meaningful.

_____   5. He married her neither for her ability to cook nor her ability to clean house.

_____   6. The discussion was both exciting and interest.

_____   7. He withdrew all the money not only from the checking account but also from the savings account.

_____   8. Neither the teacher or the students are ready to leave the classroom.

_____   9. You can meet with me either in the next few minutes or at 4:00.

_____   10. John is an adventurous person who enjoys not only skydiving but also goes parasailing.

EXERCISE (Skills 14–15): Each of the following sentences contains words or groups of words that should be parallel. Circle the word or words that indicate that the sentence should have parallel parts. Underline the parts that should be parallel. Then indicate if the sentences are correct (C) or incorrect (I).

_____   1. The advertisements appeared in the newspaper and on the radio.

_____   2. She is trained as both an accountant and in nursing.

_____   3. We can take either my car or yours to the party.

_____   4. The coffee is too hot, too bitter, and too strength.

_____   5. He not only passed the test but also receiving the highest score in the class.

_____   6. Your ideas are neither more important or less important than the ideas of the others.

_____ 7. The meeting lasted only an hour but still seeming too long.

_____ 8. The novel was both emotional and description.

_____ 9. Either the counselor or her secretary can help you with that problem.

_____ 10. The leaves from the tree fell in the yard, in the pool, the driveway, and on the
            sidewalk.

TOEFL EXERCISE (Skills 14–15): Choose the letter of the underlined word or
group of words that is not correct.

_____ 1. Ballpoint pens <u>are</u> less versatile <u>but</u> more <u>population</u> than fountain <u>pens</u>.
                         A   B   C   D

_____ 2. Riddles <u>vary</u> <u>greatly</u> in both grammatical and <u>phonology</u> <u>form</u>.
                        A   B   C   D

_____ 3. Blood pressure is <u>measured</u> by feeling the pulse and <u>apply</u> a <u>force</u> to the <u>arm</u>.
                               A   B   C   D

_____ 4. The Moon <u>has</u> <u>no</u> atmosphere, no air, <u>and</u> no <u>watery</u>.
                           A B   C   D

_____ 5. The first <u>matches</u> <u>were</u> too hard to ignite, <u>a mess</u>, or too <u>dangerously</u> easy to
                          A   B   C   D
            ignite.

_____ 6. A 1971 U.S. <u>government</u> policy not only put warnings on cigarette <u>packs</u> but
                               A   B
            also <u>banning</u> television <u>advertising</u> of cigarettes.
                   C   D

_____ 7. <u>Demand</u>, beauty, durability, <u>rare</u>, and perfection of cutting <u>determine</u> the
              A   B   C
            <u>value</u> of a gemstone.
              D

_____ 8. The Harvard Yard, <u>which</u> was Harvard's <u>original</u> campus, is still a <u>major</u>
                                  A   B   C
            attraction for both students and <u>visiting</u>.
                                      D

_____ 9. In 1862, the American Confederacy <u>raised</u> the *Merrimack*, renamed it the
             A   B
            Virginia, covered it with iron <u>plates</u>, and <u>an outfit</u> it with ten guns.
                                     C   D

_____ 10. The liquid crystals in a liquid crystal <u>display</u> (LCD) <u>affect</u> the <u>polarized</u> light
                                                A   B   C
            so that it is either blocked <u>and</u> reflected by the segments of the display.
                                           D

TOEFL REVIEW EXERCISE (Skills 1–15): Choose the letter of the word or group of words that best completes the sentence.

1. Most cells in multicelled organisms perform _____ functions.

    (A) specialize
    (B) specialized
    (C) they specialize
    (D) specialization

2. The big island of Hawaii, in the middle of the Pacific Ocean, _____ by five volcanoes.

    (A) creation
    (B) it was created
    (C) creating
    (D) was created

3. The Sun uses up over 4 million tons of hydrogen per second, _____ still has enough hydrogen to last for the next 5 billion years.

    (A) it does not
    (B) it
    (C) but it
    (D) to it

4. For Katherine L. Bates, who _____ the top of Pikes Peak in 1893, the view provided the inspiration for her hymn "America the Beautiful."

    (A) reached
    (B) she reached
    (C) reaching
    (D) she was reaching

Choose the letter of the underlined word or group of words that is not correct.

_____ 5. Coal, petroleum, and natural gaseous are all fossil fuels.
               A   B   C   D

_____ 6. The mass of neutron stars generally range from one-tenth to twice the mass
                        A   B   C   D
          of the Sun.

_____ 7. Grasses grow in ways that help them to survive being nibbled, chilly, or dried.
                  A   B   C   D

_____ 8. Most of Hemingway's novels glorifies heroic exploits such as bullfighting or
                                      A   B   C
          boxing.
          D

_____ 9. Paleographers study ancient and medieval handwriting in order to establish
                          A   B   C
          not only its age and also its background.
                          D

_____ 10. The sounds produced by bullfrogs and toads vary greatly because each
                          A   B
          species have its own particular call.
                   C   D

SKILL 16: PAST PARTICIPLES AFTER *HAVE* _____

Whenever you see the verb *have* in any of its forms (*have, has, having, had*), be sure that the verb that follows it is in the past participle form.

> We *had complete** the work.
>
> They *have went** to the market.

In the first example, *complete* should be the past participle *completed* because it is after *had*. In the second example, *went* should be the past participle *gone* because it is after *have*.

The following chart outlines the use of verb forms after *have*.

VERB FORMS AFTER *HAVE*
have + past participle

> NOTE: Exercises to practice irregular verb forms are included at the back of the text in Appendix D. You may want to complete these exercises before you continue with Skills 16 through 18.

EXERCISE 16: Each of the following sentences contains a verb formed with *have*. Underline the verbs twice. Then indicate if the sentences are correct (C) or incorrect (I).

__I__ 1. We <u>have</u> already <u>hearing</u> the good news.

__C__ 2. She <u>has ridden</u> her bicycle to school every day.

_____ 3. I have always believe you.

_____ 4. He has find the missing car keys.

_____ 5. They have put their money in a savings account.

_____ 6. Their parents have allowed them to stay up late.

_____ 7. She has never ran away from home before.

_____ 8. Have you ever saw a ghost?

_____ 9. They have taken three tests already this week.

_____ 10. He has offer me a high-paying job.

SKILL 17: PRESENT PARTICIPLES OR PAST PARTICIPLES AFTER *BE*

The verb *be* in any of its forms (*am, is, are, was, were, be, been, being*) can be followed by another verb. This verb should be in either the present participle or the past participle form.

> They *are turn on** all the lamps.
>
> The office door *is lock** in the evening.

In the first example, *turn on* should be *turning on* because it is after *are*. In the second example, *lock* should be *locked* because it is after *is*.

The following chart outlines the use of verb forms after *be*.

VERB FORMS AFTER *BE*		
be	+	(1) present participle
		(2) past participle

EXERCISE 17: Each of the following sentences contains a verb formed with *be*. Underline the verbs twice. Then indicate if the sentences are correct (C) or incorrect (I).

__I__   1. She <u>was study</u> the textbooks all night long.

__C__   2. The pie <u>was cut</u> into six equal pieces.

_____   3. Today the teacher is allow the students to leave class a few minutes early.

_____   4. The class is teach every other semester.

_____   5. Tom is bringing some drinks to the party.

_____   6. The sick child was taken to see a doctor.

_____   7. The children are swim in the backyard pool.

_____   8. The diamond jewelry is always keep in a safe place.

_____   9. The teacher is preparing a difficult exam for the students.

_____ 10. Dinner is served from 6:00 to 8:00.

Skill 18: BASE FORM VERBS AFTER MODALS _____

Whenever you see a modal such as *will, would, shall, should, can, could, may, might,* or *must,* you should be sure that the verb that follows it is in its base form.

> You *must telling** her the truth.
>
> The child *may comes** in now.

In the first example, *telling* should be the base form *tell* because it follows *must*. In the second example, *comes* should be the base form *come* because it follows *may*.

The following chart outlines the use of verb forms after modals.

VERB FORMS AFTER MODALS
modal   +   base form of the verb

EXERCISE 18: Each of the following sentences contains a verb formed with a modal. Underline the verbs twice. Then indicate if the sentences are correct (C) or incorrect (I).

_C_ 1. You <u>should try</u> to respond politely.

_I_ 2. Everyone <u>must leaves</u> the room immediately.

_____ 3. I could sat on the beach for hours.

_____ 4. She will asking you many difficult questions.

_____ 5. You can look at the book, but you cannot borrow it.

_____ 6. He may lies to you because he is not very truthful.

_____ 7. He knew that he would forgot the phone number.

_____ 8. The weatherman said that it might snowing tonight.

_____ 9. Perhaps we could bought a new car this year.

_____ 10. This course will satisfy the graduation requirement.

EXERCISE (Skills 16–18): Each of the following sentences contains a verb formed with several parts. Underline the verbs twice. Then indicate if the sentences are correct (C) or incorrect (I).

_____ 1. We have became good friends in the last year.

_____ 2. Your name will be list in the new directory.

_____ 3. The new movie is receive good reviews.

_____ 4. She must have feel sorry about her bad behavior.

_____ 5. They have always given their family many presents.

_____ 6. We may be taking a vacation next week.

_____ 7. We could have taking a vacation last week.

_____ 8. The package might had been deliver by an express mail service.

_____ 9. I have not wrote very many letters to my friends.

_____ 10. The car should not have be drive anymore today.

TOEFL EXERCISE (Skills 16–18): Choose the letter of the underlined word or group of words that is not correct.

_____ 1. By the 1920s, many radio transmitters had been build.
             A   B   C   D

_____ 2. Fish farming has rose in the United States in recent years.
          A   B   C   D

_____ 3. In areas of volcanic activity, beach sand may contains dark minerals and
             A   B   C
little quartz.
D

_____ 4. Cro-Magnon man was names after the caves in southwest France where the
                          A   B
first remains were discovered.
      C   D

_____ 5. Lassie, the famous collie who made her first screen appearance in 1943, has
                                     A   B
always be played by a male dog.
       C   D

_____ 6. A blue bigwig lizard stakes out a territory and will defending females within
                              A   B   C
it against courting males.
           D

_____ 7. President George Washington was <u>inaugurates</u> on the <u>steps</u> <u>of</u> the Federal
                                                 A   B   C

<u>Building</u> in New York City.
D

_____ 8. <u>By</u> 1627, Plymouth had <u>became</u> a viable and <u>growing</u> community of 50
     A   B   C

families, 25 goats, 15 cows, and <u>more than</u> 50 pigs.
D

_____ 9. Tobacco <u>was</u> the crop on which the <u>eminence</u> of Williamsburg and the
            A   B

<u>prosperity</u> of Virginia were <u>base</u>.
C   D

_____ 10. Because there <u>may be</u> scores of genes in each suspect DNA region, scientists
                A

must <u>identifying</u> and <u>sequence</u> the actual genes <u>contributing</u> to Type I
         B   C   D

diabetes.

TOEFL REVIEW EXERCISE (Skills 1–18): Choose the letter of the word or group of words that best completes the sentence.

1. _____ the deepest valleys and canyons on the Earth.

   (A) In the Pacific Ocean with
   (B) In the Pacific Ocean
   (C) The Pacific Ocean
   (D) The Pacific Ocean has

2. In the United States, the participation of females in the labor force _____ from 37 percent in 1965 to 51 percent in 1980.

   (A) it jumped
   (B) jump
   (C) jumping
   (D) jumped

3. Some composers, such as Richard Wagner, have felt that _____ the action of the opera too much and have written operas without them.

   (A) arias interrupt
   (B) interrupt arias
   (C) the interruption of arias
   (D) areas of interruption

Choose the letter of the underlined word or group of words that is not correct.

_____ 4. Water <u>stored</u> behind a <u>dam</u> can <u>used</u> to <u>drive</u> turbines.
              A   B   C   D

_____ 5. Our universe may <u>continue</u> to <u>expand</u> as it <u>gets</u> colder, <u>empty</u>, and deader.
                        A   B   C   D

_____ 6. Every <u>form</u> of matter in the world <u>are</u> <u>made up</u> of <u>atoms</u>.
                 A   B C   D

_____ 7. The <u>lens</u> and cornea are <u>supply</u> with <u>nutrients</u> and oxygen by the <u>aqueous</u>
              A   B   C   D
fluid.

_____ 8. Dodge City, laid out in 1872, <u>owed</u> both its prosperity and its <u>famous</u> to the
                                     A   B
buffalo in <u>its</u> early <u>years</u>.
               C   D

_____ 9. The amount of the <u>two kinds</u> of cholesterol in the blood <u>have</u> been <u>shown</u> to
                           A   B   C
have an <u>effect</u> on the risk of heart attack.
               D

_____ 10. By the time Noah Webster <u>reached</u> <u>his</u> mid-twenties, he had already <u>publish</u>
                                   A B   C
an <u>elementary</u> speller.
   D

SKILL 19: SINGULAR AND PLURAL NOUNS_____

A problem that is common in the Written Expression section of the TOEFL test is a singular noun used where a plural noun is needed, or a plural noun used where a singular noun is needed.

> He just finished several *book**.
>
> She studied each *chapters**.

In the first example, *several* indicates that the plural *books* is needed. In the second example, *each* indicates that the singular *chapter* is needed.

In the Written Expression section of the TOEFL test you should watch very carefully for key words such as *each, every, a,* and *single* that indicate that a noun should be singular. You should also watch carefully for key words such as *many, several,* and *three* that indicate that a noun should be plural.

The following chart lists the key words that indicate to you whether a noun should be singular or plural.

KEY WORDS FOR SINGULAR AND PLURAL NOUNS					
For singular nouns	*each*	*every*	*single*	*one*	*a*
For plural nouns	*both*	*two*	*many*	*several*	*various*

EXERCISE 19: Each of the following sentences contains at least one key word to tell you if a noun should be singular or plural. Circle the key words. Draw arrows to the nouns they describe. Then indicate if the sentences are correct (C) or incorrect (I).

__I__ 1. She talked to (each) people in the room.

__C__ 2. There is not (a single) bit of food in the refrigerator.

_____ 3. You need two piece of identification to cash a check.

_____ 4. Both classes started on time.

_____ 5. We took a new routes to the beach house.

_____ 6. He gave many different reasons for his actions.

_____ 7. You must answer every questions on the test.

____   8. She tried several times to call me.

____   9. He offered me only one glass of water.

____ 10. We had various kind of drinks with the meal.

SKILL 20: COUNTABLE AND UNCOUNTABLE NOUNS_____

In English, nouns are classified as countable or uncountable. For certain questions on the TOEFL test, it is necessary to distinguish countable and uncountable nouns in order to use the correct modifiers with them.

As the name implies, countable nouns are nouns that can be counted. Countable nouns can come in quantities of one, or two, or a hundred, etc. The noun *book* is countable because you can have one book or several books.

Uncountable nouns, on the other hand, are nouns that cannot be counted because they come in some indeterminate quantity or mass. A noun such as *milk* or *happiness* cannot be counted; you cannot have one milk or two milks, and you cannot find one happiness or two happinesses. Uncountable nouns are often liquid items such as *water, oil,* or *shampoo*. Uncountable nouns can also refer to abstract ideas such as *security, friendship,* or *hope*.

It is important for you to recognize the difference between countable and uncountable nouns when you come across such key words as *much* and *many*.

> They have taken *much** trips recently.
>
> There was not *many** water in the pool.

In the first example, *much* is incorrect because *trips* is countable. This sentence should say *many trips*. In the second example, *many* is incorrect because *water* is uncountable. This sentence should say *much water*.

The following chart lists the key words that indicate to you whether a noun is countable or uncountable.

KEY WORDS FOR COUNTABLE AND UNCOUNTABLE NOUNS				
For countable nouns	*many*	*number*	*few*	*fewer*
For uncountable nouns	*much*	*amount*	*little*	*less*

EXERCISE 20: Each of the following sentences contains at least one key word to tell you if a noun is countable or uncountable. Circle the key words. Draw arrows to the nouns they describe. Then indicate if the sentences are correct (C) or incorrect (I).

_C_   1. She will visit in a (few) months.

_I_   2. (Many) risk are unnecessary.

_____   3. You need to show a little kindness.

_____   4. You have a number of choice.

_____   5. There was a large amount of apples in the bowl.

_____   6. We have fewer opportunities now.

_____   7. How much money is left?

_____   8. He caused less problems this time.

_____   9. They need a little times to finish their work.

_____   10. He visited many exotic places.

EXERCISE (Skills 19–20): Each of the following sentences contains at least one key word to tell you if a noun is singular, plural, countable, or uncountable. Circle the key words. Draw arrows to the nouns they describe. Then indicate if the sentences are correct (C) or incorrect (I).

_____   1. She enjoys food from many culture.

_____   2. He could not give me much good reasons.

_____   3. Each owner must register his or her car.

_____   4. They came up with a number of ideas.

_____   5. Various new law go into effect on the first of the year.

_____   6. The car now uses less oil.

_____ 7. The meal did not cost a single cents.

_____ 8. You need to make fewer mistake.

_____ 9. You can take one course or both courses.

_____ 10. He only smokes a small amount of cigarettes.

TOEFL EXERCISE (Skills 19–20): Choose the letter of the underlined word or group of words that is not correct.

_____ 1. Cone shells <u>live</u> in <u>much</u> different seas and feed mainly on <u>small</u> fish and
                A   B   C
     <u>worms</u>.
       D

_____ 2. The leaves of the <u>common</u> sunflower <u>are</u> <u>rough</u> to the touch on both <u>side</u>.
                        A   B   C   D

_____ 3. Hemoglobin <u>enables</u> the red <u>blood cells</u> to carry oxygen and <u>small</u> <u>numbers</u>
                 A   B   C   D
     of carbon dioxide.

_____ 4. <u>Those</u> with narcolepsy experience the uncontrollable <u>desire</u> to sleep, perhaps
      A   B
     several <u>time</u> in one <u>day</u>.
           C   D

_____ 5. Another <u>great</u> <u>artists</u> of the <u>time</u> and possibly <u>the most</u> gifted silversmith in
                   A   B   C
     the colonies was Paul Revere.
          D

_____ 6. Alzheimer's disease afflicts two <u>in</u> <u>ten</u> <u>person</u> <u>over</u> the age of seventy in the
                                    A   B   C   D
     United States.

_____ 7. The red cardinal <u>spends</u> <u>many</u> of <u>its</u> time <u>feeding</u> on the ground.
                       A   B   C   D

_____ 8. In the 1920s, Tulsa had a <u>higher</u> number of <u>millionaire</u> than <u>any</u> <u>other</u> U.S. city.
                               A   B   C   D

_____ 9. Because Washington is <u>a district</u> and not a state, <u>its</u> residents have <u>less</u> rights
                           A   B   C
     than <u>other</u> citizens.
           D

_____ 10. Implosive <u>consonants</u> <u>occur</u> in many different <u>language</u>, but <u>they</u> are
                    A   B   C   D
     particularly common in American Indian and African languages.

TOEFL REVIEW EXERCISE (Skills 1–20): Choose the letter of the word or group of words that best completes the sentence.

1. _____ the second most common metal in the Earth's crust, and it always occurs in combination with other substances.

   (A) Iron
   (B) Iron is
   (C) With iron
   (D) With iron is

2. In most parts of the globe, the _____ not exceed roughly 31 degrees centigrade.

   (A) ocean surface
   (B) ocean has a surface
   (C) ocean surface does
   (D) ocean has surfaced

3. _____ which climatologists have determined is the wettest place on Earth not under water is a spot on the island of Kauai.

   (A) The place
   (B) It is the place
   (C) The place is
   (D) In the place is

Choose the letter of the underlined word or group of words that is not correct.

____ 4. A single protein molecule may being composed of tens of thousands of atoms.
        A   B   C   D

____ 5. Less plants grow in the poor taiga soils beneath the trees.
        A   B   C   D

____ 6. Vast reserves of oil and gas is located in the Gulf of Mexico.
        A   B   C   D

____ 7. Helium is a colorless, odorless, taste element often used to inflate balloons.
               A   B   C   D

____ 8. The common was the heart of every New England villages built in the
                   A   B   C   D
        eighteenth century.

____ 9. Some of the regulations that bind U.S. institutions allows foreign banks to
                                   A   B   C
        package loans at hard-to-beat interest rates.
                                      D

____ 10. In angioplasty, a catheter is thread through an artery and guided through the
                                       A   B
         body to the blocked area.
         C   D

SKILL 21: SUBJECT AND OBJECT PRONOUNS_____

Pronouns are words such as *he, she,* or *it* that take the place of nouns. One common problem with pronouns on the TOEFL test is that subject and object pronouns are confused, so you should be able to recognize these two types of pronouns.

SUBJECT	OBJECT
I	*me*
you	*you*
he	*him*
she	*her*
it	*it*
we	*us*
they	*them*

A subject pronoun is used as the subject of a verb. An object pronoun can be used as the object of a verb or the object of a preposition. Compare the following two sentences.

Marie saw *the film* with *Barry.*

She saw *it* with *him.*

In the second sentence, the subject pronoun *she* is replacing the noun *Marie.* The object of the verb *it* is replacing the noun phrase *the film,* and the object of the preposition *him* is replacing the noun *Barry.*

The following are examples of the types of subject or object pronoun errors that you might see on the TOEFL test.

*Me** and my friend are taking a trip.

Our neighbors are going with you and *I*.*

In the first example, the object pronoun *me* is incorrect because this pronoun serves as the subject of the sentence. The object pronoun *me* should be changed to the subject pronoun *I.* It can be difficult to recognize that *me* is the subject because the verb *are* has a double subject, *me* and *my friend.* In the second example, the subject pronoun *I* is incorrect because this pronoun serves as the object of the preposition *with.* The subject pronoun *I* should be changed to the object pronoun *me.* It can be difficult to recognize that *I* is the object of the preposition *with* because the preposition *with* has two objects: the correct object *you* and the incorrect object *I.*

EXERCISE 21: Each of the following sentences contains at least one subject or object pronoun. Circle the pronouns. Then indicate if the sentences are correct (C) or incorrect (I).

__C__   1. (You) should do (it) for (her.)

__I__   2. (They) helped (she) with the work.

_____   3. Her and Bob came over to visit me.

_____   4. I brought it for you and them.

_____   5. He opened the refrigerator and took some food from it.

_____   6. She lent it to you and I.

_____   7. She spent all the money on them.

_____   8. You forgot to give it to they.

_____   9. We offered she a place to stay.

_____   10. They watched us play with it.

Skill 22: POSSESSIVES

Possessive adjectives and pronouns both show who or what "owns" a noun. However, possessive adjectives and possessive pronouns do not have the same function, and these two kinds of possessives can be confused on the TOEFL test. A possessive adjective describes a noun: it must be accompanied by a noun. A possessive pronoun takes the place of a noun: it cannot be accompanied by a noun.

> Beth gave us *her* television.
> **ADJECTIVE**

> Beth gave us *hers*.
> **PRONOUN**

Notice that in the first example the possessive adjective *her* is accompanied by the noun *television*. In the second example, the possessive pronoun *hers* is not accompanied by a noun.

The following chart outlines the possessives and their uses.

POSSESSIVE ADJECTIVES	POSSESSIVE PRONOUNS
my your his her its our their	mine yours his hers — ours theirs
must be accompanied by a noun	*cannot* be accompanied by a noun

These examples show the types of errors that are possible with possessive adjectives and possessive pronouns on the TOEFL test.

> The students turned in *theirs** papers.

> I would like to borrow *your**.

In the first example, the possessive pronoun *theirs* is incorrect because it is accompanied by the noun *papers,* and a possessive pronoun cannot be accompanied by a noun. The possessive adjective *their* is needed in the first example. In the second example, the possessive adjective *your* is incorrect because it is not accompanied by a noun, and a possessive adjective must be accompanied by a noun. The possessive pronoun *yours* is needed in the second example.

EXERCISE 22: Each of the following sentences contains at least one possessive pronoun or adjective. Circle the possessives in these sentences. Then indicate if the sentences are correct (C) or incorrect (I).

__I__   1. She cut (hers) hair recently.

__C__   2. We will take (our) car or (theirs.)

_____   3. Please lend me yours notes from the history lecture.

_____   4. I like his ideas and hers.

_____   5. The tree fell on its side during the storm.

_____   6. My desk is located near hers.

_____   7. Theirs suggestion was unrealistic.

_____   8. Our appointment is just after your.

_____ 9. Your friends and my friends are coming to our party.

_____ 10. You don't have yours gloves with you, but I have mine.

Skill 23: PRONOUN REFERENCE

After you have checked that the subject and object pronouns and the possessives are used correctly, you should also check each of these pronouns and possessives for agreement. The following are examples of errors of this type that you might find on the TOEFL test.

> The cookies are for you, so please take *it**.
>
> Each person has to sign *their** application form.

In the first example, the singular pronoun *it* is incorrect because it refers to the plural noun *cookies*. This pronoun should be replaced with the plural pronoun *them*. In the second example, the plural possessive adjective *their* is incorrect because it refers to the singular *each person*. This adjective should be replaced with the singular *his* or *his or her*.

The following chart outlines what you should remember about checking pronoun reference.

PRONOUN AGREEMENT
1. Be sure that every pronoun and possessive agrees with the noun it refers to.
2. You generally check *earlier* in the sentence for agreement.

EXERCISE 23: Each of the following sentences contains at least one pronoun or possessive. Circle the pronouns and possessives. Draw arrows to the nouns they refer to. Then indicate if the sentences are correct (C) or incorrect (I).

__I__ 1. If my friend calls, please tell (them) that I will return the call.

__C__ 2. I don't like the idea because (it) is too costly.

_____ 3. The tables at the restaurant are so large that it can seat 12 people.

_____ 4. The soup needs more salt because he does not taste very good.

_____ 5. The girls ran too fast, and she fell down.

_____ 6. In the autumn, the tree lost its leaves.

_____ 7. The windows were open, so I closed it.

_____ 8. The travelers lost their way in the storm.

_____ 9. The boy got the box, and he opened it carefully.

_____ 10. The woman left their earrings at home, so she wasn't wearing them.

EXERCISE (Skills 21–23): Each of the following sentences contains at least one pronoun or possessive. Circle the pronouns and possessives. Then indicate if the sentences are correct (C) or incorrect (I).

_____ 1. They sold the car to you and I.

_____ 2. Please tell your brother that I need to talk to him.

_____ 3. The bicycle lost it front wheel.

_____ 4. Martha was happy when her boss gave her a pay raise.

_____ 5. Just between us, I am not sure if we can trust them.

_____ 6. The mother talked to her son about his behavior.

_____ 7. I told his the truth, but he didn't believe me.

_____ 8. You and she should look for they.

_____ 9. The student left his notebooks in the class, so he went back to get it.

_____ 10. If they don't have their car, we will lend them ours.

TOEFL EXERCISE (Skills 21–23): Choose the letter of the underlined word or group of words that is not correct.

_____ 1. Animals like frogs <u>have</u> waterproof skin <u>that</u> prevents <u>they</u> from drying out
                             A   B   C

   quickly in air, sun, or <u>wind</u>.
                            D

_____ 2. Because of <u>its</u> ability to survive <u>close to</u> human habitations, the Virginia deer
                    A   B

   <u>has</u> actually increased <u>their</u> range and numbers.
    C   D

_____ 3. John D. Rockefeller was the <u>founder</u> of the Standard Oil Company, and <u>he</u>
                                  A   B

   was the richest man in the world at <u>the time</u> of <u>her</u> retirement.
                                  C   D

_____ 4. The aorta arches <u>out of</u> the heart, <u>and</u> then <u>its</u> moves down toward the <u>lower</u>
                               A   B   C   D

   body.

_____ 5. <u>Global</u> average temperatures <u>are</u> now .6 degrees Celsius warmer <u>than</u> <u>we</u>
          A   B   C D

   were 100 years ago.

_____ 6. During the Civil War, Clara Barton <u>became</u> <u>known</u> as the "Angel of the
                                                      A   B

   Battlefield" for <u>hers</u> fearless <u>care</u> of wounded soldiers.
                  C   D

_____ 7. Our Sun is a <u>medium-sized</u> star orbiting near the <u>edge</u> of a collection of stars
          A   B   C

   that <u>our</u> call the Milky Way.
       D

_____ 8. Francis Scott Key <u>wrote</u> the <u>words</u> to "The Star-Spangled Banner" as <u>they</u>
                            A   B   C

   stood <u>alone</u> watching the British bombardment of Fort McHenry.
        D

_____ 9. <u>Some</u> scallops can open and close <u>theirs</u> valves and swim away rapidly when
          A   B

   <u>they</u> are <u>disturbed</u>.
    C   D

_____ 10. Pearl S. Buck <u>began</u> <u>her</u> first novel, _East Wind, West Wind_, in 1925, while <u>her</u>
                          A   B   C

   was <u>traveling</u> between the United States and China.
       D

TOEFL REVIEW EXERCISE (Skills 1–23): Choose the letter of the word or group of words that best completes the sentence.

1. Although knives and forks _____ of prehistoric origin, spoons are relatively new.

   (A) are
   (B) they are
   (C) are they
   (D) which are

2. Neptune's _____ the planet in the direction opposite to the other seven moons.

   (A) moon Triton orbiting
   (B) moon Triton orbits
   (C) moon Triton in orbit
   (D) moon is in Triton's orbit

3. A dip pen's nib is split into two halves _____ at the point of the nib.

   (A) who meet
   (B) which meet
   (C) they meet
   (D) meet

Choose the letter of the underlined word or group of words that is not correct.

_____ 4. In 1785, Henry Knox was appoint the new republic's first secretary of war.
                    A   B   C   D

_____ 5. Biophysics is one of the various branch of physics.
                       A B   C   D

_____ 6. Unlike many great writers, Longfellow was an enormously popular poet in
                 A   B   C
        him day.
        D

_____ 7. After Lincoln's assassination, Ford's Theater was closed and parts of it was
                                                          A   B C
        converted to government office space.
                                        D

_____ 8. Most of the Earth's ice is found either in the two great ice caps of Antarctica
                            A   B   C
        and Greenland and on the tall mountains of the world.
                            D

_____ 9. Except for a few species, such as the spotted salamander, the courtship of
                     A
        salamanders are secretive and not often observed.
                     B   C   D

_____ 10. Unlike most mollusks, crustaceans outgrow their shells and need to build
                  A   B
        several completely new casings throughout they lives.
                  C   D

SKILL 24: ADJECTIVES AND ADVERBS

Sometimes in the Written Expression section of the TOEFL test, adjectives are incorrectly used in place of adverbs, or adverbs are incorrectly used in place of adjectives. Adjectives and adverbs have very different uses in sentences. Adjectives have only one job: they describe nouns or pronouns.

It is a *delicious* meal.
   ADJ. NOUN

It is *delicious*.
PRON. ADJ.

In the first example, the adjective *delicious* describes the noun *meal*. In the second example, the adjective *delicious* describes the pronoun *it*.

  Adverbs have three different uses. They can describe verbs, adjectives, or other adverbs.

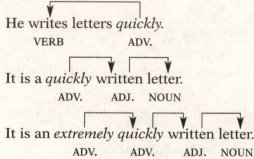

He writes letters *quickly*.
 VERB   ADV.

It is a *quickly* written letter.
  ADV. ADJ. NOUN

It is an *extremely quickly* written letter.
   ADV. ADV. ADJ. NOUN

In the first example, the adverb *quickly* describes the verb *writes*. In the second example, the adverb *quickly* describes the adjective *written* (which describes the noun *letter*). In the third example, the adverb *extremely* describes the adverb *quickly*, which describes the adjective *written* (which describes the noun *letter*).

  The following are examples of incorrect sentences as they might appear on the TOEFL test.

They were seated at a *largely** table.
     ADV. NOUN

The child talked *soft** to her mother.
   VERB ADJ.

We read an *extreme** long* story.
    ADJ. ADJ.

She speaks *unbelievable** quickly.
   ADJ.   ADV.

In the first example, the adverb *largely* is incorrect because the adjective *large* is needed to describe the noun *table*. In the second example, the adjective *soft* is incorrect because the adverb *softly* is needed to describe the verb *talked*. In the third example, the adjective *extreme* is incorrect because the adverb *extremely* is needed to describe the adjective *long*. In the last example, the adjective *unbelievable* is incorrect because the adverb *unbelievably* is needed to describe the adverb *quickly*.

The following chart outlines the important information that you should remember about the use of adjectives and adverbs.

USE OF ADJECTIVES AND ADVERBS	
Adjectives	Adjectives describe *nouns* or *pronouns*.
Adverbs	Adverbs describe *verbs, adjectives,* or other *adverbs*.

> NOTE: A list of common word endings (including adjective and adverb endings) and exercises to practice their use are included at the back of the text in Appendix C. You may want to complete these exercises (if you have not already done so) before you continue with Skills 24 through 25.

EXERCISE 24: Each of the following sentences has at least one adjective or adverb. Circle the adjectives and adverbs, and label them. Draw arrows to the words they describe. Then indicate if the sentences are correct (C) or incorrect (I).

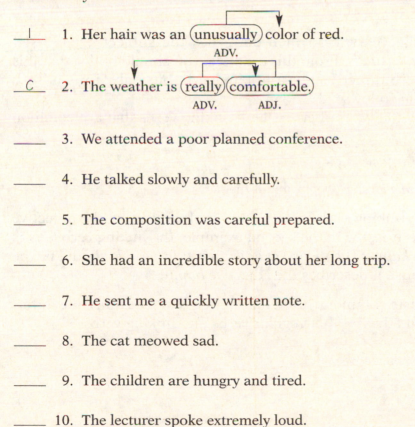

__I__   1. Her hair was an (unusually) color of red.
                              ADV.

__C__   2. The weather is (really) (comfortable.)
                            ADV.   ADJ.

_____   3. We attended a poor planned conference.

_____   4. He talked slowly and carefully.

_____   5. The composition was careful prepared.

_____   6. She had an incredible story about her long trip.

_____   7. He sent me a quickly written note.

_____   8. The cat meowed sad.

_____   9. The children are hungry and tired.

_____   10. The lecturer spoke extremely loud.

SKILL 25: ADJECTIVES AFTER LINKING VERBS

Generally an adverb rather than an adjective will come directly after a verb because the adverb is describing the verb.

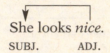

She spoke *nicely.*
VERB   ADV.

In this example, the verb *spoke* is followed by the adverb *nicely.* This adverb describes the verb *spoke.*

However, you must be very careful if the verb is a *linking* verb. A *linking* verb is followed by an adjective rather than an adverb.

She looks *nice.*
SUBJ.   ADJ.

In this example, the linking verb *looks* is followed by the adjective *nice.* This adjective describes the subject *she.*

You should be sure to use an adjective rather than an adverb after a linking verb. Be careful, however, because the adjective that goes with the linking verb does not always directly follow the linking verb.

He seems *unusually nice.*
SUBJ.   ADV.   ADJ.

In this example, the adjective *nice,* which describes the subject *he,* is itself described by the adverb *unusually.* From this example, you should notice that it is possible to have an adverb directly after a linking verb, but only if the adverb describes an adjective that follows.

These sentences show the types of errors with linking verbs that are common on the TOEFL test.

The test looks *easily** to me.

Sally feels *unbelievable** happy* about the news.

In the first example, the linking verb *looks* should be followed by the adjective *easy* rather than the adverb *easily.* In the second example, the linking verb *feels* is followed by the adjective *happy.* The incorrect adjective *unbelievable* should be the adverb *unbelievably* because it describes the adjective *happy.*

The following chart lists commonly used linking verbs and outlines the different uses of adjectives and adverbs after regular verbs and linking verbs.

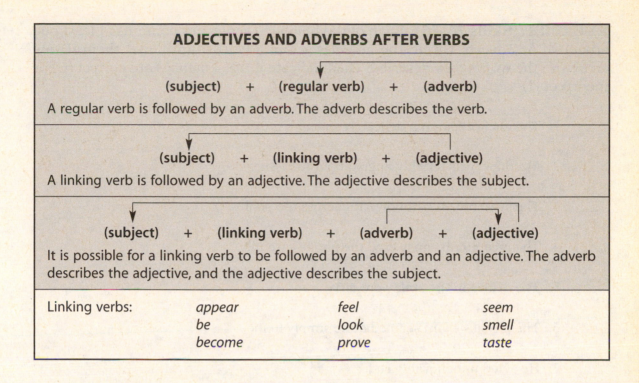

ADJECTIVES AND ADVERBS AFTER VERBS

(subject)   +   (regular verb)   +   (adverb)

A regular verb is followed by an adverb. The adverb describes the verb.

(subject)   +   (linking verb)   +   (adjective)

A linking verb is followed by an adjective. The adjective describes the subject.

(subject)   +   (linking verb)   +   (adverb)   +   (adjective)

It is possible for a linking verb to be followed by an adverb and an adjective. The adverb describes the adjective, and the adjective describes the subject.

Linking verbs:	*appear*	*feel*	*seem*
	be	*look*	*smell*
	become	*prove*	*taste*

EXERCISE 25: Each of the following sentences contains at least one adjective or adverb. Circle the adjectives and adverbs, and label them. Draw arrows to the words they describe. Then indicate if the sentences are correct (C) or incorrect (I).

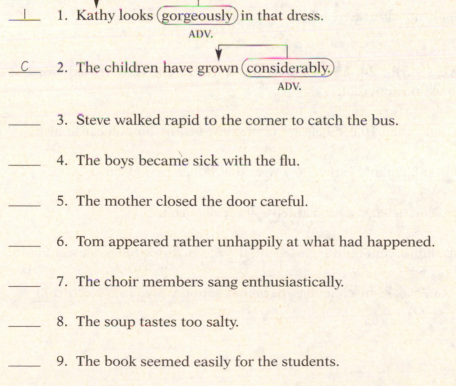

__I__   1. Kathy looks (gorgeously) in that dress.
                    ADV.

__C__   2. The children have grown (considerably.)
                    ADV.

_____   3. Steve walked rapid to the corner to catch the bus.

_____   4. The boys became sick with the flu.

_____   5. The mother closed the door careful.

_____   6. Tom appeared rather unhappily at what had happened.

_____   7. The choir members sang enthusiastically.

_____   8. The soup tastes too salty.

_____   9. The book seemed easily for the students.

_____   10. In the late afternoon, the sun set slow in the west.

EXERCISE (Skills 24–25): Each of the following sentences contains at least one adjective or adverb. Circle the adjectives and adverbs, and label them. Draw arrows to the words they describe. Then indicate if the sentences are correct (C) or incorrect (I).

_____ 1. The chef prepared a delicately sauce.

_____ 2. Matthew feels terribly angry about the issue.

_____ 3. The swimmer swam powerful across the pool.

_____ 4. The receptionist answered the phone carefully.

_____ 5. The dishes in the sink were dirty.

_____ 6. The physics exam seemed quite simply to me.

_____ 7. He acted unbelievably rude.

_____ 8. The burned toast did not taste very good.

_____ 9. His decision was absolutely necessary.

_____ 10. The job applicant dressed carefully for the important interview.

TOEFL EXERCISE (Skills 24–25): Choose the letter of the underlined word or group of words that is not correct.

_____ 1. Sounds quieter than 10 decibels are impossibly for the human ear to hear.
               A   B   C   D

_____ 2. Often the best farmland is next to a river that floods periodical.
               A   B   C   D

_____ 3. The planet Mercury has a moderately elliptically orbit.
          A   B   C   D

_____ 4. An 18-watt fluorescent bulb seems as brightly as a 75-watt incandescent bulb.
   A   B C   D

_____ 5. The telephone works by changing the voice's sound waves into electrically
                             A   B   C   D

signals.

_____ 6. In the northern United States, two European species of <u>small</u> <u>white</u> birch are
                                                                  A   B
extensive planted as <u>ornamentals</u>.
   C   D

_____ 7. Fifty million Americans <u>continue</u> to smoke despite <u>abundant</u> evidence that
                                  A   B
smoking is <u>extremely</u> <u>unhealthfully</u>.
            C   D

_____ 8. The U.S. Military Academy <u>sits</u> on <u>scenic</u> heights <u>overlooking</u> a <u>strategically</u>
                                    A   B   C   D
bend in the Hudson River.

_____ 9. The Erie Canal became so <u>successfully</u> at providing <u>cheap</u> transportation that
                                   A   B
it was <u>greatly</u> <u>enlarged</u> between 1835 and 1862.
        C   D

_____ 10. The Infra-Red Astronomy Satellite (IRAS), <u>launched</u> in 1983, contained a
                                                    A
<u>special</u> <u>coded</u> <u>reflecting</u> telescope that detected infrared rays.
 B   C   D

TOEFL REVIEW EXERCISE (Skills 1–25): Choose the letter of the word or group of words that best completes the sentence.

1. On December 17, 1903, the *Flyer* _____ near Kitty Hawk, North Carolina, with Orville Wright as pilot.

   (A) took off
   (B) it took off
   (C) taking off
   (D) took it off

2. Comets are relatively small celestial bodies _____ up chiefly of dirt and icy materials.

   (A) make
   (B) made
   (C) they make
   (D) make them

3. Researchers have long debated about _____ moon Titan contains hydrocarbon oceans or lakes.

   (A) Saturn's
   (B) whether it is Saturn's
   (C) whether Saturn's
   (D) whether Saturn is a

Choose the letter of the underlined word or group of words that is not correct.

_____   4. The <u>abrasively</u> action of the wind <u>wears</u> away <u>softer</u> <u>layers</u> of rock.
               A   B   C   D

_____   5. There are two <u>way</u> of <u>making</u> a gas <u>condense</u>: cooling it or <u>putting</u> it under
                    A   B   C   D

        pressure.

_____   6. Researchers have <u>discovered</u> that the <u>application</u> of bright light can
                              A   B

        sometimes be <u>uses</u> to <u>overcome</u> jet lag.
                       C   D

_____   7. Salmon <u>migrations</u> may <u>include</u> having to jump up waterfalls, swim up
                     A   B

        rapids, or <u>climbing</u> fish <u>ladders</u> at dams.
                C   D

_____   8. If a strike <u>is called</u> in <u>violation</u> of an <u>existing</u> contract between labor and
                    A   B   C

        management, <u>its</u> a wildcat strike.
                 D

_____   9. Snapping turtles are <u>easily</u> recognized because of the <u>large</u> head, the <u>long</u> tail,
                           A   B   C

        and the shell that seems <u>insufficiently</u> to protect the body.
                               D

_____   10. The <u>long</u> string of genes <u>making</u> up a chromosome <u>have</u> been <u>likened</u> to a
               A   B   C   D

        string of pearls.

TOEFL POST-TEST

SECTION 2
STRUCTURE AND WRITTEN EXPRESSION
Time—25 minutes
(including the reading of the directions)
Now set your clock for 25 minutes.

This section is designed to measure your ability to recognize language that is appropriate for standard written English. There are two types of questions in this section, with special directions for each type.

Structure

Directions: These questions are incomplete sentences. Beneath each sentence you will see four words or phrases, marked (A), (B), (C), and (D). Choose the **one** word or phrase that best completes the sentence. Then, on your answer sheet, find the number of the question and fill in the space that corresponds to the letter of the answer you have chosen.

Look at the following examples.

Example I   **Sample Answer**
                                                                     ●
The president _____ the election by a landslide.   Ⓑ
                                                                     Ⓒ
(A) won   Ⓓ
(B) he won
(C) yesterday
(D) fortunately

The sentence should read, "The president won the election by a landslide." Therefore, you should choose answer (A).

Example II   **Sample Answer**
                                                                     Ⓐ
When _____ the conference?   ●
                                                                     Ⓒ
(A) the doctor attended   Ⓓ
(B) did the doctor attend
(C) the doctor will attend
(D) the doctor's attendance

The sentence should read, "When did the doctor attend the conference?" Therefore, you should choose answer (B).

GO ON TO THE NEXT PAGE ➡

1. _____ lived on Earth for nearly 150 million years.

    (A) Dinosaurs
    (B) Dinosaurs who
    (C) If dinosaurs
    (D) Since dinosaurs

2. Early printers arranged type into _____ a small, flat composing stick.

    (A) words
    (B) are words on
    (C) words on
    (D) the words are on

3. _____ along most of its length into an upper chamber and a lower chamber.

    (A) The divided cochlea
    (B) Dividing the cochlea
    (C) The cochlea is divided
    (D) With a divided cochlea

4. Yeast is an organic catalyst _____ known to prehistoric humanity.

    (A) was
    (B) which was
    (C) which it
    (D) which

5. Many communities _____ a complex system of linguistic levels in order to show respect.

    (A) useful
    (B) use already made
    (C) making it useful
    (D) make use of

6. The ear is a flexible organ, _____ simply was not designed to withstand the noise of modern living.

    (A) but it
    (B) it
    (C) but
    (D) its

7. In 1934, chemist Wallace Carothers produced a plastic which _____ nylon.

    (A) his call
    (B) he called
    (C) to call him
    (D) calling

8. As _____ grows, the shell in which it lives grows, too.

    (A) a mollusk
    (B) a mollusk it
    (C) has a mollusk
    (D) it has a mollusk

9. The first _____ the Civil War was fired from Fort Johnson upon Fort Sumter on April 12, 1861.

    (A) shot
    (B) shot in
    (C) shot was in
    (D) it was shot

10. Stalactites are formed in caves by groundwater _____ dissolved lime.

    (A) it contains
    (B) containing
    (C) contains
    (D) containment

GO ON TO THE NEXT PAGE →

11. By studying the movements of the Sun and Moon, even early astronomers could _____ eclipses would take place.

    (A) predicting when
    (B) when it predicts
    (C) the prediction when
    (D) predict when

12. Coffee probably originally grew wild in Ethiopia in the province of Kaffe, and from there _____ to southern Arabia.

    (A) bringing it
    (B) it was brought
    (C) brought it
    (D) brought with it

13. Alabama was occupied by the French and Spanish before _____ to England in 1763.

    (A) was ceded
    (B) ceded to it
    (C) it was ceded
    (D) ceded it

14. A group of winged reptiles _____ pterosaurs is believed to have been the first vertebrates with the power of flight.

    (A) call
    (B) calls
    (C) called
    (D) is called

15. On November 23, 1863, Grant stunned the Confederates on Missionary Ridge with what _____ to be a full-dress military parade of troops who unexpectedly opened fire.

    (A) appeared
    (B) appearing
    (C) appearance
    (D) apparent

GO ON TO THE NEXT PAGE ➡

Written Expression

Directions: In these questions, each sentence has four underlined words or phrases. The four underlined parts of the sentence are marked (A), (B), (C), and (D). Identify the **one** underlined word or phrase that must be changed in order for the sentence to be correct. Then, on your answer sheet, find the number of the question and fill in the space that corresponds to the letter of the answer you have chosen.

Look at the following examples.

Example I   **Sample Answer**

The four string on a violin are tuned
A   B   C   D

in fifths.

(A)
●
(C)
(D)

The sentence should read, "The four strings on a violin are tuned in fifths." Therefore, you should choose answer (B).

Example II   **Sample Answer**

The research for the book *Roots* taking
A   B   C

Alex Haley twelve years.
D

(A)
(B)
●
(D)

The sentence should read, "The research for the book *Roots* took Alex Haley twelve years." Therefore, you should choose answer (C).

GO ON TO THE NEXT PAGE →

TOEFL® test directions and format are reprinted by permission of ETS, the copyright owner. However, all examples and test questions are provided by Pearson Education, Inc.

16. Vast flows of information is carried on hair-thin fiber-optic cables.
    A   B   C   D

17. The crafting of fine violins has been proceeding for several century as a secret art.
                      A   B   C   D

18. Linguistic conflicts due to divided ethnic and national loyalties can be both bitter or violent.
                       A   B   C   D

19. In 1851, with the publication of hers antislavery novel, Harriet Beecher Stowe rocketed to fame.
                                     A   B   C   D

20. The smallest and simple living organisms on Earth are bacteria.
                     A   B   C   D

21. The effort to determine the exact numerical value of *pi* has now reach 2.16 billion decimal digits.
        A   B   C   D

22. The hammerhead shark is usual found in warm, temperate waters.
                           A   B   C   D

23. Princeton University, which was establish in 1746, is one of the oldest universities in the United
                                   A   B   C   D

    States.

24. According to a World Resources Institute report, a significant part of forest acreage disappear
    A   B   C

    each year.
    D

25. The Earth's crust is composed of 15 plates which float on the partially molten layer below they.
                                        A   B   C   D

26. As one climbs high up a mountain, the air becomes both colder or thinner.
           A   B   C   D

27. When a bone is broke into several pieces, doctors may pin the pieces together for proper healing.
                   A   B   C   D

28. The long necks of much plant-eating dinosaurs were useful for reaching up to the treetops to feed.
                      A   B   C   D

29. Hippocrates believed that good health was dependently on the balance of the four fluids of the
                A   B   C   D

    body.

GO ON TO THE NEXT PAGE

30. A jet stream is a flat and narrow tube of air that moves more rapid than the surrounding air.
               A   B   C   D

31. Because mistletoe berries are poisonous, everyone with Christmas decorations containing
                           A   B

    mistletoe need to be aware of the potential danger.
             C   D

32. When Pierre L'Enfant designed the national capital in 1791, her envisioned a broad boulevard
                       A   B   C

    linking the White House and the Capitol.
        D

33. In a copperhead snake, the venom flows from a single venom glands to a pair of hollow teeth.
                  A   B   C   D

34. A hawk swallows its food in large pieces, digests some of it, and regurgitating the rest.
                   A   B   C   D

35. Defects can occurring when liquid helium undergoes a phase transition to its superfluid phase.
       A   B   C   D

36. Cavemen created a large amount of early works of art using a mixture of clay, chalk, and burned
                       A   B   C

    wood and bones.
          D

37. Variations in melody, rhythm, and tone of voice becomes a major feature of child speech toward
                    A   B   C   D

    the end of the first year.

38. As a protective protein molecule, an antibody can combines with a foreign virus protein.
          A   B   C   D

39. The water moccasin is a high venomous and extremely dangerous pit viper.
                        A   B   C   D

40. Though aluminum is more common than iron, it is extremely difficult to break their hold on
     A   B   C

    other atoms.
      D

**This is the end of Section 2.
If you finish before 25 minutes has ended,
check your work on Section 2 only.**

2 ● 2 ● 2 ● 2 ● 2 ● 2 ● 2 ● 2

When you finish the test, you may do the following:

- Turn to the **Diagnostic Chart** on pages 357–363, and circle the numbers of the questions that you missed.

- Turn to the **Progress Chart** on page 353, and add your score to the chart.

SECTION THREE

READING COMPREHENSION

DIAGNOSTIC PRE-TEST

SECTION 3
READING COMPREHENSION
Time—55 minutes
(including the reading of the directions)
Now set your clock for 55 minutes.

This section is designed to measure your ability to read and understand short passages similar in topic and style to those that students are likely to encounter in North American universities and colleges. This section contains reading passages and questions about the passages.

Directions: In this section you will read several passages. Each one is followed by a number of questions about it. You are to choose the **one** best answer, (A), (B), (C), or (D), to each question. Then, on your answer sheet, find the number of the question and fill in the space that corresponds to the letter of the answer you have chosen.

Answer all questions about the information in a passage on the basis of what is **stated** or **implied** in that passage.

Read the following passage:

John Quincy Adams, who served as the sixth president of the United States from 1825 to 1829, is today recognized for his masterful statesmanship and diplomacy. He dedicated his life to public service, both in the presidency and in the various other political offices that he held.
Line Throughout his political career he demonstrated his unswerving belief in freedom of speech, the
(5) antislavery cause, and the right of Americans to be free from European and Asian domination.

Example I   **Sample Answer**

To what did John Quincy Adams devote his life?   Ⓐ
                                                                                                       ●
(A) Improving his personal life   Ⓒ
(B) Serving the public   Ⓓ
(C) Increasing his fortune
(D) Working on his private business

According to the passage, John Quincy Adams "dedicated his life to public service." Therefore, you should choose answer (B).

Example II   **Sample Answer**

In line 4, the word "unswerving" is closest in meaning to   Ⓐ
                                                                                                       Ⓑ
(A) moveable   ●
(B) insignificant   Ⓓ
(C) unchanging
(D) diplomatic

The passage states that John Quincy Adams demonstrated his unswerving belief "throughout his career." This implies that the belief did not change. Therefore, you should choose answer (C).

GO ON TO THE NEXT PAGE ➡

TOEFL® test directions and format are reprinted by permission of ETS, the copyright owner. However, all examples and test questions are provided by Pearson Education, Inc.

Questions 1–9

The largest diamond ever found is the Cullinan Diamond. This diamond weighed 3,106 carats in its uncut state when it was discovered in South Africa on January 25, 1905.

Line The Cullinan Diamond was cut into 9 major stones and 96 smaller ones. The largest of the cut stones, and still the largest cut diamond in the world, is the pear-shaped Cullinan I at 530 carats. (5) This diamond, which is also known as the Greater Star of Africa, is more than 2 inches (5.4 cm) long and 1.75 inches (4.4 cm) wide. It became part of the British crown jewels in 1907.

1. What is the best title for this passage?

    (A) Diamond Cutting
    (B) The World's Biggest Diamond, Uncut
        and Cut
    (C) Measuring Diamonds in Carats
    (D) The British Crown Jewels

2. The word "uncut" in line 2 is closest in meaning to which of the following?

    (A) Finished
    (B) Unnatural
    (C) Pear
    (D) Whole

3. The word "discovered" in line 2 is closest in meaning to

    (A) created
    (B) found
    (C) buried
    (D) weighed

4. It can be inferred from the passage that the Cullinan Diamond was cut into how many total stones?

    (A) 9
    (B) 96
    (C) 105
    (D) 3,106

5. The word "major" in line 3 could best be replaced by

    (A) well-known
    (B) military
    (C) natural
    (D) big

GO ON TO THE NEXT PAGE

6. Which of the following is NOT true about Cullinan I?

   (A) It was cut from the Cullinan Diamond.
   (B) It weighs 3,106 carats.
   (C) It is the biggest cut diamond in the world.
   (D) It is sometimes called the Greater Star of Africa.

7. All of the following are true about the shape of the Greater Star of Africa EXCEPT that

   (A) it is in the shape of a pear
   (B) it is 5.4 centimeters long
   (C) it is longer than it is wide
   (D) it is 4.4 inches wide

8. According to the passage, what happened to Cullinan I?

   (A) It remained in Africa.
   (B) It was cut into smaller stones.
   (C) It was cut and changed into the Greater Star of Africa.
   (D) It became the property of the British Royal family.

9. Where in the passage does the author mention the Cullinan Diamond's weight when it was mined?

   (A) Lines 1–2
   (B) Line 3
   (C) Lines 4–5
   (D) Line 6

GO ON TO THE NEXT PAGE ➡

Questions 10–20

Coca-Cola was invented in 1886 by Atlanta pharmacist John S. Pemberton. The name for the product was actually proposed by Pemberton's assistant, Frank Robinson. The name was taken from the two most unusual ingredients in the drink, the South American coca leaf and the African
Line cola nut.
(5)   The recipe for today's Coca-Cola is very well guarded. Many of the ingredients are known; in addition to coca leaves and cola nut, they include lemon, orange, lime, cinnamon, nutmeg, vanilla, caramel, and sugar. The proportions of the ingredients and the identity of Coke's secret ingredients are known by only a few of the Coca-Cola Company's senior corporate officers.

10. The passage mainly discusses

    (A) the success of the Coca-Cola Company
    (B) the unusual ingredients in Coca-Cola
    (C) John S. Pemberton
    (D) Coca-Cola's recipe and who developed it

11. According to the passage, who created Coca-Cola?

    (A) The Coca-Cola Company
    (B) John S. Pemberton
    (C) Pemberton's assistant
    (D) Frank Robinson

12. The word "unusual" in line 3 is closest in meaning to

    (A) uncommon
    (B) important
    (C) unused
    (D) tasty

13. Which of the following is NOT true about the name Coca-Cola?

    (A) The name "coca" comes from the coca leaf.
    (B) The name "cola" comes from the cola nut.
    (C) Frank Robinson suggested the name.
    (D) The inventor came up with the name.

14. A "recipe" in line 5 is

    (A) information about drugs for a pharmacy
    (B) a description of how to prepare something
    (C) an accounting statement
    (D) a corporate organizational plan

15. The passage states that the recipe for Coca-Cola is

    (A) well known
    (B) known by only a limited number of people
    (C) unknown
    (D) published information

16. Which of the following is NOT mentioned as an ingredient of Coca-Cola?

    (A) Orange leaves
    (B) Nutmeg
    (C) Citrus fruits
    (D) Sugar

17. The word "secret" in line 7 could best be replaced by

    (A) unrevealed
    (B) delicious
    (C) business
    (D) speechless

GO ON TO THE NEXT PAGE

18. It can be inferred from the passage that

    (A) the public knows all the ingredients in Coca-Cola
    (B) the public is not sure that coca leaves are used in Coca-Cola
    (C) the public does not know how many cola nuts are used in a batch of Coca-Cola
    (D) no one knows the exact proportions of ingredients used in Coca-Cola

19. The word "senior" in line 8 could best be replaced by

    (A) trustworthy
    (B) high-level
    (C) more mature
    (D) really decisive

20. Where in the passage does the author mention who gave Coca-Cola its name?

    (A) Lines 1–2
    (B) Lines 3–4
    (C) Line 5
    (D) Lines 7–8

GO ON TO THE NEXT PAGE

Questions 21–30

Most people would say that the world's tallest mountain is Mount Everest. This mountain in the Himalayas is just over 29,000 feet high.

However, if mountains are measured a little bit differently, then the tallest mountain on Earth is
Line Mauna Kea, in the Hawaiian Islands. Mauna Kea is only about 14,000 feet above sea level, so in
(5) comparison to Mount Everest it just does not look anywhere near as high as Mount Everest to a person standing at sea level.

Mauna Kea, however, does not begin at sea level. It rises from an ocean floor that is more than 16,000 feet below the surface of the water. This mountain therefore measures more than 30,000 feet from its base to its top, making it a higher mountain than Mount Everest.

21. The main idea of the passage is that

    (A) Mount Everest is the world's tallest mountain
    (B) Mount Everest and Mauna Kea are located in different parts of the world
    (C) Mauna Kea's base is below sea level
    (D) Mauna Kea could be considered the tallest mountain in the world

22. Which of the following is NOT stated about Mount Everest?

    (A) Many people believe it is the world's tallest mountain.
    (B) It is part of the Himalayas.
    (C) It is over 29,000 feet high.
    (D) It rises from the ocean floor.

23. The word "just" in line 2 could best be replaced by

    (A) noticeably
    (B) soon
    (C) barely
    (D) recently

24. The expression "a little bit" in line 3 is closest in meaning to

    (A) a small size
    (B) quite
    (C) somewhat
    (D) extremely

25. According to the passage, Mauna Kea is how far above the level of the water?

    (A) 14,000 feet
    (B) 16,000 feet
    (C) 29,000 feet
    (D) 30,000 feet

26. The expression "in comparison to" in lines 4 and 5 could best be replaced by

    (A) close to
    (B) in relation to
    (C) as a result of
    (D) because of

27. It is implied in the passage that Mauna Kea does not seem as tall as Mount Everest because

    (A) people do not want to look at it
    (B) part of Mauna Kea is under water
    (C) Mount Everest has more snow
    (D) Mauna Kea is in a different part of the world than Mount Everest

28. The word "floor" in line 7 could best be replaced by

    (A) carpet
    (B) bottom
    (C) roof
    (D) water

GO ON TO THE NEXT PAGE →

29. The passage indicates that Mauna Kea

    (A) measures 16,000 feet from top to bottom
    (B) is completely covered with water
    (C) is more than half covered by water
    (D) is 1,000 feet shorter than Mount Everest

30. Where in the passage does the author mention Mount Everest's total height?

    (A) Lines 1–2
    (B) Lines 4–6
    (C) Line 7
    (D) Lines 8–9

GO ON TO THE NEXT PAGE →

Questions 31–40

When Columbus arrived in the Americas in 1492, there were already an estimated thirty to forty million people living in North and South America. It has therefore been quite easy for some to refute the idea that Columbus "discovered" America. How and when these inhabitants came to
Line America has been the source of much scientific research and discussion.
(5) Most archeologists agree that the first Americans, the true "discoverers" of America, came from northeastern Asia. There is also a considerable amount of proof that inhabitants have been in the Americas for at least 15,000 years.

To get to the Americas, these people had to cross over the 55-mile-wide Bering Strait that separates Asia and North America. According to one theory, these people crossed over during
(10) periods when a land bridge existed between the two continents. During Ice Ages, so much of the Earth's water was frozen that the sea levels dropped, and it was possible to walk from Asia to North America.

31. What is the author's main purpose?

    (A) To explain how Columbus discovered America
    (B) To show how people came to America before Columbus
    (C) To demonstrate the importance to archeologists of northeastern Asia
    (D) To explain how to cross the Bering Strait

32. In 1492, how many people were probably in the Americas?

    (A) Fewer than thirty million
    (B) Exactly thirty million
    (C) Forty million or fewer
    (D) At least forty million

33. The word "refute" in line 3 is closest in meaning to

    (A) theorize
    (B) support
    (C) contradict
    (D) defend

34. It is implied in the passage that

    (A) Columbus was really the first person in America
    (B) scientists are sure about America's first inhabitants
    (C) Columbus arrived at almost the same time as America's first inhabitants
    (D) all is not known about America's first inhabitants

35. There is general agreement that the first people who came to North America came from

    (A) Europe
    (B) South America
    (C) northeastern Asia
    (D) Africa

36. The word "considerable" in line 6 could best be replaced by which of the following?

    (A) Large
    (B) Weak
    (C) Well-known
    (D) Considerate

GO ON TO THE NEXT PAGE

37. The word "separates" in line 9 is closest in meaning to

    (A) differentiates
    (B) divides
    (C) joins
    (D) crosses

38. Which of the following is NOT stated about the Bering Strait?

    (A) It is 55 miles wide.
    (B) It separates North America and Asia.
    (C) It was probably a land bridge during the Ice Ages.
    (D) It is a land bridge today.

39. The word "frozen" in line 11 could best be replaced by

    (A) cool
    (B) dirty
    (C) solid
    (D) wet

40. Where in the passage does the author mention how long people have probably been in the Americas?

    (A) Lines 1–2
    (B) Lines 3–4
    (C) Lines 6–7
    (D) Lines 8–9

GO ON TO THE NEXT PAGE

Questions 41–50

Alpha Centauri is a triple-star system. One of the three stars in Alpha Centauri is Proxima Centauri, which is the nearest star to the Earth, except of course for the Sun. The name "Proxima" comes from a Latin word which means "close."

Line
(5) Even though Proxima Centauri is the closest star to the Earth outside of our solar system, it is not really close. Interstellar distances are so large that they are almost impossible to imagine. A person traveling in a modern spacecraft would not arrive at Proxima Centauri within this lifetime, or the next, or even ten lifetimes because the distance is so great. Light travels at a speed of 186,000 miles per second, and it still takes light more than four years to travel from Proxima Centauri to the Earth.

(10) Alpha Centauri can be easily seen in the night sky without a telescope from certain parts of the Earth. It is the third brightest star in the sky, out of approximately 6,000 visible stars. It cannot be seen from most parts of the United States because most of the United States is too far north; however, it can be seen from the southern parts of the southernmost states.

41. The main subject of this passage is

    (A) the closest stars to the Earth
    (B) modern space travel
    (C) the speed of light
    (D) interstellar distances

42. The passage indicates that which of the following is NOT true?

    (A) Alpha Centauri is composed of three stars.
    (B) Proxima Centauri is the closest star to the Earth.
    (C) Proxima Centauri is one of the stars in Alpha Centauri.
    (D) It is possible to see Alpha Centauri from the Earth.

43. The word "comes" in line 3 could best be replaced by

    (A) travels
    (B) is derived
    (C) is directed
    (D) visits

44. "Interstellar distances" in line 5 are

    (A) distances between stars
    (B) distances between the Earth and various stars
    (C) distances measured by the speed of light
    (D) distances from the Sun to each of the planets, including the Earth

45. It can be inferred from the passage that if a person left in one of today's spacecrafts, he or she would arrive at Alpha Centauri

    (A) within this lifetime
    (B) within the next lifetime
    (C) within ten lifetimes
    (D) after more than ten lifetimes

46. The word "great" in line 7 could best be replaced by which of the following?

    (A) Famous
    (B) Well-known
    (C) Accomplished
    (D) Big

GO ON TO THE NEXT PAGE →

47. Which of the following is true according to the passage?

    (A) Light travels at 186,000 miles per hour.
    (B) A person could travel from Earth to Proxima Centauri in four years.
    (C) Light from Proxima Centauri reaches the Earth in more than four years.
    (D) It is 186,000 miles from the Earth to Proxima Centauri.

48. The word "brightest" in line 11 could best be replaced by

    (A) smartest
    (B) palest
    (C) shiniest
    (D) largest

49. It can be inferred from the passage that from Alaska Alpha Centauri is

    (A) always visible
    (B) frequently visible
    (C) occasionally visible
    (D) never visible

50. Where in the passage does the author explain how fast light can travel?

    (A) Lines 1–2
    (B) Line 5
    (C) Lines 7–9
    (D) Lines 10–11

This is the end of the Reading Comprehension Pre-Test.

When you finish the test, you may do the following:

- Turn to the **Diagnostic Chart** on pages 357–363, and circle the numbers of the questions that you missed.

- Turn to the **Progress Chart** on page 353, and add your score to the chart.

READING COMPREHENSION

The third section of the TOEFL test is the Reading Comprehension section. This section consists of fifty questions (some tests may be longer). You have fifty-five minutes to complete the fifty questions in this section.

In this part of the test you will be given reading passages, and you will be asked two types of questions about the reading passages:

1. **Reading Comprehension** questions ask you to answer questions about the information given in the reading passages. There will be a variety of questions about each reading passage, including main idea questions, directly answered detail questions, and implied detail questions.

2. **Vocabulary** questions ask you to identify the meanings of vocabulary words in the reading passages. To answer these questions, you may have to know the meanings of the words. You can also identify the meanings of some of the words by understanding the context surrounding the words.

GENERAL STRATEGIES

1. **Be familiar with the directions.** The directions on every TOEFL test are the same, so it is not necessary to spend time reading the directions carefully when you take the test. You should be completely familiar with the directions before the day of the test.

2. **Do not spend too much time reading the passages!** You do not have time to read each reading passage in depth, and it is quite possible to answer the questions correctly without first reading the passages in depth. Some students prefer to spend a minute or two on each passage reading for the main idea before starting on the questions. Other students prefer to move directly to the questions without reading the passages first.

3. **Do not worry if a reading passage is on a topic that you are unfamiliar with.** All of the information that you need to answer the questions is included in the passages. You do not need any background knowledge to answer the questions.

4. **Never leave any questions blank on your answer sheet.** Even if you are unsure of the correct response, you should answer the question. There is no penalty for guessing.

THE READING COMPREHENSION QUESTIONS

The Reading Comprehension section of the TOEFL test consists of five reading passages, each followed by a number of reading comprehension and vocabulary questions. Topics of the reading passages are varied, but they are often informational subjects that might be studied in an American university: American history, literature, art, architecture, geology, geography, and astronomy, for example.

Time is definitely a factor in the Reading Comprehension section. Many students who take the TOEFL test note that they are unable to finish all the questions in this section. Therefore, you need to make the most efficient use of your time in this section to get the highest score. The following method is the best way of attacking a reading passage to get the most questions correct in a limited amount of time.

STRATEGIES FOR THE READING COMPREHENSION QUESTIONS

1. **Skim the reading passage to determine the main idea and the overall organization of ideas in the passage.** You do not need to understand every detail in a passage to answer the questions correctly. It is therefore a waste of time to read the passage with the intent of understanding every single detail before you try to answer the questions.

2. **Look ahead at the questions to determine what types of questions you must answer.** Each type of question is answered in a different way.

3. **Find the section of the passage that deals with each question.** The question type tells you exactly where to look in the passage to find correct answers.
   - For *main idea questions,* look at the first line of each paragraph.
   - For *directly* and *indirectly answered detail questions,* choose a key word in the question, and skim for that key word (or a related idea) in order in the passage.
   - For *vocabulary questions,* the question will tell you where the word is located in the passage.
   - For *where questions,* the answers are found anywhere in the passage.

4. **Read the part of the passage that contains the answer carefully.** The answer will probably be in the same sentence (or one sentence before or after) the key word or idea.

5. **Choose the best answer to each question from the four answer choices listed in your test book.** You can choose the best answer according to what is given in the appropriate section of the passage, eliminate definitely wrong answers, and mark your best guess on the answer sheet.

The following skills will help you to implement these strategies in the Reading Comprehension section of the TOEFL test.

SKILL 1: MAIN IDEA QUESTIONS

Almost every reading passage on the TOEFL test will have a question about the main idea of a passage. Such a question may be worded in a variety of ways; you may, for example, be asked to identify the *topic, subject, title, primary idea,* or *main idea.* These questions are all really asking what primary point the author is trying to get across in the passage. Since TOEFL passages are generally written in a traditionally organized manner, it is not difficult to find the main idea by studying the topic sentence, which is most probably found at the beginning of a paragraph.

If a passage consists of only one paragraph, you should study the beginning of that paragraph to determine the main idea.

Example I

The passage:

Basketball was invented in 1891 by a physical education instructor in Springfield, Massachusetts, by the name of James Naismith. Because of the terrible weather in winter, his physical
Line education students were indoors rather than outdoors. They
(5) really did not like the idea of boring, repetitive exercises and preferred the excitement and challenge of a game. Naismith figured out a team sport that could be played indoors on a gymnasium floor, that involved a lot of running, that kept all team members involved, and that did not allow the tackling and
(10) physical contact of American-style football.

The question:

What is the main idea of this passage?

(A) The life of James Naismith
(B) The history of sports
(C) Physical education and exercise
(D) The origin of basketball

The first sentence of this passage discusses the *invention of basketball,* so this is probably the topic. A quick check of the rest of the sentences in the passage confirms that the topic is in fact the beginnings of the sport of basketball. Now you should check each of the answers to determine which one comes closest to the topic that you have determined. Answer (A) mentions James Naismith but not basketball, so it is not the topic. Answer (B) is too general; it mentions sports but does not mention basketball. Answer (C) is also too general; it mentions physical education but does not mention basketball. The best answer is therefore answer (D); the *origin* of basketball means that the *invention* of basketball is going to be discussed.

If a passage consists of more than one paragraph, you should study the beginning of each paragraph to determine the main idea.

Example II

The passage:

Early maps of the North American continent showed a massive river that began in the Rocky Mountains, flowed into the Great Salt Lake, and from there continued westward into *Line* the Pacific Ocean. This river, named the Buenaventura River, on (5) some maps rivaled the great Mississippi River.

This mythical river of course does not exist. Perhaps an early mapmaker hypothesized that such a river probably existed; perhaps a smaller river was seen and its path from the Rockies to the Pacific was assumed. As late as the middle of the (10) nineteenth century, this river was still on maps and explorers were still searching for it.

The question:

Which of the following would be the best title for this passage?

(A) Early Maps of North America
(B) A Non-Existent River on Maps
(C) A Comparison of the Buenaventura and the Mississippi Rivers
(D) Rivers in Mythology

In a passage with more than one paragraph, you should be sure to read the first sentence of each paragraph to determine the subject, title, or main idea. In this example, the first sentence of the first paragraph indicates that the first paragraph is about *a river on early maps of North America*. If you look at only the first paragraph, you might choose the incorrect answer (A). The first sentence of the second paragraph indicates the *river does not exist*. Answer (C) is incorrect because a comparison with the Mississippi River is only one small detail in the first paragraph. Answer (D) is incorrect because this passage is not about mythology. The best answer to this question is answer (B); the first paragraph says that the *river is on maps,* and the second paragraph says that the *river does not exist.*

The following chart outlines the key information that you should remember about main idea questions.

MAIN IDEA QUESTIONS	
HOW TO IDENTIFY THE QUESTION	*What is the **topic** of the passage?* *What is the **subject** of this passage?* *What is the **main idea** of the passage?* *What is the author's **main point** in the passage?* *With what is the author **primarily concerned**?* *Which of the following would be the best **title**?*
WHERE TO FIND THE ANSWER	The answer to this type of question can generally be determined by looking at the first sentence of each paragraph.
HOW TO ANSWER THE QUESTION	1. Read the first line of each paragraph. 2. Look for a common theme or idea in the first lines. 3. Pass your eyes quickly over the rest of the passage to check that you really have found the topic sentence(s). 4. Eliminate any definitely wrong answers and choose the best answer from the remaining choices.

TOEFL EXERCISE 1: Study each of the passages, and choose the best answers to the questions that follow. In this exercise, each paragraph is followed by *two* main idea, topic, or title questions so that you can practice this type of question. On the TOEFL test, one passage would probably not have two such questions because they are so similar.

PASSAGE ONE (Questions 1–2)

Most of the ice on the Earth, close to 90 percent of it, is covering the surface of the continent Antarctica. It does not snow very much in Antarctica, but whatever snow does fall remains and grows deeper and deeper. In some areas of Antarctica, the ice has perhaps been around for as much as a million years and now is more than two miles deep.

1. The main idea of the passage is that

(A) the Earth is a cold planet
(B) most of the Earth's ice is found in Antarctica
(C) it snows more in Antarctica than in any other place on Earth
(D) Antarctica is only two miles wide but is 90 percent ice

2. The best title for the passage is

(A) Snowfall in Antarctica
(B) The Icy Earth
(C) The Cold, Cold Snow
(D) The Causes of Antarctica's Ice Pack

PASSAGE TWO (Questions 3–4)

The extremely hot and humid weather that occurs in the United States in July and August is commonly called the "dog days" of summer. This name comes from the star Sirius, which is known as the Dog Star. Sirius is the brightest visible star, and in the hot *Line* summer months it rises in the east at approximately the same time as the Sun. As *(5)* ancient people saw this star rising with the Sun when the weather was at its hottest, they believed that Sirius was the cause of the additional heat; they believed that this bright star added its heat to the heat of the Sun, and these two together made summer weather so unbearably hot.

3. The topic of this passage is

   (A) how dogs like to play during the summer
   (B) the causes of hot and humid weather
   (C) why the hot summer days are known as the "dog days"
   (D) the days that dogs prefer

4. The main idea of this passage is that

   (A) the name for the summer days came from Sirius, the Dog Star
   (B) dogs generally prefer hot summer days
   (C) the hottest days occur in the summer because of the movements of the Sun and stars
   (D) Sirius rises at almost the same time as the Sun during the summer months

PASSAGE THREE (Questions 5–6)

The term "primitive art" has been used in a variety of ways to describe works and styles of art. One way that this term has been used is to describe the early period within the development of a certain style of art. Another way that this term has been used is to *Line* describe artists who have received little professional training and who demonstrate a *(5)* nontraditional naivete in their work.

A wonderful example of this second type of primitive artist is Grandma Moses, who spent all her life living on a farm and working at tasks normally associated with farm life. She did not begin painting until she reached the age of seventy-six, when she switched to painting from embroidery because the arthritis in her hands made *(10)* embroidery too difficult. Totally without formal education in art, she began creating panoramic images of everyday life on the farm that have achieved international fame.

5. The subject of this passage is

   (A) an example of one of the types of primitive art
   (B) Grandma Moses's life on the farm
   (C) how primitive art differs from formal art
   (D) Grandma Moses's primitive lifestyle

6. Which of the following best expresses the main idea of the passage?

   (A) Grandma Moses spent her life on a farm.
   (B) Art critics cannot come to any agreement on a definition of primitive art.
   (C) Grandma Moses is one type of primitive artist because of her lack of formal training.
   (D) Many artists receive little professional training.

PASSAGE FOUR (Questions 7–8)

In the first half of the nineteenth century, a New York newspaper, the *New York Sun*, successfully carried out a hoax on the American public. Because of this trick, readership of the paper rose substantially.

Line
(5) On August 25, 1835, the *Sun* published reports that some wonderful new discoveries had been made on the moon. The article described strange, never-before-seen animals and temples covered in shining jewels. Many members of the American public were fooled by the story, even some prominent members of the scientific community.

The effect of the false story on sales of the paper was dramatic. Paper sales increased considerably as people eagerly searched out details of the new discoveries.
(10) Later, the newspaper company announced that it had not been trying to trick the public; instead, the company explained the moon stories as a type of literary satire.

7. Which of the following best states the topic of the passage?

   (A) A nineteenth-century discovery on the moon
   (B) The *New York Sun*
   (C) A hoax and its effect
   (D) The success of a newspaper

8. The main point of the passage is that

   (A) the *New York Sun* was one of the earliest American newspapers
   (B) the *Sun* increased sales when it tricked the public with a false story
   (C) a newspaper achieved success by writing about the moon
   (D) in 1835 some amazing new discoveries were made about the moon

SKILL 2: STATED DETAIL QUESTIONS _____

A stated detail question asks about one piece of information in the passage rather than the passage as a whole. The answers to these questions are generally given in order in the passage, and the correct answer is often a restatement of what is given in the passage. This means that the correct answer often expresses the same idea as what is written in the passage, but the words are not exactly the same.

Example

The passage:

Flutes have been around for quite some time, in all sorts of shapes and sizes and made from a variety of materials. The oldest known flutes are about 20,000 years

Line old; they were made from hollowed-out bones with holes

(5) cut in them. In addition to bone, older flutes were often constructed from bamboo or hollowed-out wood.

Today's flutes are generally made of metal, and in addition to the holes they have a complicated system of keys, levers, and pads. The instrument belonging to well-

(10) known flautist James Galway is not just made of any metal; it is made of gold.

The questions:

1. According to the passage, the oldest flutes

   (A) had holes cut in them
   (B) were made of metal
   (C) were made 200,000 years ago
   (D) had a complicated set of levers and pads

2. The passage indicates that James Galway's flute is made of

   (A) bones
   (B) bamboo
   (C) wood
   (D) gold

The answers to the questions are generally found in order in the passage, so you should look for the answer to the first question near the beginning of the passage. Since the first question asks about *the oldest flutes,* you should see that this question is answered in the second sentence. The passage states that the oldest flutes were bones *with holes cut in them,* so the best answer is answer (A). Answers (B) and (D) are true about today's flutes, but not the oldest flutes, so they are incorrect. Answer (C) is an incorrect number; the oldest flutes are 20,000 years old, not 200,000 years old.

The answer to the second question will probably be located in the passage after the answer to the first question. Since the second question is about *James Galway's flute,* you should skim through the passage to find the part of the passage that discusses this topic. The answer to this question is found in the statement that *the instrument belonging to well-known flautist James Galway is not just made of any metal; it is made of gold.* The best answer to this question is therefore answer (D).

The following chart outlines the key information that you should remember about stated detail questions.

STATED DETAIL QUESTIONS	
HOW TO IDENTIFY THE QUESTION	*According to the passage, . . .* *It is **stated** in the passage that . . .* *The passage **indicates** that . . .* *The author **mentions** that . . .* *Which of the following is **true** . . . ?*
WHERE TO FIND THE ANSWER	The answers to these questions are found in order in the passage.
HOW TO ANSWER THE QUESTION	1. Choose a *key word* in the question. 2. Skim the appropriate part of the passage for the *key word* (or related *idea*). 3. Read the sentence that contains the *key word* or *idea* carefully. 4. Look for the answer that restates an idea in the passage. 5. Eliminate the definitely wrong answers and choose the best answer from the remaining choices.

TOEFL EXERCISE 2: Study each of the passages, and choose the best answers to the questions that follow.

PASSAGE ONE (Questions 1–2)

Many parts of the Southwestern United States would become deserts again without the waters of the Colorado River. A system of thousands of miles of canals, hundreds of miles of tunnels and aqueducts, and numerous dams and reservoirs bring Colorado
Line River water to the area. The Imperial Valley in Southern California is an example of
(5) such a place; it is a vast and productive agricultural area that was once a desert. Today, 2,000 miles of canals irrigate the fertile land and keep it productive.

1. Which of the following is mentioned in the passage as a way that Colorado River water gets to the Southwest?

   (A) By truck
   (B) In bottles
   (C) In wells
   (D) Through canals

2. According to the passage, the Imperial Valley

   (A) is a desert today
   (B) is located in Colorado
   (C) produces a lot of agricultural goods
   (D) does not require irrigation

PASSAGE TWO (Questions 3–5)

The ancestors of humans had a lot more hair than the humans of today; in fact, they had thick hair all over their bodies. This thick hair was necessary for protection against the cold of the Ice Ages.

Line
(5)
As the Earth got warmer, the hair began to thin out, except for on the head. The head hair has remained through the evolutionary process, both as a sort of pillow to cushion the sensitive head when it gets banged around and as a sort of hat to keep the head warm and prevent so much heat from escaping through the scalp.

3. Which of the following is true about the hair of the ancestors of humans?

   (A) There was not much of it.
   (B) It covered their entire bodies.
   (C) It was thin.
   (D) It was not useful.

4. According to the passage, what happened as the temperature on the Earth increased?

   (A) The hair on the head began to thin out.
   (B) The hair on the body remained the same.
   (C) The hair on the body got thicker.
   (D) The hair on the body began to thin out.

5. The author indicates that one of the purposes of hair on the head is to

   (A) fill up pillows
   (B) help heat escape through the scalp
   (C) ensure that the head is warm
   (D) make it easier to think

PASSAGE THREE (Questions 6–10)

The plane with the largest wingspan ever built was nicknamed the *Spruce Goose*. The wingspan of the *Spruce Goose* was 320 feet (almost 100 meters), and the plane weighed 200 tons. It was so big that it needed eight engines to power it.

Line
(5)   The plane was designed by Howard Hughes in response to a U.S. government request for a plane that was able to carry a large cargo for the war effort. It was made of wood because wood is a less critical material in wartime than metal.

The plane was so difficult to build that it never really got used. It was flown one time only, by Hughes himself, on November 2, 1947; during that flight it traveled a distance of less than one mile over the Los Angeles Harbor, but it did fly. Today, the
(10)   *Spruce Goose* is on exhibit for the public to see in Long Beach, California.

6. Which of the following is true about the *Spruce Goose*?

   (A) Each of its wings measures 100 meters.
   (B) It weighs 200 pounds.
   (C) It has eight wings to help it to fly.
   (D) It has a wingspan larger than the wingspan of any other plane.

7. The passage indicates that the plane was designed

   (A) as a cargo plane
   (B) as a racing plane
   (C) to carry wood
   (D) for exhibition

8. According to the passage, the *Spruce Goose* is constructed from

   (A) wood
   (B) lightweight metal
   (C) plastic
   (D) steel

9. According to the passage, when the *Spruce Goose* flew,

   (A) it went only a short distance
   (B) it fell into the Los Angeles Harbor
   (C) it flew 100 miles
   (D) it carried a large cargo

10. The passage indicates that the *Spruce Goose* today

   (A) flies regularly for the U.S. government
   (B) is in the Los Angeles Harbor
   (C) is in storage
   (D) can be seen by the public

TOEFL REVIEW EXERCISE (Skills 1–2): Study each of the passages, and choose the best answers to the questions that follow.

PASSAGE ONE (Questions 1–3)

The center part of a hurricane is called the eye of the storm. In the eye of a hurricane, winds are calm and no rain falls. There can even be blue sky and sunshine in the eye of the storm.

Line
(5)

This dry and calm spot is caused as the air spins around the center of the hurricane. The spinning air rises and pulls moisture with it. What remains in the center is dry, clear air.

1. The topic of the passage is

   (A) the destruction of hurricanes
   (B) the harsh weather during a hurricane
   (C) the calm in the center of a hurricane
   (D) the beautiful weather that follows a hurricane

2. The passage indicates that in the eye of a hurricane

   (A) it is windy
   (B) there is a lot of rain
   (C) there is cloudy, gray sky
   (D) it can be sunny

3. According to the passage, what causes the calm spot?

   (A) The air circling around the center
   (B) The blue sky and sunshine
   (C) The high temperatures
   (D) The heavy rainfall

PASSAGE TWO (Questions 4–8)

The invention of the phonograph happened quite by accident. Thomas Edison moved to Menlo Park, New Jersey, in 1876, where he established an industrial research laboratory. There, Edison was working on a carbon telephone transmitter to improve *Line* the existing Bell telephone system.

(5)   In that laboratory a year later, Edison invented the phonograph while he was trying to improve a telegraph repeater. He attached a telephone diaphragm to the needle in the telegraph repeater; in this way, he was able to reproduce a recording that could be played back. After he made some improvements to the machine, he tested it. He recited "Mary Had a Little Lamb" into the machine and played his voice back to a very (10)   surprised audience.

4. What is the best title for the passage?

(A) Thomas Edison's Many Inventions
(B) Improvements in the Telephone and Telegraph
(C) The History of Menlo Park
(D) An Accidental Invention

5. According to the passage, the invention of the phonograph

(A) was quite unplanned
(B) was Edison's principal project
(C) was surprising to no one
(D) took many years

6. In what year did the invention of the phonograph occur?

(A) 1876
(B) 1877
(C) 1878
(D) The article does not say.

7. According to the passage, how was the phonograph made?

(A) With a telephone needle and a recorder
(B) From a recording of a telegraph
(C) With only a telegraph repeater
(D) From a combination of telephone and telegraph parts

8. According to the passage, how did Edison test his new invention?

(A) He made improvements to the machine.
(B) He used a carbon transmitter.
(C) He read a children's rhyme.
(D) He reproduced the audience's voice.

PASSAGE THREE (Questions 9–14)

The Sears and Roebuck catalogue was a fixture in American society for many decades. Practically anything needed in the American home could be ordered through this comprehensive catalogue and delivered by mail. The catalogue made it easier for
Line homeowners in urban areas to track down items they were trying to find; the catalogue
(5) was an absolute necessity for residents in out-of-the-way areas where many types of home supplies were not available for hundreds of miles.

In the early twentieth century, it was not possible to buy just home supplies from the Sears and Roebuck catalogue. It was actually possible to buy a mail-order house. If you ordered a house through the mail, you would receive all the necessary building
(10) materials as well as plans for constructing the house; all of this could be had for prices starting around $600.

9. This passage mainly discusses

  (A) products sold in the Sears and Roebuck stores
  (B) the design of the Sears and Roebuck catalogue
  (C) how to shop using catalogues
  (D) shopping through the Sears and Roebuck catalogue in the past

10. The passage indicates that items ordered through the Sears and Roebuck catalogue

  (A) had to be picked up at a Sears and Roebuck store
  (B) were delivered by mail
  (C) arrived in Sears and Roebuck trucks
  (D) had to be small

11. According to the passage, why was the Sears and Roebuck catalogue important to people in remote areas?

  (A) It contained the only products they could afford.
  (B) They did not like the products in local stores.
  (C) It had a lot of products they could not get in their local areas.
  (D) It was the only way to get a new home.

12. The passage mentions that which of the following large items could be purchased through the Sears and Roebuck catalogue?

  (A) A home
  (B) A car
  (C) A boat
  (D) A train

13. The mail-order house in the Sears and Roebuck catalogue

  (A) was for urban areas only
  (B) was set up by Sears and Roebuck workers
  (C) needed to be put together
  (D) arrived in one piece

14. The price of $600 mentioned in the passage was

  (A) the lowest price for the item
  (B) the average price for the item
  (C) the only price for the item
  (D) the highest price for the item

Skill 3: UNSTATED DETAIL QUESTIONS _____

You will sometimes be asked in the Reading Comprehension section of the TOEFL test to find an answer that is *not stated* or *not mentioned* or *not true* in the passage. This type of question really means that three of the answers are *stated, mentioned,* or *true* in the passage, while one answer is not. Your actual job is to find the three correct answers and then choose the letter of the one remaining answer.

You should note that there are two kinds of answers to this type of question: (1) there are three true answers and one answer that is *not discussed* in the passage, or (2) there are three true answers and one that is *false* according to the passage.

Example

The passage:

    The Florida Keys are a beautiful <u>chain</u> of almost 1,000 <u>coral and limestone islands</u>. These islands form an <u>arc</u> that heads first southwest and then west from the mainland. U.S. Highway 1,
Line called <u>the Overseas Highway</u>, connects the main islands in the
(5) chain. On this highway, it is necessary to cross <u>42 bridges</u> over the ocean to <u>cover the 159 miles from Miami</u>, on the mainland, to <u>Key West</u>, the farthest island on the highway and the southernmost city in the United States.

The questions:

1. Which of the following is NOT mentioned about the Florida Keys?

    (A) The Florida Keys are a <u>chain</u> of islands.
    (B) The Florida Keys contain <u>coral and limestone</u>.
    (C) The Florida Keys are in the shape of an <u>arc</u>.
    (D) The Florida Keys are not all inhabited.

2. Which of the following is NOT true about U.S. Highway 1?

    (A) It is also known as <u>the Overseas Highway</u>.
    (B) It joins all of the islands in the Florida Keys.
    (C) It has <u>more than 40 bridges</u>.
    (D) It <u>connects Miami and Key West</u>.

The first question asks for the one answer that is *not mentioned* about the Florida Keys. The passage states that the Florida Keys are a *chain* (answer A) with *coral and limestone* (answer B) in the shape of an *arc* (answer C), so these answers are not correct. The best answer is therefore answer (D). The passage does not discuss whether or not the keys are all inhabited.

    The second question asks for the answer that is *not true* about U.S. Highway 1. The passage states that it is called *the Overseas Highway* (answer A), that it has *42 bridges* (answer C), and that it *cover(s) the 159 miles from Miami . . . to Key*

West (answer D), so these answers are not correct. The best answer is answer (B). The passage states that the Overseas Highway *connects the main islands in the chain,* so it does not connect *all* of the islands.

The following chart outlines the key information that you should remember about unstated detail questions.

UNSTATED DETAIL QUESTIONS	
HOW TO IDENTIFY THE QUESTION	*Which of the following is **not stated** . . . ?* *Which of the following is **not mentioned** . . . ?* *Which of the following is **not discussed** . . . ?* *All of the following are true **except** . . .*
WHERE TO FIND THE ANSWER	The answers to these questions are found in order in the passage.
HOW TO ANSWER THE QUESTION	1. Choose a *key word* in the question. 2. Scan the appropriate place in the passage for the *key word* (or related *idea*). 3. Read the sentence that contains the *key word* or *idea* carefully. 4. Look for the answers that are definitely true according to the passage. Eliminate those answers. 5. Choose the answer that is *not true* or *not discussed* in the passage.

TOEFL EXERCISE 3: Study each of the passages, and choose the best answers to the questions that follow.

PASSAGE ONE (Questions 1–2)

Blood pressure measurement has two components: systolic and diastolic. Systolic pressure is taken when the heart is contracting to pump blood; diastolic pressure is taken when the heart is resting between beats. In the usual blood pressure reading, the systolic measurement is given first and is the higher of the two.

Line
(5)

Normal blood pressure is a systolic measurement of 120–140, and when the systolic pressure is 160 or higher, then hypertension exists. Systolic pressure between 140 and 160 indicates borderline hypertension.

1. Which of the following is NOT true about systolic blood pressure?

   (A) It is taken during the contraction of the heart.
   (B) It is usually given first in a blood pressure reading.
   (C) A normal systolic measurement is 120–140.
   (D) Hypertension exists when the systolic pressure is below 140.

2. Which of the following is NOT stated about diastolic pressure?

   (A) It is one of the two components of blood pressure measurement.
   (B) It is taken when the heart is resting.
   (C) It is lower than systolic pressure.
   (D) A diastolic measurement of 140 is normal.

PASSAGE TWO (Questions 3–4)

In the 1960s, as space travel was becoming a subject of much discussion, Pan American Airlines began receiving some fairly unusual requests for flight information. People began making requests to be on the first flight that Pan Am made to the Moon.

Line
(5)

On a whim, Pan Am started a waiting list for the first flight to the Moon. Similar requests have come to Pan Am over the years, and Pan Am has responded by adding the names of the requesters to the list.

Unfortunately for Pan Am, the original company is no longer in business, and it never got to the Moon. However, when it went out of business, it had a waiting list of more than 90,000 names for its first lunar flight.

3. All of the following are mentioned about Pan American Airlines, EXCEPT that

   (A) it started business in the 1960s
   (B) it received requests for its first flight to the Moon
   (C) it kept some people on a long waiting list
   (D) it went out of business

4. Which of the following is NOT true about Pan Am's Moon flights?

   (A) People asked Pan Am about its flights to the Moon.
   (B) Pan Am kept a waiting list for its Moon flights.
   (C) Pan Am never really made any Moon flights.
   (D) Pan Am's waiting list had only a few names on it.

PASSAGE THREE (Questions 5–8)

The tunnel trees in Yosemite Valley are an amazing attraction to people who visit there. The tunnel trees are huge trees, giant redwoods, which have had tunnels carved in them, and cars can actually drive through some of the trees. The fact that the trees are large enough to have cars drive through them should give you some indication of just how big the trees are.

Line
(5)

There are currently two existing tunnel trees in Yosemite Valley. One of them is called the "Dead Giant." This is just the stump, or bottom part, of a much larger tree. The hole was cut through the base of the tree in 1878, and stagecoaches used to drive through it. Today the Dead Giant still exists, but the stagecoaches do not. Passenger cars can and do drive through the 10-foot-wide opening in the tree stump.

(10)

The other existing tunnel tree is the 230-foot high California Tree, which had a hole carved through it in 1895. This tree is no longer open to the public, so it is not possible to take a car through it.

Unfortunately, a third tunnel tree no longer exists. The Wawona Tunnel Tree was a 2,100-year-old tree which was carved in 1881. A terrible snowstorm in 1969 caused this ancient giant of a tree to fall.

(15)

5. Which of the following is NOT true about the tunnel trees in Yosemite Valley?

   (A) They are trees with holes cut in them.
   (B) They are giant redwoods.
   (C) Three tunnel trees currently exist.
   (D) Cars have driven through some of them.

6. All of the following are stated about the Dead Giant, EXCEPT that

   (A) it is still a tunnel tree today
   (B) it is just the stump of a tree
   (C) it was cut less than a century ago
   (D) it has a 10-foot opening

7. Which of the following is NOT true about the California Tree?

   (A) Its tunnel still exists.
   (B) Its tunnel is 230 feet high.
   (C) Its tunnel was cut in 1895.
   (D) Cars are not allowed to go through it.

8. All of the following are true about the Wawona Tunnel Tree, EXCEPT that

   (A) it does not exist anymore
   (B) the tree lived for more than 2,000 years
   (C) the tunnel tree was destroyed in a snowstorm
   (D) the tunnel was destroyed in 1881

TOEFL REVIEW EXERCISE (Skills 1–3): Study each of the passages, and choose the best answers to the questions that follow.

PASSAGE ONE (Questions 1–4)

When the typewriter was first invented, its keys were arranged alphabetically. This made the keys easy to find. However, this arrangement also caused the bars of the machine to jam, or get stuck.

Line
(5)
To solve this problem, a new letter arrangement was introduced by Christopher Latham Scholes in 1872. His system, the standard keyboard system, is still used on typewriters today. He arranged the letters in such a way that the bars hit the inked ribbon from opposite directions as much as possible. This resulted in far less jamming than had occurred with the alphabetical models.

1. The main topic of this passage is

   (A) the invention of the typewriter
   (B) a problem and solution concerning the early typewriter
   (C) how to write a letter on the typewriter
   (D) why the keys stick on today's typewriter

2. According to the passage, on the first typewriters

   (A) the keys were in alphabetical order
   (B) the keys were hard to find
   (C) the bars on the machine never jammed
   (D) Scholes's system worked quite well

3. Which of the following is NOT true about the system invented by Scholes?

   (A) It was introduced in 1872.
   (B) It is still used today.
   (C) It became the standard system.
   (D) It was alphabetical.

4. The passage indicates that under Scholes's system, the bars hit the ribbon

   (A) in alphabetical order
   (B) from opposite directions
   (C) and caused the keys to jam
   (D) in the same way as they had on the original typewriter

PASSAGE TWO (Questions 5–9)

Desert tundra, or cold desert, occurs on the Arctic edges of North America, Europe, and Asia. In these areas the temperatures are almost always freezing, and they cause an environment in which plant life is virtually impossible. The existence of ice rather than water for the majority of the year means that vegetation does not have enough moisture for growth to take place. During the short period of time when the temperature increases enough for the ice to melt, there is generally a large volume of water. Too much water and not enough drainage through the frozen subsoil make it difficult for plants to grow.

Line
(5)

5. Which of the following is the best title for the passage?

   (A) Where Desert Tundra Is Found
   (B) The Weather in the Arctic
   (C) The Effect of Desert Tundra on Plant Life
   (D) The Variety of Plant Life in Desert Tundra

6. According to the passage, desert tundra is found

   (A) throughout North America, Europe, and Asia
   (B) in Antarctica
   (C) on the Arctic borders of the northern continents
   (D) at the North Pole

7. According to the passage, what makes plant life almost impossible in areas of desert tundra during most of the year?

   (A) Excessive water on the plants
   (B) The frozen state of the water
   (C) The increase in temperature
   (D) The lack of ice

8. According to the passage, which of the following does NOT happen when the weather heats up?

   (A) Plants grow well.
   (B) The ice melts.
   (C) There is not enough drainage.
   (D) There is too much water.

9. According to the passage, why is it impossible for the water to drain after it melts?

   (A) The land beneath the surface is still frozen.
   (B) The temperature is too high.
   (C) The period of time is too short.
   (D) The vegetation is flourishing.

PASSAGE THREE (Questions 10–14)

Whales are mammals rather than fish, yet they live in the world's oceans rather than on land. Because of the fact that they are mammals, scientists have believed for quite some time that whales are descendants of land mammals.

Line
(5)   Some interesting evidence to support this theory has recently been found. In Egypt, fossils have been found of a forty-million-year-old whale leg, kneecap, ankle, footbones, and toes. It appears from the fossil evidence that the bones were not very strong and not very large in comparison to the size of the whale.

Based on this fossil evidence, the following evolutionary path has been hypothesized. As the whale began its evolution toward the water, its legs weakened and
(10)   decreased in size. Then, during its millions of years in the water, the legs slowly disappeared, leaving only the front flippers today.

10. The main idea of this passage is that

   (A) numerous whale fossils have been found in the world's oceans
   (B) there is evidence that whales may have descended from land mammals
   (C) whales are mammals and not fish
   (D) whales have not evolved very much over the last millions of years

11. All of the following are true about whales, EXCEPT that

   (A) they are mammals
   (B) they live in the ocean
   (C) they are fish
   (D) they may have come from the land

12. Which of the following is NOT mentioned about the whale fossils in the passage?

   (A) They were found in Egypt.
   (B) They support the theory that whales came from land.
   (C) They are forty million years old.
   (D) They showed that ancient whales had flippers.

13. Which of the following was NOT mentioned in the list of whale fossils found in Egypt?

   (A) A whale's kneecap
   (B) A whale's ankle
   (C) A whale's footbones
   (D) A whale's fingers

14. According to the hypothesis in the passage, what happened to whales' legs?

   (A) They got stronger over time.
   (B) They got larger over time.
   (C) They disappeared quickly.
   (D) They became front flippers.

SKILL 4: IMPLIED DETAIL QUESTIONS

Some questions in the Reading Comprehension section of the TOEFL test will require answers that are not directly stated in the passage. To answer these questions correctly, you will have to draw conclusions from information that is given in the passage. Questions of this type contain the words *implied*, *inferred*, *likely*, or *probably* to let you know that the answer to the question is not directly stated.

Example

The passage:

The number of rings in a tree can be used to determine how old a tree really is. Each year a tree produces a ring that is composed of one light-colored wide band and one dark-colored
Line   narrow band. The wider band is produced during the spring
(5)   and early summer, when tree stem cells grow rapidly and become larger. The narrower band is produced in fall and early winter, when cell growth is much slower and cells do not get very large. No cells are produced during the harsh winter and summer months.

The questions:

1. It is implied in the passage that if a tree has 100 wide bands and 100 narrow bands, then it is

   (A) a century old
   (B) two centuries old
   (C) fifty years old
   (D) two hundred years old

2. It can be inferred from the passage that cells do not grow

   (A) when the tree is ill
   (B) during extreme heat or cold
   (C) when it rains too much
   (D) if there are more light-colored bands than dark-colored bands

---

The first question asks about the age of a tree with *100 wide bands* and *100 narrow bands*. The passage does not tell the age of a tree with 100 wide and narrow bands, but it does indicate that *one . . . wide band* and *one . . . narrow band* are produced each year. From this you can draw the conclusion that a tree with 100 wide and narrow bands is 100 years, or *a century*, old. The best answer to this question is therefore answer (A). The second question asks when *cells do not grow*. The passage indicates that *no cells are produced* during the *harsh winter and summer months*. From this you can draw the conclusion that cells do not grow during the *extreme heat* of summer or the *extreme cold* of winter. The best answer to this question is therefore answer (B).

The following chart outlines the key information that you should remember about implied detail questions.

IMPLIED DETAIL QUESTIONS	
HOW TO IDENTIFY THE QUESTION	*It is **implied** in the passage that ...* *It can be **inferred** from the passage that ...* *It is most **likely** that ...* *What **probably** happened ...?*
WHERE TO FIND THE ANSWER	The answers to these questions are found in order in the passage.
HOW TO ANSWER THE QUESTION	1. Choose a *key word* in the question. 2. Scan the passage for the *key word* (or related *idea*). 3. Read the sentence that contains the *key word* carefully. 4. Look for an answer that *could be* true, according to that sentence.

TOEFL EXERCISE 4: Study each of the passages, and choose the best answers to the questions that follow.

PASSAGE ONE (Questions 1–3)

Until 1996 the Sears Tower was the tallest building in the world, with more than a hundred stories. It is located in Chicago, whose nickname is the Windy City. The combination of a very tall building in a city with such weather conditions leads to a lot of swaying in the breeze.

Line
(5)   On a windy day, the top of the building can move back and forth as much as three feet every few seconds. The inside doors at the top of the building open and close, and water in sinks sloshes back and forth.

1. The Sears Tower is probably

    (A) as tall as the Empire State Building
    (B) no longer the tallest building in the world
    (C) taller than any other building
    (D) still the highest building in the world

2. It can be inferred from the passage that Chicago

    (A) has moderate weather
    (B) is generally warm
    (C) has humid weather
    (D) usually has a lot of wind

3. It is implied in the passage that the upper-level doors in the Sears Tower open and close because

    (A) the building was poorly constructed
    (B) people go in and out so often
    (C) the building moves in the wind
    (D) there is water in the sinks

PASSAGE TWO (Questions 4–6)

The most common last name in the English-speaking world is Smith, which was taken from the job of working with metals. A silversmith, for example, is someone who works with the metal silver. Historical records indicate that the use of this last name is at least 700 years old. Today, there are more than 3.3 million Smiths living in the United States and perhaps another million Smiths living in other English-speaking countries worldwide.

Line
(5)

4. It can be inferred from the passage that family names

   (A) were always taken from the area where a family lived
   (B) were short names
   (C) had little or no meaning
   (D) could be taken from jobs

5. Which of the following is implied about the Smith family name?

   (A) It is definitely not more than 700 years old.
   (B) It existed 600 years ago.
   (C) It did not exist 500 years ago.
   (D) It definitely was not in use 1,000 years ago.

6. In England there are probably

   (A) more Smiths than there are in the United States
   (B) more than a million Smiths
   (C) fewer than a million Smiths
   (D) no families with the name of Smith

PASSAGE THREE (Questions 7–9)

On the hardness scale, corundum immediately follows diamond, which is the hardest mineral in the world. Corundum is perhaps better known by the names of its gemstones, ruby and sapphire. Basically, gem corundum is divided into two groups: corundum that is red in color is called ruby, and corundum that is any other color is called sapphire.

Pure corundum is clear, but pure corundum is rarely found in nature. If small amounts of the chemical substance chromic oxide (Cr_2O_3) got into the crystal structure when it formed millions of years ago, then the corundum turned a deep, rich red and became ruby.

Red is not the only color that corundum can take on. Other chemical substances enter into the crystal structure of corundum, and it can take on a variety of other colors. Most people associate blue with sapphires, and certainly when corundum contains impurities that turn it blue, it is called sapphire. However, corundum can have a variety of other colors—e.g., green or purple—and still be called sapphire.

7. It can be inferred from the passage that corundum is

   (A) the hardest mineral in the world
   (B) not as hard as sapphire
   (C) the second hardest mineral
   (D) a rather soft mineral

8. Chromic oxide is probably what color?

   (A) Clear
   (B) Blue
   (C) Red
   (D) Green

9. Yellow corundum is most likely called

   (A) gold
   (B) chromic oxide
   (C) ruby
   (D) sapphire

TOEFL REVIEW EXERCISE (Skills 1–4): Study each of the passages, and choose the best answers to the questions that follow.

PASSAGE ONE (Questions 1–5)

Before ballpoint pens or fountain pens, pens were made from goose feathers. These goose feathers, called quills, were sharpened and dipped into inkwells, where they absorbed enough ink to write a few words. It was necessary to keep an inkwell very *Line* close by, as frequent dipping was necessary.

(5)   These quill pens were one of the earliest products "designed" specifically for left- and right-handed people. Feathers from the left wing of the goose worked best for right-handers because of the way that the feathers arched. Feathers from the right wing were preferred by left-handers.

1. Which of the following is the best title for this passage?

   (A) Early Ballpoint and Fountain Pens
   (B) Quill Pens for Lefties and Righties
   (C) Where Quill Pens Came From
   (D) Various Uses for Goose Feathers

2. According to the passage, a quill came from

   (A) a tree
   (B) a bird
   (C) a piece of metal
   (D) a fountain pen

3. The passage indicates that a quill pen could hold enough ink to write

   (A) one or two pages
   (B) for about one hour
   (C) a couple of words
   (D) numerous sentences

4. Which of the following is NOT true about quill pens, according to the passage?

   (A) Left-handers were unable to use quill pens.
   (B) Left-handed people generally preferred quills from the right wing.
   (C) Right-handers could use quill pens.
   (D) Right-handed people generally preferred quills from the left wing.

5. It can be inferred from the passage that quill pens

   (A) are still used regularly today
   (B) are preferred over ballpoint pens
   (C) are the best pens for left-handers
   (D) are no longer used much

PASSAGE TWO (Questions 6–10)

The English names of the last four months of the Gregorian calendar (September, October, November, December) have rather interesting histories. The Gregorian calendar is a twelve-month calendar, so these months are the ninth, tenth, eleventh, and
Line
(5)
twelfth months respectively. However, their names do not reflect their positioning in the calendar. The name September comes from the Latin word *septum*, which means "seven." This month was originally the name of the seventh rather than the ninth month. Similarly, the name October comes from the Latin *octo* ("eight"); the name November comes from the Latin *novem* ("nine"); the name December comes from the Latin *decem* ("ten").

6. The main topic of this passage is

   (A) the origin of certain month names
   (B) the Gregorian calendar
   (C) the numbers in Latin
   (D) ten- and twelve-month calendars

7. The first month on the Gregorian calendar is probably

   (A) March
   (B) May
   (C) January
   (D) December

8. The passage states that in the original version of the calendar, September was the name of

   (A) the sixth month
   (B) the seventh month
   (C) the eighth month
   (D) the ninth month

9. It can be inferred from the passage that November

   (A) used to be the ninth month of the year
   (B) is no longer part of the Gregorian calendar
   (C) has always been the eleventh month
   (D) was not part of the original Gregorian calendar

10. Which of the following is NOT mentioned in the passage about December?

    (A) It is the twelfth month on the Gregorian calendar.
    (B) Its name is derived from a Latin word.
    (C) Its meaning comes from the number ten.
    (D) It has 31 days.

PASSAGE THREE (Questions 11–15)

Different types of relationships exist between living things. One type of relationship is parasitism, in which one partner benefits while the other loses. A very different type of relationship is symbiosis, in which both partners benefit.

Line
(5)   An example of a parasitic relationship exists between the stone crab and sacculina, a type of barnacle. The sacculina attaches itself to the stone crab. It then eats into the crab, and the stone crab becomes disabled.

An example of a symbiotic relationship exists between the hermit crab and the calliactis anemone. The anemone attaches itself to the crab, but it is not a parasite because it does not harm the crab; it feeds on food that is dropped by the crab. The
(10) anemone even helps the crab by protecting the crab from other predators with its tentacles.

11. The subject of this passage is

(A) two different kinds of
relationships among living
things
(B) parasitic relationships
(C) relationships that are mutually
beneficial to living things
(D) symbiosis

12. Which of the following is NOT true
about parasitic relationships?

(A) There are two partners in a
parasitic relationship.
(B) One partner in a parasitic
relationship hurts the other.
(C) The stone crab can be part of a
parasitic relationship.
(D) A parasitic relationship is usually
symbiotic.

13. According to the passage, what does
sacculina eat?

(A) The stone crab
(B) Barnacles
(C) Food dropped by the crab
(D) Other parasites

14. The calliactis anemone

(A) is a parasite
(B) harms the hermit crab
(C) eats into the hermit crab
(D) assists the hermit crab

15. Which of the following can be
inferred from the passage?

(A) All crabs are involved in parasitic
relationships.
(B) All crabs are involved in
symbiotic relationships.
(C) Some crabs are involved in
symbiotic relationships, while
others are not.
(D) Crabs are involved in neither
parasitic nor symbiotic
relationships.

SKILL 5: VOCABULARY IN CONTEXT QUESTIONS

On the TOEFL test you will sometimes be asked to determine the meaning of a difficult word or expression, a word or expression that you do not know. In this case, the passage often gives you a clear indication of what the word or expression means.

Example

A line in the passage:

. . . She has a large <u>geranium</u> growing in a pot in the corner of her apartment. . . .

The question:

A "geranium" is probably which of the following?

(A) A sofa
(B) A chair
(C) A fish
(D) <u>A plant</u>

In this type of question, you are not expected to know the meaning of the word *geranium*. Instead, you should understand from the context that if the *geranium* is *growing in a pot,* then it is probably a plant. Answer (D) is therefore the best answer.

The following chart outlines the key information that you should remember about vocabulary questions on the TOEFL test.

VOCABULARY QUESTIONS CONTAINING DIFFICULT WORDS	
HOW TO IDENTIFY THE QUESTION	*What is the **meaning** . . . ?* *Which of the following is closest in **meaning** to . . . ?* *. . . could **best be replaced** by which of the following?*
WHERE TO FIND THE ANSWER	The question usually tells you in which line of the passage the words or expression can be found.
HOW TO ANSWER THE QUESTION	1. Find the word or expression in the passage. 2. Read the sentence that contains the word *carefully*. 3. Look for context clues to help you understand the meaning. 4. Choose the answer that the context indicates.

TOEFL EXERCISE 5: Study each of the passages, and choose the best answers to the questions that follow.

PASSAGE ONE (Questions 1–4)

When babies are born, they always have blue eyes. This is because the melanin, the pigment that colors the eyes, is not on the surface of the iris. Instead, it is within the creases of the iris. Because there is little melanin on the surface of the iris, the eyes appear blue.

After a few months, the melanin moves to the surface of the iris. It is the amount of melanin on the surface that determines a person's permanent eye color, so it is at this point that a baby's eyes develop the color they will have for a lifetime.

Line
(5)

1. The word "pigment" in line 2 is closest in meaning to

   (A) skin
   (B) muscle
   (C) tissue
   (D) color

2. The word "surface" in line 2 is closest in meaning to

   (A) top
   (B) inside
   (C) back
   (D) bottom

3. The word "permanent' in line 6 could best be replaced by

   (A) changeable
   (B) lasting
   (C) dark
   (D) possible

4. The word "point" in line 7 could best be replaced by which of the following?

   (A) Dot
   (B) Era
   (C) Time
   (D) Place

PASSAGE TWO (Questions 5–9)

The chili pepper is native to the Americas, but nowadays it is found all over the world. It is an extremely popular spice in many cultures and is, in fact, the world's second favorite spice, after salt. There are more than a hundred species of chili peppers, some which are quite mild and others which are incredibly hot and spicy.

Line
(5)

Today chili peppers are used to spice a variety of foods, e.g., salsa, meat and rice dishes, and even jam and jelly. In the past, chili peppers had some other, more unusual uses. In ancient Mexico, for example, chilies could be used to pay taxes. In addition, in Panama, these peppers were used to protect against sharks.

5. The word "favorite" in line 3 is closest in meaning to

   (A) most popular
   (B) most delicious
   (C) best known
   (D) most recognized

6. The word "species" in line 3 is closest in meaning to which of the following?

   (A) Plants
   (B) Uses
   (C) Types
   (D) Sizes

7. The word "mild" in line 4 could best be replaced by

   (A) strong tasting
   (B) cold
   (C) delicate tasting
   (D) amiable

8. "Jam" in line 6 is probably

   (A) a type of chili
   (B) something to eat
   (C) something to wear
   (D) a container for chilies

9. The expression "protect against" in line 8 could best be replaced by

   (A) lean against
   (B) hunt for
   (C) flirt with
   (D) defend against

PASSAGE THREE (Questions 10–15)

At the end of the Revolutionary War, America was no longer a colony; instead, America was a new, young country that needed to set up its own government. There was a lot of disagreement throughout the country as to the type of government that was
Line best. One of the major issues was whether there should be a strong federal government
(5) with little power in the hands of the individual states or a weak central government and powerful states.

It is interesting to note that it was many of the Revolutionary War veterans who were in favor of a strong central government. Because of their efforts in winning the war over the British, after the war they became a powerful political force, and as a
(10) whole they were extremely nationalistic.

There were also financial reasons that veterans supported a strong national government. The revolutionary congress had ended the war with a large amount of debt, and a large portion of this debt was in back pay and pensions to soldiers. Many soldiers believed that with a strong federal government, they had a better chance of
(15) collecting the money owed to them.

10. A "colony" in line 1 is

    (A) an independent country
    (B) a type of government
    (C) a dependent area
    (D) a continent

11. The expression "set up" in line 2 could best be replaced by which of the following?

    (A) Defend
    (B) Organize
    (C) Argue about
    (D) Protect

12. The word "federal" in line 4 is closest in meaning to

    (A) state
    (B) weak
    (C) central
    (D) new

13. In line 7, "veterans" refers to

    (A) government officials
    (B) former soldiers
    (C) voters
    (D) current members of the armed forces

14. The word "financial" in line 11 is closest in meaning to

    (A) monetary
    (B) important
    (C) military
    (D) national

15. The word "back" in line 13 could best be replaced by which of the following?

    (A) Reverse
    (B) Low-income
    (C) Returnable
    (D) Already earned

TOEFL REVIEW EXERCISE (Skills 1–5): Study each of the passages, and choose the best answers to the questions that follow.

PASSAGE ONE (Questions 1–9)

     Geographically, California's diversity is breathtaking, and the state's coastline from north to south is no exception. Measuring 840 miles in length, the coast consists of the rugged cliffs of the Coast Ranges in the north and wide sandy beaches in the south. Along the coastline there are two major harbors, one in the north at San Francisco, the other in the south at San Diego. Near Humboldt and Monterey are smaller natural harbors.

Line
(5)

1. The topic of this passage is

   (A) how the state of California is divided into north and south
   (B) the variations in California's coastal geography
   (C) the breathtaking beauty of California
   (D) the exceptions in coastal geography

2. The word "breathtaking" in line 1 probably means

   (A) breathing
   (B) amazing
   (C) stolen
   (D) usual

3. According to the passage, what measures 840 miles in length?

   (A) The California coastline
   (B) The Coast Ranges
   (C) The rugged cliffs
   (D) The exceptional part of northern California

4. The Coast Ranges are probably

   (A) flat, sandy areas on the coast of California
   (B) found in southern California
   (C) a series of mountains
   (D) hundreds of miles north of the cliffs

5. "Harbors" in line 4 are

   (A) cliffs
   (B) ports
   (C) beaches
   (D) mountains

6. It is implied in the passage that northern California

   (A) has more beaches than southern California
   (B) has the same type of coastline as southern California
   (C) has fewer major harbors than southern California
   (D) has a different coastline from southern California

7. According to the passage, where are the major harbors located in California?

   (A) In San Diego
   (B) Only in northern California
   (C) Near Humboldt and Monterey
   (D) In the north and in the south

8. In line 5, "natural harbors" are

   (A) not human-made
   (B) always small in size
   (C) evenly shaped
   (D) constructed of natural materials

9. Which of the following geographical features is NOT mentioned in the passage?

   (A) Cliffs
   (B) Canyons
   (C) Beaches
   (D) Harbors

PASSAGE TWO (Questions 10–18)

Among some groups of people, cats have a reputation as rather silly animals that are always getting themselves stuck in trees. Cats have often been known to become frightened of something, run up a tree, and then cry sadly until they are rescued.

Line
(5)
There is, in reality, a reasonable explanation for this type of behavior, and it has to do with the shape of the cat's claws. A cat's claws are hooked in a direction that makes climbing up a tree a rather easy task. However, when it comes to climbing back down the tree, these claws are not very helpful.

10. The main idea of the passage is that

    (A) cats really are silly animals
    (B) cats have good reason for their behavior
    (C) cats enjoy climbing trees
    (D) cats' sharp claws are unnecessary for survival

11. The passage indicates that some people think that cats are silly because the cats

    (A) have funny-looking claws
    (B) frighten other cats
    (C) climb trees and cannot get down
    (D) are unable to rescue other cats

12. The word "rescued" in line 3 is closest in meaning to

    (A) left
    (B) saved
    (C) scared
    (D) tired

13. The expression "in reality" in line 4 could best be replaced by

    (A) in contrast
    (B) in fact
    (C) in agreement
    (D) in all probability

14. The word "hooked" in line 5 is closest in meaning to

    (A) curved
    (B) straightened
    (C) sharpened
    (D) shortened

15. According to the passage, a cat CANNOT

    (A) climb up a tree
    (B) get stuck in a tree
    (C) cry easily
    (D) climb down easily

16. The passage states that a cat gets stuck in a tree because

    (A) it is crying
    (B) of the shape of its claws
    (C) it does not know how to climb
    (D) it is afraid of other cats

17. It is implied in the passage that if a cat tries to climb down a tree, it will

    (A) be able to do it easily
    (B) move very quickly
    (C) cry to other cats
    (D) perhaps fall

18. The word "helpful" in line 7 could best be replaced by

    (A) friendly
    (B) useful
    (C) nice
    (D) sincere

PASSAGE THREE (Questions 19–27)

In the 1890s, bicycles became quite popular in the United States as the new "safety" bicycles replaced the older penny-farthing bicycles. On the penny-farthing bicycles, one wheel was much larger than the other, and these bicycles were not very stable; they
Line were always falling over. On the new "safety" bicycles, both wheels were equal in size,
(5) and they were much easier to control.

Many women also enjoyed these new "safety" bicycles, but they had to take measures to deal with their clothing while riding the bicycles. The fashion at the time was for long, full skirts that did not go well with bicycles. Some women put lead weights in their skirts to keep their skirts from blowing up. Other women changed from
(10) long skirts to bloomers, which were long, full, wide pants, but some people felt that bloomers were inappropriate for women to wear; in fact, some newspapers and magazines of the day criticized the new bicycle fashion as a danger to ladies' morals.

19. The passage is mainly about

    (A) the popularity of safety bicycles, even among women
    (B) the differences between safety and penny-farthing bicycles
    (C) women's fashions in the nineteenth century
    (D) the lack of stability of the penny-farthing bicycles

20. According to the passage, the penny-farthing bicycle had

    (A) two small wheels
    (B) two large wheels
    (C) two equal wheels
    (D) two unequal wheels

21. The word "stable" in line 3 is closest in meaning to

    (A) dangerous
    (B) expensive
    (C) big
    (D) steady

22. Which of the following is NOT true about the safety bicycle?

    (A) It had equal wheels.
    (B) It was fairly simple to control.
    (C) It preceded the penny-farthing bicycle.
    (D) It became popular in the 1890s.

23. The word "measures" in line 7 could best be replaced by

    (A) counts
    (B) numbers
    (C) steps
    (D) problems

24. The passage indicates that it was fashionable in the 1890s for women to wear

    (A) long skirts
    (B) short pants
    (C) small hats
    (D) men's clothing

25. It is implied in the passage that lead is

    (A) heavy
    (B) soft
    (C) delicate
    (D) light

26. In line 10, "bloomers" are

    (A) shirts
    (B) skirts
    (C) hats
    (D) pants

27. It is implied in the passage that newspapers expressed the opinion that women

    (A) should wear bloomers
    (B) should not ride bicycles
    (C) should not wear long, full skirts
    (D) should always follow the fashion

SKILL 6: "WHERE" QUESTIONS

Sometimes the final question in a reading passage will ask you to determine where in the passage a piece of information is found. The answer choices will list possible locations for that information. The best way to approach this type of question is to study the question to determine the information that you are looking for and then to go to the lines listed in the answers and skim for that information.

Example

The passage:

The words "capital" and "capitol" are confused in spelling and in meaning by a lot of people who try to use them. Both their spellings and their meanings are quite closely related. A
Line "capital" is the location of the center of government, while a
(5) "capitol" is the actual building where the government officials meet. Thus, in the United States, for example, the Capitol building is located in Washington, D.C., which is the *capital* city of the United States.

The questions:

1. Where in the passage does the author define the word "capital"?

   (A) Lines 1–2
   (B) Line 3
   (C) Line 4
   (D) Lines 6–8

2. Where in the passage does the author mention where the U.S. Capitol can be found?

   (A) Lines 1–2
   (B) Line 3
   (C) Lines 4–5
   (D) Line 6–8

To answer the first question, you should skim for the word *capital* and then look for its meaning. A *capital* is *the location of the center of government,* and this definition is given in the fourth line. The best answer to this question is therefore answer (C).

To answer the second question, you should skim for *U.S. Capitol* and then look for where the U.S. Capitol is found. The U.S. Capitol is *located in Washington, D.C.,* and this information is given in the sixth through eighth lines. The best answer to this question is therefore answer (D).

The following chart outlines the key information that you should remember when you are trying to determine where in the passage something is found.

QUESTIONS ABOUT WHERE IN THE PASSAGE ...	
HOW TO IDENTIFY THE QUESTION	*Where* in the passage ...?
WHERE TO FIND THE ANSWER	The question can be in any of the lines listed in the answers to the question.
HOW TO ANSWER THE QUESTION	1. Chose a *key word* or *idea* in the question. 2. Skim the lines in the passage that are listed in the answers to the question. You should skim for the *key word* or *idea*. 3. Choose the answer that contains the line numbers of a *restatement* of the key word or idea in the question.

TOEFL EXERCISE 6: Study each of the passages and choose the best answers to the questions that follow.

PASSAGE ONE (Questions 1–3)

A geyser occurs when rainwater seeps into the ground and volcanic magma beneath the surface heats it. The rainwater then turns into steam. The pressurized steam rises to the surface and bursts out as a geyser.

Line
(5)

Yellowstone National Park has more geysers than all of the rest of the world together. The most famous of these geysers is Old Faithful, which erupts in a high arc of steam about once an hour.

There have not been any volcanic eruptions in the Yellowstone area for 70,000 years. However, the existence of the geysers is proof that the area is volcanically active.

1. Where in the passage does the author mention what heats the water in a geyser?

   (A) Lines 1–2
   (B) Line 4
   (C) Lines 5–6
   (D) Line 7

2. The author indicates how often Old Faithful erupts in

   (A) lines 1–2
   (B) line 4
   (C) lines 5–6
   (D) line 7

3. Where in the passage does the author state how long it has been since a volcano erupted at Yellowstone?

   (A) Lines 2–3
   (B) Lines 5–6
   (C) Line 7
   (D) Line 8

PASSAGE TWO (Questions 4–7)

By 1963 the one-man space flights of Project Mercury had successfully taken place, and NASA (the National Aeronautics and Space Administration) was ready for a new challenge. That new challenge was to send two men into space at the same time, rather than one, so that it would be possible to conduct a wide variety of new maneuvers and tests.

An appropriate name was found for that new project: the new project was called Project Gemini. The name "Gemini" might seem appropriate because it is the name of one of the constellations of stars in the sky, but that is not the real reason for the choice of the name. "Gemini" comes from the Latin word *geminus,* which means "twin." The constellation Gemini received its name because it consists of two very bright stars with no other bright stars close by, and those stars seem like twins. The NASA project received its name because of the number of men who would be together in the space capsule orbiting the Earth.

Line (5) and *(10)* mark line numbers.

4. Where in the passage does the author state what the initials NASA represent?

   (A) Lines 1–3
   (B) Lines 6–7
   (C) Line 9
   (D) Lines 11–13

5. Where in the passage does the author describe NASA's new challenge after Project Mercury?

   (A) Lines 3–5
   (B) Lines 6–7
   (C) Line 9
   (D) Lines 11–13

6. The author explains the derivation of the word "Gemini" in

   (A) lines 1–3
   (B) lines 6–7
   (C) line 9
   (D) lines 11–13

7. Where in the passage does the author describe the composition of the Gemini constellation?

   (A) Lines 3–5
   (B) Lines 6–7
   (C) Line 9
   (D) Lines 10–11

PASSAGE THREE (Questions 8–12)

One of the best-known stories in American history—that Betsy Ross created the first flag of the United States—is believed by a number of scholars to be somewhat questionable.

Line
(5)   The official story goes as follows: In 1776, a group that included George Washington came to the workshop in Philadelphia where Betsy Ross worked as a seamstress; they brought a drawing of a flag with stars and stripes on it and asked if Betsy could make it.

The flag with the stars and stripes was definitely adopted by Congress on June 14, 1777. In the minutes on that day there is a resolution accepting a flag with 13 stars and 13 stripes as the official flag of the nation. However, there is no mention of Betsy Ross
(10)   as the one who had made the flag.

The first time that there is a documented reference to Betsy Ross as the one who made the flag came more than a century later, when her grandson gave a speech to the Philadelphia Historical Society indicating that the family had passed down the story for a hundred years that grandmother Betsy had made the first flag. Philadelphians
(15)   enthusiastically supported the story. Betsy Ross's house was restored and renamed Flag House, and it was opened to the public as a memorial to Betsy Ross.

Many historians dispute this story, and certainly no one has been able to come up with indisputable proof that it was Betsy who made the first flag. This much *is* known about Betsy Ross: She did exist, she was a seamstress, and she did sometimes make
(20)   flags for the ships of the Pennsylvania State Navy. If the story about the first flag is not completely true—and who is to know at this point—at least it makes a good story.

8. Where in the passage does the author mention a group that came to visit Betsy Ross?

(A) Lines 1–3
(B) Lines 4–6
(C) Lines 7–8
(D) Lines 9–10

9. Where in the passage does the author state when the flag was adopted by Congress?

(A) Lines 1–3
(B) Lines 4–6
(C) Lines 7–9
(D) Lines 11–14

10. The author describes the first historical reference to Betsy Ross as the creator of the first U.S. flag in

(A) lines 4–6
(B) lines 9–10
(C) lines 11–14
(D) lines 17–18

11. The author discusses how Philadelphians responded to the Betsy Ross story in

(A) lines 9–10
(B) lines 14–16
(C) lines 17–18
(D) lines 20–21

12. Where in the passage does the author discuss how historians have reacted to the Betsy Ross story?

(A) Lines 8–9
(B) Lines 11–14
(C) Lines 17–18
(D) Lines 19–20

TOEFL REVIEW EXERCISE (Skills 1–6): Study each of the passages, and choose the best answers to the questions that follow.

PASSAGE ONE (Questions 1–10)

The deer is a distinctive animal easily recognized by the antlers that adorn most species of male deer. These antlers are used by the males primarily to fight, either for mates or for leadership of the herd. Deer generally lose their antlers each winter and *Line* begin growing new ones in late spring. The new antlers are soft knobs covered with (5) velvety hairs. Later in the year as the seasons progress, the antlers grow and harden into solid branches. In the middle of winter, the full-grown antlers fall off and decay on the ground. The following spring the process begins again.

1. This passage mainly discusses

    (A) the lifestyle of the deer
    (B) the seasons of the year
    (C) the antlers of the deer
    (D) how antlers are used

2. The deer is called a distinctive animal because it

    (A) uses its antlers to recognize others
    (B) has many species
    (C) has antlers
    (D) has to fight for its mates

3. The word "adorn" in line 1 is closest in meaning to which of the following?

    (A) Cover
    (B) Decorate
    (C) Bother
    (D) Hide

4. The word "primarily" in line 2 is closest in meaning to

    (A) primitively
    (B) only
    (C) mainly
    (D) once

5. It is NOT mentioned in the passage that the deer uses its antlers

    (A) to battle other deer
    (B) to get a mate
    (C) to become a leader
    (D) to climb branches

6. In which month would a deer in North America probably have short, soft, velvety antlers?

    (A) May
    (B) December
    (C) October
    (D) January

7. The word "velvety" in line 5 could best be replaced by

    (A) soft
    (B) long
    (C) gray
    (D) coarse

8. The word "solid" in line 6 could best be replaced by which of the following?

    (A) Firm
    (B) Thin
    (C) Leafy
    (D) Tiny

9. In winter the mature antlers

    (A) are soft knobs
    (B) come off
    (C) are covered with velvety hair
    (D) begin again

10. Where in the passage does the author explain how a deer uses its antlers?

    (A) Lines 2–3
    (B) Lines 4–5
    (C) Line 6
    (D) Line 7

PASSAGE TWO (Questions 11–20)

REM (rapid eye movement) sleep is a type of sleep that is important to humans. This type of sleep generally occurs four or five times during one night of sleep, in periods of time ranging from five minutes to forty minutes for each occurrence. The *Line* periods of REM sleep become longer and longer as the night progresses.
(5)   Physical changes occur in the body to show that a person has transitioned from NREM (non-rapid eye movement) sleep to REM sleep. Breathing becomes faster, the heart rate increases, and, as the name implies, the eyes begin to move quickly.

Accompanying these physical changes in the body is a very important characteristic of REM sleep. It is during REM sleep that dreams occur.

11. The subject of this passage is

(A) the human need for REM sleep
(B) physical changes in the human body
(C) the characteristics of REM sleep
(D) why people sleep

12. According to the passage, how often does REM sleep occur in one night?

(A) Once
(B) Twice
(C) Four or five times
(D) Forty times

13. A REM sleep period of forty minutes would most likely be which period of REM sleep?

(A) The first period
(B) The second period
(C) The third period
(D) The fourth period

14. The word "progresses" in line 4 is closest in meaning to

(A) continues
(B) darkens
(C) falls
(D) sleeps

15. The word "transitioned" in line 5 could best be replaced by which of the following?

(A) Breathed
(B) Increased
(C) Fallen
(D) Moved

16. The N in NREM probably stands for which of the following words?

(A) Nine
(B) Non
(C) Name
(D) Night

17. According to the passage, all of the following occur during REM sleep EXCEPT that

    (A) the rate of breathing increases
    (B) the heart rate speeds up
    (C) the eyes remain steady
    (D) dreams take place

18. The word "Accompanying" in line 8 could best be replaced by which of the following?

    (A) Along with
    (B) In spite of
    (C) In contrast to
    (D) Because of

19. Where in the passage does the author discuss the length of periods of REM sleep?

    (A) Line 1
    (B) Lines 2–3
    (C) Lines 6–7
    (D) Lines 8–9

20. The author mentions a nonphysical occurrence during REM sleep in

    (A) line 1
    (B) lines 3–4
    (C) lines 5–6
    (D) lines 8–9

PASSAGE THREE (Questions 21–30)

In the 1930s, Chester F. Carlson was working in the patents department of a large electronics firm in New York City. One of the major problems in his work was the length of time and expense involved in getting patents copied; patents were lengthy legal documents, and the only ways to get them copied were to take them to a typist or to a photographer. Either way of copying patents took a lot of time and cost a lot of money.

He came up with the idea for a machine that would copy documents quickly and efficiently. He researched the idea in the library and then worked over a three-year period on developing a machine that used a light, an electrostatically charged plate, and powder to duplicate images on paper. The result of this work was a machine that produced the first xerographic copy on October 22, 1938. He named the process "Xerox," which is derived from a word meaning "dry writing."

Carlson felt that he had a good idea, one that would be extremely helpful in the business world. He tried to sell his idea to a number of large corporations, but they were not terribly interested in his machine. He was able to get some help in developing the machine from a nonprofit institute, and a few years later he sold the process to a small family-owned company. This small company grew into the giant Xerox Corporation, and both Carlson and Xerox became rather wealthy in the process.

21. This passage is mainly about

    (A) Carlson's job in a patent office
    (B) how the Xerox machine works
    (C) Carlson's success in business
    (D) the development of the Xerox machine

22. Which of the following is NOT mentioned as a problem that Carlson encountered in getting patents copied?

    (A) The time needed for copying
    (B) The expense of the copying
    (C) The length of the patents
    (D) The dependability of the photographers

23. The word "expense" in line 3 is closest in meaning to

    (A) cost
    (B) difficulty
    (C) legality
    (D) payment

24. The word "researched" in line 7 is closest in meaning to which of the following?

    (A) Searched for
    (B) Came up with
    (C) Looked for information about
    (D) Returned to

25. Which of the following is NOT mentioned as a component of the machine that Carlson developed?

    (A) A light
    (B) A charged plate
    (C) Powder
    (D) A typewriter

26. It can be inferred from the passage that Carlson began work on the machine in

    (A) 1930
    (B) 1935
    (C) 1938
    (D) 1941

27. The passage indicates that the large corporations that Carlson tried to sell his process to

(A) were family owned
(B) were nonprofit institutions
(C) helped to develop the process
(D) did not want to buy his machine

28. The word "giant" in line 16 could best be replaced by

(A) monster
(B) tiny
(C) familiar
(D) huge

29. Where in the passage does the author indicate what a patent is?

(A) Lines 1–2
(B) Lines 3–5
(C) Lines 6–7
(D) Lines 9–11

30. The author describes what happened to the company that eventually bought Carlson's process in

(A) lines 1–2
(B) lines 9–11
(C) lines 13–14
(D) lines 16–17

TOEFL POST-TEST

SECTION 3
READING COMPREHENSION
Time—55 minutes
(including the reading of the directions)
Now set your clock for 55 minutes.

This section is designed to measure your ability to read and understand short passages similar in topic and style to those that students are likely to encounter in North American universities and colleges. This section contains reading passages and questions about the passages.

Directions: In this section you will read several passages. Each one is followed by a number of questions about it. You are to choose the **one** best answer, (A), (B), (C), or (D), to each question. Then, on your answer sheet, find the number of the question and fill in the space that corresponds to the letter of the answer you have chosen.

Answer all questions about the information in a passage on the basis of what is **stated** or **implied** in that passage.

Read the following passage:

John Quincy Adams, who served as the sixth president of the United States from 1825 to 1829, is today recognized for his masterful statesmanship and diplomacy. He dedicated his life to public service, both in the presidency and in the various other political offices that he held.
Line Throughout his political career he demonstrated his unswerving belief in freedom of speech, the
(5) antislavery cause, and the right of Americans to be free from European and Asian domination.

Example I	**Sample Answer**

To what did John Quincy Adams devote his life?

(A) Improving his personal life
(B) Serving the public
(C) Increasing his fortune
(D) Working on his private business

According to the passage, John Quincy Adams "dedicated his life to public service." Therefore, you should choose answer (B).

Example II	**Sample Answer**

In line 4, the word "unswerving" is closest in meaning to

(A) moveable
(B) insignificant
(C) unchanging
(D) diplomatic

The passage states that John Quincy Adams demonstrated his unswerving belief "throughout his career." This implies that the belief did not change. Therefore, you should choose answer (C).

GO ON TO THE NEXT PAGE →

Questions 1–8

The tiniest bird in the world is the male bee hummingbird. Because it is so small, it is often mistaken for a bee or some other type of insect of that size.

As a hummingbird, it is able to flap its wings extremely quickly, up to eighty times per second.
Line With this really fast wing speed, the bee hummingbird can hover like a helicopter, fly forward, fly
(5) backward, or even fly upside down.

1. What is the topic of this passage?

    (A) The bee
    (B) One type of hummingbird
    (C) How fast hummingbirds fly
    (D) How helicopters fly

2. The word "tiniest" in line 1 is closest in meaning to

    (A) fastest
    (B) most dangerous
    (C) noisiest
    (D) smallest

3. It can be inferred from the passage that the female bee hummingbird

    (A) is really a bee
    (B) does not exist
    (C) is larger than the male
    (D) eats insects

4. According to the passage, when people see a male bee hummingbird, they often incorrectly think it is

    (A) a bird
    (B) an insect
    (C) a bat
    (D) a helicopter

5. In line 3, to "flap" wings is to

    (A) hold them still
    (B) stretch them out
    (C) fold them
    (D) move them up and down

6. According to the passage, how fast can a bee hummingbird flap its wings?

    (A) A hundred times each second
    (B) Eighty times per minute
    (C) Eighty times each second
    (D) Eight times in a second

7. In line 4, to "hover" is to

    (A) fly forward quickly
    (B) land
    (C) stay in place in the air
    (D) use fuel

8. The passage indicates that a bee hummingbird can do all of the following EXCEPT

    (A) hover
    (B) fly backward
    (C) fly in an inverted position
    (D) fly a helicopter

GO ON TO THE NEXT PAGE →

Questions 9–18

One mystery about elephants that seems to have been solved is how elephants communicate with each other. Humans have heard a whole variety of sounds coming from elephants, but these sounds are not the only way that elephants communicate.

Line
(5) A new explanation about elephant communication is being proposed. Elephants vibrate the air in their trunks and foreheads. The sound that is created during this vibration has an extremely low pitch; the pitch, in fact, is so low that humans cannot hear it. However, it seems that other elephants can and do hear and understand these low rumblings.

9. The passage mainly discusses

    (A) the answer to a question about how elephants communicate
    (B) how elephants vibrate the air in their trunks
    (C) communication between animals and humans
    (D) the sounds that elephants make

10. A "mystery" in line 1 is

    (A) a speech
    (B) something unknown
    (C) a funny story
    (D) a detective

11. According to the passage, people

    (A) cannot hear any elephant sounds
    (B) are not interested in elephant sounds
    (C) hear only one elephant sound
    (D) can hear numerous elephant sounds

12. It can be inferred from the passage that the elephant sounds that humans hear are

    (A) one of the ways that elephants communicate
    (B) not part of elephant communication
    (C) how elephants communicate with humans
    (D) the only sounds that elephants make

13. The word "way" in line 3 could best be replaced by

    (A) direction
    (B) method
    (C) path
    (D) road

14. Where do elephants vibrate air?

    (A) In their throats
    (B) In their trunks
    (C) In their mouths
    (D) In their ears

15. The word "pitch" in line 6 is closest in meaning to which of the following?

    (A) Meaning
    (B) Voice
    (C) Height
    (D) Sound

16. Which of the following is NOT true about the extremely low sound created by elephants?

    (A) Humans cannot understand it.
    (B) Humans hear it.
    (C) Elephants hear it.
    (D) Elephants understand it.

GO ON TO THE NEXT PAGE

17. The word "rumblings" in line 7 is closest in meaning to

   (A) words
   (B) ears
   (C) vibrations
   (D) melodies

18. Where in the passage does the author describe the sound that elephants create in their trunks and foreheads?

   (A) Lines 1–2
   (B) Lines 2–3
   (C) Line 4
   (D) Lines 5–6

GO ON TO THE NEXT PAGE ➡

Questions 19–28

George Gershwin grew up in New York City, and he first made his living playing popular music on the piano in "Tin Pan Alley," the music publishing district of New York. It was there that he developed a strong feel for the popular music of the time that served as a basis for the popular
Line songs that he composed.
(5)   In addition to his love of popular songs, he enjoyed jazz and believed that jazz was the primary source of truly American folk music. Jazz had, prior to Gershwin's time, been performed by small jazz bands and soloists, but Gershwin believed that jazz could serve as the basis for serious symphonic works. Gershwin became the link between jazz and serious classical music with such works as his jazz concerto *Rhapsody in Blue* and the jazz-inspired orchestral piece *An American in*
(10) Paris.

19. The passage mainly discusses

    (A) George Gershwin's popular music
    (B) Tin Pan Alley
    (C) American jazz
    (D) the variety of music by Gershwin

20. The word "made" in line 1 could best be replaced by

    (A) constructed
    (B) earned
    (C) worked
    (D) built

21. According to the passage, Tin Pan Alley is

    (A) a piano shop
    (B) a music studio
    (C) an area in New York City
    (D) a street where Gershwin lived

22. Which of the following is NOT true about George Gershwin's relationship with popular music?

    (A) He played popular music on the piano.
    (B) Popular music was the foundation of some of his songs.
    (C) He wrote some popular songs.
    (D) Popular music was the only type of music that he enjoyed.

23. Gershwin believed that jazz

    (A) was real American traditional music
    (B) should only be played in small bands
    (C) was not serious music
    (D) was not as enjoyable as popular music

24. The word "primary" in line 5 is closest in meaning to

    (A) main
    (B) only
    (C) first
    (D) unknown

25. The expression "prior to" in line 6 is closest in meaning to

    (A) during
    (B) after
    (C) in
    (D) before

GO ON TO THE NEXT PAGE ➤

26. It can be inferred from the passage that Gershwin

    (A) wrote the first jazz music
    (B) wrote jazz music for larger groups
    (C) did not like writing jazz music
    (D) wrote only for small jazz bands

27. The word "link" in line 8 is closest in meaning to

    (A) divider
    (B) separation
    (C) judge
    (D) connection

28. Where in the passage does the author mention the names of some of Gershwin's works?

    (A) Lines 1–2
    (B) Lines 2–4
    (C) Lines 5–6
    (D) Lines 8–10

GO ON TO THE NEXT PAGE

Questions 29–39

Like a lot of other ideas, chewing gum developed when an inventive person was trying to
develop something else. In 1870, Thomas Adams was trying to create a substance similar to rubber.
He knew that in the past, natives of Mexico had enjoyed chewing chicle, which was the gum of the
Line sapodilla tree; he thought that this chicle might possibly be useful as a replacement for rubber.
(5) While he was working with it, he decided to try chewing it, just as had been done in Mexico. He
enjoyed the sensation and decided that he should try selling it. Unfortunately, however, not many
people bought it. He then improved the product by adding flavorings and sugar to it, and he gave
out free samples until the product caught on. Though he never succeeded in his original search for
a replacement for rubber, he became highly successful as a chewing gum producer.

29. The main idea of the passage is that

    (A) chicle was commonly chewed in
        Mexico
    (B) Thomas Adams invented chewing gum
        by accident
    (C) Thomas Adams enjoyed chewing
        chicle
    (D) Thomas Adams was unsuccessful in
        finding a substitute for rubber

30. In line 1, the expression "an inventive
    person" could best be replaced by

    (A) a creative person
    (B) an illogical person
    (C) a destructive person
    (D) a mistaken person

31. According to the passage, what did
    Thomas Adams originally want to create?

    (A) Chewing gum
    (B) The sapodilla tree
    (C) A rubber substitute
    (D) Flavorings

32. Which of the following is NOT true about
    chicle?

    (A) It comes from a tree.
    (B) Some people like chewing it.
    (C) It is part of the rubber plant.
    (D) Adams thought he might find a use
        for it.

33. In line 3, "natives" are

    (A) trees
    (B) people
    (C) places
    (D) plastics

34. The word "sensation" in line 6 is closest in
    meaning to

    (A) thought
    (B) feeling
    (C) taste
    (D) look

35. According to the passage, what happened
    when Thomas Adams first tried selling his
    chicle product?

    (A) It did not sell very well.
    (B) It was successful because of the taste.
    (C) People thought it was rubber.
    (D) Adams became immediately
        successful.

36. "Flavorings" in line 7 are used to improve a
    product's

    (A) appearance
    (B) feel
    (C) taste
    (D) smell

GO ON TO THE NEXT PAGE ➡

37. It is implied in the passage that Adams gave out free samples of gum because

    (A) he had a lot that he did not want
    (B) he did not care about making money
    (C) he was not a very smart businessman
    (D) he wanted to improve future sales

38. According to the passage, in his search for a rubber substitute, Adams

    (A) was not successful
    (B) found the original rubber plant
    (C) succeeded late in his life
    (D) was highly successful

39. Where in the passage does the author explain what chicle is?

    (A) Lines 1–2
    (B) Lines 3–4
    (C) Line 5
    (D) Lines 8–9

GO ON TO THE NEXT PAGE

Questions 40–50

Sometimes mail arrives at the post office, and it is impossible to deliver the mail. Perhaps there is an inadequate or illegible address and no return address. The post office cannot just throw this mail away, so this becomes "dead mail." This dead mail is sent to one of the U.S. Postal Service's
Line dead-mail offices in Atlanta, New York, Philadelphia, St. Paul, or San Francisco. Seventy-five
(5) million pieces of mail can end up in the dead-mail office in one year.

The staff of the dead-mail offices have a variety of ways to deal with all of these pieces of dead mail. First of all, they look for clues that can help them deliver the mail; they open packages in the hope that something inside will show where the package came from or is going to. Dead mail will also be listed on a computer so that people can call in and check to see if a missing item is there.
(10) However, all of this mail cannot simply be stored forever; there is just too much of it. When a lot of dead mail has piled up, the dead-mail offices hold public auctions. Every three months, the public is invited in and bins containing items found in dead-mail packages are sold to the highest bidder.

40. The best title for the passage is

    (A) The U.S. Postal Service
    (B) Staff Responsibilities at the U.S. Postal Service
    (C) Why Mail Is Undeliverable
    (D) Dead-Mail Offices

41. Dead mail is mail that

    (A) has no use
    (B) has been read and thrown away
    (C) is unwanted
    (D) is undeliverable

42. The word "illegible" in line 2 is closest in meaning to which of the following?

    (A) Incomplete
    (B) Missing
    (C) Unreadable
    (D) Incorrect

43. According to the passage, how many dead-mail offices does the U.S. Postal Service have?

    (A) 3
    (B) 5
    (C) 15
    (D) 75

44. The word "staff" in line 6 is closest in meaning to

    (A) workers
    (B) machines
    (C) rules
    (D) pieces of furniture

45. Which of the following is NOT mentioned as a way that post office staff members deal with dead mail?

    (A) They search for clues.
    (B) They throw dead mail away.
    (C) They open dead mail.
    (D) They list dead mail on a computer.

46. It is implied in the passage that the dead-mail staff would be happy if they opened a package and found

    (A) money
    (B) jewelry
    (C) a computer
    (D) an address

GO ON TO THE NEXT PAGE →

47. In line 9, the expression "call in" could best be replaced by

    (A) visit
    (B) phone
    (C) shout
    (D) talk

48. The word "auctions" in line 11 is closest in meaning to

    (A) sales
    (B) deliveries
    (C) meetings
    (D) demonstrations

49. The passage indicates that dead-mail auctions are held

    (A) once a year
    (B) twice a year
    (C) three times a year
    (D) four times a year

50. Where in the passage does the author explain why the post office cannot store dead mail forever?

    (A) Lines 2–3
    (B) Lines 4–5
    (C) Lines 7–8
    (D) Line 10

This is the end of Section 3.

When you finish the test, you may do the following:

- Turn to the **Diagnostic Chart** on pages 357–363, and circle the numbers of the questions that you missed.

- Turn to the **Progress Chart** on page 353, and add your score to the chart.

TEST OF
WRITTEN ENGLISH
(TWE)

TEST OF WRITTEN ENGLISH (TWE)

The Test of Written English (TWE) is a writing section that appears on the TOEFL test several times a year. You should check the *Bulletin of Information for TOEFL, TWE, and TSE* for the dates that the TWE will be administered. If you are required to take the TWE, be sure to sign up for the TOEFL test in one of the months that the TWE is given.

On the TWE you will be given a specific topic and you will be asked to write an essay on that topic in thirty minutes. The TWE will be given at the beginning of the TOEFL test, before the Listening Comprehension, Structure and Written Expression, and Reading Comprehension sections.

Because you must write a complete essay in such a short period of time, it is best for you to aim to write a basic, clear, concise, and well-organized essay. The following strategies should help you to write this type of essay.

STRATEGIES FOR THE TEST OF WRITTEN ENGLISH (TWE)

1. **Read the topic carefully and write about it exactly as it is presented.** Take several minutes at the beginning of the test to be sure that you understand the topic and to outline a response.

2. **Organize your response very clearly.** You should think of having an introduction, body paragraphs that develop the introduction, and a conclusion to end your essay. Use transitions to help the reader understand the organization of ideas.

3. **Whenever you make any general statement, be sure to support that statement.** You can use examples, reasons, facts, or similar details to support any general statement.

4. **Stick to vocabulary and sentence structures that you know.** This is not the time to try out new words or structures.

5. **Finish writing your essay a few minutes early so that you have time to proof what you wrote.** You should spend that last three to five minutes checking your essay for errors.

THE WRITING SCORE

The score of the TWE is included on the same form as your regular TOEFL score, but it is not part of your overall TOEFL score. It is a separate score on a scale of 1 to 6, where 1 is the worst score and 6 is the best score. The following chart outlines what each of the scores essentially means.

TEST OF WRITTEN ENGLISH (TWE) SCORE

6. The writer has very strong organizational, structural, and grammatical skills.

5. The writer has good organizational, structural, and grammatical skills. However, the essay contains some errors.

4. The writer has adequate organizational, structural, and grammatical skills. The essay contains a number of errors.

3. The writer shows evidence of organizational, structural, and grammatical skills that still need to be improved.

2. The writer shows a minimal ability to convey ideas in written English.

1. The writer is not capable of conveying ideas in written English.

SAMPLE ESSAYS

This section contains six essays, one demonstrating each of the six possible scores. These essays can give you some idea of the type of essay you need to write to achieve a good score. They can also demonstrate some of the major errors you should avoid when you take the TWE.

The strengths and weaknesses of each essay have been outlined at the end of each. It would be helpful to study each answer in order to understand what is good and what is not so good in each of these essays.

This is the topic that was used:

Sample Essay Topic
Time—30 minutes

Do you agree or disagree with the following statement?

Some people place a high value on loyalty to the employer. To others, it is perfectly acceptable to change jobs every few years to build a career. Discuss these two positions. Then indicate which position you agree with and why.

Use specific reasons and details to support your answer. Write your answer on the forms provided.

The following essay received a score of 6:

Different cultures place varying values on loyalty to the employer. In some countries, most notably in Asia, there is a high degree of loyalty to one company. However, in most European countries and the United States, loyalty to one's employer is not highly valued; instead it is considered more rationel and reasonable for an employee to change jobs whenever it is waranted to achieve the optimal overall career. Both of these positions have advantages and disadvantages.

In cultures that value loyalty to the employer, a kind of family relationship seems to develop between employer and employee. It is a reciprocal arrangement which the employer is concerned with asisting the employee to develop to his/her full potential and the employee is concerned about optimizing the welfare of the company. The negative aspect to absolute loyalty to one company is that an employee may stay in one job that he/she has outgrows and may miss out on opportunities to develop in new directions. From the employer's point of view, the employee may be burdened with employees whose skills no longer match the needs of the company.

In cultures in which it is quite acceptable to change jobs every few years, employees can build the career they choose for themself. They can stay with one company as long as it is mutually beneficial to company and employee. As long as good relationship exists and the employee's career is advancing at an acceptable pace, the employee can remain with a company. But at any time the employee is free to move to another company, perhaps to achieve a higher position, to move into a new area, or to find a work situation that is more suitable to his/her personality. The disadvantage of this situation is employees tend to move around a lot.

Although both these systems have advantages and disadvantages, it is much better for employees have the opportunity to move from job to job if it is necessary to have a better career.

THE "6" ESSAY

Strengths of This Essay

1. It discusses all aspects of the topic.
2. It is clearly organized.
3. The ideas are well developed.
4. It has good, correct sentence structure.
5. It has only a few spelling and grammar errors.

Weaknesses of This Essay

1. The concluding paragraph is rather weak.

The following essay received a score of 5:

Some people place high value on loyalty to employer. They believe the company is responsible for the employee's career. The company will make decisions for the employee about his job. The company will decide to raise employee to new position or keep him in the old position. In this way the company will have overall plan for the good of the company and everyone in the company.

Other people believe it is perfectly acceptable to change jobs every few years to build a career. They believe employee is responsible for his own career. The employee will make decisions about his career. Employee will choose what is good for employee rather than the company.

The best system is one when employer takes responsibility for the careers of employees. Employer should take responsibility. It is his duty. Employee knows that employer is watching out for his career. Then employee will work hard and do good job. He will be loyal to the company. This system works out best for everyone. It is best for both the company and employees.

THE "5" ESSAY

Strengths of This Essay

1. It discusses the topic fully.
2. It is clearly organized.
3. It has correct sentence structure.

Weaknesses of This Essay

1. The sentence structure is very simple.
2. There are some grammatical errors, particularly with articles.

The following essay received a score of 4:

Every one is not in agreement about how loyal people should be to their employers. Some people place a high value on loyalty to the employer. These people believe that they should work hard for their employer and so their employer will take care of them. To others it is perfectly acceptable to change jobs every few years to build a career. They believe that having only one employer and one job in a career will not be the best for them.

In my culture people stay with one employer for their whole life. They have a job they will work their hardest at that job because it is the only job they will have. They do not look for another job they already have one because that would be unloyal. This way is better because when you old the company will take care you and your family.

THE "4" ESSAY

Strengths of This Essay

1. It answers the question fairly well.
2. It is clearly organized.

Weaknesses of This Essay

1. It copies too directly from the question.
2. The ideas are not very well developed.
3. There are several examples of incorrect sentence structure.

The following essay received a score of 3:

Some people stay with one employeer for their entire career, but anothers build a career by changing jobs every few years. There are three reasens people should staying with on employer for their entire career.

First, the people should staying with one employer because it is best for the workers. If workers stay with one employer they will not having to move and they can learning all abou the company and advence in the company.

Second, people should staying with one employer because it is best for the compeny. The people will knowing how to do their jobs and they will having a big producton and the compeny will be very success.

Finally, people should staying with one employer because it is best for soceity. If people stay with one compeny than all the compenies will being very success. If all the compenie are very success then soceity will be success.

THE "3" ESSAY

Strengths of This Essay

1. It is clearly organized.
2. It has good, correct sentence structure.

Weaknesses of This Essay

1. It does not discuss the topic completely.
2. There are errors in spelling and grammar.

The following essay received a score of 2:

First, there is a disadvantage to place a high value on loyalty to the employer if your employer is no a good employer and your job is no a good job then you should no be loyal to a bad employer. Many employer are no good employers and if you are loyal to a bad employer it is a waste because a bad employer he will no be good to you.

Next, there is a advantage to change jobs every few years to build a carere if you get boring with your job and you want to move from one job to other so yo can get a better job instead of stay in your old boring job.

Finally, people should decide for themself where they want to work, if they decide one plce when they are young, how can they be sure whe they are older that they will still want to work there?

THE "2" ESSAY

Strengths of This Essay

1. The overall organization is clear.
2. The writer's main point is clear.

Weaknesses of This Essay

1. The sentence structure is poor.
2. There are numerous errors in spelling and grammar.
3. The ideas are not very well developed.

The following essay received a score of 1:

I think people should staying only one job for his hole careere. Because it is important loyal to your jop. If you not loyal. Th company didn't be able has good business. If the employees keep change. New employees alway needs be train, and so on.

THE "1" ESSAY

Weaknesses of This Essay

1. It does not discuss the topic completely.
2. The ideas are disorganized and difficult to follow.
3. There are many errors in spelling and grammar.
4. There are many errors in sentence structure.
5. It is too short.

BEFORE WRITING

Skill 1: THE WRITING TOPIC

The first and most important step when you are writing an essay on the TOEFL test is to read the writing topic carefully. The writing topic will show you how to organize your response, so you must read the topic and think about how you will organize your essay. Study the following writing topic.

Essay Topic

Some people prefer warm weather, while others prefer cool weather. Discuss the advantages of each type of weather. Then indicate which you prefer and why.

As you read this topic, you should think about the organization of your response. Your essay should start with an introduction, and that introduction should mention *warm weather, cool weather,* and *the advantages of each.* This introduction should be followed by supporting paragraphs describing *the advantages of warm weather* and *the advantages of cool weather.* In the final paragraph, you should discuss whether you prefer *warm weather* or *cool weather* and *why.* The final paragraph is your conclusion; it brings together the ideas in the previous paragraphs about warm and cool weather. The following is a good outline for an essay on this topic.

Paragraph 1:   INTRODUCTORY PARAGRAPH
(mentioning the advantages of warm and cool weather)

Paragraph 2:   FIRST SUPPORTING PARAGRAPH
(listing and discussing the advantages of warm weather)

Paragraph 3:   SECOND SUPPORTING PARAGRAPH
(listing and discussing the advantages of cool weather)

Paragraph 4:   CONCLUDING PARAGRAPH
(saying whether you prefer warm or cool weather and why)

The following chart outlines the key information that you should remember about writing topics on the TOEFL test.

THE WRITING TOPIC

Each writing topic on the TOEFL test shows you *what* to discuss and *how* to organize your response. You must read the topic carefully to determine the best way to organize your response.

EXERCISE 1: For each of the writing topics, indicate the type of information that you will include in each paragraph of your response.

> 1. What are the characteristics of a good teacher? Support your response with examples.

INTRODUCTORY PARAGRAPH: *mentioning the characteristics of a good teacher*

SUPPORTING PARAGRAPH 1:   *the first characteristic, with an example*

SUPPORTING PARAGRAPH 2:   *the second characteristic, with an example*

SUPPORTING PARAGRAPH 3:   *the third characteristic, with an example*

CONCLUDING PARAGRAPH: *summary of the characteristics of a good teacher*

> 2. What kind of music do you like most? Give reasons to support your response.

INTRODUCTORY PARAGRAPH: _____

SUPPORTING PARAGRAPH 1:   _____

SUPPORTING PARAGRAPH 2:   _____

SUPPORTING PARAGRAPH 3:   _____

CONCLUDING PARAGRAPH: _____

> 3. Some people like to try new kinds of food, while other people always eat the same kind of food. Which type of person are you? Give examples to support your response.

INTRODUCTORY PARAGRAPH: _____

SUPPORTING PARAGRAPH 1:   _____

SUPPORTING PARAGRAPH 2:   _____

SUPPORTING PARAGRAPH 3:   _____

CONCLUDING PARAGRAPH: _____

4. Do you agree or disagree with the following statement?
    It is best to work for only one company in your career.
    Use specific reasons to support your response.

INTRODUCTORY PARAGRAPH: _____

SUPPORTING PARAGRAPH 1: _____

SUPPORTING PARAGRAPH 2: _____

SUPPORTING PARAGRAPH 3: _____

CONCLUDING PARAGRAPH: _____

5. Some people prefer to attend large universities, while others prefer to attend small schools. Discuss the advantages of each. Then indicate which you prefer and why.

INTRODUCTORY PARAGRAPH: _____

SUPPORTING PARAGRAPH 1: _____

SUPPORTING PARAGRAPH 2: _____

SUPPORTING PARAGRAPH 3: _____

CONCLUDING PARAGRAPH: _____

6. Do you agree or disagree with the following statement?
    It is important to follow the wishes of your family.
    Support your response with reasons and examples.

INTRODUCTORY PARAGRAPH: _____

SUPPORTING PARAGRAPH 1: _____

SUPPORTING PARAGRAPH 2: _____

SUPPORTING PARAGRAPH 3: _____

CONCLUDING PARAGRAPH: _____

SKILL 2: THE SUPPORTING IDEAS

After you decide how to organize your essay, you need to plan your supporting ideas. Your ideas need to support the topic clearly and provide the type of support that the question asks for. Study the following writing topic.

> **Essay Topic**
>
> What kinds of classes do you dislike the most? Use examples to support your response.

As you read this topic, you should see that the overall organization of your essay should be an introduction, supporting paragraphs with examples of the kinds of classes you dislike, and a conclusion. You should take a few minutes before you begin writing to develop your supporting ideas.

INTRODUCTION	*kinds of classes that I dislike the most*
SUPPORTING PARAGRAPH 1 (example)	*classes that are too disorganized* • *a history class that I once took that had no syllabus, no clear reading schedule, no clear written assignments, no clear basis for grades*
SUPPORTING PARAGRAPH 2 (example)	*classes that are too large* • *a chemistry course that I once took in a large auditorium with 500 students enrolled, no possibility of discussion with other students, no possibility of asking the professor questions*
SUPPORTING PARAGRAPH 3 (example)	*classes that are too boring* • *a psychology class that I once took where the professor basically read from the textbook during each class period*
CONCLUSION	*three least favorite kinds of class: too disorganized, too large, too boring*

In this example, there are three kinds of classes that the writer most dislikes: classes that are too disorganized, too large, or too boring. Each of these ideas is supported with an example.

The following chart outlines the key information that you should remember about supporting ideas.

THE SUPPORTING IDEAS
1. Your ideas should *support* the topic clearly.
2. Your ideas should *follow* what the question asks for.

EXERCISE 2: For each of the following topics, develop ideas to support it.

> 1. What is your favorite holiday of the year? Give reasons to support your response.

INTRODUCTORY IDEA: _____

REASON 1: _____

REASON 2: _____

REASON 3: _____

> 2. Some people are very careful with their money, while other people are not very careful with their money. Which kind of person are you? Use examples to support your response.

INTRODUCTORY IDEA: _____

EXAMPLE 1: _____

EXAMPLE 2: _____

EXAMPLE 3: _____

> 3. Do you agree or disagree with the following statement?
>   *Money cannot buy happiness.*
>   Support your response with specific reasons.

INTRODUCTORY IDEA: _____

REASON 1: _____

REASON 2: _____

REASON 3: _____

4. What types of music do you enjoy the most? Use specific examples to support your response.

INTRODUCTORY IDEA: _____

TYPE AND EXAMPLE 1: _____

TYPE AND EXAMPLE 2: _____

TYPE AND EXAMPLE 3: _____

5. Some people really like pets, while other people do not like pets at all. Which type of person are you? Use reasons to support your response.

INTRODUCTORY IDEA: _____

REASON 1: _____

REASON 2: _____

REASON 3: _____

6. Do you agree or disagree with the following statement?
    Parents should push their children to work as hard as possible.
    Use specific examples to support your response.

INTRODUCTORY IDEA: _____

EXAMPLE 1: _____

EXAMPLE 2: _____

EXAMPLE 3: _____

WHILE WRITING

SKILL 3: THE INTRODUCTORY PARAGRAPH

A good introduction should do two things. First it should show the reader exactly what the topic is. Then it should show the reader how the rest of the essay will be organized. Here is a possible topic for an essay.

> **Essay Topic**
>
> Some students like to study only one subject, while other students like to study a number of different subjects. Which type of student are you? Use reasons to support your response.

The following example shows one possible introduction to an essay on this topic.

> INTRODUCTION 1
>
> *Some students enjoy studying a single subject, while other students enjoy studying a variety of subjects. I am the type of student who wants to study a large number of subjects. I have two very good reasons why I want to study a variety of subjects.*

The first part of the introduction shows the topic of the essay. It shows that the essay could be about students who enjoy studying either a single subject or a variety of subjects. Then it shows that this essay is about a student who enjoys studying a large number of subjects. The last part of the introduction shows the organization of the essay. It shows that the writer is going to present two very good reasons for wanting to study a variety of subjects.

The next example shows a different way that an essay on this topic could be introduced.

> INTRODUCTION 2
>
> *Students may like to study only one subject, or they may like to study a number of subjects. For me, there is only one subject that interests me greatly, and that subject is astronomy. I have two very strong reasons why: this is a subject that has interested me for a long time, and this is a subject that I want to have as a career.*

The first part of the introduction shows the topic of the essay. It shows that the essay could be about students who like to study only one subject or a number of subjects. Then it shows that this essay is about a student who enjoys one subject. The last part of the introduction shows the organization of the essay. The writer has two strong reasons for enjoying the study of one subject, and the writer is going to present these reasons.

The following chart outlines the important information that you should remember about writing introductory paragraphs.

THE INTRODUCTORY PARAGRAPH

1. Be sure to state the *topic* of the essay in your introductory paragraph.

2. Be sure to state the author's *view* of the topic in your introductory paragraph.

3. Be sure to show the *organization* of the essay in your introductory paragraph.

EXERCISE 3: Write introductory paragraphs for essays on the following topics. In each introductory paragraph that you write, circle the *topic* of the essay. Put parentheses around the author's *view* of the topic. Underline the information that shows the *organization* of the topic.

1. What is the funniest movie you have ever seen, and why did it make you laugh? Support your response with specific reasons.

2. Some people worry all the time, while other people seem to worry very little. Which type of person are you? Give examples to support your response.

3. Do you agree or disagree with the following statement?
   It is important to marry before the age of thirty.
   Support your response with specific examples.

4. What are the three hardest things about learning a new language? Use specific examples to support your response.

5. Some students prefer to write papers, while others prefer to give oral presentations. What are the advantages of each? Which do you prefer and why?

6. Do you agree or disagree with the following statement?
   Teachers should be very strict in class.
   Support your response with specific reasons and examples.

Skill 4: THE SUPPORTING PARAGRAPHS

An essay needs two or more supporting paragraphs to develop the ideas in an introductory paragraph. A good supporting paragraph should do three things. First, it should have a transition to show that it is a supporting paragraph. Then it should have a topic sentence to introduce the main idea of the supporting paragraph. Finally, it should have details to develop the main idea of the paragraph. Refer to the essay topic and sample introductions in Skill 3.

Essay Topic

Some students like to study only one subject, while other students like to study a number of different subjects. Which type of student are you? Use reasons to support your response.

The following paragraphs are the supporting paragraphs for the essay that began with INTRODUCTION 1 (in Skill 3).

SUPPORTING PARAGRAPHS 1

   My first reason for wanting to study a variety of subjects is that I like learning about many different subjects. In high school, I have never had a favorite subject, one subject that I like more than the rest. For example, I liked history as much as math, and I liked biology as much as literature. I have always been interested in many different subjects, so in my university studies I want to study a variety of subjects. I am not interested in focusing on just one subject.

   My second reason for wanting to study a variety of subjects is that I want to have a career in elementary education. As an elementary teacher, I will be responsible for teaching the children a variety of subjects. It will be my responsibility to teach math and science, literature and writing, history and government, art and music. Thus, it is best for me to study a variety of subjects while I am in school.

In the first supporting paragraph above, there is a transition *my first reason* to show that this is a supporting paragraph that presents a reason. This paragraph also introduces the topic *I like learning about many different subjects*. Then it has details about having *never had a favorite subject* and about liking *history as much as math* and *biology as much as literature* to develop the topic. In the second supporting paragraph, there is a transition *my second reason* to show that this is a supporting paragraph that presents another reason. This paragraph also has the topic *I want to have a career in elementary education*. Then it has details about *teaching the children a variety of subjects . . . math and science, literature and writing, history and government, art and music* to develop the topic.

   The next paragraphs are the supporting paragraphs for the essay that began with INTRODUCTION 2 (in Skill 3).

SUPPORTING PARAGRAPHS 2

Astronomy has been my main interest for much of my life, and this is one of the reasons why I want to focus my studies on astronomy. When I was young, I learned all about the planets and the stars. I could name the planets, and I could name many of the constellations and tell the stories behind them. As I grew older, I was always aware of happenings in the sky. I read all about comets or meteors in the news. I knew all about any eclipse that was about to occur.

I also want to focus my studies on astronomy because I want to have a career in the future in astronomy. Because I find astronomy so fascinating, I know that I want to spend my life involved in astronomy. In order to be prepared for a successful career in astronomy, I want to focus my university studies on this subject. In this way, I will be as knowledgeable as I can about astronomy and will be as prepared as I can for a career in astronomy.

In the first supporting paragraph above, there is a transition *this is one of the reasons* to show that this is a supporting paragraph that presents a reason. This paragraph also has the topic *astronomy has been my main interest for much of my life.* Then it has details about *planets, stars, constellations, comets,* and *meteors* to develop the topic. In the second supporting paragraph, there is a transition *also* to show that this is a supporting paragraph that presents another reason. This paragraph also has the topic *I want to have a career in the future in astronomy.* Then it has details about being *involved in astronomy,* being *prepared for a successful career in astronomy,* and being *as knowledgeable as I can about astronomy* to develop the topic.

The following chart outlines the important information that you should remember about writing supporting paragraphs.

THE SUPPORTING PARAGRAPHS
1. Use a transition to show that a paragraph is a supporting paragraph.
2. Use a topic sentence to introduce the main idea of the paragraph.
3. Use details to develop the main idea of the paragraph.

EXERCISE 4: Write supporting paragraphs for the essays that you introduced in Skill 3. In each supporting paragraph, circle the *transition*. Underline the *topic* of the paragraph one time. Underline the key *details* two times.

1. What is the funniest movie you have ever seen, and why did it make you laugh? Support your response with specific reasons.

2. Some people worry all the time, while other people seem to worry very little. Which type of person are you? Give examples to support your response.

3. Do you agree or disagree with the following statement?
   It is important to marry before the age of thirty.
   Support your response with specific examples.

4. What are the three hardest things about learning a new language? Use specific examples to support your response.

5. Some students prefer to write papers, while others prefer to give oral presentations. What are the advantages of each? Which do you prefer and why?

6. Do you agree or disagree with the following statement?
   Teachers should be very strict in class.
   Support your response with specific reasons and examples.

SKILL 5: THE CONCLUDING PARAGRAPH

A good conclusion should do two things. First, it should summarize the key points of your essay. Then it should make sure that the overall idea and supporting ideas are very clear. Refer to the essay topic and sample introductions in Skill 3.

Essay Topic

Some students like to study only one subject, while other students like to study a number of different subjects. Which type of student are you? Use reasons to support your response.

The following paragraph is the conclusion to the essay that began with INTRO-DUCTION 1 (in Skill 3).

CONCLUSION 1

You can see from this that I am the type of student who enjoys studying lots of subjects. Because I have chosen a career in elementary education, it is good that I enjoy dealing with lots of subjects. Throughout my career, I will be responsible for teaching all these different subjects to many, many young children.

In this conclusion, the writer clearly mentions the interest in studying lots of subjects. The writer also summarizes the reasons for wanting to study a variety of subjects: the writer's enjoyment of lots of subjects and the need for lots of subjects in the career that the writer has chosen.

The next paragraph is the conclusion to the essay that began with INTRO-DUCTION 2 (in Skill 3).

CONCLUSION 2

I have found astronomy to be quite fascinating for a long time, and I know that I will have a career in astronomy. For these reasons, I am mainly interested in the study of one subject when I am in school, and that subject is astronomy.

In this conclusion, the writer summarizes the reasons for wanting to concentrate on the study of astronomy: astronomy has been fascinating to the writer for a long time, and astronomy will be the writer's career. The writer also clearly mentions the interest in studying one particular subject.

The following chart outlines the important information that you should remember about writing concluding paragraphs.

THE CONCLUDING PARAGRAPH

1. *Summarize* the key points of your essay.

2. Be sure that the *overall idea* and *supporting ideas* are all very clear.

EXERCISE 5: Write concluding paragraphs for the essays that you introduced in Skill 3. In each concluding paragraph, circle your *overall idea.* Underline the *supporting ideas* of your discussion.

1. What is the funniest movie you have ever seen, and why did it make you laugh? Support your response with specific reasons.

2. Some people worry all the time, while other people seem to worry very little. Which type of person are you? Give examples to support your response.

3. Do you agree or disagree with the following statement?
    It is important to marry before the age of thirty.
    Support your response with specific examples.

4. What are the three hardest things about learning a new language? Use specific examples to support your response.

5. Some students prefer to write papers, while others prefer to give oral presentations. What are the advantages of each? Which do you prefer and why?

6. Do you agree or disagree with the following statement?
    Teachers should be very strict in class.
    Support your response with specific reasons and examples.

AFTER WRITING

SKILL 6: EDIT SENTENCE STRUCTURE

6A. Simple Sentence Structure

A *simple* sentence is a sentence that has only one **clause.**[1] This means that the sentence has one subject and verb.

> The <u>cat</u> quickly <u>ran</u> into the bushes.
>   SUBJECT   VERB

> The <u>information</u> <u>seems</u> unimportant.
>   SUBJECT   VERB

The first sentence is correct because it has a subject *cat* and a verb *ran*. The second sentence is correct because it has the subject *information* and the verb *seems*.

For each simple sentence, you should check that the sentence has both a subject and a verb.

> A <u>book</u> describing the historical events.*

> Often <u>is</u> necessary to fill out several forms.*

> In a drawer in the bedroom at the top of the stairs.*

The first sentence is incorrect because it has the subject *book* but is missing a verb. The second sentence is incorrect because it has the verb *is* but is missing a subject. The third sentence is incorrect because it is missing both a subject and a verb.

EDITING SIMPLE SENTENCES
1. A simple sentence is a sentence with *one clause*.
2. A simple sentence must have both a *subject* and a *verb*.

---

[1]**A clause** is a group of words that has both a subject and a verb. Simple sentences with only one clause are covered in great detail in Skill 1 of the Structure section of this book.

EXERCISE 6A: Underline the subjects once and the verbs twice. Then indicate if the sentences are correct (C) or incorrect (I).

__I__   1. Recently <u>has not rained</u> enough for the plants to be healthy.

_____   2. I could not start the car this morning.

_____   3. The large fountain in the courtyard of the building it was beautiful.

_____   4. In the room at the top of the stairs.

_____   5. The forecaster predicted thunderstorms for this afternoon.

_____   6. Soon will be starting a new job in a lawyer's office.

_____   7. The restaurant serves various types of food.

_____   8. Of all the courses in the program, this the most difficult.

_____   9. With a cry of delight at her good fortune.

_____   10. The doctor prescribed some medicine for her allergies.

_____   11. Now am making plans to travel to New York.

_____   12. Reservations need to be made at least two weeks in advance.

_____   13. The exam on the first three chapters of the textbook.

_____   14. Until the midterm exam at the end of the sixth week of the course.

_____   15. One leg of the chair is shorter than the others.

_____   16. During the storm, lightning it was everywhere in the sky.

_____   17. In the morning will be moving into a new room in the dormitory.

_____   18. The important papers are filed in the locked cabinet.

_____   19. On the shelves at the back of the third-floor room of the library.

_____   20. Several passwords are required to turn on the computer.

6B. Compound Sentence Structure

A *compound* sentence is a sentence that has more than one **main clause.**[2] This means that the sentence has more than one subject and verb and that each subject and verb is joined to another subject and verb with a coordinate connector (*and, but, so, or, yet*) and a comma.

The <u>cook</u> <u>must stir</u> the stew, **or** the <u>dinner</u> <u>will burn</u>.
   SUBJECT VERB   SUBJECT VERB

The <u>woman</u> <u>dropped</u> her watch, **and** then <u>she</u> <u>stepped</u> on it, **but** <u>it</u> still <u>worked</u>.
  SUBJECT VERB   SUBJECT VERB   SUBJECT VERB

The first sentence is correct because it has two main clauses, *cook must stir* and *dinner will burn*. These two main clauses are joined with a comma and the coordinate connector *or*. The second sentence is correct because it has three main clauses, *woman dropped, she stepped,* and *it . . . worked*. These main clauses are joined with commas and the coordinate connectors *and* and *but*.

For each compound sentence, you should check that each main clause has a subject and a verb. Then you should check that each pair of main clauses is connected with a comma and a coordinate connector.

The <u>students</u> <u>found</u> some empty chairs, <u>they</u> quickly <u>took</u> their seats.*
   SUBJECT VERB   SUBJECT   VERB

The <u>accountants</u> <u>have finished</u> the report, **so** <u>can be distributed</u> tomorrow.*
   SUBJECT   VERB   VERB

The first sentence is incorrect because it has two complete main clauses, *we found* and *we . . . took,* but it is missing a connector. The second sentence is incorrect because it has a complete main clause, *accountants have finished,* and an incomplete main clause, *can be distributed,* which are joined by a comma and the coordinate connector *so*. The incomplete main clause needs a subject to be complete.

EDITING COMPOUND SENTENCES

1. A compound sentence is a sentence with two (or more) *main clauses.*

2. Each *main clause* must have a subject and a verb.

3. Each pair of main clauses must be joined with a comma and a coordinate connector (*and, but, or, so, yet*).

---

[2]**A main clause** is an independent clause that has both a subject and a verb. Compound sentences with two or more main clauses are covered in Skill 5 of the Structure section of this book.

EXERCISE 6B: Underline the subjects once and the verbs twice in the main clauses. Put boxes around the punctuation and connectors that join the main clauses. Then indicate if the sentences are correct (C) or incorrect (I).

_C_   1. You must work much harder , or you will not succeed.

_____   2. Steve had a bad headache he took some aspirin.

_____   3. Yet Pam decided not to go to the concert.

_____   4. His studies very thorough, yet he did not do well on the exam.

_____   5. The exam was too long, and it had too many questions, so I could not finish it.

_____   6. We can meet after class or we can wait until tomorrow.

_____   7. It was raining this morning, but now the sun is out.

_____   8. You should return his phone call, he will be angry.

_____   9. By the end of the day had not finished the project, so we will work on it some more tomorrow.

_____   10. I mailed the package on Monday, and it arrived on Wednesday.

_____   11. Our alarm went off, but did not wake up.

_____   12. The train departed late, yet it still managed to arrive on time.

_____   13. The sun set, and the sky turned dark we went home.

_____   14. The fog heavy, and it seems to be getting worse, yet the airport is still open.

_____   15. The bill is due tomorrow, so they must pay it immediately.

_____   16. Someone should go to the market tonight, or no food for breakfast.

_____   17. And the interview was good, so she expected to get the job, but it was not offered to her.

_____   18. I parked in front of the store and then I went inside.

_____   19. You may look at the book here, you may not take it with you.

_____   20. She was feeling quite sick, yet she was still able to finish the work.

6C. Complex Sentence Structure

A *complex* sentence is a sentence that has a main clause and at least one **subordinate clause.**[3] This means that the sentence has a subject and verb in the main clause and another subject and verb in each subordinate clause and that each subordinate clause is joined to the main clause with a subordinate connector.

Adverb clauses are one of three types of subordinate clauses (the other two are adjective clauses and noun clauses). Adverb clauses may come either before the main clause or after the main clause. If an adverb clause comes before the main clause, it is followed by a comma. Adverb clauses are introduced by connectors such as *after, as, before, since, until, when, while, because, if, whether, although, even though,* and *though.*

The <u>store</u> <u>has been</u> in the same location **since** <u>it</u> first <u>opened.</u>
    SUBJECT VERB   SUBJECT   VERB

When the <u>concert</u> <u>ended,</u> the <u>audience</u> <u>left</u> the theater.
         SUBJECT VERB   SUBJECT VERB

The <u>student</u> <u>turned in</u> his exam **before** <u>time</u> <u>was</u> up **because** <u>he</u> <u>finished</u> early.
   SUBJECT   VERB   SUBJECT VERB   SUBJECT VERB

The first sentence is correct because it has the main clause *store has been* and the subordinate clause *it . . . opened,* which is joined to the main clause with the subordinate connector *since.* The second sentence is correct because it has the subordinate clause *concert ended,* which is followed by a comma and is joined to the main clause *audience left* with the subordinate connector *when.* The third sentence is also correct. It has a main clause, *student turned in,* and two subordinate clauses, *time was* and *he finished.* The first subordinate clause is joined to the main clause with the subordinate connector *before,* and the second subordinate clause is joined to the main clause with the subordinate connector *because.*

For each complex sentence containing one or more adverb clauses, you should check that the main clause has a subject and a verb. Then you should check that each adverb clause has a subject and a verb and is joined to the main clause with a subordinate connector. Also, if the adverb clause comes before the main clause, the adverb clause should be followed by a comma.

The <u>professor</u> <u>left</u> the room **after** <u>returned</u> the papers.*
    SUBJECT VERB   VERB

Because the <u>problems</u> <u>are</u> difficult <u>we</u> <u>need</u> to get some help.*
        SUBJECT VERB   SUBJECT VERB

The first sentence is incorrect because it has a complete main clause, *professor left,* and an incomplete subordinate clause, *returned,* which is joined to the main clause with the subordinate connector *after.* The incomplete subordinate clause needs a

---

[3]**A subordinate clause** is a dependent clause. It has both a subject and a verb and is introduced by a subordinate connector. Complex sentences with adverb clauses are covered in Skill 6 of the Structure section of this book.

subject to be complete. The second sentence has a complete subordinate clause, *problems are,* which is joined to the main clause *we need* with the subordinate connector *because.* This sentence is incorrect because the subordinate clause comes before the main clause, but there is no comma following the subordinate clause.

EDITING COMPLEX SENTENCES

1. A complex sentence is a sentence with *one main clause* and at least one *subordinate clause.*

2. Each clause must have a subject and a verb.

3. Each subordinate clause must be joined to the main clause with a subordinate connector.

4. An adverb clause may come before or after the main clause.

5. If an adverb clause comes before the main clause, the adverb clause must be followed by a comma.

EXERCISE 6C: Underline the subjects once and the verbs twice. Put boxes around the subordinate connectors and punctuation used with the connectors. Then indicate if the sentences are correct (C) or incorrect (I).

_C_   1. If the cake bakes much longer, it will burn.

_____ 2. I have been studying English I have been in junior high school.

_____ 3. She a student in this course because it seems so interesting.

_____ 4. After the workers have turned in their time cards.

_____ 5. The teacher collected the papers when everyone had finished.

_____ 6. You must stir the soup often while is cooking on the stove.

_____ 7. Although the exam was relatively short, it was extremely difficult.

_____ 8. Until we find out our grades we will not be able to relax.

_____ 9. Because we lived on the east coast before we moved across the country.

_____ 10. Though no one realized it at first, we had the winning ticket.

_____ 11. Should get some new shoes if your shoes are too small.

_____ 12. Since the news came on the radio, I have been quite upset.

_____ 13. Our friends have a vacation, they will come and visit us.

_____ 14. We will not stop working, until everything is finished.

_____ 15. After the players scored a goal, the crowd roared its approval.

_____ 16. As the end of the semester closer and closer, the students got more and more excited.

_____ 17. The fine was increased because it was not paid on time.

_____ 18. Whether you have time or not, must complete the project.

_____ 19. She was still very angry even though I apologized to her.

_____ 20. Before the semester starts the students hunt for places to live.

EXERCISE 6 (A–C): Find and correct the sentence structure errors in the following essay. (The number in parentheses at the end of each paragraph indicates the number of errors in that paragraph.) The essay discusses the following topic.

> What are the important characteristics of a good roommate? Support your response with specific reasons and details.

1. *Because many different types of people can be good roommates. Three characteristics, to me, important in a good roommate. Let's see if you agreeing with me about these three important characteristics of a good roommate. (3 errors)*

2. *The first characteristic of a good roommate it is a sense of humor. Any two roommates will be very different people, they will disagree about many things. However, if they each have a sense of humor. Then they can laugh about these disagreements instead of arguing about them. A good sense of humor necessary in a roommate. (4 errors)*

3. *The next characteristic of a good roommate it is respect for each other's belongings. When two people are roommates they each come into this situation with their own belongings. Because each roommate's belongings are important to him or her, is important for each of the roommates to respect the other roommate's belongings. So respect for each other's belongings will help to prevent problems between roommates. (4 errors)*

4. *The final important characteristic of a good roommate may surprise you. But this characteristic is quite important to me. This final characteristic of a good roommate a lack of neatness. I myself am not a very neat person so it would be very hard for me to have a neat roommate. A neat roommate would probably be upset with me much of the time because am a little messy. If I had a neat roommate. This roommate and I would probably have problems. So the best roommate for me is therefore a rather messy roommate. (6 errors)*

5. *Thus, many different types of people they can be good roommates. However, certain characteristics important to me in a roommate: a sense of humor, respect for each other's belongings, and not too much need for neatness. A roommate with these important characteristics be a successful roommate for me. (3 errors)*

SKILL 7: EDIT WRITTEN EXPRESSION

7A. Agreement and Parallel Structure

Errors in agreement and parallel structure are covered in the Written Expression section of this book. You may want to review these skills.

> **Skill 11: Agreement after prepositional phrases**
> **Skill 12: Agreement after expressions of quantity**
> **Skill 13: Agreement after certain words**
> **Skill 14: Parallel structure with coordinate conjunctions**
> **Skill 15: Parallel structure with paired conjunctions**

EXERCISE 7A: Find and correct the errors in the following essay. (The number in parentheses at the end of each paragraph indicates the number of errors in that paragraph.) The essay discusses the following topic.

> Do you agree or disagree with the following statement?
> *Money is the best measure of success.*
> Support your response with details and examples.

1.   *Everybody have a different way of measuring success. Money may be one measure of success, but it is not the best measure of success. Better ways of measuring success is available. Some of the better measures of a successful life is family, friendly, and career.* (4 errors)

2.   *One way to measure the success of a life are the strength and deep of family relationships. Perhaps someone either without a family nor with a very unhappy family have a lot of money, but this person has not really had a successful life. Anybody with family relationships that are both strong and love have had a successful life.* (6 errors)

3.   *Another way to measure the success of a life are the strength of friendships. Someone with a lot of money but no friends to share it with are not a successful person. In contrast, somebody with lots of close, thoughtfully, and caring friends have achieved success in life.* (4 errors)

4.   *A final way to measure the success of a life are the amount of enjoyment in a career. A career with a lot of money but without enjoyment are neither fulfilling nor desirably. On the other hand, a career that provides true enjoyment day after day is a successful career even if it does not provide a lot of money.* (3 errors)

5.   *It is not really a good idea to measure the success of a life by the amount of money that a person has made. Instead, the success of a life should be measured in a number of other ways, not only by the family relations and the friends and also by the career that a person has developed over a lifetime. All of these measures of success is far more meaningful and accurately than using money to measure success.* (3 errors)

7B. Verbs and Nouns

Errors with verbs and nouns are covered in the Written Expression section of this book. You may want to review these skills.

Skill 16: Past participles after *have*
Skill 17: Present participles or past participles after *be*
Skill 18: Base form verbs after modals
Skill 19: Singular and plural nouns
Skill 20: Countable and uncountable nouns

EXERCISE 7B: Find and correct the errors in the following essay. (The number in parentheses at the end of each paragraph indicates the number of errors in that paragraph.) The essay discusses the following topic.

> Some people always arrive on time or early, while other people are always late. Which type of person are you? Use specific examples and details to support your response.

1.   I have always dream of being a person who is always on time. However, in reality, I am always, always late. The following three example show that, even in several very important situation, I cannot seeming to arrive on time. (4 errors)

2.   One example of my terrible tardiness is a job interviews that I had soon after I graduated from college. I was give the opportunity to interview for a wonderful job that much other people wanted. The interview was schedule for 10:00. However, I overslept and did not arrive at the interview until 11:00. I am sure that my lateness was the major reason that I did not get the job. (4 errors)

3.   Another example of my terrible lateness is an appearance in court that I had to make after I had receiving a ticket. I, of course, could not arrives on time for this court date. Because I missed my court time, I had to pay the original ticket, and a large fine was add to the number of money that I had to pay. (4 errors)

4.   The final example of my terrible lateness was my wedding. I was engaged to be married to the most wonderful woman, and the wedding had be scheduled for 2:00 on Saturday afternoon. As you can probably guess from both of the earlier example, I just could not managing to arrive at my own wedding on time. I was very lucky that my bride was wait for me when I arrived an hour late. (4 errors)

5.   These examples show that there is few doubt that I have a serious problem with lateness. My lateness has causing me much serious problems in my life, as the examples of the job interview and the court appointment show. At least my lateness did not cause me to lose out on the single most important occasions of my life, my wedding. (4 errors)

7C. Pronouns and Adjectives

Errors with pronouns and adjectives are covered in the Written Expression section of this book. You may want to review these skills.

> **Skill 21: Subject and object pronouns**
> **Skill 22: Possessives**
> **Skill 23: Pronoun reference**
> **Skill 24: Adjectives and adverbs**
> **Skill 25: Adjectives after linking verbs**

EXERCISE 7C: Find and correct the errors in the following essay. (The number in parentheses at the end of each paragraph indicates the number of errors in that paragraph.) The essay discusses the following topic.

> When you receive a nice surprise, how do you react? Use examples to support your response.

1.   *When I receive a pleasant surprise, my reaction differs considerable from the reactions of most people, I think. Most other people react to a nicely surprise by showing theirs reaction and by telling other people around them about its. However, I do not react this way. I react to a pleasant surprise by keeping them to myself for a while. (5 errors)*

2.   *One example of my reaction to a pleasant surprise was a grade that me received on a chemistry exam. After I took this exam, I did not think that I had done extreme well. When the professor returned the exam, him announced that only one exam paper had received an A. I felt quite happily when I looked at my paper and saw the A on them. I kept the news to myself for some time because I wanted to enjoy this myself. Perhaps a week later, I told some of my friends about my grade. It was unbelievably to they that I had kept this news to myself for so long. (7 errors)*

3.   *Another example of my reaction to a pleasant surprise was my admission to a specially Honors Program at my school. When I received the letter saying that I had been admitted, I did not run and shout this news out to everyone immediate. Instead, I wanted to keep the news to myself. It was four or five days before I told my family and friends. Then I told him quiet, without shouting the news. I did not seem very happily about the situation because I was not jumping up and down and shouting, but I was really quite happy about him. (6 errors)*

4.   *These examples show that I usually keep specially news to myself for a while. I think that I want to be the only one to know about it for a while. I want to enjoy it myself before I share it with family and friends of my. (2 errors)*

PRACTICE TESTS

Essay Topic # 1
Time—30 minutes

Do you agree or disagree with the following statement?

It is sometimes better to lie than to tell the truth.

Use specific reasons and details to support your answer.

Essay Topic # 2
Time—30 minutes

Some professors give exams or quizzes often, perhaps once a week; in contrast, other professors give only one comprehensive exam at the end of the course. Discuss the advantages and disadvantages of each type of exam schedule. Then indicate which you prefer and why.

Essay Topic # 3
Time—30 minutes

Do you agree or disagree with the following statement?

It can be a great pleasure to take vacations alone.

Use specific reasons and details to support your answer.

Essay Topic # 4
Time—30 minutes

Some people believe that you should work hard today to prepare for the future, while others believe in the philosophy that "tomorrow never comes," so you should enjoy life to the fullest today. Discuss the advantages of each of these philosophies. Then indicate which one you believe in and why.

COMPLETE PRACTICE TESTS

Two different types of complete practice tests are included in this text, and each test fulfills different purposes.

1. *Practice Tests One and Two—The Introductory-Level Practice Tests*—only include questions that are based on the skills covered in this text; they do not include some of the more advanced types of questions that also appear on the official TOEFL test. You should expect to score very well on these tests after all the skills in this book have been thoroughly covered. *Practice Tests One and Two* serve two purposes:

   - You can use these tests as a review of all of the skills taught throughout the text.
   - You can determine which skills are still a problem by completing the analysis section at the end of each test.

   Please note that *Practice Tests One and Two* cannot be used to determine an approximate TOEFL score because the level of the tests is lower than the level of an official TOEFL test.

2. *Practice Test Three—The TOEFL-Level Practice Test*—is at the same level as the official TOEFL test. It includes the introductory skills taught in this text as well as some of the advanced types of questions that also appear on the official TOEFL test. You should score well on the more basic questions on this test at the end of a course in which all the skills in this text have been covered, but you may not do as well on the questions involving more advanced skills. *Practice Test Three* serves a number of purposes:

   - You can see the level of an official TOEFL test.
   - You can recognize and answer the introductory-level questions on a test that also includes some more advanced questions.
   - You can try to answer some of the more advanced types of questions that appear on an official TOEFL test.
   - You can determine an approximate TOEFL score using the scoring information provided in the text.

1 □ 1 □ 1 □ 1 □ 1 □ 1 □ 1 □ 1

COMPLETE TEST ONE
INTRODUCTORY LEVEL

SECTION 1
LISTENING COMPREHENSION
Time—approximately 35 minutes
(including the reading of the directions for each part)

In this section of the test, you will have an opportunity to demonstrate your ability to understand conversations and talks in English. There are three parts to this section, with special directions for each part. Answer all the questions on the basis of what is **stated** or **implied** by the speakers you hear. Do **not** take notes or write in your test book at any time. Do **not** turn the pages until you are told to do so.

Part A

Directions: In Part A you will hear short conversations between two people. After each conversation, you will hear a question about the conversation. The conversations and questions will not be repeated. After you hear a question, read the four possible answers in your test book and choose the best answer. Then, on your answer sheet, find the number of the question and fill in the space that corresponds to the letter of the answer you have chosen.

Here is an example.

On the recording, you will hear:

Sample Answer

Ⓐ
Ⓑ
Ⓒ
●

(man)   *That exam was just awful.*
(woman)   *Oh, it could have been worse.*
(narrator) *What does the woman mean?*

In your test book, you will read: (A) The exam was really awful.
                                   (B) It was the worst exam she had ever seen.
                                   (C) It couldn't have been more difficult.
                                   (D) It wasn't that hard.

You learn from the conversation that the man thought the exam was very difficult and that the woman disagreed with the man. The best answer to the question, "What does the woman mean?" is (D), "It wasn't that hard." Therefore, the correct choice is (D).

Wait

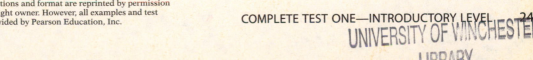

1. (A) Her trip will last only a few days.
   (B) She departs in several days.
   (C) She's leaving in a few hours.
   (D) Her trip began a few days ago.

2. (A) A salesclerk.
   (B) A lawyer.
   (C) A painter.
   (D) An apartment manager.

3. (A) His paper was on the top of the pile.
   (B) He received the highest mark.
   (C) He's a graduate student in math.
   (D) He had a tough math exam.

4. (A) He's upset.
   (B) He's not present.
   (C) He's seated in his chair.
   (D) He's where he should be.

5. (A) A rainstorm is coming.
   (B) He'd like to tell the woman about the storm.
   (C) He agrees with the woman.
   (D) The storm damage was minimal.

6. (A) He said he was sorry.
   (B) He was temporarily lost.
   (C) He finally polished the silver.
   (D) He was the last to appear.

7. (A) Marking the pages in red.
   (B) Buying some bread.
   (C) Reading more often.
   (D) Jogging to the market.

8. (A) The letters were sent.
   (B) She picked up some mail from the post office.
   (C) She spent a lot of time at the post office.
   (D) The post office delivered some letters.

9. (A) He has a problem understanding a certain book.
   (B) He never browses through books.
   (C) He needs to return to the library.
   (D) He'll give the book back soon.

10. (A) The chair is not soft enough.
    (B) The set of jars is unaffordable.
    (C) It's hard to find a comfortable chair.
    (D) He hardly has time to sit.

11. (A) At a ball game.
    (B) At an exam.
    (C) At a dance.
    (D) At a concert.

12. (A) She's like most people.
    (B) She reaches out to most people.
    (C) She's nice to almost everyone.
    (D) She has a lot of money.

13. (A) Helping him solve a personal problem.
    (B) Only working on the harder problems.
    (C) Getting some assistance.
    (D) Solving the problems herself.

14. (A) The apartment has a nice closet.
    (B) It's not far to the school from his apartment.
    (C) He was able to find the university from his apartment.
    (D) The university apartments are closed.

15. (A) She was certain about the time of the party.
    (B) She traveled several miles to the party.
    (C) She planned the surprise party.
    (D) She looked happy.

16. (A) The rain is really heavy.
    (B) She shares the man's opinion.
    (C) The heavy traffic was expected.
    (D) The man should repeat what he said.

17. (A) A general.
    (B) A runner.
    (C) A police officer.
    (D) A truck driver.

GO ON TO THE NEXT PAGE →

18. (A) Recopy her paper.
    (B) Check the spelling on her homework.
    (C) Give the right answers.
    (D) Have another cup of coffee.

19. (A) He doesn't like warm water.
    (B) The weather is not very warm.
    (C) He's going swimming anyway.
    (D) The water's too cool.

20. (A) Visiting a different store.
    (B) Closing the door.
    (C) Storing things in a closet.
    (D) Buying something else.

21. (A) There are three new buildings at the
        university.
    (B) The theater is under construction.
    (C) The university is accepting bids on a
        theater.
    (D) The university has to pay the bill for
        the theater.

22. (A) She also thinks they should not leave
        now.
    (B) They will both live until tomorrow.
    (C) The leaves will be falling tomorrow.
    (D) She thinks they should leave today.

23. (A) The teacher assigned the work
        carefully.
    (B) The grade was not really low.
    (C) She didn't do her homework.
    (D) Her homework contained a lot of
        errors.

24. (A) His weekend was relaxing.
    (B) He spent the weekend on the beach.
    (C) He needed a piece of paper.
    (D) He preferred a more relaxing
        weekend.

25. (A) In the dining room.
    (B) At school.
    (C) In a hospital.
    (D) At a concert.

26. (A) Sitting up in bed.
    (B) Waking up without an alarm.
    (C) Turning on the alarm clock.
    (D) Setting the alarm clock on the floor.

27. (A) Additional writing supplies are
        necessary.
    (B) The man needs to bring the test.
    (C) Pencils and paper are not necessary.
    (D) The man needs to take an extra test.

28. (A) It is unusual to play hide-and-seek.
    (B) The baby's temperature is not normal.
    (C) She is taking care of the baby
        temporarily.
    (D) The baby is not sick.

29. (A) Only Alex went on the trip.
    (B) He was given the chance to go.
    (C) The trip was a good opportunity.
    (D) No one went on the trip.

30. (A) She has several children.
    (B) She doesn't believe what he says.
    (C) She is only a child.
    (D) She behaves immaturely.

GO ON TO THE NEXT PAGE

Part B

Directions: In this part of the test, you will hear longer conversations. After each conversation, you will hear several questions. The conversations and questions will not be repeated.

After you hear a question, read the four possible answers in your test book and choose the best answer. Then, on your answer sheet, find the number of the question and fill in the space that corresponds to the letter of the answer you have chosen.

Remember, you are **not** allowed to take notes or write in your test book.

31. (A) A boat trip.
    (B) A bus trip.
    (C) A plane trip.
    (D) A train trip.

32. (A) Spring.
    (B) Summer.
    (C) Autumn.
    (D) Winter.

33. (A) They are heading north.
    (B) They are looking for warmer water.
    (C) They are returning to their home.
    (D) They are heading toward Alaska.

34. (A) One hour.
    (B) Two hours.
    (C) Three hours.
    (D) Four hours.

35. (A) How to enroll in university classes.
    (B) What is bad about mail service.
    (C) How to fill out university applications.
    (D) The location of a campus building.

36. (A) It is a long process.
    (B) It is the only way to enroll.
    (C) It is easy to complete.
    (D) It begins in the administration building.

37. (A) It takes place in one office.
    (B) It involves many hours in line.
    (C) It is very efficient.
    (D) It takes almost no time.

38. (A) Write a letter to a friend.
    (B) Go to the administration building.
    (C) Stand in line.
    (D) Register by mail.

GO ON TO THE NEXT PAGE

Part C

Directions: In Part C of this section, you will hear several talks. After each talk, you will hear some questions. The talks and questions will not be repeated.

After you hear a question, you will read the four possible answers in your test book and choose the best answer. Then, on your answer sheet, find the number of the question and fill in the space that corresponds to the letter of the answer you have chosen.

Here is an example.

On the recording, you will hear:

(narrator) *Listen to an instructor talk to his class about painting.*
(man)   *Artist Grant Wood was a guiding force in the school of painting known as American regionalist, a style reflecting the distinctive characteristics of art from rural areas of the United States. Wood began drawing animals on the family farm at the age of three, and when he was thirty-eight one of his paintings received a remarkable amount of public notice and acclaim. This painting, called* American Gothic, *is a starkly simple depiction of a serious couple staring directly out at the viewer.*

Now listen to a sample question.   **Sample Answer**
                                                                        Ⓐ
(narrator)   *What style of painting is known as American regionalist?*   Ⓑ
                                                                        Ⓒ
In your test book, you will read: (A) Art from America's inner cities.   ⬤
                                   (B) Art from the central region of the
                                        United States.
                                   (C) Art from various urban areas in the
                                        United States.
                                   (D) Art from rural sections of America.

The best answer to the question, "What style of painting is known as American regionalist?" is (D), "Art from rural sections of America." Therefore, the correct choice is (D).

Now listen to another sample question.   **Sample Answer**
                                                                        Ⓐ
(narrator)   *What is the name of Wood's most successful painting?*   Ⓑ
                                                                        ⬤
In your test book, you will read: (A) *American Regionalist.*   Ⓓ
                                   (B) *The Family Farm in Iowa.*
                                   (C) *American Gothic.*
                                   (D) *A Serious Couple.*

The best answer to the question, "What is the name of Wood's most successful painting?" is (C), *American Gothic.* Therefore, the correct choice is (C).

Remember, you are **not** allowed to take notes or write in your test book.

(**Wait**)

39. (A) A professor.
    (B) A tour guide.
    (C) A furniture salesman.
    (D) An apartment manager.

40. (A) One.
    (B) Two.
    (C) Three.
    (D) Four.

41. (A) It is not large.
    (B) It has a fireplace.
    (C) It has some windows.
    (D) It does not have a refrigerator.

42. (A) There is none.
    (B) It has already been rented.
    (C) The apartment owner will give them some.
    (D) The apartment has great furniture.

43. (A) The New York City subway system.
    (B) The development of the subway.
    (C) The history of the railroad system.
    (D) The IRT.

44. (A) The railroads.
    (B) Private businesses in New York City.
    (C) The mayor of New York City.
    (D) The subway in New York City.

45. (A) It was more important than the railroads.
    (B) It took a long time to develop.
    (C) It was developed by the government of New York.
    (D) It was quite easy to accomplish.

46. (A) In 1870.
    (B) In 1874.
    (C) In 1900.
    (D) In 1904.

47. (A) Studying animals in the wild.
    (B) Animal songs on the radio.
    (C) Problems with radio signals.
    (D) Weather satellites.

48. (A) By using radio transmitters.
    (B) By following their tracks.
    (C) With weather balloons.
    (D) With satellites.

49. (A) With radio collars.
    (B) With atmospheric pressure.
    (C) With radio receivers.
    (D) With satellites.

50. (A) Geography.
    (B) Botany.
    (C) Zoology.
    (D) Communication.

This is the end of Section 1.
Stop work on Section 1.

Turn off the recording.

Read the directions for Section 2 and begin work.
Do NOT read or work on any other section
of the test during the next 25 minutes.

GO ON TO THE NEXT PAGE

SECTION 2
STRUCTURE AND WRITTEN EXPRESSION
Time—25 minutes
(including the reading of the directions)
Now set your clock for 25 minutes.

This section is designed to measure your ability to recognize language that is appropriate for standard written English. There are two types of questions in this section, with special directions for each type.

Structure

Directions: These questions are incomplete sentences. Beneath each sentence you will see four words or phrases, marked (A), (B), (C), and (D). Choose the **one** word or phrase that best completes the sentence. Then, on your answer sheet, find the number of the question and fill in the space that corresponds to the letter of the answer you have chosen.

Look at the following examples.

Example I

The president _____ the election by a landslide.

(A) won
(B) he won
(C) yesterday
(D) fortunately

Sample Answer

● Ⓑ Ⓒ Ⓓ

The sentence should read, "The president won the election by a landslide." Therefore, you should choose answer (A).

Example II

When _____ the conference?

(A) the doctor attended
(B) did the doctor attend
(C) the doctor will attend
(D) the doctor's attendance

Sample Answer

Ⓐ ● Ⓒ Ⓓ

The sentence should read, "When did the doctor attend the conference?" Therefore, you should choose answer (B).

GO ON TO THE NEXT PAGE

1. The Arctic Circle _____ through northern North America, Europe, and Asia.

   (A) the pass
   (B) passing
   (C) it passes
   (D) passes

2. Earth's gravity pulls everything toward _____ the Earth.

   (A) it centers
   (B) the center of
   (C) centered it
   (D) the center

3. The forces _____ earthquakes are the same ones that build mountains.

   (A) unleash
   (B) unleashes
   (C) that unleash
   (D) that unleashing

4. Since the eighteenth century, _____ the major genre of literature in most literate societies.

   (A) becoming the novel
   (B) has the novel become
   (C) a becoming novel
   (D) the novel has become

5. Under a microscope, _____ of a computer chip looks like a network of aluminum tracks.

   (A) the circuitry
   (B) with the circuitry
   (C) after the circuitry
   (D) it circulates

6. Dinosaurs became extinct 64 million years _____ first people ever appeared on Earth.

   (A) prior to the
   (B) the preceding time
   (C) before the
   (D) the

7. Venus is almost the same size as the Earth, _____ mountain ranges are much higher.

   (A) they
   (B) but they
   (C) its
   (D) but its

8. In concrete poetry the primary consideration is the way that _____ in the poem.

   (A) words are arranged
   (B) the arrangement of words
   (C) arranging the words
   (D) words in an arrangement

9. Scientists are now only beginning to understand the factors _____ cigarette addiction.

   (A) cause
   (B) causing
   (C) they cause
   (D) causes

10. Agricultural _____ largely responsible for the unfolding of nutritional knowledge of vitamins and minerals early in the last century.

    (A) was
    (B) chemists
    (C) with chemists
    (D) chemists were

11. Each summer the Roanoke Historical Association sponsors a play that shows _____ about the fate of the early colony.

    (A) known
    (B) what is known
    (C) what knowing
    (D) is known

GO ON TO THE NEXT PAGE

12. Agriculture requires a steady supply of water to keep the plants alive, so _____ in areas with a lot of rainfall.

    (A) naturally started
    (B) starting nature
    (C) it naturally started
    (D) its natural start

13. Even though _____ about $4,000 to fully train a hearing dog, these dogs are generally given without charge to qualified candidates.

    (A) it costs
    (B) the cost of it
    (C) the cost
    (D) costs

14. The reactor core of a nuclear reactor is housed in a steel vessel _____ by a thick layer of concrete.

    (A) is surrounded
    (B) it surrounds
    (C) surrounds
    (D) surrounded

15. The properties of every protein depend on how _____ are arranged in the molecular chain.

    (A) all the amino acids
    (B) all of the amino acid
    (C) all of the aminos acidify
    (D) of all the amino acids

GO ON TO THE NEXT PAGE

Written Expression

Directions: In these questions, each sentence has four underlined words or phrases. The four underlined parts of the sentence are marked (A), (B), (C), and (D). Identify the **one** underlined word or phrase that must be changed in order for the sentence to be correct. Then, on your answer sheet, find the number of the question and fill in the space that corresponds to the letter of the answer you have chosen.

Look at the following examples.

Example I

The four string on a violin are tuned
  A   B   C D

in fifths.

Sample Answer

   Ⓐ
   ●
   Ⓒ
   Ⓓ

The sentence should read, "The four strings on a violin are tuned in fifths." Therefore, you should choose answer (B).

Example II

The research for the book *Roots* taking
     A   B   C

Alex Haley twelve years.
           D

Sample Answer

   Ⓐ
   Ⓑ
   ●
   Ⓓ

The sentence should read, "The research for the book *Roots* took Alex Haley twelve years." Therefore, you should choose answer (C).

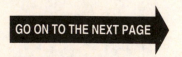

GO ON TO THE NEXT PAGE

TOEFL® test directions and format are reprinted by permission of ETS, the copyright owner. However, all examples and test questions are provided by Pearson Education, Inc.

16. Polar winters are length, dark, and cold enough to kill most plants.
               A   B   C   D

17. The remains of very ancient wood have turn into coal.
         A   B   C   D

18. In 1893, Henry Ford built his first car engine in he home workshop in Detroit.
                   A B   C   D

19. Armies of laborers toiled for eight year to build the Erie Canal.
     A   B   C   D

20. Some of the stars in the closing stages of their lives becomes white dwarfs.
            A   B   C   D

21. The normally force of gravity at the Earth's surface is called *1g*.
        A   B   C   D

22. Edward McDowell is remember as the composer of such perennial favorites as "To a Wild Rose."
                  A   B   C   D

23. Because hc is gravitationally bound to the Milky Way, the Andromeda galaxy is currently
         A   B   C

    approaching Earth.
       D

24. CAT scanners are used not only for detecting conditions but also for observation the effects of
               A   B   C

    therapy.
     D

25. The chain of rider stations along the way were crucial to the success of the Pony Express.
             A   B C   D

26. The functional relationship between the brain's two hemispheres has been a major focus of much
                     A   B   C   D

    studies in neuropsychology.

27. The Great Salt Lake is the remnant of a vast inland seas.
          A   B   C   D

28. A desire to eradicate irregular spellings in English can being traced back to the sixteenth century.
     A   B   C   D

GO ON TO THE NEXT PAGE →

29. Jade can <u>actually</u> refer to either the less common and <u>more valuable</u> jadeite <u>and</u> the more
         A   B   C

    common and <u>less</u> valuable nephrite.
               D

30. The number of electrons in <u>an atom</u> <u>match</u> the number of <u>charged</u> particles, <u>or</u> protons.
                             A   B   C   D

31. The neocortex <u>becomes</u> <u>progressive</u> more <u>developed</u> in the more <u>advanced</u> mammals.
                   A   B   C   D

32. During <u>their</u> first <u>attempts</u> as a songwriter, George Gershwin diligently <u>continued</u> to study the
           A   B   C

    piano, harmony, <u>theory</u>, and orchestration.
                     D

33. Alexander Graham Bell <u>was</u> twenty-nine when <u>him</u> was <u>granted</u> a telephone patent <u>in</u> 1876.
                           A   B   C   D

34. Early television sets such as the RCA Victor <u>model</u> had <u>small</u> screens but <u>containing</u> a mass of
                                           A   B   C

    <u>additional</u> components.
       D

35. A huge <u>amount</u> of immigrants <u>passed</u> <u>through</u> the Great Hall on Ellis Island <u>between</u> 1892 and
            A   B   C   D

    1954.

36. The <u>cliff</u> dwellings in Mesa Verde were <u>build</u> in the thirteenth century by Native Americans <u>who</u>
        A   B   C

    farmed <u>the green</u> plateau.
            D

37. The poet Walt Whitman <u>was</u> an <u>easy</u> recognized <u>figure</u> with his <u>long</u>, white beard and wide-
                        A   B   C   D

    brimmed hat.

38. The sand dollars <u>are</u> a <u>distinctive</u> group of sea urchins <u>that</u> have <u>adapt</u> especially to lie on sandy
                 A   B   C   D

    shores.

GO ON TO THE NEXT PAGE

39. Someone who personifies the "American Dream" are Andrew Carnegie, who immigrated to the
    A   B

United States from Scotland without money and made millions in the steel industry.
                              C   D

40. The Nez Perce lived peacefully with the trappers and traders who traveled theirs lands until the
                      A   B   C

discovery of gold in 1860 brought miners and settlers into the region.
                          D

**This is the end of Section 2.
If you finish before 25 minutes has ended,
check your work on Section 2 only.**

**At the end of 25 minutes, go on to Section 3.
Use exactly 55 minutes to work on Section 3.**

SECTION 3
READING COMPREHENSION
Time—55 minutes
(including the reading of the directions)
Now set your clock for 55 minutes.

This section is designed to measure your ability to read and understand short passages similar in topic and style to those that students are likely to encounter in North American universities and colleges. This section contains reading passages and questions about the passages.

Directions: In this section you will read several passages. Each one is followed by a number of questions about it. You are to choose the **one** best answer, (A), (B), (C), or (D), to each question. Then, on your answer sheet, find the number of the question and fill in the space that corresponds to the letter of the answer you have chosen.

Answer all questions about the information in a passage on the basis of what is **stated** or **implied** in that passage.

Read the following passage:

John Quincy Adams, who served as the sixth president of the United States from 1825 to 1829, is today recognized for his masterful statesmanship and diplomacy. He dedicated his life to public service, both in the presidency and in the various other political offices that he held.
Line Throughout his political career he demonstrated his unswerving belief in freedom of speech, the
(5) antislavery cause, and the right of Americans to be free from European and Asian domination.

Example I	**Sample Answer**
To what did John Quincy Adams devote his life?	Ⓐ
	●
(A) Improving his personal life	Ⓒ
(B) Serving the public	Ⓓ
(C) Increasing his fortune	
(D) Working on his private business	

According to the passage, John Quincy Adams "dedicated his life to public service." Therefore, you should choose answer (B).

Example II	**Sample Answer**
In line 4, the word "unswerving" is closest in meaning to	Ⓐ
	Ⓑ
(A) moveable	●
(B) insignificant	Ⓓ
(C) unchanging	
(D) diplomatic	

The passage states that John Quincy Adams demonstrated his unswerving belief "throughout his career." This implies that the belief did not change. Therefore, you should choose answer (C).

GO ON TO THE NEXT PAGE ➡

Questions 1–9

Romantic music of the nineteenth century differed greatly from the classical music of the eighteenth century. Classical music was primarily concerned with strict form and style. Romantic composers, however, wanted to express their feelings and thoughts through music. Their music was
Line less structured than the music of the classicists; its goal was to fill the listener with emotion, with
(5) thoughts of beauty, wonder, and nature, and with poetry.

1. What is the topic of this passage?

    (A) The characteristics of romantic music
    (B) Various types of music
    (C) Popular music in the eighteenth century
    (D) A comparison of romantic and classical music

2. The word "greatly" in line 1 could best be replaced by which of the following?

    (A) Famously
    (B) Tremendously
    (C) Structurally
    (D) Slightly

3. According to the passage, classical music

    (A) expresses feelings and thoughts
    (B) was popular in the nineteenth century
    (C) has rigid forms
    (D) is less structured than romantic music

4. The word "form" in line 2 is closest in meaning to

    (A) structure
    (B) meter
    (C) meaning
    (D) use

5. It can be inferred from the passage that romantic music

    (A) developed prior to the eighteenth century
    (B) did not have a strict form
    (C) came before classical music
    (D) was more concerned with form than feeling

6. The word "goal" in line 4 is NOT close in meaning to which of the following?

    (A) Aim
    (B) Objective
    (C) Result
    (D) Purpose

7. The word "emotion" in line 4 is closest in meaning to

    (A) feeling
    (B) logic
    (C) sound
    (D) movement

8. According to the passage, romantic music filled the listener with all of the following EXCEPT

    (A) thoughts of poetry
    (B) thoughts of wonder
    (C) thoughts of loveliness
    (D) thoughts of strictness

9. Where in the passage does the author mention when the different types of music were popular?

    (A) Lines 1–2
    (B) Line 3
    (C) Line 4
    (D) Line 5

GO ON TO THE NEXT PAGE ➡

Questions 10–19

In the American colonies, Benjamin Franklin worked as a printer; from his work, he clearly understood how difficult and costly it was to make books. However, he and his friends really enjoyed reading and wanted to get hold of as many books as they could.

Line
(5) One of Franklin's good ideas, and he had many good ideas, was to set up a club where people could share their books. The 50 members who joined the club when it was started in 1732 donated books and also pooled their money to buy additional books. Anyone who wanted to could stop in and read the books; club members were also allowed to take the books home with them, provided they returned them on time. This "club" became America's first circulating library.

10. The passage mainly discusses

    (A) the American colonies
    (B) Benjamin Franklin's work as a printer
    (C) Franklin's many good ideas
    (D) America's first circulating library

11. A "printer" in line 1 is a person who

    (A) works in a library
    (B) runs a book club
    (C) reads a lot of books
    (D) produces books and pamphlets

12. The passage indicates that Franklin had

    (A) no good ideas
    (B) one good idea
    (C) few good ideas
    (D) numerous good ideas

13. According to the passage, how many people were in the original club?

    (A) 5
    (B) 15
    (C) 50
    (D) 500

14. The word "pooled" in line 6 could best be replaced by

    (A) watered
    (B) swam
    (C) earned
    (D) shared

15. Which of the following is NOT mentioned in the passage as something that club members did?

    (A) They gave books to the club.
    (B) They started new clubs.
    (C) They took books home.
    (D) They helped buy additional books.

16. It can be inferred from the passage that nonmembers of Franklin's club could NOT

    (A) enter the club
    (B) look at the club's books
    (C) read
    (D) take books out of the club

17. The word "provided" in line 7 could best be replaced by which of the following?

    (A) If
    (B) Before
    (C) Where
    (D) Although

GO ON TO THE NEXT PAGE

18. In line 8, the books in a "circulating" library are probably

  (A) spun in circles
  (B) moved up and down on the library shelves
  (C) checked in and out of the library
  (D) turned upside-down

19. Where in the passage does the author explain why Franklin started the book club?

  (A) Lines 1–2
  (B) Lines 4–5
  (C) Lines 6–7
  (D) Line 8

GO ON TO THE NEXT PAGE

Questions 20–29

The Hopi are part of the Pueblo Indian culture. Today they live mostly in northeastern Arizona, at the edge of the Painted Desert. Something that sets the Hopi culture off from other cultures is that it is in some senses a maternal rather than a paternal culture.

Line
(5)
The Hopi are divided into clans, or families, along maternal lines, and as a result a child becomes a member of the mother's clan rather than the father's. In addition, ownership of property, such as land and houses, passes from mother to daughter instead of from father to son, as it does in other Native American cultures. However, women do not have all the power in this culture. Societal authority still rests in the hands of men, but that authority does pass to men from their mothers.

20. The main idea of the passage is that

    (A) the Hopi are one type of Pueblo Indian
    (B) the Hopi have a maternal culture
    (C) most Indian cultures are paternal cultures
    (D) today the Hopi live in northeastern Arizona

21. The passage states that the Hopi

    (A) are enemies of the Pueblo Indians
    (B) all live in northeastern Arizona
    (C) live inside the Painted Desert
    (D) may be found on the borders of the Painted Desert

22. In line 3, something that is "maternal" is related to

    (A) the culture
    (B) the mother
    (C) the Hopi
    (D) the clan

23. It is implied in the passage that most Native American cultures

    (A) live in the Painted Desert
    (B) are part of the Hopi tribe
    (C) are paternal cultures
    (D) do not have strong families

24. A "clan" in line 5 is a

    (A) mother
    (B) father
    (C) family
    (D) child

25. Which of the following is true about Hopi property ownership, according to the passage?

    (A) Hopi do not own property.
    (B) Hopi property passes from father to son.
    (C) Property ownership in the Hopi culture is similar to property ownership in most other cultures.
    (D) A Hopi daughter will probably inherit property from her mother.

26. The expression "such as" in line 6 is closest in meaning to

    (A) then
    (B) for example
    (C) as a result
    (D) also

GO ON TO THE NEXT PAGE

27. Which of the following is NOT true about power in Hopi society?

    (A) Women do not have all the power in Hopi society.
    (B) Men have power in Hopi society.
    (C) A man will probably inherit power from his mother.
    (D) A man inherits power from his father.

28. The word "rests" in line 8 could best be replaced by

    (A) sleeps
    (B) remains
    (C) naps
    (D) tires

29. Where in the passage does the author describe where the Hopi live today?

    (A) Lines 1–2
    (B) Lines 4–5
    (C) Lines 5–7
    (D) Lines 7–8

GO ON TO THE NEXT PAGE

Questions 30–39

Some kinds of animals that are still around today were in existence millions of years ago during the time of the dinosaur.

One of these survivors is the crocodile, which has been around for about 100 million years.
Line Today's crocodiles can grow to a length of 20 feet and weigh about a ton. Their prehistoric ancestors
(5) were about two-and-a-half times the size of today's animals.

Another survivor from the past is the Galapagos tortoise, whose history goes back around 200 million years. The tortoise of today has not evolved much over the last 200 million years; it looks about the same now as it did way back then.

The oldest survivor from prehistoric times is, can you believe it, the cockroach. Cockroaches
(10) have been able to stick around for more than 250 million years. The main reason for their incredible endurance is their ability to live in all kinds of conditions and survive on all kinds of food.

30. This passage is mainly about

(A) the dinosaur
(B) how the crocodile has survived
(C) animals that live to be very old
(D) types of animals that have existed for
     a long time

31. The word "time" in line 2 could best be replaced by

(A) hour
(B) era
(C) clock
(D) moment

32. According to the passage, the crocodile

(A) survived an attack by dinosaurs
(B) first appeared 100,000 years ago
(C) has increased in size over time
(D) has existed for millions of years

33. It can be inferred from the passage that prehistoric crocodiles could reach a maximum length of

(A) 10 feet
(B) 20 feet
(C) 50 feet
(D) 100 feet

34. The word "ancestors" in line 4 is closest in meaning to which of the following?

(A) Predecessors
(B) Descendants
(C) Monsters
(D) Enemies

35. The passage indicates that the Galapagos tortoise

(A) has changed considerably
(B) has been around for 250 million years
(C) is about the same as it was in the era
     of the dinosaur
(D) is much larger than prehistoric
     tortoises

GO ON TO THE NEXT PAGE →

36. Which of the following is NOT mentioned about the cockroach?

    (A) It has evolved considerably over the years.
    (B) It has been around for a quarter of a billion years.
    (C) It lived at the time of the dinosaur.
    (D) It eats many kinds of food.

37. The expression "stick around" in line 10 is closest in meaning to

    (A) endure
    (B) attack
    (C) travel around
    (D) look around

38. Which of the animals mentioned in the passage has been around for the longest time?

    (A) The dinosaur
    (B) The crocodile
    (C) The Galapagos tortoise
    (D) The cockroach

39. Where in the passage does the author explain why the cockroach has been able to endure?

    (A) Lines 1–2
    (B) Lines 7–8
    (C) Line 9
    (D) Lines 10–12

GO ON TO THE NEXT PAGE

Questions 40–50

The three phases of the human memory are sensory memory, short-term memory, and long-term memory. This division of memory into phases is based on the length of time of the memory.

Line
(5) Sensory memory is instantaneous memory. It is an image or a memory that enters your mind only for a short period of time; it comes and goes in under a second. The memory will not last longer than that unless the information enters short-term memory.

Information can be held in short-term memory for about 20 seconds or as long as you are actively using it. If you repeat a fact to yourself, that fact will stay in your short-term memory as long as you keep repeating it. Once you stop repeating it, either it is forgotten or it moves into long-term memory.

(10) Long-term memory is the huge memory tank that can hold ideas and images for years and years. Information can be added to your long-term memory when you actively try to put it there through memorization or when an idea or image enters your mind on its own.

40. The best title for this passage would be

(A) The Difference Between Sensory and Short-Term Memory
(B) How Long It Takes to Memorize
(C) The Stages of Human Memory
(D) Human Phases

41. The three phases of memory discussed in this passage are differentiated according to

(A) location in the brain
(B) the period of time it takes to remember something
(C) how the senses are involved in the memory
(D) how long the memory lasts

42. The expression "is based on" in line 2 could best be replaced by

(A) is on top of
(B) is at the foot of
(C) depends on
(D) is below

43. According to the passage, which type of memory is the shortest?

(A) Sensory memory
(B) Active memory
(C) Short-term memory
(D) Long-term memory

44. According to the passage, when will information stay in your short-term memory?

(A) For as long as 20 minutes
(B) As long as it is being used
(C) After you have repeated it many times
(D) When it has moved into long-term memory

45. The word "keep" in line 8 could best be replaced by

(A) hold
(B) continue
(C) retain
(D) save

46. The word "Once" in line 8 could best be replaced by which of the following?

(A) Just after
(B) Although
(C) Just before
(D) Because

GO ON TO THE NEXT PAGE →

47. All of the following are true about long-term memory EXCEPT that

    (A) it has a very large capacity
    (B) it can hold information for a long time
    (C) it is possible to put information into it through memorization
    (D) memorization is the only way that information can get there

48. The expression "on its own" in line 12 could best be replaced by

    (A) by itself
    (B) in its own time
    (C) with its possessions
    (D) in only one way

49. It can be inferred from the passage that if a person remembers a piece of information for two days, this information is probably in

    (A) three phases of memory
    (B) sensory memory
    (C) short-term memory
    (D) long-term memory

50. Where in the passage does the author explain what happens when someone stops repeating information?

    (A) Lines 4–5
    (B) Lines 6–7
    (C) Lines 8–9
    (D) Lines 11–12

This is the end of Section 3.

STOP STOP STOP STOP STOP STOP STOP

**If you finish in less than 55 minutes,
check your work on Section 3 only.
Do NOT read or work on any other section of the test.**

TEST OF WRITTEN ENGLISH:
TWE ESSAY TOPIC
Time—30 minutes

Do you agree or disagree with the following statement?

It is always important to put family before career.

Use specific reasons and details to support your answer.

COMPLETE TEST TWO
INTRODUCTORY LEVEL

SECTION 1
LISTENING COMPREHENSION
Time—approximately 35 minutes
(including the reading of the directions for each part)

In this section of the test, you will have an opportunity to demonstrate your ability to understand conversations and talks in English. There are three parts to this section, with special directions for each part. Answer all the questions on the basis of what is **stated** or **implied** by the speakers you hear. Do **not** take notes or write in your test book at any time. Do **not** turn the pages until you are told to do so.

Part A

Directions: In Part A you will hear short conversations between two people. After each conversation, you will hear a question about the conversation. The conversations and questions will not be repeated. After you hear a question, read the four possible answers in your test book and choose the best answer. Then, on your answer sheet, find the number of the question and fill in the space that corresponds to the letter of the answer you have chosen.

Here is an example.

Sample Answer
Ⓐ
Ⓑ
Ⓒ
●

On the recording, you will hear:

(man)   *That exam was just awful.*
(woman)   *Oh, it could have been worse.*
(narrator) *What does the woman mean?*

In your test book, you will read: (A) The exam was really awful.
(B) It was the worst exam she had ever seen.
(C) It couldn't have been more difficult.
(D) It wasn't that hard.

You learn from the conversation that the man thought the exam was very difficult and that the woman disagreed with the man. The best answer to the question, "What does the woman mean?" is (D), "It wasn't that hard." Therefore, the correct choice is (D).

Wait

1. (A) Taking a math class.
   (B) Answering some math problems.
   (C) Checking the math homework.
   (D) Seeing their professor.

2. (A) He's getting a bite to eat.
   (B) He has four meetings today.
   (C) He'll arrive after 4:00.
   (D) He needs a bit of luck.

3. (A) She did not request it.
   (B) It did not come.
   (C) It came quickly.
   (D) It came slowly.

4. (A) She agrees with the man.
   (B) She can't find where she parked.
   (C) She had a hard time getting up this morning.
   (D) She would like the man to repeat himself.

5. (A) The exams were placed in the office.
   (B) The woman can take the exam in the office.
   (C) The exams will be graded in the office.
   (D) The woman should put her exam in the office.

6. (A) A librarian.
   (B) A jeweler.
   (C) A doctor.
   (D) A seamstress.

7. (A) Playing tennis now.
   (B) Playing a different sport.
   (C) Going to the store now.
   (D) Leaving the shopping for later.

8. (A) It's delicious.
   (B) She hasn't tasted it.
   (C) It needs more spices.
   (D) It's not very good.

9. (A) The professor just assigned a paper to be written.
   (B) He is not sure when he should see the professor.
   (C) The professor changed the date the paper is due.
   (D) The professor changed the date of the class.

10. (A) She disagrees with the man.
    (B) She doesn't want to do the problems.
    (C) They can finish the problems in class.
    (D) She shares the man's opinion.

11. (A) The time he suggested is fine.
    (B) She'd prefer to meet later.
    (C) She'd prefer never to meet.
    (D) She'd prefer to meet earlier.

12. (A) To a service station.
    (B) To a doctor's office.
    (C) To a gym.
    (D) To a pharmacy.

13. (A) The words were too small.
    (B) The professor did not write anything.
    (C) She could not hear the words.
    (D) The board was very tiny.

14. (A) They have the same answer.
    (B) He will change his answer.
    (C) He's uncertain of his response.
    (D) He doesn't want to respond to her question.

15. (A) Helping some other people.
    (B) Asking when the assignment is due.
    (C) Helping each other with the assignment.
    (D) Finding someone to help them.

16. (A) He has also written an article.
    (B) He shares the woman's opinion.
    (C) The meeting is in front of the school.
    (D) What was in the article was fair.

17. (A) An auto mechanic.
    (B) A bicycle repairman.
    (C) An engineer.
    (D) A train station attendant.

GO ON TO THE NEXT PAGE ➡

18. (A) She was asked to be a guest speaker.
    (B) She became president of the club.
    (C) She started her own business.
    (D) She invited someone to hear a speech.

19. (A) She's going to a different part of campus.
    (B) She likes the apartment.
    (C) She wants to be closer to school.
    (D) She didn't see the apartment.

20. (A) Driving to the game.
    (B) Walking to the game.
    (C) Not going to the game.
    (D) Not walking to the game.

21. (A) The window was partially open.
    (B) Someone shut the window.
    (C) He couldn't see the window.
    (D) It wasn't really very cold.

22. (A) He didn't get his paper back.
    (B) He made a big mistake.
    (C) He wrote a very long paper.
    (D) He spilled something on his paper.

23. (A) He had enough time.
    (B) He sent the fax.
    (C) The fax didn't come.
    (D) The fax has not been read.

24. (A) To a flight school.
    (B) To a travel agency.
    (C) To a restaurant.
    (D) To a train station.

25. (A) The concepts were disorganized.
    (B) The ideas were not very good.
    (C) She disagreed with the ideas.
    (D) The organization was excellent.

26. (A) He has something to say to her.
    (B) The teacher gave a very hard lecture.
    (C) He shares the woman's opinion.
    (D) The woman should pay attention to him.

27. (A) Leave on a cruise in seven days.
    (B) Visit with seven crew members.
    (C) Take a seven-hour cruise.
    (D) Take a week-long boat trip.

28. (A) Trying to cool off.
    (B) Getting something warm to drink.
    (C) Warming up a drink.
    (D) Exercising to warm up.

29. (A) He answered all the professor's questions.
    (B) He phoned the professor three times.
    (C) The professor couldn't answer all his questions.
    (D) The professor called on him a number of times.

30. (A) To see a ballet.
    (B) To listen to a lecture.
    (C) To hear a concert.
    (D) To watch a debate.

GO ON TO THE NEXT PAGE

Part B

Directions: In this part of the test, you will hear longer conversations. After each conversation, you will hear several questions. The conversations and questions will not be repeated.

After you hear a question, read the four possible answers in your test book and choose the best answer. Then, on your answer sheet, find the number of the question and fill in the space that corresponds to the letter of the answer you have chosen.

Remember, you are **not** allowed to take notes or write in your test book.

31. (A) She was mistaken about the date of the exam.
    (B) She missed Tuesday's class.
    (C) She is unsure of today's date.
    (D) She missed the exam.

32. (A) Tuesday of this week.
    (B) Wednesday of this week.
    (C) Tuesday of next week.
    (D) Wednesday of next week.

33. (A) The third.
    (B) The twelfth.
    (C) The thirteenth.
    (D) The twentieth.

34. (A) Get some sleep now.
    (B) Talk to the professor.
    (C) Put off studying until later.
    (D) Begin studying immediately.

35. (A) In a new dorm.
    (B) In an old dorm.
    (C) In an off-campus house.
    (D) In an off-campus apartment.

36. (A) In a new dorm.
    (B) In an old dorm.
    (C) In an off-campus house.
    (D) In an off-campus apartment.

37. (A) Because it is old-fashioned.
    (B) Because it is off-campus.
    (C) Because it is near the middle of campus.
    (D) Because it is modern.

38. (A) Because it is modern.
    (B) Because it is off-campus.
    (C) Because it is near the middle of campus.
    (D) Because it is far away from school.

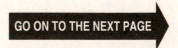
GO ON TO THE NEXT PAGE

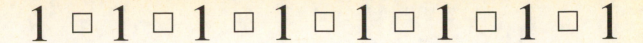

Part C

Directions: In Part C of this section, you will hear several talks. After each talk, you will hear some questions. The talks and questions will not be repeated.

After you hear a question, you will read the four possible answers in your test book and choose the best answer. Then, on your answer sheet, find the number of the question and fill in the space that corresponds to the letter of the answer you have chosen.

Here is an example.

On the recording, you will hear:

(narrator) *Listen to an instructor talk to his class about painting.*
(man) *Artist Grant Wood was a guiding force in the school of painting known as American regionalist, a style reflecting the distinctive characteristics of art from rural areas of the United States. Wood began drawing animals on the family farm at the age of three, and when he was thirty-eight one of his paintings received a remarkable amount of public notice and acclaim. This painting, called* American Gothic, *is a starkly simple depiction of a serious couple staring directly out at the viewer.*

Now listen to a sample question.

Sample Answer
Ⓐ
Ⓑ
Ⓒ
●

(narrator) *What style of painting is known as American regionalist?*

In your test book, you will read: (A) Art from America's inner cities.
(B) Art from the central region of the United States.
(C) Art from various urban areas in the United States.
(D) Art from rural sections of America.

The best answer to the question, "What style of painting is known as American regionalist?" is (D), "Art from rural sections of America." Therefore, the correct choice is (D).

Now listen to another sample question.

Sample Answer
Ⓐ
Ⓑ
●
Ⓓ

(narrator) *What is the name of Wood's most successful painting?*

In your test book, you will read: (A) *American Regionalist.*
(B) *The Family Farm in Iowa.*
(C) *American Gothic.*
(D) *A Serious Couple.*

The best answer to the question, "What is the name of Wood's most successful painting?" is (C), *American Gothic.* Therefore, the correct choice is (C).

Remember, you are **not** allowed to take notes or write in your test book.

Wait

39. (A) The octopus.
    (B) Another vertebrate.
    (C) Backbones.
    (D) Other invertebrates.

40. (A) It is a vertebrate.
    (B) It has no backbone.
    (C) It has no tentacles.
    (D) It has eight backbones.

41. (A) It has eight parts.
    (B) It has its own eyes.
    (C) It is quite big.
    (D) It has the largest brain of all animals.

42. (A) An octopus has very good eyesight.
    (B) The eyesight of an octopus is limited.
    (C) An octopus is able to see into its brain.
    (D) The eyesight of an octopus is unclear.

43. (A) Getting work done on time.
    (B) Attending meetings.
    (C) Taking a lot of courses.
    (D) Avoiding deadlines.

44. (A) Copying each class syllabus.
    (B) Obtaining a calendar.
    (C) Asking to extend deadlines.
    (D) Writing down presentations.

45. (A) The date when an assignment is due.
    (B) The date when a paper must be turned in.
    (C) The date when a student will watch a presentation.
    (D) The date when an exam will be given.

46. (A) To help other students.
    (B) To stay busy.
    (C) To clear off their desks.
    (D) To identify busy periods of time.

47. (A) Individually.
    (B) Along with two others.
    (C) Along with three others.
    (D) In groups of ten.

48. (A) The students have selected the groups.
    (B) The groups have been randomly chosen.
    (C) The professor has made the assignments.
    (D) The students have signed up on a list on the wall.

49. (A) Eight ten-minute presentations.
    (B) Three hour-and-a-half presentations.
    (C) Ten eight-minute presentations.
    (D) Three ten-minute presentations.

50. (A) Find out who is in each group.
    (B) Check the wall to see which poem to read.
    (C) Read the selected poem thoroughly.
    (D) Discuss the poem with group members.

This is the end of Section 1.
Stop work on Section 1.

Turn off the recording.

Read the directions for Section 2 and begin work.
Do NOT read or work on any other section
of the test during the next 25 minutes.

GO ON TO THE NEXT PAGE ➔

SECTION 2
STRUCTURE AND WRITTEN EXPRESSION
Time—25 minutes
(including the reading of the directions)
Now set your clock for 25 minutes.

This section is designed to measure your ability to recognize language that is appropriate for standard written English. There are two types of questions in this section, with special directions for each type.

Structure

Directions: These questions are incomplete sentences. Beneath each sentence you will see four words or phrases, marked (A), (B), (C), and (D). Choose the **one** word or phrase that best completes the sentence. Then, on your answer sheet, find the number of the question and fill in the space that corresponds to the letter of the answer you have chosen.

Look at the following examples.

Example I

The president _____ the election by a landslide.

(A) won
(B) he won
(C) yesterday
(D) fortunately

Sample Answer
● Ⓑ Ⓒ Ⓓ

The sentence should read, "The president won the election by a landslide." Therefore, you should choose answer (A).

Example II

When _____ the conference?

(A) the doctor attended
(B) did the doctor attend
(C) the doctor will attend
(D) the doctor's attendance

Sample Answer
Ⓐ ● Ⓒ Ⓓ

The sentence should read, "When did the doctor attend the conference?" Therefore, you should choose answer (B).

GO ON TO THE NEXT PAGE

TOEFL® test directions and format are reprinted by permission of ETS, the copyright owner. However, all examples and test questions are provided by Pearson Education, Inc.

1. Kansas _____ at the geographical center of the United States.

   (A) it is located
   (B) the location is
   (C) its location
   (D) is located

2. _____ first pizza restaurant opened in New York City in 1895.

   (A) The
   (B) It was the
   (C) At the
   (D) It was at the

3. _____ without a backbone is the Atlantic squid.

   (A) For the largest creature
   (B) It is the largest creature
   (C) The largest creature
   (D) The largest creature is

4. The last star on the handle of _____ Polaris, or the North Star.

   (A) to call the Little Dipper
   (B) calling the Little Dipper
   (C) the Little Dipper calling
   (D) the Little Dipper is called

5. Societies _____ to at least 1500 B.C. made use of molds to treat superficial infections.

   (A) they date back
   (B) the date is back
   (C) dating back
   (D) date back

6. Eugene Debs ran for the presidency of the United States five times, _____ was never elected.

   (A) he
   (B) but he
   (C) to him
   (D) for his

7. The oldest known daggers are ones that Neolithic humans _____ out of flint.

   (A) skillfully chipped
   (B) skillful chips
   (C) chipping skillfully
   (D) chips are skillful

8. Woodrow Wilson served as president of Princeton _____ was elected president of the United States.

   (A) before
   (B) to him
   (C) he
   (D) before he

9. Sound waves are produced when _____ quickly.

   (A) objects vibrate
   (B) vibrating objects
   (C) objects to vibrate
   (D) the vibration of objects

10. A genetic predisposition determines _____ is most likely to form freckles.

    (A) he
    (B) it
    (C) who
    (D) when

11. The vast west-central section of North America, _____ from Texas to Canada, is one of the world's largest grasslands.

    (A) it stretches
    (B) stretches
    (C) which stretches
    (D) is stretching

GO ON TO THE NEXT PAGE →

12. Characteristically, the dulcimer features three or four strings _____ along a fingerboard.

    (A) stretched
    (B) are stretched
    (C) stretch them
    (D) they are stretched

13. Diamond Head is what _____ of an extinct volcano.

    (A) to remain
    (B) remains
    (C) remaining
    (D) the remnants

14. Any member of a group of drugs _____ barbituric acid is a barbiturate.

    (A) the derivation of
    (B) is derived from
    (C) derived from
    (D) derives from

15. Henry VIII ruled that people born on February 29 _____ their birthdays on February 28 in non-leap years.

    (A) a celebrity
    (B) a celebration
    (C) celebrating
    (D) would celebrate

GO ON TO THE NEXT PAGE ➤

Written Expression

Directions: In these questions, each sentence has four underlined words or phrases. The four underlined parts of the sentence are marked (A), (B), (C), and (D). Identify the **one** underlined word or phrase that must be changed in order for the sentence to be correct. Then, on your answer sheet, find the number of the question and fill in the space that corresponds to the letter of the answer you have chosen.

Look at the following examples.

Example I

The four string on a violin are tuned
  A   B   C   D

in fifths.

Sample Answer

Ⓐ
●
Ⓒ
Ⓓ

The sentence should read, "The four strings on a violin are tuned in fifths." Therefore, you should choose answer (B).

Example II

The research for the book *Roots* taking
     A   B   C

Alex Haley twelve years.
          D

Sample Answer

Ⓐ
Ⓑ
●
Ⓓ

The sentence should read, "The research for the book *Roots* took Alex Haley twelve years." Therefore, you should choose answer (C).

GO ON TO THE NEXT PAGE

16. Areas of rock may shifts up or down on each side of a fault.
        A   B   C   D

17. When someone take a depressant, the level of activity in the central nervous system is lowered.
               A   B   C   D

18. The world's largest deposits of asbestos have be located in the Appalachian Mountains.
             A   B   C   D

19. Both Thomas Jefferson or John Adams died on the very same day, July 4, 1826.
                A   B C   D

20. Most tundra plant are mosses and lichens that hug the ground.
            A   B C   D

21. Uranium atoms in a nuclear reaction is split into smaller atoms to produce heat.
                       A B   C   D

22. Virginia Dare, the first child born to English parents in the New World, was named after the
                         A   B   C

    Virginia colony where her was born.
                 D

23. The apple tree appears in the mythology, traditions, historical, and archeology of the most
              A   B   C

    ancient nations.
       D

24. The first horse-drawn chariots were introduce around 2500 B.C.
       A   B   C   D

25. In 1917, Clyde Cessna designed an innovative monoplane, and later the Cessna Aircraft company
                         A   B   C

    was started by he.
             D

26. Not only the Etruscan alphabet and the Latin alphabet are descendants of the Greek alphabet.
     A   B   C   D

27. All of the oceans of the world is home to members of the dolphin family.
                         A B   C   D

28. The Earth rotates on its axis and follows an elliptically orbit around the Sun.
                 A   B   C   D

GO ON TO THE NEXT PAGE →

29. Theodore Roosevelt <u>was</u> the first president <u>to ride</u> in a car, fly in an airplane, and <u>submerging</u> in a
           A   B   C

    <u>submarine</u>.
     D

30. The carbonation of water and soft drinks <u>were</u> one of the first <u>uses</u> <u>found</u> for <u>gaseous</u> carbon
                                       A   B C   D

    dioxide.

31. After an apple is <u>cut</u>, chemicals inside <u>her</u> <u>combine</u> with oxygen <u>to form</u> a brown coat.
                   A   B   C   D

32. Cribbage <u>is</u> a card game <u>in which</u> points are <u>tally</u> by <u>moving</u> pegs on a board.
            A   B   C   D

33. Most of the birds <u>living</u> in desert regions <u>inhabits</u> the <u>fringes</u> of the <u>desert</u>.
                     A   B   C   D

34. The U.S. Constitution, in Article 1, Section 2, <u>provided</u> for a <u>census</u> of the <u>population</u> every
                                               A   B   C

    <u>decades</u>.
     D

35. The constellation Aquarius was <u>associated</u> with the <u>rainy</u> seasons by a <u>large</u> <u>amount</u> of ancient
                                    A   B   C D

    civilizations.

36. <u>Only</u> a small percentage of <u>mined</u> diamonds are actually <u>suitably</u> for <u>use</u> as gemstones.
     A   B   C   D

37. A turkey <u>that</u> Abraham Lincoln had <u>save</u> from Thanksgiving dinner became a <u>beloved</u> family <u>pet</u>.
             A   B   C   D

38. The game of dominoes is played with <u>flat, oblong</u> blocks <u>identified</u> by the <u>number</u> of dots on
                                          A   B   C

    <u>theirs</u> faces.
      D

GO ON TO THE NEXT PAGE

2 • 2 • 2 • 2 • 2 • 2 • 2 • 2

39. Sodium hydroxide and <u>other</u> alkali <u>solutions</u> work <u>effective</u> as <u>degreasing</u> agents.
　　　　　　　　　　　　　　A　　　　　　　B　　　　　　C　　　　　　D

40. The flintlock pistol was <u>popular</u> as a weapon in the seventeenth century <u>because</u> <u>they</u> could be
　　　　　　　　　　　　　A　　　　　　　　　　　　　　　　　　　　　　　B　　　　C

fired one-handed by a rider on <u>horseback</u>.
　　　　　　　　　　　　　　　　D

This is the end of Section 2.
If you finish before 25 minutes has ended,
check your work on Section 2 only.

At the end of 25 minutes, go on to Section 3.
Use exactly 55 minutes to work on Section 3.

SECTION 3
READING COMPREHENSION
Time—55 minutes
(including the reading of the directions)
Now set your clock for 55 minutes.

This section is designed to measure your ability to read and understand short passages similar in topic and style to those that students are likely to encounter in North American universities and colleges. This section contains reading passages and questions about the passages.

Directions: In this section you will read several passages. Each one is followed by a number of questions about it. You are to choose the **one** best answer, (A), (B), (C), or (D), to each question. Then, on your answer sheet, find the number of the question and fill in the space that corresponds to the letter of the answer you have chosen.

Answer all questions about the information in a passage on the basis of what is **stated** or **implied** in that passage.

Read the following passage:

> John Quincy Adams, who served as the sixth president of the United States from 1825 to
> 1829, is today recognized for his masterful statesmanship and diplomacy. He dedicated his life to
> public service, both in the presidency and in the various other political offices that he held.
> *Line* Throughout his political career he demonstrated his unswerving belief in freedom of speech, the
> *(5)* antislavery cause, and the right of Americans to be free from European and Asian domination.

Example I

To what did John Quincy Adams devote his life?

(A) Improving his personal life
(B) Serving the public
(C) Increasing his fortune
(D) Working on his private business

Sample Answer
Ⓐ
●
Ⓒ
Ⓓ

According to the passage, John Quincy Adams "dedicated his life to public service." Therefore, you should choose answer (B).

Example II

In line 4, the word "unswerving" is closest in meaning to

(A) moveable
(B) insignificant
(C) unchanging
(D) diplomatic

Sample Answer
Ⓐ
Ⓑ
●
Ⓓ

The passage states that John Quincy Adams demonstrated his unswerving belief "throughout his career." This implies that the belief did not change. Therefore, you should choose answer (C).

GO ON TO THE NEXT PAGE

Questions 1–10

Most icebergs are formed in the waters of the world's polar and subpolar regions. These are the regions in and around the North and South Poles. Icebergs melt as they encounter warmer ocean waters and warmer ocean breezes closer to the equator. This happens with most, but not all,
Line icebergs.
(5)   One record-setting iceberg managed to travel further from the frigid waters near the poles than any other iceberg has been known to travel. In 1894, an iceberg broke off from Antarctica in the south and began moving slowly northward. It eventually left the very cold waters near the pole and entered warmer waters. This unusual iceberg managed to get amazingly close to the equator. It was observed at a latitude of about 26 degrees south of the equator. This is on the same latitude as Rio de
(10) Janeiro, Brazil, which is famous for its comfortably warm waters and weather throughout the year.

1. The subject of this passage is

   (A) the world's polar and subpolar regions
   (B) how icebergs are formed
   (C) one unusual iceberg
   (D) the climate of Brazil

2. The passage indicates that icebergs form

   (A) only in the north
   (B) only in the south
   (C) near the equator
   (D) in both the north and south

3. According to the passage, where are subpolar regions located?

   (A) At the poles
   (B) Close to the poles
   (C) Close to the equator
   (D) At the equator

4. The word "encounter" in line 2 could best be replaced by the expression

   (A) run after
   (B) run into
   (C) run around
   (D) run up

5. The record-setting iceberg discussed in the passage traveled

   (A) into unusually warm waters
   (B) unusually close to the North Pole
   (C) unusually far south
   (D) unusually far from the equator

6. The word "frigid" in line 5 is closest in meaning to

   (A) warm
   (B) calm
   (C) cold
   (D) deep

7. When did the record-setting iceberg discussed in the passage exist?

   (A) In the first half of the eighteenth century
   (B) In the last half of the eighteenth century
   (C) In the first half of the nineteenth century
   (D) In the last half of the nineteenth century

8. It is NOT stated in the passage that the iceberg

   (A) was moving in a northerly direction
   (B) ended up near the equator
   (C) was seen south of the equator
   (D) was observed from Rio de Janeiro

9. The word "amazingly" in line 8 is closest in meaning to

   (A) comfortably
   (B) surprisingly
   (C) possibly
   (D) unquestionably

10. Where in the passage does the author indicate what usually happens to icebergs in warm water?

    (A) Lines 2–3
    (B) Lines 5–6
    (C) Lines 7–8
    (D) Lines 9–10

GO ON TO THE NEXT PAGE

Questions 11–19

Paul Revere was recognized in Longfellow's poem "The Midnight Ride of Paul Revere" for his act of heroism during Revolutionary times. In this well-known poem, Longfellow describes how Paul Revere made a nighttime ride on horseback from Lexington to Concord. The purpose of this

Line famous ride was to warn the Concord militia that the British were planning to attack.

(5)   However, Longfellow's poem does not recount the historical events accurately. In reality, Paul Revere did not travel alone on his important ride. Instead, he met up with William Dawes in Lexington. These two set out for Concord with a Dr. Samuel Prescott, who was on his way home.

On the way between Lexington and Concord, the three were stopped by some British soldiers. Revere became a prisoner of the British, and Dawes managed to escape. It was Dr. Prescott rather

(10) than Paul Revere who got through to Concord to warn the militia of the British attack that was coming. However, it was Paul Revere and not Dr. Prescott who received the credit for the heroic deed in Longfellow's poem.

11. The main idea of this passage is that

    (A) Paul Revere's ride was essential to the Revolution
    (B) Longfellow's description of Revere's actions was heroic but inaccurate
    (C) Paul Revere should have been given more credit in Longfellow's poem
    (D) Longfellow did not really write the poem about Paul Revere's ride

12. It is stated in the passage that "The Midnight Ride of Paul Revere"

    (A) was really written by Dr. Samuel Prescott
    (B) is about an attack on the British
    (C) was written before the Revolutionary War
    (D) is a famous piece of literature

13. In the poem, Paul Revere

    (A) was a coward
    (B) rode at midday
    (C) issued a warning
    (D) attacked the British

14. The word "militia" in line 4 is closest in meaning to

    (A) defenders
    (B) advisors
    (C) leaders
    (D) workers

15. It is implied in the passage that, in Longfellow's poem, Paul Revere

    (A) made his ride by himself
    (B) did not travel on horseback
    (C) met up with William Dawes
    (D) rode with Dr. Prescott

16. The word "recount" in line 5 is closest in meaning to

    (A) number
    (B) tell
    (C) deny
    (D) invent

17. What happened after the trio was stopped by the British?

    (A) Paul Revere escaped.
    (B) Dr. Prescott was taken prisoner.
    (C) Paul Revere was taken captive.
    (D) Dr. Prescott failed to get through.

GO ON TO THE NEXT PAGE →

18. The word "deed" in line 12 is closest in meaning to

    (A) speech
    (B) story
    (C) battle
    (D) act

19. Where in the passage does the author indicate who actually carried out the warning?

    (A) Lines 2–3
    (B) Line 5
    (C) Line 8
    (D) Lines 9–11

GO ON TO THE NEXT PAGE

Questions 20–29

The name Studebaker is well known today because of the actions of five Studebaker brothers. These five brothers were responsible for one of the oldest vehicle manufacturing companies in the United States.

Line
(5) These brothers were born in the first half of the nineteenth century. In 1852, two of the Studebaker brothers opened a wagon-building shop. Their entire resources were some tools for building wagons and 68 dollars. They managed to build three wagons in their first year of operations, and they sold two of the three wagons. Their business continued to increase steadily. By the time of the Civil War in the 1860s, they had a government contract to build wagons for the war effort.

(10) After the war, the brothers added a carriage division. The carriages created by the Studebaker Company became famous. At the end of the nineteenth century, the Studebaker Company was the largest and best-known manufacturer of horse-drawn wagons and carriages in the world.

In 1897, the company started experimenting with vehicles that ran under their own power. The company began making electric automobiles first and later worked on gasoline automobiles. By
(15) 1920, the company had stopped making wagons and was producing cars. The Studebaker Company stayed in business until 1966, when it stopped producing automobiles.

20. The best title for this passage would be

(A) One Family's Joys and Sorrows
(B) Building Better Wagons
(C) A Long-Lived Company
(D) The Effort to Win the War

21. When the Studebaker brothers started their first company, they had

(A) a number of wagons
(B) a government contract to build wagons
(C) some tools for working on cars
(D) a small amount of money

22. The word "managed" in line 6 could best be replaced by

(A) organized
(B) were able
(C) directed
(D) were available

23. It can be inferred from the passage that, right after the Civil War, the Studebaker brothers

(A) continued building wagons
(B) stopped producing carriages
(C) started producing automobiles
(D) stopped building wagons

24. The word "famous" in line 11 is closest in meaning to

(A) profitable
(B) well built
(C) attractive
(D) well known

25. According to the passage, the Studebaker brothers

(A) developed gasoline cars before electric cars
(B) stopped producing wagons in 1897
(C) developed electric cars before gasoline cars
(D) began making cars in 1920

26. The word "stayed" in line 16 is closest in meaning to

(A) remained
(B) held
(C) left
(D) managed

GO ON TO THE NEXT PAGE

27. What is NOT mentioned in the passage as something that the Studebaker brothers produced?

    (A) Wagons
    (B) Carriages
    (C) Cars
    (D) Boats

28. Which paragraph describes the business activities of the Studebaker brothers prior to the Civil War?

    (A) The first paragraph
    (B) The second paragraph
    (C) The third paragraph
    (D) The fourth paragraph

29. Where in the passage does the author explain what the Studebaker brothers did in their first year of business?

    (A) Lines 2–3
    (B) Lines 6–7
    (C) Line 10
    (D) Line 14

GO ON TO THE NEXT PAGE

Questions 30–38

Not all humans have the same type of blood. In different types of blood, certain antibodies and antigens may or may not be present. There are different systems for classifying blood, and one of the systems is the ABO system. In this system, a person's blood is classified as either type A, type B, type AB, or type O. The purpose of this system is to describe which types of blood are compatible. This means which types of blood can be taken from or given to a person. There are three principles that govern which types of blood are compatible.

The first principle is that a particular blood type is always compatible with itself. This means, for example, that a person with type A blood can receive type A blood and that a person with type B blood can accept type B blood. It also means that a person with type AB blood can receive type AB blood and that a person with type O blood can receive type O blood.

The second principle is that type O blood can be given to any of the other blood groups. Type O can be given to a patient with types A, B, or AB blood. For this reason, type O is called the universal donor.

The last of the principles is that patients with type AB blood can receive blood from types A, B, or O. This means that patients with type AB blood can compatibly receive any other type of blood.

Line
(5)

(10)

(15)

30. The topic of this passage is

   (A) a particular type of blood
   (B) a system for classifying types of blood
   (C) examples of problems with blood
   (D) the principle of universal donors

31. It is stated in the passage that certain antibodies and antigens in the blood

   (A) are omitted from the ABO system
   (B) have not been classified
   (C) are universal donors
   (D) may not be in all blood

32. "Principles" in line 6 are

   (A) leaders
   (B) effects
   (C) rules
   (D) trials

33. The word "particular" in line 7 is closest in meaning to

   (A) rare
   (B) strange
   (C) specific
   (D) normal

34. It can be inferred from the passage that type A blood can

   (A) accept type A or O blood
   (B) accept type O or AB blood
   (C) accept type A or AB blood
   (D) accept type A or B blood

35. A "donor" in line 13 is most likely someone who

   (A) receives
   (B) gives
   (C) shows
   (D) takes

36. It can be inferred from the passage that type AB blood can be donated to

   (A) type A, B, O, or AB
   (B) type A or AB blood only
   (C) type O or AB blood only
   (D) type AB blood only

GO ON TO THE NEXT PAGE ➜

37. Which paragraph describes the author's third important concept about blood compatibility?

   (A) The first paragraph
   (B) The second paragraph
   (C) The third paragraph
   (D) The fourth paragraph

38. Where in the passage does the author indicate how many types of blood there are in the ABO system?

   (A) Lines 3–4
   (B) Line 5
   (C) Lines 9–10
   (D) Lines 14–15

GO ON TO THE NEXT PAGE ➡

Questions 39–50

The U.S. manned space flight program of the 1960s and 1970s consisted of three distinct phases: Mercury, Gemini, and Apollo. Each of these distinct phases of the space flight program served a very different purpose.

Line
(5) Mercury was the first phase of the manned space flight program. Its purpose was to get a person into orbital flight. The tiny Mercury capsule carried only a single astronaut. Alan Shepard and Virgil Grissom piloted the first two Mercury flights, which were suborbital flights, in 1961. John Glenn, in the next Mercury flight, orbited the Earth in 1962. Three more Mercury flights followed.

The next phase of the manned space flight program was Gemini. The purpose of the ten crewed Gemini flights in 1965 and 1966 was to conduct training tests necessary for longer space flights.
(10) Gemini, for example, carried out training in orbital clocking techniques and tests of the effects of long-term weightlessness on astronauts. Unlike Mercury capsules, which held only one astronaut, the Gemini capsules were designed to carry two astronauts. The name Gemini was taken from the name of the constellation, which means "twins."

The Apollo flights followed the Gemini flights with the goal of landing astronauts on the Moon.
(15) The Apollo spacecraft consisted of three modules. The command module carried three astronauts to and from the Moon, the service module housed the propulsion and environmental systems, and the lunar module separated from the command module to land two astronauts on the Moon. There were seventeen total Apollo flights, of which the first six carried no crew. The seventh through tenth Apollo flights (1968–1969) circumnavigated the Moon without landing and then returned to Earth.
(20) The next seven Apollo flights (1969–1972) were intended to land on the Moon. All of them did, except *Apollo 13*, which developed serious problems and had to abort the intended landing but still managed to return safely to Earth.

39. The subject of this passage is

    (A) lunar landings
    (B) the Gemini flights
    (C) phases of the U.S. space flight program
    (D) space exploration through the decades

40. According to the passage, the Mercury flights

    (A) were all suborbital flights
    (B) did not include any orbital flights
    (C) were all orbital flights
    (D) included suborbital and orbital flights

41. It is implied in the passage that there were how many total Mercury flights?

    (A) Three
    (B) Four
    (C) Five
    (D) Six

42. The word "crewed" in line 8 is closest in meaning to

    (A) endangered
    (B) manned
    (C) organized
    (D) tested

43. The purpose of the Gemini flights was

    (A) to prepare for longer space flights
    (B) to attempt suborbital flights
    (C) to circumnavigate the Moon
    (D) to land on the Moon

44. It is NOT stated in the passage

    (A) how many astronauts a Mercury flight carried
    (B) how many astronauts a Gemini flight carried
    (C) how the Mercury flights were named
    (D) how the Gemini flights were named

GO ON TO THE NEXT PAGE

45. It can be inferred from the passage that how many of the Apollo flights carried astronauts?

    (A) 6
    (B) 11
    (C) 16
    (D) 17

46. The word "circumnavigated" in line 19 is closest in meaning to

    (A) traveled around
    (B) returned from
    (C) studied about
    (D) headed toward

47. It can be determined from the passage that how many Apollo flights landed on the moon?

    (A) 1
    (B) 6
    (C) 11
    (D) 17

48. The word "abort" in line 21 is closest in meaning to

    (A) postpone
    (B) schedule
    (C) try
    (D) stop

49. It can be determined from the passage that the manned space flight program discussed in the passage lasted for

    (A) two years
    (B) just over 6 years
    (C) almost 12 years
    (D) three decades

50. Which paragraph describes the flights that carried one astronaut each?

    (A) The first paragraph
    (B) The second paragraph
    (C) The third paragraph
    (D) The fourth paragraph

This is the end of Section 3.

**If you finish in less than 55 minutes,
check your work on Section 3 only.
Do NOT read or work on any other section of the test.**

TEST OF WRITTEN ENGLISH:
TWE ESSAY TOPIC
Time—30 minutes

Do you agree or disagree with the following statement?

There is too much violence in movies and on television.

Use specific details and examples to support your response.

COMPLETE TEST THREE
TOEFL LEVEL

SECTION 1
LISTENING COMPREHENSION
Time—approximately 35 minutes
(including the reading of the directions for each part)

In this section of the test, you will have an opportunity to demonstrate your ability to understand conversations and talks in English. There are three parts to this section, with special directions for each part. Answer all the questions on the basis of what is **stated** or **implied** by the speakers you hear. Do **not** take notes or write in your test book at any time. Do **not** turn the pages until you are told to do so.

Part A

Directions: In Part A you will hear short conversations between two people. After each conversation, you will hear a question about the conversation. The conversations and questions will not be repeated. After you hear a question, read the four possible answers in your test book and choose the best answer. Then, on your answer sheet, find the number of the question and fill in the space that corresponds to the letter of the answer you have chosen.

Here is an example.

On the recording, you will hear:

(man)   *That exam was just awful.*
(woman)   *Oh, it could have been worse.*
(narrator) *What does the woman mean?*

Sample Answer
Ⓐ
Ⓑ
Ⓒ
●

In your test book, you will read: (A) The exam was really awful.
                                    (B) It was the worst exam she had ever seen.
                                    (C) It couldn't have been more difficult.
                                    (D) It wasn't that hard.

You learn from the conversation that the man thought the exam was very difficult and that the woman disagreed with the man. The best answer to the question, "What does the woman mean?" is (D), "It wasn't that hard." Therefore, the correct choice is (D).

Wait

1. (A) She doesn't want to do it.
   (B) It is simple to do.
   (C) She doesn't know what it is.
   (D) It is fun to watch.

2. (A) It was boring.
   (B) It was exactly right.
   (C) It was too literal.
   (D) It was quite interesting.

3. (A) Not fighting anymore.
   (B) Flying in the fall instead.
   (C) Training the pets.
   (D) Going by railroad.

4. (A) They had some soup.
   (B) They gave her a present.
   (C) They have been fed.
   (D) They prepared supper.

5. (A) She was mainly at home.
   (B) She stayed at school during vacation.
   (C) She went camping during the holidays.
   (D) She was captain of the team for the remaining days.

6. (A) A doctor.
   (B) A secretary.
   (C) A waiter.
   (D) A police officer.

7. (A) The stereo is chipped.
   (B) He's going to try the system.
   (C) The stereo's too expensive.
   (D) He decided to buy the system.

8. (A) Sing a little louder.
   (B) Start the song one more time.
   (C) Begin studying music.
   (D) Try to learn to play the game.

9. (A) Mail the papers quickly.
   (B) Send the information to the newspaper office.
   (C) Wrap a box in tissue paper.
   (D) Read the papers soon.

10. (A) He doesn't like to talk about work.
    (B) He works very hard at school.
    (C) He goes to the same school as the woman.
    (D) He agrees with the woman.

11. (A) In a department store.
    (B) In a barber shop.
    (C) In a flower shop.
    (D) In a restaurant.

12. (A) She's not running.
    (B) Her hat is not ruined.
    (C) The weather is dry.
    (D) It's going to rain.

13. (A) No more money can be spent.
    (B) The money has to last.
    (C) An estimation is satisfactory.
    (D) The numbers must be exact.

14. (A) Robin is looking for a new car.
    (B) She thinks that Robin's car is pretty great, too.
    (C) Robin is certain about the changes.
    (D) The tire pressure in Robin's car is not right.

15. (A) The desk is disorganized.
    (B) He needs to measure the desk.
    (C) Wanda's dress is a mess.
    (D) Wanda's always at her desk.

16. (A) A detective.
    (B) A store clerk.
    (C) A librarian.
    (D) A writer.

17. (A) Buying a new computer.
    (B) Attending a course.
    (C) Watching a television program.
    (D) Computing the correct answer.

GO ON TO THE NEXT PAGE

18. (A) He is trying to become a ticket agent.
    (B) All the tickets have been sold.
    (C) The ticket agent bought the tickets.
    (D) He was able to sell his concert tickets.

19. (A) He dropped out of school.
    (B) He wanted to know when school ended.
    (C) He questioned her reasons.
    (D) He dropped her off at school.

20. (A) The post office was close by.
    (B) She was scared of what was in the package.
    (C) The post office was closed when she got there.
    (D) She was able to send the package.

21. (A) He was late for the boat.
    (B) He could have taken the boat to the bank.
    (C) He lost a good opportunity.
    (D) He missed seeing his friend at the bank.

22. (A) Her best guess is that the lecture's about to start.
    (B) She's not really sure.
    (C) The man's lecture is as good as hers.
    (D) She guesses the lecture will be good.

23. (A) He's heard of a new program for next semester.
    (B) It's been done before.
    (C) Only fools take five courses.
    (D) He can handle four courses.

24. (A) They should visit their new neighbors.
    (B) The new family called to her.
    (C) They should move to the apartment across the hall.
    (D) It would be a good idea to phone the new family.

25. (A) The police officer didn't really stop him.
    (B) He is quite unhappy about what happened.
    (C) He's not unhappy even though he got a ticket.
    (D) He didn't get a ticket.

26. (A) He should have his head examined.
    (B) He should run in the race, too.
    (C) He needs to hit the nails harder.
    (D) He's exactly right.

27. (A) The scholarship was not a surprise.
    (B) He was amazed that he won.
    (C) The music was surprisingly beautiful.
    (D) The Music Department won a prize.

28. (A) He has a date tonight.
    (B) He needs to brush off his clothes.
    (C) He knows the date of the history exam.
    (D) He needs to review a bit.

29. (A) He would not attend the wedding.
    (B) He had already made the decision to go.
    (C) He was deciding what to wear.
    (D) He would wear a different suit to the wedding.

30. (A) It wasn't really his first time skiing.
    (B) He didn't try the steepest slope.
    (C) He tried to do too much.
    (D) He didn't need to learn how to ski.

GO ON TO THE NEXT PAGE

Part B

Directions: In this part of the test, you will hear longer conversations. After each conversation, you will hear several questions. The conversations and questions will not be repeated.

After you hear a question, read the four possible answers in your test book and choose the best answer. Then, on your answer sheet, find the number of the question and fill in the space that corresponds to the letter of the answer you have chosen.

Remember, you are **not** allowed to take notes or write in your test book.

31. (A) At a museum.
    (B) In the park.
    (C) At a shopping center.
    (D) In an artist's studio.

32. (A) Every afternoon.
    (B) Each week.
    (C) Twice a month.
    (D) Once a year.

33. (A) Paintings.
    (B) Jewelry
    (C) Animals.
    (D) Pottery.

34. (A) Buy something.
    (B) Lose her wallet.
    (C) Head for home.
    (D) Stay away from the fair.

35. (A) He's attending the same physics
        lecture as she is.
    (B) He knows about the physics course.
    (C) He works in the physics laboratory.
    (D) They are working on a lab report
        together.

36. (A) One.
    (B) Two.
    (C) Three.
    (D) Four.

37. (A) One.
    (B) Two.
    (C) Three.
    (D) Four.

38. (A) It is fun.
    (B) It is interesting.
    (C) It requires little time.
    (D) It is difficult to understand.

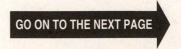

GO ON TO THE NEXT PAGE

Part C

Directions: In Part C of this section, you will hear several talks. After each talk, you will hear some questions. The talks and questions will not be repeated.

After you hear a question, you will read the four possible answers in your test book and choose the best answer. Then, on your answer sheet, find the number of the question and fill in the space that corresponds to the letter of the answer you have chosen.

Here is an example.

On the recording, you will hear:

(narrator) *Listen to an instructor talk to his class about painting.*

(man) *Artist Grant Wood was a guiding force in the school of painting known as American regionalist, a style reflecting the distinctive characteristics of art from rural areas of the United States. Wood began drawing animals on the family farm at the age of three, and when he was thirty-eight one of his paintings received a remarkable amount of public notice and acclaim. This painting, called* American Gothic, *is a starkly simple depiction of a serious couple staring directly out at the viewer.*

Now listen to a sample question.

Sample Answer

(narrator) *What style of painting is known as American regionalist?*

Ⓐ
Ⓑ
Ⓒ
●

In your test book, you will read: (A) Art from America's inner cities.
(B) Art from the central region of the United States.
(C) Art from various urban areas in the United States.
(D) Art from rural sections of America.

The best answer to the question, "What style of painting is known as American regionalist?" is (D), "Art from rural sections of America." Therefore, the correct choice is (D).

Now listen to another sample question.

Sample Answer

(narrator) *What is the name of Wood's most successful painting?*

Ⓐ
Ⓑ
●
Ⓓ

In your test book, you will read: (A) *American Regionalist.*
(B) *The Family Farm in Iowa.*
(C) *American Gothic.*
(D) *A Serious Couple.*

The best answer to the question, "What is the name of Wood's most successful painting?" is (C), *American Gothic.* Therefore, the correct choice is (C).

Remember, you are **not** allowed to take notes or write in your test book.

Wait

39. (A) Just before the start of the semester.
    (B) Just before class.
    (C) At the end of a class.
    (D) After the end of the semester.

40. (A) Two days.
    (B) Two weeks.
    (C) Two months.
    (D) Two semesters.

41. (A) By seven o'clock.
    (B) By five o'clock.
    (C) By ten o'clock.
    (D) By twelve o'clock.

42. (A) Ten.
    (B) Eleven.
    (C) Twelve.
    (D) Thirteen.

43. (A) They fight fires.
    (B) They start fires.
    (C) They smoke.
    (D) They build roads.

44. (A) By walking.
    (B) By firetruck.
    (C) By road.
    (D) By parachute.

45. (A) When the fire is small.
    (B) When there are no roads leading to
        the fire.
    (C) When there is a lot of smoke.
    (D) When there is a lot of time to fight the
        fire.

46. (A) Rest.
    (B) Return to their airplanes.
    (C) Walk to a road.
    (D) Go for a parachute jump.

47. (A) Geology.
    (B) Biology.
    (C) Art History.
    (D) Food and Nutrition.

48. (A) By drilling into volcanoes.
    (B) By counting the layers of ice.
    (C) By studying volcanoes.
    (D) By dusting the glacier.

49. (A) Layers of rust.
    (B) Active volcanoes.
    (C) Volcanic dust.
    (D) Old drills.

50. (A) Visit a glacier.
    (B) Prepare for a test.
    (C) Learn about volcanoes.
    (D) Read the next chapter.

This is the end of Section 1.
Stop work on Section 1.

Turn off the recording.

Read the directions for Section 2 and begin work.
Do NOT read or work on any other section
of the test during the next 25 minutes.

SECTION 2
STRUCTURE AND WRITTEN EXPRESSION
Time—25 minutes
(including the reading of the directions)
Now set your clock for 25 minutes.

This section is designed to measure your ability to recognize language that is appropriate for standard written English. There are two types of questions in this section, with special directions for each type.

Structure

Directions: These questions are incomplete sentences. Beneath each sentence you will see four words or phrases, marked (A), (B), (C), and (D). Choose the **one** word or phrase that best completes the sentence. Then, on your answer sheet, find the number of the question and fill in the space that corresponds to the letter of the answer you have chosen.

Look at the following examples.

Example I

The president _____ the election by a landslide.

(A) won
(B) he won
(C) yesterday
(D) fortunately

Sample Answer

● (B) (C) (D)

The sentence should read, "The president won the election by a landslide." Therefore, you should choose answer (A).

Example II

When _____ the conference?

(A) the doctor attended
(B) did the doctor attend
(C) the doctor will attend
(D) the doctor's attendance

Sample Answer

(A) ● (C) (D)

The sentence should read, "When did the doctor attend the conference?" Therefore, you should choose answer (B).

GO ON TO THE NEXT PAGE

1. _____ on the first Saturday in May at Churchill Downs.

   (A) For the running of the Kentucky Derby
   (B) The Kentucky Derby is run
   (C) To run the Kentucky Derby
   (D) When the Kentucky Derby is run

2. According to _____ quantum mechanics, it is normally impossible to pinpoint the orbit of an electron bond to an atom.

   (A) the related laws
   (B) the laws are related
   (C) the laws of
   (D) the laws are related to

3. Chicago is home to more than 4 million people _____ as many as 54 languages and dialects.

   (A) speak
   (B) they speak
   (C) spoke
   (D) speaking

4. When Mexico ceded California to the United States in 1848, signers of the treaty did not know _____ had been discovered there.

   (A) golden
   (B) that with gold
   (C) that gold
   (D) with gold

5. Rubber came to the attention of Europeans _____ found Native Americans using it.

   (A) explorers
   (B) after explorers
   (C) when explored
   (D) after explorers they

6. Most asteroids are located in _____ called the asteroid belt.

   (A) what is
   (B) what is in
   (C) is what
   (D) is it

7. About three-fourths of the books published in the United States are put out by publishers _____ in New York City.

   (A) locates
   (B) located
   (C) they locate
   (D) they are located

8. The physical phenomenon _____ use to obtain water from the soil is osmosis.

   (A) plants have roots
   (B) that plant roots
   (C) what plant roots
   (D) plants are rooted

9. More books have been written about the Civil War _____ any other war in history.

   (A) that there is
   (B) about
   (C) of
   (D) than about

10. A sheet of clear glass, _____ with a film of metal, results in a luminously clear mirror.

    (A) when backed
    (B) it is backed
    (C) is backed
    (D) when is it backed

11. The Liberty Bell, _____ its own pavilion on Independence Mall, hung for nearly a century at Independence Hall.

    (A) that now has
    (B) now has
    (C) when does it have
    (D) which now has

GO ON TO THE NEXT PAGE →

12. Not until about 8,000 years ago _____ come into use.

   (A) bronze tools for weapons
   (B) bronze tools for weapons have
   (C) bronze tools for weapons were to
   (D) did bronze tools for weapons

13. The state of Michigan can rightfully claim to be a "Water Wonderland" _____ has a 3,121-mile shoreline.

   (A) because
   (B) that
   (C) in that it
   (D) that it

14. _____ glacial sediment, the moister the surface soil becomes.

   (A) It is thicker
   (B) In the thick
   (C) The thicker the
   (D) The thick

15. _____ cut away, the wheel could be strengthened with struts or crossbars.

   (A) Were large sections of a wheel
   (B) Large sections of a wheel
   (C) Large sections of a wheel were
   (D) Large sections of a wheel to

GO ON TO THE NEXT PAGE →

Written Expression

Directions: In these questions, each sentence has four underlined words or phrases. The four underlined parts of the sentence are marked (A), (B), (C), and (D). Identify the **one** underlined word or phrase that must be changed in order for the sentence to be correct. Then, on your answer sheet, find the number of the question and fill in the space that corresponds to the letter of the answer you have chosen.

Look at the following examples.

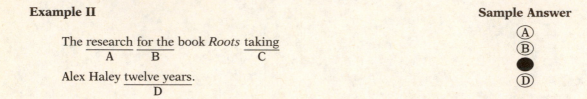

Example I   **Sample Answer**

The four string on a violin are tuned

  A   B   C   D

in fifths.

Ⓐ ● Ⓒ Ⓓ

The sentence should read, "The four strings on a violin are tuned in fifths." Therefore, you should choose answer (B).

Example II   **Sample Answer**

The research for the book *Roots* taking

    A   B   C

Alex Haley twelve years.

          D

Ⓐ Ⓑ ● Ⓓ

The sentence should read, "The research for the book *Roots* took Alex Haley twelve years." Therefore, you should choose answer (C).

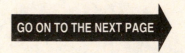

GO ON TO THE NEXT PAGE

16. Various chemical element have more than one isotope.
            A   B   C D

17. Top management must took a hard look at its current product lines to see if resources can be
                     A   B C   D

    reallocated.

18. Today, the glaciers of the world occupies about 10 percent of the Earth's surface.
      A   B   C   D

19. Polystyrene comes in both a hard form or a lightweight foam.
                A   B   C   D

20. Although the bow and arrow were first invented in the Mesolithic Period, it continued to be used
                               A   B   C

    for hunting in the early Neolithic Period.
        D

21. An understanding of latent heat became importantly in the improvement of the steam engine.
     A   B   C   D

22. Only a few mineral can resist weathering by rain water, which is a weak acid.
        A   B   C   D

23. The Stanley brothers built their first small steam car in 1897, and 200 were sell by the end of the
                   A   B   C D

    first year.

24. All of the Great Lakes is in the United States and Canada except Lake Michigan, which is entirely
                     A   B   C   D

    in the United States.

25. Kangaroos sometimes rest or groom themselves while they are sitting on them hind legs.
                       A   B   C   D

26. Despite the turmoil of the Civil War, the relative new game of "base-ball" attracted great numbers
     A   B   C   D

    of spectators.

27. Anyone who takes the Rorschach test for personality traits are asked to interpret a series of
         A B   C   D

    inkblots.

GO ON TO THE NEXT PAGE ➡

28. Alexander Hamilton's financial program included a central bank to serve the Treasury, provide a
                                            A   B
depository for public money, and regulation of the currency.
                                     C   D

29. In 1890, the city of Pasadena has started sponsorship of the Tournament of Roses Parade on New
                                   A   B   C
Year's morning.
       D

30. The Louisiana state legal system is based with the legal system established by Napoleon.
                           A   B   C   D

31. The White House was designed by James Hobar, an Irishman whom the proposal in the design
                              A   B   C
competition won $500.
          D

32. Fuel cells, alike batteries, generate electricity by chemical reaction.
          A   B   C   D

33. The Virginia Company, which founded colony at Jamestown, sent over glassmakers from Poland
                            A   B
with the intention of developing the glass-making industry in the New World.
                  C   D

34. Of the more than 1,300 volcanoes in the world, only about 600 can classify as active.
                   A   B   C   D

35. Ben Franklin, needing one set of lenses for distant vision and other for near vision, devised
                 A   B   C   D
bifocals in 1784.

36. Key West traces its modern settlement to an American business who purchased the island in 1882.
             A   B   C   D

37. The Indianapolis 500 race is run each Memorial Day weekend on the two-and-a-half-miles Motor
                        A   B   C
Speedway track outside of Indianapolis.
                  D

38. The streets of Salt Lake City were laid out wide enough for an ox cart to do a turn
                                A   B   C
without brushing the curb.
    D

GO ON TO THE NEXT PAGE →

39. Most of the vertebrae have two flanges, or wings, one on each side, calling transverse processes.
    A   B   C   D

40. Overlooking the Hudson River in New York, the Cloisters includes parts several medieval
    A   B   C

monasteries and chapels brought from Europe.
                       D

This is the end of Section 2.
If you finish before 25 minutes has ended,
check your work on Section 2 only.

At the end of 25 minutes, go on to Section 3.
Use exactly 55 minutes to work on Section 3.

SECTION 3
READING COMPREHENSION
Time—55 minutes
(including the reading of the directions)
Now set your clock for 55 minutes.

This section is designed to measure your ability to read and understand short passages similar in topic and style to those that students are likely to encounter in North American universities and colleges. This section contains reading passages and questions about the passages.

Directions: In this section you will read several passages. Each one is followed by a number of questions about it. You are to choose the **one** best answer, (A), (B), (C), or (D), to each question. Then, on your answer sheet, find the number of the question and fill in the space that corresponds to the letter of the answer you have chosen.

Answer all questions about the information in a passage on the basis of what is **stated** or **implied** in that passage.

Read the following passage:

> John Quincy Adams, who served as the sixth president of the United States from 1825 to 1829, is today recognized for his masterful statesmanship and diplomacy. He dedicated his life to public service, both in the presidency and in the various other political offices that he held.
> *Line* Throughout his political career he demonstrated his unswerving belief in freedom of speech, the
> *(5)* antislavery cause, and the right of Americans to be free from European and Asian domination.

Example I   **Sample Answer**

To what did John Quincy Adams devote his life?   Ⓐ
                                                                ●
(A) Improving his personal life   Ⓒ
(B) Serving the public   Ⓓ
(C) Increasing his fortune
(D) Working on his private business

According to the passage, John Quincy Adams "dedicated his life to public service." Therefore, you should choose answer (B).

Example II   **Sample Answer**

In line 4, the word "unswerving" is closest in meaning to   Ⓐ
                                                                Ⓑ
(A) moveable   ●
(B) insignificant   Ⓓ
(C) unchanging
(D) diplomatic

The passage states that John Quincy Adams demonstrated his unswerving belief "throughout his career." This implies that the belief did not change. Therefore, you should choose answer (C).

GO ON TO THE NEXT PAGE

Questions 1–10

The Hollywood sign in the hills that line the northern border of Los Angeles is a famous landmark recognized the world over. The white-painted, 50-foot-high, sheet metal letters can be seen from great distances across the Los Angeles basin.

Line
(5) The sign was not constructed, as one might suppose, by the movie business as a means of celebrating the importance of Hollywood to this industry; instead, it was first constructed in 1923 as a means of advertising homes for sale in a 500-acre housing subdivision in a part of Los Angeles called "Hollywoodland." The sign that was constructed at the time of course said "Hollywoodland." Over the years, people began referring to the area by the shortened version "Hollywood," and after the sign and its site were donated to the city in 1945, the last four letters were removed.

(10) The sign suffered from years of disrepair, and in 1973 it needed to be completely replaced, at a cost of $27,700 per letter. Various celebrities were instrumental in helping to raise needed funds. Rock star Alice Cooper, for example, bought an O in memory of Groucho Marx, and Hugh Hefner of *Playboy* fame held a benefit party to raise the money for the Y. The construction of the new sign was finally completed in 1978.

1. What is the topic of this passage?

   (A) A famous sign
   (B) A famous city
   (C) World landmarks
   (D) Hollywood versus Hollywoodland

2. The expression "the world over" in line 2 could best be replaced by

   (A) in the northern parts of the world
   (B) on top of the world
   (C) in the entire world
   (D) in the skies

3. It can be inferred from the passage that most people think that the Hollywood sign was first constructed by

   (A) an advertising company
   (B) the movie industry
   (C) a construction company
   (D) the city of Los Angeles

4. The pronoun "it" in line 5 refers to

   (A) the sign
   (B) the movie business
   (C) the importance of Hollywood
   (D) this industry

5. According to the passage, the Hollywood sign was first built in

   (A) 1923
   (B) 1949
   (C) 1973
   (D) 1978

6. Which of the following is NOT mentioned about Hollywoodland?

   (A) It used to be the name of an area of Los Angeles.
   (B) It was formerly the name on the sign in the hills.
   (C) There were houses for sale there.
   (D) It was the most expensive area of Los Angeles.

7. The passage indicates that the sign suffered because

   (A) people damaged it
   (B) it was not fixed
   (C) the weather was bad
   (D) it was poorly constructed

GO ON TO THE NEXT PAGE →

8. It can be inferred from the passage that the Hollywood sign was how old when it was necessary to totally replace it?

   (A) Ten years old
   (B) Twenty-six years old
   (C) Fifty years old
   (D) Fifty-five years old

9. The word "replaced" in line 10 is closest in meaning to which of the following?

   (A) Moved to a new location
   (B) Destroyed
   (C) Found again
   (D) Exchanged for a newer one

10. According to the passage, how did celebrities help with the new sign?

    (A) They played instruments.
    (B) They raised the sign.
    (C) They helped get the money.
    (D) They took part in work parties to build the sign.

GO ON TO THE NEXT PAGE →

Questions 11–20

For hundreds of years in the early history of America, pirates sailed through coastal waters, pillaging and plundering all in their path. They stole from other ships and stole from coastal towns; not content only to steal, they destroyed everything they could not carry away. Some of the pirate
Line ships amassed large treasures, the fates of which are unknown, leaving people of today to wonder at
(5) their whereabouts and to dream of one day coming across some lost treasure.

One notoriously large treasure was on the pirate ship *Whidah,* which sank in the waters off Cape Cod during a strong storm in 1717. A hundred of the crew members went down with the ship, along with its treasure of coins, gold, silver, and jewels. The treasure on board had an estimated value, on today's market, of more than 100 million dollars.
(10) The remains of the *Whidah* were discovered in 1984 by Barry Clifford, who had spent years of painstaking research and tireless searching, only to finally locate the ship about 500 yards from shore. A considerable amount of treasure from the centuries-old ship has been recovered from its watery grave, but there is clearly still a lot more out there. Just as a reminder of what the waters off the coast have been protecting for hundreds of years, occasional pieces of gold, or silver, or jewels
(15) still wash up on the beaches, and lucky beachgoers find pieces of the treasure.

11. The passage mainly discusses

    (A) early pirates
    (B) a large pirate treasure
    (C) what really happened to the *Whidah*'s pirates
    (D) why people go to the beach

12. It is NOT mentioned in the passage that pirates did which of the following?

    (A) They killed lots of people.
    (B) They robbed other ships.
    (C) They took things from towns.
    (D) They gathered big treasures.

13. The word "amassed" in line 4 is closest in meaning to

    (A) sold
    (B) hid
    (C) transported
    (D) gathered

14. It is implied in the passage that the *Whidah*'s crew

    (A) died
    (B) went diving
    (C) searched for the treasure
    (D) escaped with parts of the treasure

15. Which of the following is NOT mentioned as part of the treasure of the *Whidah*?

    (A) Art objects
    (B) Coins
    (C) Gold and silver
    (D) Jewels

16. The word "estimated" in line 8 is closest in meaning to which of the following?

    (A) Known
    (B) Sold
    (C) Approximate
    (D) Decided

17. The passage indicates that the cargo of the *Whidah* is worth about

    (A) $10,000
    (B) $100,000
    (C) $10,000,000
    (D) $100,000,000

GO ON TO THE NEXT PAGE ➤

18. The work that Barry Clifford did to locate the *Whidah* was NOT

    (A) successful
    (B) effortless
    (C) detailed
    (D) lengthy

19. It is mentioned in the passage that the treasure of the *Whidah*

    (A) is not very valuable
    (B) is all in museums
    (C) has not all been found
    (D) was taken to shore by the pirates

20. The paragraph following the passage most likely discusses

    (A) what Barry Clifford is doing today
    (B) the fate of the *Whidah*'s crew
    (C) other storms in the area of Cape Cod
    (D) additional pieces that turn up from the *Whidah*'s treasure

GO ON TO THE NEXT PAGE

Questions 21–30

It is a characteristic of human nature that people like to get together and have fun, and people living during America's frontier days were no exception. However, because life was hard and the necessities of day-to-day living took up their time, it was common for recreation to be combined
Line with activities necessary for survival.
(5)   One example of such a form of recreation was logrolling. Many frontier areas were heavily wooded, and in order to settle an area it was necessary to remove the trees. A settler could cut down the trees alone, but help was needed to move the cut trees. After a settler had cut a bunch of trees, he would then invite his neighbors over for a logrolling.
    A logrolling was a community event where families got together for a combination of work and
(10) fun. The women would bring food and have a much needed and infrequent opportunity to relax and chat with friends, the children would play together exuberantly, and the men would hold lively competitions that involved rolling logs from place to place as quickly as possible. This was a day of fun for everyone involved, but at its foundation was the need to clear the land.

21. The main idea of the passage is that in America's frontier days

    (A) people combined work with recreation
    (B) people cleared land by rolling logs
    (C) it was necessary for early settlers to clear the land
    (D) a logrolling involved the community

22. The expression "day-to-day" in line 3 could best be replaced by which of the following?

    (A) Daytime
    (B) Everyday
    (C) Day after day
    (D) Today's

23. The word "survival" in line 4 is closest in meaning to

    (A) existence
    (B) a lifetime
    (C) physical exercise
    (D) society

24. According to the passage, what did people have to do first to settle an area?

    (A) Develop recreation ideas
    (B) Build farms
    (C) Get rid of the trees
    (D) Invite neighbors over

25. According to the passage, which of the following is NOT true about a logrolling?

    (A) It involved a lot of people.
    (B) It could be enjoyable.
    (C) There could be a lot of movement.
    (D) It was rather quiet.

26. The word "chat" in line 11 means

    (A) work
    (B) talk
    (C) cook
    (D) eat

27. The word "exuberantly" in line 11 is closest in meaning to

    (A) privately
    (B) laboriously
    (C) enthusiastically
    (D) neatly

28. It can be inferred from the passage that competitions were held because

    (A) it was the only way to move the logs
    (B) competition made the work fun
    (C) men refused to help unless there was competition
    (D) the children could then help move the logs

GO ON TO THE NEXT PAGE ➡

29. Where in the passage does the author indicate what a settler did when he had a number of cut trees?

    (A) Lines 2–4
    (B) Line 5
    (C) Lines 7–8
    (D) Lines 9–10

30. This passage would most probably be assigned reading in which of the following courses?

    (A) Forestry
    (B) Environmental Studies
    (C) Psychology
    (D) History

GO ON TO THE NEXT PAGE

Questions 31–40

Most people picture sharks as huge, powerful, frightening predators, ready at any moment to use their sharp teeth to attack unwary swimmers without provocation. There are numerous fallacies, however, in this conception of sharks.

Line
(5) First, there are about 350 species of shark, and not all of them are large. They range in size from the dwarf shark, which can be only 6 inches (.5 feet) long and can be held in the palm of the hand, to the whale shark, which can be more than 55 feet long.

A second fallacy concerns the number and type of teeth, which can vary tremendously among the different species of shark. A shark can have from one to seven sets of teeth at the same time, and some types of shark can have several hundred teeth in each jaw. It is true that the fierce and
(10) predatory species do possess extremely sharp and brutal teeth used to rip their prey apart; many other types of shark, however, have teeth more adapted to grabbing and holding than to cutting and slashing.

Finally, not all sharks are predatory animals ready to strike out at humans on the least whim. In fact, only 12 of the 350 species of shark have been known to attack humans, and a shark needs to be
(15) provoked in order to attack. The types of shark that have the worst record with humans are the tiger shark, the bull shark, and the great white shark. However, for most species of shark, even some of the largest types, there are no known instances of attacks on humans.

31. The author's main purpose in the passage is to

    (A) categorize the different kinds of sharks throughout the world
    (B) warn humans of the dangers posed by sharks
    (C) describe the characteristics of shark teeth
    (D) clear up misconceptions about sharks

32. The word "unwary" in line 2 is closest in meaning to

    (A) strong
    (B) combative
    (C) careless
    (D) fearful

33. "Dwarf" in line 5 refers to something that is probably

    (A) large
    (B) powerful
    (C) dangerous
    (D) short

34. The longest shark is probably the

    (A) whale shark
    (B) great white shark
    (C) bull shark
    (D) tiger shark

35. Which of the following is NOT true about a shark's teeth?

    (A) All sharks have teeth.
    (B) A shark can have six rows of teeth.
    (C) A shark can have hundreds of teeth.
    (D) All sharks have extremely sharp teeth.

36. A "jaw" in line 9 is

    (A) a part of the shark's tail
    (B) a part of the stomach
    (C) a backbone
    (D) a bone in the mouth

GO ON TO THE NEXT PAGE

37. "Prey" in line 10 is something that is

    (A) fierce
    (B) hunted
    (C) religious
    (D) shared

38. The passage indicates that a shark attacks a person

    (A) for no reason
    (B) every time it sees one
    (C) only if it is bothered
    (D) only at night

39. It can be inferred from the passage that a person should probably be the least afraid of

    (A) a dwarf shark
    (B) a tiger shark
    (C) a bull shark
    (D) a great white shark

40. Where in the passage does the author give the proportion of shark species that act aggressively toward people?

    (A) Lines 4–6
    (B) Lines 9–12
    (C) Lines 13–14
    (D) Lines 16–17

GO ON TO THE NEXT PAGE

Questions 41–50

Quite different from storm surges are the giant sea waves called *tsunamis*, which derive their name from the Japanese expression for "high water in a harbor." These waves are also referred to by the general public as tidal waves, although they have relatively little to do with tides. Scientists
Line often refer to them as seismic sea waves, far more appropriate in that they do result from undersea
(5) seismic activity.

Tsunamis are caused when the sea bottom suddenly moves, during an underwater earthquake or volcano for example, and the water above the moving earth is suddenly displaced. This sudden shift of water sets off a series of waves. These waves can travel great distances at speeds close to 700 kilometers per hour. In the open ocean, tsunamis have little noticeable amplitude, often no more
(10) than one or two meters. It is when they hit the shallow waters near the coast that they increase in height, possibly up to 40 meters.

Tsunamis often occur in the Pacific because the Pacific is an area of heavy seismic activity. Two areas of the Pacific well accustomed to the threat of tsunamis are Japan and Hawaii. Because the seismic activity that causes tsunamis in Japan often occurs on the ocean bottom quite close to the
(15) islands, the tsunamis that hit Japan often come with little warning and can therefore prove disastrous. Most of the tsunamis that hit the Hawaiian Islands, however, originate thousands of miles away near the coast of Alaska, so these tsunamis have a much greater distance to travel and the inhabitants of Hawaii generally have time for warning of their imminent arrival.

Tsunamis are certainly not limited to Japan and Hawaii. In 1755, Europe experienced a
(20) calamitous tsunami, when movement along the fault lines near the Azores caused a massive tsunami to sweep onto the Portuguese coast and flood the heavily populated area around Lisbon. The greatest tsunami on record occurred on the other side of the world in 1883 when the Krakatoa volcano underwent a massive explosion, sending waves more than 30 meters high onto nearby Indonesian islands; the tsunami from this volcano actually traveled around the world and was
(25) witnessed as far away as the English Channel.

41. The paragraph preceding this passage most probably discusses

   (A) tidal waves
   (B) tides
   (C) storm surges
   (D) underwater earthquakes

42. According to the passage, all of the following are true about tidal waves EXCEPT that

   (A) they are the same as tsunamis
   (B) they are caused by sudden changes in high and low tides
   (C) this terminology is not used by the scientific community
   (D) they refer to the same phenomenon as seismic sea waves

43. The word "displaced" in line 7 is closest in meaning to

   (A) located
   (B) not pleased
   (C) filtered
   (D) moved

44. It can be inferred from the passage that tsunamis

   (A) cause severe damage in the middle of the ocean
   (B) generally reach heights greater than 40 meters
   (C) are far more dangerous on the coast than in the open ocean
   (D) are often identified by ships on the ocean

GO ON TO THE NEXT PAGE

45. In line 10, water that is "shallow" is NOT

    (A) clear
    (B) deep
    (C) tidal
    (D) coastal

46. A main difference between tsunamis in Japan and in Hawaii is that tsunamis in Japan are more likely to

    (A) arrive without warning
    (B) come from greater distances
    (C) be less of a problem
    (D) originate in Alaska

47. The possessive "their" in line 18 refers to

    (A) the Hawaiian Islands
    (B) thousands of miles
    (C) these tsunamis
    (D) the inhabitants of Hawaii

48. A "calamitous" tsunami, in line 20, is one that is

    (A) expected
    (B) extremely calm
    (C) at fault
    (D) disastrous

49. From the expression "on record" in line 22, it can be inferred that the tsunami that accompanied the Krakatoa volcano

    (A) occurred before efficient records were kept
    (B) was not as strong as the tsunami in Lisbon
    (C) was filmed as it was happening
    (D) might not be the greatest tsunami ever

50. The passage suggests that the tsunami resulting from the Krakatoa volcano

    (A) caused volcanic explosions in the English Channel
    (B) was far more destructive close to the source than far away
    (C) was unobserved outside of the Indonesian islands
    (D) resulted in little damage

This is the end of Section 3.

**If you finish in less than 55 minutes,
check your work on Section 3 only.
Do NOT read or work on any other section of the test.**

When you finish the test, you may do the following:

- Turn to the **Diagnostic Chart** on pages 357–363, and circle the numbers of the questions that you missed.

- Turn to **Scoring Information** on pages 354–356, and determine your TOEFL score.

- Turn to the **Progress Chart** on page 353, and add your score to the chart.

TEST OF WRITTEN ENGLISH:
TWE ESSAY TOPIC
Time—30 minutes

Do you agree or disagree with the following statement?

I learn more when I study with classmates than when I study alone.

Use specific reasons and details to support your answer.

APPENDIXES

APPENDIX A: **Similar Sounds**

DIRECTIONS: Practice pronouncing the words in the box and the words in the exercise. Then listen to each sentence on the recording (or as your teacher reads it to you) and circle the letter of the word or words that you hear.

CONSONANT SOUNDS: *L* AND *R*
L: *lip, link, lock, loot, laid, lag, late*
R: *rip, rink, rock, root, raid, rag, rate*

EXERCISE A1

1. A. ramp   B. lamp

2. A. road   B. load

3. A. reaped   B. leaped

4. A. robbed   B. lobbed

5. A. roar   B. lore   C. role

6. A. leer   B. rear   C. real

7. A. rare   B. lair   C. rail

8. A. rule   B. lure   C. rural

9. A. row . . . low   B. low . . . row

10. A. rain . . . lane   B. lane . . . rain

11. A. rent . . . lent   B. lent . . . rent

12. A. room . . . loom   B. loom . . . room

13. A. rid . . . rice   B. lid . . . lice   C. rid . . . lice

14. A. raced . . . rake   B. laced . . . lake   C. raced . . . lake

15. A. robes . . . rack   B. lobes . . . lack   C. robes . . . lack

> **CONSONANT SOUNDS:** *SH, CH, J*
>
> SH: *shout, shirt, should, share, shoot, shine*
> CH: *chair, chain, chap, child, cheap, chore*
> J: *jail, just, jar, judge, job, jazz, jam*

EXERCISE A2

1. A. sheet   B. cheat

2. A. sheaf   B. chief

3. A. gel   B. shell

4. A. chop   B. shop

5. A. jest . . . junk   B. chest . . . junk   C. chest . . . chunk

6. A. chill . . . Jill   B. chill . . . shill   C. Jill . . . chill

7. A. shin . . . chair   B. chin . . . chair   C. gin . . . share

8. A. jam . . . jar   B. sham . . . jar   C. jam . . . char

9. A. joked . . . chunk B. choked . . . junk   C. choked . . . chunk

10. A. chip . . . chore   B. ship . . . shore   C. chip . . . shore

11. A. cheap . . . jeep   B. cheap . . . sheep   C. jeep . . . cheap

12. A. choke . . . jest   B. joke . . . jest   C. choke . . . chest

13. A. share . . . ships B. chair . . . chips   C. share . . . chips

14. A. jot . . . sheet   B. shot . . . sheet   C. jot . . . cheat

15. A. shore . . . sheer B. chore . . . shear   C. chore . . . cheer
       . . . sheep   . . . sheep   . . . cheap

CONSONANT SOUNDS: *P, B, V, F*

P: *pay, pit, pun, pale, poor, pear*

B: *bay, bind, bit, bone, bag, bomb*

V: *vow, vane, vote, very, vast, veil*

F: *find, fit, fun, four, fig, fear, fate*

EXERCISE A3

1. A. ban . . . van	B. pan . . . van	C. pan . . . fan
2. A. file . . . vile	B. pile . . . bile	C. pile . . . vile
3. A. best . . . pest	B. pest . . . best	C. vest . . . best
4. A. veal . . . pie	B. veal . . . buy	C. feel . . . buy
5. A. pet . . . vet	B. pet . . . bet	C. bet . . . vet
6. A. view . . . fast	B. view . . . vast	C. few . . . past
7. A. van . . . veer	B. fan . . . fear	C. ban . . . veer
8. A. pew . . . fine . . . pine	B. few . . . pine . . . vine	C. view . . . fine . . . vine
9. A. peel . . . veil . . . face	B. feel . . . bale . . . vase	C. feel . . . veil . . . face
10. A. bat . . . vile . . . filled	B. vast . . . pile . . . built	C. fat . . . file . . . filled
11. A. fan . . . vets . . . pain	B. ban . . . bets . . . bane	C. van . . . pets . . . pain
12. A. pace . . . fast . . . few	B. base . . . last . . . few	C. pace . . . past . . . view
13. A. pale . . . veil . . . failed	B. bail . . . pail . . . failed	C. fail . . . pail . . . bailed
14. A. bat . . . fast . . . face	B. vat . . . fast . . . pace	C. bat . . . past . . . face
15. A. very buy . . . berry pest	B. berry pie . . . very best	C. very pie . . . berry best

VOWEL SOUNDS: LONG *E*, SHORT *I*, SHORT *E*

Long E: *bean, weak, peel, meat, seem*

Short I: *sick, hit, mint, kid, win, lip, risk*

Short E: *bend, men, sent, red, less, get*

EXERCISE A4

1. A. set . . . seat	B. sit . . . set	C. seat . . . set
2. A. feel . . . fill	B. feel . . . fell	C. fill . . . fell
3. A. picked . . . peck	B. peeked . . . pick	C. pecked . . . peek
4. A. tin . . . ten	B. teen . . . tin	C. teen . . . ten
5. A. pet . . . pit	B. pit . . . pet	C. pit . . . Pete
6. A. bet . . . beat	B. bit . . . beat	C. bit . . . bet
7. A. red . . . rid	B. red . . . read	C. rid . . . red
8. A. deed . . . did	B. dead . . . deed	C. deed . . . dead
9. A. net . . . knit	B. neat . . . knit	C. neat . . . net
10. A. dean . . . din . . . den	B. din . . . dean . . . den	C. dean . . . den . . . din

VOWEL SOUNDS: LONG *I*, LONG *A*, SHORT *A*
Long I: *hide, bike, dime, tile, sign*
Long A: *make, play, date, fade, same*
Short A: *cap, bad, rash, man, hat*

EXERCISE A5

1. A. dime   B. dame   C. dam

2. A. lime   B. lame   C. lam

3. A. bite . . . bat   B. bat . . . bait   C. bite . . . bait

4. A. pane . . . pine   B. pan . . . pane   C. pan . . . pine

5. A. might . . . mate   B. might . . . mat   C. mate . . . mat

6. A. Kate . . . cat   B. cat . . . kite   C. Kate . . . kite

7. A. fate . . . fight   B. fate . . . fat   C. fight . . . fate

8. A. vain . . . vine   B. vain . . . vein   C. van . . . vane

9. A. hate . . . hat . . . height   B. hide . . . height . . . hat   C. hate . . . height . . . hat

10. A. main . . . man . . . mine   B. man . . . main . . . mine   C. man . . . mine . . . main

VOWEL SOUNDS: LONG *O*, *OO*, SHORT *U*
Long O: *boat, load, home, toes, soak*
OO: *noon, boot, tool, room, mood*
Short U: *cup, bud, fun, hug, luck*

EXERCISE A6

1. A. soon . . . sun   B. sun . . . soon

2. A. pole . . . pool   B. pool . . . pole

3. A. bum . . . boon   B. boom . . . bun   C. boom . . . boon

4. A. boot . . . but   B. boat . . . but   C. boat . . . boot

5. A. cooped . . . cupped   B. cupped . . . coped   C. coped . . . cooped

6. A. mood . . . mud   B. mode . . . mud   C. mood . . . mode

7. A. rut . . . root   B. road . . . rut   C. root . . . rut
       . . . road   . . . root   . . . road

8. A. room . . . roam   B. roam . . . room   C. roam . . . rum
       . . . rum   . . . rum   . . . room

9. A. nun . . . known   B. noon . . . nun   C. nun . . . noon
       . . . noon   . . . known   . . . known

10. A. doom . . . dome   B. dumb . . . doom   C. dumb . . . dome
        . . . dumb   . . . domed   . . . doomed

EXERCISE A7

This exercise includes all of the sounds. Listen to the sentences on the recording. Then fill in the blanks with the words that you hear.

1. Tom told a _____ _____ about the _____.

2. Mae enjoyed the sun's _____ as she _____ on the sand.

3. It's really _____ for _____ to get so _____.

4. We want to get _____ of the _____ who are making a _____.

5. I _____ on the _____ of the _____ as it crossed the _____.

6. Mike _____ in _____ and _____ down a few _____.

7. I'm going to _____ for first _____ in the _____.

8. I had to _____ my friend out of _____ when he _____ to _____ the _____.

9. You _____ to _____ the _____ advice and respect the _____ on _____.

10. Please _____ in the closest _____ and _____ the _____ on the _____ in the _____ of the _____.

11. _____ _____ out the window, where he had a _____ of a _____ on the _____.

12. The _____ _____ out a _____ when the _____ hit the _____.

13. At the _____, he _____ up some _____ and watched the _____ _____ by.

14. The _____ _____ and _____ at the terrible _____.

15. Steve had a _____ of _____ vegetables and _____ in his _____. When the _____ _____ on the floor, he had a _____ _____ _____ on his _____.

APPENDIX B: **Prepositions**

DIRECTIONS: Study the list of prepositions. Then underline the prepositions in each sentence. Circle the prepositional phrases (prepositions + modifiers + objects). In each passage, you should find *ten* prepositions.

PREPOSITIONS				
about	*before*	*for*	*on*	*under*
across	*behind*	*from*	*outside*	*unlike*
after	*beside*	*in*	*over*	*until*
against	*between*	*inside*	*past*	*up*
along	*beyond*	*into*	*since*	*upon*
among	*by*	*like*	*through*	*versus*
around	*despite*	*near*	*throughout*	*with*
as	*down*	*of*	*to*	*within*
at	*during*	*off*	*toward*	*without*

EXERCISE B1

A local construction site has been in an uproar since yesterday, when the fossilized bones of an extinct dinosaur were discovered under several feet of soil by incredulous construction workers. The bones are being removed from the ditch, and work on the construction site has temporarily been halted for further scientific study of the location.

EXERCISE B2

The Computer Department at the local community college is offering a computer course for computer-phobics, people who have never had their hands on a computer and cannot tell the difference between a computer monitor and a keyboard. If you want to learn about this course, you can call the local office, which is open until six o'clock daily. The course is offered during the fall semester at a low fee to residents throughout the county.

EXERCISE B3

While a major hurricane churns its way across the Atlantic, scientists are carefully monitoring its progress. Winds inside the storm are circling at 130 miles an hour, and the storm is still strengthening over the warm southern waters. The storm appears to be making a beeline toward the southern coast. Despite the current distance of the storm from land, forecasters are urging residents near the coast to begin taking precautions. Expected landfall should occur within 36 hours.

EXERCISE B4

The mansion down the street is without a doubt the most amazing building of its type that I have ever seen. Unlike most homes in this neighborhood, it is four stories high and stands behind a massive stone wall covered with ivy. A bolted gate through the wall affords the only entrance to the compound from the street.

EXERCISE B5

The annual car rally is now ready to begin. The race course leads through the downtown area, along the edge of the Saugus River, and across the Township Bridge into the wide open spaces outside the town. Among the expected leaders are three local drivers known for their fearless performances in previous races against strong competitors.

APPENDIX C: **Word Endings**

Word endings in English often tell you how a word is used grammatically in English; therefore, it is very important for you to recognize some common word endings. If you recognize a word ending on a word that you do not know, you can tell how the word should be used grammatically, even if you do not understand the meaning of the word.

The following chart lists some common word endings in English.

WORD ENDINGS IN ENGLISH				
NOUN (person)	**NOUN (thing)**	**VERB**	**ADJECTIVE**	**ADVERB**
-er	-nce	-ate	-ful	-ly
-or	-ism	-ize	-nt	
-ist	-ness	-fy	-al	
-ian	-logy		-ble	
	-ion		-ous	
	-ty			

EXERCISE C1

Indicate whether each of the following words is a noun person (NP), a noun thing (NT), a verb (V), an adjective (ADJ), or an adverb (ADV).

1. ___ identify   ___ identical   ___ identity   ___ identically   ___ identification

2. ___ observer   ___ observant   ___ observantly   ___ observance   ___ observation

3. ___ personable   ___ personal   ___ personally   ___ personality   ___ personalize

4. ___ dictate   ___ dictator   ___ dictation   ___ diction   ___ dictatorial

5. ___ user   ___ useful   ___ usable   ___ usual   ___ usefulness

6. ___ technical   ___ technicality   ___ technology   ___ technician   ___ technically

7. ___ credence   ___ credulous   ___ credible   ___ credibly   ___ credulousness

8. ___ presence   ___ presenter   ___ presentation   ___ presentable   ___ presently

9. ___ humanist   ___ humanize   ___ humanity   ___ humanly   ___ humanitarian

10. ___ violently   ___ violate   ___ violator   ___ violence   ___ violent

11. ___ colonial   ___ colonialism   ___ colonialize   ___ colonialist   ___ colonialization

12. ___ ideology   ___ ideal   ___ idealism   ___ idealize   ___ idealist

13. ___ civilian   ___ civilize   ___ civilly   ___ civility   ___ civilization

14. ___ gracious   ___ graceful   ___ gracefully   ___ graciously   ___ graciousness

15. ___ verify   ___ verifiable   ___ verily   ___ verity   ___ verification

EXERCISE C2

Circle the letter of the word that correctly completes each sentence.

1. It is doubtful that the government will _____ marijuana in the near future.
   A. legalize   B. legality   C. legally

2. The student did not do well in the class because he had a problem with _____.
   A. absent   B. absently   C. absenteeism

3. The sick child must stay away from others because he has a _____ disease.
   A. communicable   B. communicator   C. communication

4. The merger of the two companies was funded by a _____.
   A. capitalist   B. capitalism   C. capitalize

5. When he heard what had happened, he was _____ angry.
   A. murderous   B. murderer   C. murderously

6. I do not understand what these results _____.
   A. significance   B. signify   C. significant

7. A major _____ disturbance occurred early this morning.
   A. seismology   B. seismological   C. seismologist

8. The information in that article is _____ inaccurate.
   A. historian   B. historical   C. historically

9. A large amount of _____ exists between the two former friends.
   A. antagonism   B. antagonize   C. antagonist

10. The charitable organization received a large gift from the _____.
    A. donation   B. donor   C. donate

EXERCISE C3

Fill in the chart with word forms.

	NOUN (person)	NOUN (thing)	VERB	ADJECTIVE	ADVERB
1.					finally
2.			profess		
3.				sociable	
4.		specialization			
5.			electrify		electrically
6.	realist				
7.				beautiful	
8.					ideally
9.		terrorism			
10.	illustrator				

APPENDIX D: **Irregular Verb Forms**

DIRECTIONS: Fill in each space with the letters needed to complete the irregular verb forms.

Verb	Past	Participle

EXERCISE D1

r <u>i</u> ng	r <u>a</u> ng	r <u>u</u> ng
s __ ng	s __ ng	s __ ng
dr __ nk	dr __ nk	dr __ nk
s __ nk	s __ nk	s __ nk
sw __ m	sw __ m	sw __ m
beg __ n	beg __ n	beg __ n

EXERCISE D2

sen <u>d</u>	sen <u>t</u>	sen <u>t</u>
spen __	spen __	spen __
len __	len __	len __
buil __	buil __	buil __
los __	los __	los __
ma __ e	ma __ e	ma __ e
mean	mean __	mean __
ha __ __	ha __	ha __
hear	hear __	hear __

Verb	Past	Participle

EXERCISE D3

Verb	Past	Participle
b _e_ t	b _e_ t	b _e_ t
p __ t	p __ t	p __ t
h __ rt	h __ rt	h __ rt
c __ st	c __ st	c __ st
sh __ t	sh __ t	sh __ t
h __ t	h __ t	h __ t
l __ t	l __ t	l __ t
c __ t	c __ t	c __ t
qu __ t	qu __ t	qu __ t
f __ t	f __ t	f __ t
r __ __ d	r __ __ d	r __ __ d

EXERCISE D4

Verb	Past	Participle
s _i_ t	s _a_ t	s _a_ t
w __ n	w __ n	w __ n
d __ g	d __ g	d __ g
h __ ld	h __ ld	h __ ld
f __ nd	f __ __ nd	f __ __ nd
sh __ __ t	sh __ t	sh __ t
l __ __ d	l __ d	l __ d
m __ __ t	m __ t	m __ t
f __ __ d	f __ d	f __ d

EXERCISE D5

Verb	Past	Participle
pa _y_	pa _i_ _d_	pa _i_ _d_
sa __	sa __ __	sa __ __
s __ l __	s __ l __	s __ l __
t __ l __	t __ l __	t __ l __
st __ __ d	st __ __ d	st __ __ d
sle __ p	slep __	slep __
ke __ p	kep __	kep __
feel	fe __ __	fe __ __

Verb	Past	Participle

EXERCISE D6

Verb	Past	Participle
kn _o_ w	kn _e_ w	kn _o_ w _n_
gr __ w	gr __ w	gr __ w __
bl __ w	bl __ w	bl __ w __
thr __ w	thr __ w	thr __ w __
fl __	fl __ w	fl __ w __
sh __ w	sh __ w __ __	sh __ w __
dr __ w	dr __ w	dr __ w __

EXERCISE D7

Verb	Past	Participle
th _i_ n _k_	_t_ _h_ _o_ _u_ _g_ _h_ t	_t_ _h_ _o_ _u_ _g_ _h_ t
t __ __ ch	t __ __ __ __ t	t __ __ __ __ t
b __ y	b __ __ __ __ t	b __ __ __ __ t
f __ ght	f __ __ __ __ t	f __ __ __ __ t
c __ tch	c __ __ __ __ t	c __ __ __ __ t
br __ ng	br __ __ __ __ t	br __ __ __ __ t

EXERCISE D8

Verb	Past	Participle
g _i_ ve	g _a_ ve	g _i_ ve _n_
wr __ te	wr __ te	wr __ t __ e __
tak __	t __ __ k	tak __ __
f __ ll	f __ ll	f __ ll __ __
dr __ ve	dr __ ve	dr __ ve __
eat	__ __ e	eat __ __
r __ de	r __ de	r __ d __ e __
r __ se	r __ se	r __ se __
forg __ ve	forg __ ve	forg __ ve __

Verb	Past	Participle

EXERCISE D9

Verb	Past	Participle
st _e_ _a_ l	st _o_ l _e_	st _o_ l _e_ n
sp __ __ k	sp __ k __	sp __ k __ __
ch __ __ se	ch __ se	ch __ se __
br __ __ k	br __ k __	br __ k __ __
fr __ __ ze	fr __ ze	fr __ ze __
g __ t	g __ t	g __ t __ __ __
forg __ t	forg __ t	forg __ t __ __ __
bit __	b __ t	bit __ __ __
hid __	h __ d	hid __ __ __
beat	b __ __ t	beat __ __
prov __	prov __ __	prov __ __

EXERCISE D10

Verb	Past	Participle
bec __ me	bec __ me	bec __ me
c __ me	c __ me	c __ me
r __ n	r __ n	r __ n
t __ __ r	t __ r __	t __ r __
w __ __ r	w __ r __	w __ r __
see	s __ __	see __
do	d __ __	do __ __
go	__ __ __ __	go __ __

APPENDIX E: **Word Parts**

Prefixes are meaningful word parts that are attached to the beginnings of words. If you know the meanings of some common prefixes, they can help you to understand unknown words that contain these prefixes. Study the common prefixes in the following chart.

SOME COMMON PREFIXES		
PREFIX	**MEANING**	**EXAMPLE**
ex-	out	*ex*terior
in-	in	*in*debted
pre-	before	*pre*paid
post-	after	*post*date
sub-	under	*sub*conscious
tele-	far	*tele*phone

EXERCISE E1

Fill in each blank with the letter of the word that best completes the sentence.

A. *exile*	E. *posterity*	I. *subsoil*
B. *extract*	F. *postpones*	J. *subtitle*
C. *indented*	G. *prerequisite*	K. *teleconference*
D. *invade*	H. *preview*	L. *telemarketer*

1. The layer of earth that is *under* the top layer is the _____.

2. When a dentist must take a tooth *out,* he or she has to _____ it.

3. If the teacher changes the due date for an assignment from today until sometime *after* today, the teacher _____ the assignment.

4. A person who tries to sell you something from *far* away by using the phone is a(n) _____.

5. A course that you must take *before* you take other courses is a(n) _____.

6. When soldiers go *into* another country in order to take it over, they _____ it.

7. If there is a smaller name *under* the main name of a book, it is called a(n) _____.

8. All of your children and your children's children, the family members who come *after* you, are known as your _____.

9. A person who is forced to live *outside* of his or her country lives in ＿＿＿.

10. A movie shown *before* it is available to the general public is called a(n) ＿＿＿.

11. A meeting held using electronic equipment by people who are *far* away from each other is called a(n) ＿＿＿.

12. When the first line of a paragraph is moved *in* from the margin, the paragraph is ＿＿＿.

EXERCISE E2

Fill in each space with one letter to create words that logically complete the sentences. Each word that you create must include one of the prefixes from the list given on the facing page. (Some letters have been given.)

1. A boat that goes *under* water is a(n) ＿ ＿ ＿ M A ＿ ＿ ＿ ＿ ＿.

2. To see something from *far* away, you can use a(n) ＿ ＿ ＿ ＿ S C ＿ ＿ ＿ ＿.

3. The years just *after* a war are the ＿ ＿ ＿ T W ＿ ＿ years.

4. To leave a building, you go *out* through the ＿ ＿ I ＿.

5. A young person who is in the years just *before* becoming a teenager is a ＿ R ＿ T ＿ ＿ ＿.

6. Money that comes *into* your bank account for work that you did is your ＿ ＿ ＿ ＿ M E.

7. When you breathe *out*, you ＿ ＿ ＿ ＿ L E.

8. A train that runs *under* the ground is a(n) ＿ ＿ ＿ W ＿ ＿.

9. A ＿ ＿ ＿ ＿ ＿ G ＿ A ＿ is a short message that is written and sent electronically from *far* away.

10. If you are *inside* a building, you are ＿ ＿ D ＿ ＿ ＿ S.

11. If you put a date *before* today's date on a check, you ＿ ＿ ＿ ＿ ＿ T E the check.

12. In the period of time *after* surgery, you need ＿ ＿ ＿ O P ＿ ＿ ＿ ＿ I V E care from your doctor.

The following chart contains some additional common prefixes. Study the prefixes in the chart.

SOME MORE COMMON PREFIXES		
PREFIX	**MEANING**	**EXAMPLE**
co-/con-	together with	*co*ordination
in-	not	*in*capable
mis-	incorrect	*mis*place
re-	again	*re*view
re-	back	*re*call
un-	not	*un*fair

EXERCISE E3

Fill in each blank with the letter of the word that best completes the sentence.

A. *conspiracy*	E. *misinformed*	I. *refund*
B. *cooperation*	F. *mismanaged*	J. *reject*
C. *incredible*	G. *rearrange*	K. *unmarried*
D. *inedible*	H. *recurs*	L. *unsafe*

1. Something that you just can*not* believe is _____.

2. If you receive *incorrect* information, you are _____.

3. If you work *together with* others in a group, you work in _____.

4. If you are single, then you are _____.

5. When something happens *again*, it _____.

6. If you get your money *back*, you get a(n) _____.

7. Something that you just can*not* eat is _____.

8. Something that is dangerous is _____.

9. A company that has had *incorrect* leadership has been _____.

10. A group of people who get *together* to plan a crime are part of a(n) _____.

11. If you send something *back* because the quality is not good, you _____ it.

12. When you move the furniture *again* to put it in a different place, you _____ it.

EXERCISE E4

Fill in each space with one letter to create words that logically complete the sentences. Each word that you create must include one of the prefixes from the list given on the facing page. (Some letters have been given.)

1. Something that you do *not* know is _ _ K _ _ _ _ _.

2. If the answer to a math problem is *not* accurate, it is _ _ C _ _ _ _ _ C _.

3. When you tell a story over *again*, you _ _ _ _ L L it.

4. When you give some money *back* to a person who has lent it to you, you _ _ _ _ Y it.

5. When a word does not have all the *correct* letters in it, it is _ _ S S _ _ L L _ _.

6. Someone who works *together with* you is a(n) _ _-_ _ _ _ E R.

7. If you do not receive the same amount as someone else, you receive _ _ _ Q U _ _ amounts.

8. When you give something *back* to someone who lent it to you, you _ _ T U _ _ it.

9. An *incorrect* count of the money in a cash drawer is a(n) _ _ _ C _ _ _ T.

10. If the teacher asks you to write something over *again*, you need to _ _ C _ _ Y it.

11. When something is *not* finished, it is _ _ C O _ _ _ _ _ _ _.

12. When you join two things *together with* each other, you _ _ N N _ _ _ _ them.

Roots are meaningful word parts that come in the middle of words. If you know the meanings of some common roots, it can help you to understand unknown words that contain these roots. Study the common roots in the following chart.

SOME COMMON ROOTS		
ROOT	**MEANING**	**EXAMPLE**
-graph-	write	bio*graph*y
-jud-	judge/decide	*jud*icial
-port-	carry	sup*port*
-ven-	come	con*ven*t
-vis-	see	*vis*ion
-voc-	call/voice	*voc*al

EXERCISE E5

Fill in each blank with the letter of the word that best completes the sentence.

A. *audiovisual*	E. *graphite*	I. *seismograph*
B. *circumvent*	F. *judiciary*	J. *transport*
C. *equivocate*	G. *judicious*	K. *visor*
D. *eventually*	H. *portfolio*	L. *vociferous*

1. A type of hat that protects your eyes so that you can *see* is a(n) _____.

2. To *carry* something from one place to another is to _____ it.

3. If you speak often and in a loud *voice*, you are _____ in nature.

4. A type of carbon that is used in pencils to make them *write* is _____.

5. If you always make careful *decisions*, you are _____ in nature.

6. Something that *comes* sometime in the future comes _____.

7. Instructional materials that you can both *hear* and *see* are _____.

8. The Supreme Court is the head of the _____, the part of the government that makes final *decisions* on legal issues.

9. To avoid something by *coming* around it is to _____ it.

10. A large case that is used to *carry* pieces of artwork is a(n) _____.

11. To *voice* opinions on both sides of an issue is to _____.

12. A machine that *writes* down information whenever there is an earthquake is a(n) _____.

EXERCISE E6

Fill in each space with one letter to create words that logically complete the sentences. Each word that you create must include one of the roots from the list given on the facing page. (Some letters have been given.)

1. When you go to someone's home to *see* him, you go to __ __ S __ __ him.

2. A person who helps *carry* your baggage is a(n) __ __ R __ __ R.

3. A person who uses her *voice* to sing with a choir is a(n) __ __ __ __ L __ __ T.

4. The person who makes *decisions* in a court of law is a(n) __ __ D __ __.

5. If you *write* about your own life, you write a(n)
__ __ T O __ __ __ __ __ __ __ __ Y.

6. A social gathering or activity that is *coming* is a(n) E __ __ __ __.

7. A smaller television, one that you are able to *carry,* is a(n) __ __ __ __ A __ __ E television.

8. If you make a *decision* or express an opinion about something, you make a(n)
__ __ __ G M __ __ __.

9. A star that you are able to *see* in the sky is a(n) __ I __ I __ __ __ star.

10. If you say something in a *voice* that can be heard, you __ __ __ __ __ __ Z E it.

11. If someone *writes* his name himself, he signs a(n) A U __ __ __ __ __ __ __.

12. Money that *comes* to you in a business is R E __ __ __ __ __.

The following chart contains some additional common roots. Study the roots in the chart.

SOME MORE COMMON ROOTS		
ROOT	**MEANING**	**EXAMPLE**
-ced-/-ceed-	go	exceed
-dic-	say	diction
-mit-/-mis-	send	mission
-scrib-/-scrip-	write	tapescript
-spec-	see/look	inspect
-ver-	turn	invert

EXERCISE E7

Fill in each blank with the letter of the word that best completes the sentence.

A. *antecedent*	E. *dismiss*	I. *manuscript*
B. *avert*	F. *edict*	J. *scribble*
C. *benediction*	G. *emissary*	K. *spectacles*
D. *convertible*	H. *intercede*	L. *spectacular*

1. A long composition that is *written* by hand is a(n) _____.

2. A few nice words that are *said* to end a ceremony are called a(n) _____.

3. Glasses that you use to *see* better are also called _____.

4. Something that *goes* or happens before another is a(n) _____.

5. If you *write* in a very messy way, you _____.

6. If you *send* someone away from you, you _____ her.

7. A closed-top car that can be *turned* into an open-top car is a(n) _____.

8. Something that is *said* by an authority or government and must be followed is a(n) _____.

9. To *go* in between two people who are having an argument is to _____.

10. Something that you *see* that is truly amazing is _____.

11. If you *turn* your eyes away from something to avoid seeing it, you _____ your eyes.

12. A person that is *sent* by one government to take messages to the government of another country is a(n) _____.

EXERCISE E8

Fill in each space with one letter to create words that logically complete the sentences. Each word that you create must include one of the roots from the list given on the facing page. (Some letters have been given.)

1. When you *write* what something is like, you D _ _ _ _ _ _ E it.

2. To *say* something aloud to be recorded by someone else is to _ _ _ T _ T _ it.

3. A weapon that is *sent* through the air or the water is a(n) _ _ _ S _ L _.

4. If you decide to *go* forward with something, you P _ _ _ _ E _ with it.

5. A(n) _ _ _ _ T _ T _ _ is a person who goes to *see* a sporting event.

6. Something that is not horizontal but is instead *turned* upright is _ _ _ _ _ C A L.

7. When you *send* something electronically, you T _ _ _ S _ _ _ it.

8. When you *say* or point something out briefly, you I N _ _ _ _ T E it.

9. The *written* words of a play or movie are called the _ _ _ _ _ T.

10. To *turn* aside from a specific path is to D I _ _ _ T yourself.

11. To *look* on someone with esteem or honor is to R E _ _ _ _ _ him or her.

12. To *go* on to accomplish a goal is to S U _ _ _ _ _.

EXERCISE E9

This exercise includes all of the prefixes and roots. Match the definitions on the right to the words on the left.

____ 1. bibliography

____ 2. conference

____ 3. dictator

____ 4. extraterrestrial

____ 5. import

____ 6. incessant

____ 7. inhale

____ 8. insubordinate

____ 9. invert

____ 10. misjudge

____ 11. missive

____ 12. postlude

____ 13. prelude

____ 14. prevent

____ 15. recede

____ 16. scribe

____ 17. specter

____ 18. subvocalize

____ 19. retelevise

____ 20. unpredictable

A. breathe *in*

B. *go back*

C. *un*ending

D. *turn in*side out

E. music played just *after* a performance ends

F. make an *error* in coming to a *decision*

G. person who *writes* information in a document

H. *carry* something *into* another country

I. a meeting where people get *together* to share ideas

J. person who *says* exactly what others must do

K. a *written* list of the materials used in research

L. *un*able to say *before*hand what will happen

M. music played just *before* a performance begins

N. a written message that is to be *sent*

O. coming from *outside* this world

P. show something *again* from *far* away so that it can be *seen* on a screen

Q. something that you think you *see* but is not really there

R. take action *before* something *comes* to stop it from happening

S. acting as if you are *not under* the authority of your boss

T. say something *under* your breath in a *voice* that cannot be heard

EXERCISE E10

This exercise includes all of the prefixes and roots together. Fill in each blank with the letter of the word that best completes the sentence.

A. *circumscribe*	H. *inscription*	O. *submit*
B. *contradict*	I. *intervene*	P. *subterranean*
C. *convocation*	J. *introverted*	Q. *telecommunicate*
D. *export*	K. *mismatched*	R. *unprecedented*
E. *extrovert*	L. *postmortem*	S. *unspectacular*
F. *graphology*	M. *reconvene*	T. *visualize*
G. *injudicious*	N. *revise*	

1. If something has *never* happened *before,* it is _____.

2. Water that is *under*ground is in a(n) _____ location.

3. I need to _____ in this situation. It is important to *come in* between these two people to stop their fighting.

4. A person who is very *out*going in dealing with others is a(n) _____.

5. If you *carry* goods *out* of one country, you _____ those goods.

6. To *write* or place a limit around something is to _____ it.

7. To *look* at something *again* in order to make it better is to _____ it.

8. To *send* in something that you would like to place *under* consideration is to _____ it.

9. To exchange information electronically from *far* away is to _____.

10. If you *see* something that is *not* out of the ordinary, it is _____.

11. A large meeting where people get *together* to *speak* with each other is a(n) _____.

12. If you are *not* careful in making *decisions* or in expressing opinions, you are _____.

13. If you *come together again* for a meeting, you _____ the meeting.

14. I am trying to _____ the place you are describing; I would like to *see* it in my mind.

15. Every time I express my opinion, you always _____ me; you always *say* the opposite of what I say.

16. The _____ in the card is really meaningful; I really like what is *written inside* it.

17. My friend is studying _____; she thinks it is interesting to understand what people's hand*writing* means.

18. *After* the man's death, a(n) _____ was conducted to determine how he had died.

19. These socks are _____; they are *incorrectly* paired.

20. Tom is quite a(n) _____ person; he is *not* at all *out*going.

EXERCISE E11

Fill in the crossword puzzle using the clues on the next page. The words in the puzzle come from all of the roots and prefixes together.

WORD PARTS CROSSWORD PUZZLE

CLUES TO CROSSWORD PUZZLE

Across

3. large meeting where people *come together*
5. comprehended *incorrectly*
8. *send back*
9. *carry out* of one country and into another
10. *not* able to be mistaken
11. message *written after* the main part of a letter
13. *go out*side of or be more than
14. *under*lying meaning of a text
17. *not* possible to be *seen*
18. a *written* order by a doctor needed *before* you can get some medicine
19. *sight*

Down

1. *no* ability to *say before*hand what is going to happen
2. person who *turns* his feelings and thoughts *inside* himself
4. *not* able to be *carried*
6. action of *looking into* something to see if it is working correctly
7. put someone *under* the control of your *decisions*
11. *judgment* made *before* the facts are known
12. use *again*
15. the *written* version of the words on a tape
16. a group of people *sent* to conduct business or negotiations

SCORES AND CHARTS

PROGRESS CHART

Each time that you take a Pre-Test, a Post-Test, or a Complete Test, you should record the results in the chart that follows. In this way, you will be able to keep track of the progress that you are making. (Please note that because the TOEFL-Level Complete Test contains harder questions than the Introductory-Level Complete Tests, the number correct will be lower on the TOEFL-Level Test.) You may also turn to pages 354–356 and get a TOEFL score for the TOEFL-Level Complete Test Three.

DIRECTIONS: Fill in the number correct on each test section as you take it.

	LISTENING COMPREHENSION	STRUCTURE AND WRITTEN EXPRESSION	READING COMPREHENSION
Pre-Test			
Post-Test			
Complete Test One (Introductory Level)			
Complete Test Two (Introductory Level)			
Complete Test Three (TOEFL Level)			

SCORING COMPLETE TEST THREE _____

You can use the following chart to estimate your score on Complete Test Three—the TOEFL-Level Test. You will receive a score between 20 and 68 in each of the three sections (Listening Comprehension, Structure and Written Expression, and Reading Comprehension). You will also receive an overall score between 217 and 677.

NUMBER CORRECT	CONVERTED SCORE SECTION 1	CONVERTED SCORE SECTION 2	CONVERTED SCORE SECTION 3
50	68	—	67
49	67	—	66
48	66	—	65
47	65	—	63
46	63	—	61
45	62	—	60
44	61	—	59
43	60	—	58
42	59	—	57
41	58	—	56
40	57	68	55
39	57	67	54
38	56	65	54
37	55	63	53
36	54	61	52
35	54	60	52
34	53	58	51
33	52	57	50
32	52	56	49
31	51	55	48
30	51	54	48
29	50	53	47
28	49	52	46
27	49	51	46
26	48	50	45
25	48	49	44
24	47	48	43
23	47	47	43
22	46	46	42
21	45	45	41

NUMBER CORRECT	CONVERTED SCORE SECTION 1	CONVERTED SCORE SECTION 2	CONVERTED SCORE SECTION 3
20	45	44	40
19	44	43	39
18	43	42	38
17	42	41	37
16	41	40	36
15	41	40	35
14	39	38	34
13	38	37	32
12	37	36	31
11	35	35	30
10	33	33	29
9	32	31	28
8	32	29	28
7	31	27	27
6	30	26	26
5	29	25	25
4	28	23	24
3	27	22	23
2	26	21	23
1	25	20	22
0	24	20	21

You should first use the chart to determine your converted score for each section. Suppose that you got 30 correct in the first section, 28 correct in the second section, and 43 correct in the third section. The 30 correct in the first section means a converted score of 51. The 28 correct in the second section means a converted score of 52. The 43 correct in the third section means a converted score of 58. (See chart below.)

	SECTION 1	SECTION 2	SECTION 3
NUMBER CORRECT	30	28	43
CONVERTED SCORE	51	52	58

Next, you should determine your overall score in the following way:

1. <u>Add the three converted scores together.</u>

   $$51 + 52 + 58 = 161$$

2. <u>Divide the sum by 3.</u>

   $$161 \div 3 = 53.7$$

3. <u>Then multiply by 10.</u>

   $$53.7 \times 10 = 537$$

The overall TOEFL score in this example is 537.

After you understand the example, you can fill in the chart below with information about Complete Test Three—your TOEFL-Level Practice Test.

	SECTION 1	SECTION 2	SECTION 3
NUMBER CORRECT			
CONVERTED SCORE			
OVERALL SCORE			

DIAGNOSTIC CHARTS

LISTENING COMPREHENSION

DIRECTIONS: After you take each Listening Comprehension test, circle the number of each of the questions that you answered incorrectly. In this way, you can keep track of which language skills need more attention.

		PRE-TEST	POST-TEST	COMPLETE TEST 1	COMPLETE TEST 2	COMPLETE TEST 3
SKILL 1:	Restatements	1 3 6 9 12 15 18 21 24 27 30	1 3 6 9 12 15 18 21 24 27 30	1 3 6 9 12 15 18 21 24 27 30	2 8 13 22 23 27	1 5 8 9 13
SKILL 2:	Negatives	4 10 14 19 23 28	4 10 14 19 23 28	4 10 14 19 23 28	3 11 14 19 21 25	2 7 12 15
SKILL 3:	Suggestions	7 13 20 26	7 13 20 26	7 13 20 26	1 7 15 20 28	3 17
SKILL 4:	Passives	8 29	8 29	8 29	5 9 18 29	4 18

	PRE-TEST	POST-TEST	COMPLETE TEST 1	COMPLETE TEST 2	COMPLETE TEST 3
SKILL 5: *Who* and *Where*	2 11 17 25	2 11 17 25	2 11 17 25	6 12 17 24 30	6 11 16
SKILL 6: Agreement	5 16 22	5 16 22	5 16 22	4 10 16 26	10 14
SKILLS 7–9: Long Conversations	31 32 33 34 35 36 37 38	31 32 33 34 35 36 37 38	31 32 33 34 35 36 37 38	31 32 33 34 35 36 37 38	31 32 33 34 35 36 37 38
SKILLS 10–12: Long Talks	39 40 41 42 43 44 45 46 47 48 49 50	39 40 41 42 43 44 45 46 47 48 49 50	39 40 41 42 43 44 45 46 47 48 49 50	39 40 41 42 43 44 45 46 47 48 49 50	39 40 41 42 43 44 45 46 47 48 49 50
ADVANCED SKILLS (not covered in this book)					19 20 21 22 23 24 25 26 27 28 29 30

STRUCTURE AND WRITTEN EXPRESSION

DIRECTIONS: After you take each Structure and Written Expression test, circle the number of each of the questions that you answered incorrectly. In this way, you can keep track of which language skills need more attention.

		PRE-TEST	POST-TEST	COMPLETE TEST 1	COMPLETE TEST 2	COMPLETE TEST 3
SKILL 1:	Subjects and Verbs	1 2	1 3 5	1 10	1 2	1
SKILL 2:	Objects of Prepositions	3 6 15	2 9	2 4 5	3 4	2
SKILL 3:	Present Participles	10	10	9	5	3
SKILL 4:	Past Participles	13	14	14	12 14	7
SKILL 5:	Coordinate Connectors	5 9	6 12	7 12	6	
SKILL 6:	Adverb Clause Connectors	8 11	8 13	6 13	8 9	5
SKILL 7:	Noun Clause Connectors	7	11	15	15	4
SKILL 8:	Noun Clause Connector/Subjects	12	15	11	10 13	6
SKILL 9:	Adjective Clause Connectors	4	7	8	7	8
SKILL 10:	Adjective Clause Connector/Subjects	14	4	3	11	
SKILL 11:	Agreement after Prepositional Phrases	25 39	16 37	25 30	21 30	18
SKILL 12:	Agreement after Expressions of Quantity	17	24	20	27 33	24
SKILL 13:	Agreement after Certain Words	30	31	39	17	27
SKILL 14:	Parallel Structure with Coordinate Conjunctions	23 29	20 34	16 34	23 29	28
SKILL 15:	Parallel Structure with Paired Conjunctions	35	18 26	24 29	19 26	19

		PRE-TEST	POST-TEST	COMPLETE TEST 1	COMPLETE TEST 2	COMPLETE TEST 3
SKILL 16:	Past Participles after *Have*	26 31	21	17 38	18 37	
SKILL 17:	Present Participles or Past Participles after *Be*	32 37	23 27	22 36	24 32	23
SKILL 18:	Base Form Verbs after Modals	16 34	35 38	28	16	17
SKILL 19:	Singular and Plural Nouns	21 36	17 33	19 27	20 34	16
SKILL 20:	Countable and Uncountable Nouns	22 27	28 36	26 35	35	22
SKILL 21:	Subject and Object Pronouns	24	25	33	22 25	
SKILL 22:	Possessives	19 40	19 32	18 40	38	25
SKILL 23:	Pronoun Reference	20 33	40	23 32	31 40	20
SKILL 24:	Adjectives and Adverbs	18 38	22 30	21 37	28 39	26
SKILL 25:	Adjectives after Linking Verbs	28	29 39	31	36	21

	PRE-TEST	POST-TEST	COMPLETE TEST 1	COMPLETE TEST 2	COMPLETE TEST 3
ADVANCED SKILLS (not covered in this book)					9
					10
					11
					12
					13
					14
					15
					29
					30
					31
					32
					33
					34
					35
					36
					37
					38
					39
					40

READING COMPREHENSION

DIRECTIONS: After you take each Reading Comprehension test, circle the number of each of the questions that you answered incorrectly. In this way, you can keep track of which language skills need more attention.

		PRE-TEST	POST-TEST	COMPLETE TEST 1	COMPLETE TEST 2	COMPLETE TEST 3
SKILL 1:	Main Idea Questions	1	1	1	1	1
		10	9	10	11	11
		21	19	20	20	21
		31	29	30	28	31
		41	40	40	30	
				41	37	
					39	
					50	
SKILL 2:	Stated Detail Questions	8	4	3	2	5
		11	6	12	3	7
		15	11	13	5	10
		25	14	21	7	17
		29	21	25	12	19
		35	23	32	13	24
		47	31	35	17	38
			35	38	21	46
			38	43	25	
			41	44	31	
			43		40	
			49		43	
SKILL 3:	Unstated Detail Questions	6	8	8	8	6
		7	16	15	27	12
		13	22	27	44	15
		16	32	36		18
		22	45	47		25
		38				35
		42				42

	PRE-TEST	POST-TEST	COMPLETE TEST 1	COMPLETE TEST 2	COMPLETE TEST 3
SKILL4: Implied Detail Questions	4 18 27 32 34 45 49	3 12 26 37 46	5 16 23 33 49	15 23 34 36 41 45 47 49	3 8 14 28 34 39 44 49 50
SKILL 5: Vocabulary in Context Questions	2 3 5 12 14 17 19 23 24 26 28 33 36 37 39 43 44 46 48	2 5 7 10 13 15 17 20 24 25 27 30 33 34 36 42 44 47 48	2 4 6 7 11 14 17 18 22 24 26 28 31 34 37 42 45 46 48	4 6 9 14 16 18 22 24 26 32 33 35 42 46 48	2 9 13 16 22 23 26 27 32 33 36 37 43 45 48
SKILL 6: "Where" Questions	9 20 30 40 50	18 28 39 50	9 19 29 39 50	10 19 29 38	29 40
ADVANCED SKILLS (not covered in this book)					4 20 30 41 47

L
I.N. 996948   72701 • 004170 • TF43M171e   KAJ03045   Q2058-1/1

3049060

DO NOT WRITE IN THIS SPACE

TEST OF ENGLISH AS A FOREIGN LANGUAGE

TOEFL ANSWER SHEET   SIDE 1

1. NAME: Copy your name from your admission ticket. Use one box for each letter. First print your family name (surname), then your given name, and then your middle name, if you have one. Leave one box blank between names. Below each box, fill in the circle that contains the same letter.

2. REGISTRATION NUMBER
Start here

3. INSTITUTION AND DEPARTMENT CODES: Give the code numbers of the institutions and departments to which you want your official score report sent. Be sure to fill in the corresponding circle below each box.

INSTITUTION CODE | DEPT. CODE | INSTITUTION CODE | DEPT. CODE | INSTITUTION CODE | DEPT. CODE | INSTITUTION CODE | DEPT. CODE | INSTITUTION CODE | DEPT. CODE

Use a No. 2 (H.B.) pencil only. Do not use ink. Be sure each mark is dark and completely fills the intended circle. Erase errors or stray marks completely.

4. DO YOU PLAN TO STUDY FOR A DEGREE IN THE U.S.A. OR CANADA?
○ YES
○ NO

5. REASON FOR TAKING TOEFL (FILL IN ONLY ONE CIRCLE.)

1. To enter a college or university as an undergraduate student.
2. To enter a college or university as a graduate student.
3. To enter a school other than a college or university.
4. To become licensed to practice my profession in the U.S.A. or Canada.
5. To demonstrate my proficiency in English to the company for which I work or expect to work.
6. Other than the above (please specify).

6. NUMBER OF TIMES YOU HAVE TAKEN TOEFL BEFORE TODAY
0 1 2 3 4+

Ⓔ ® Copyright © 2003 by Educational Testing Service, Princeton, NJ 08541-0001. All rights reserved. Printed in U.S.A. (ETS)
EDUCATIONAL TESTING SERVICE, ETS and its logo, TOEFL and its logo, are registered trademarks of Educational Testing Service. The modernized ETS logo is a trademark of Educational Testing Service.

7. TEST CENTER (Print.)
CENTER NUMBER

8. PLEASE PRINT YOUR NAME AND MAILING ADDRESS
FAMILY NAME (SURNAME)
GIVEN NAME
MIDDLE NAME
STREET ADDRESS OR P. O. BOX NO.
CITY
STATE OR PROVINCE
POSTAL OR ZIP CODE
COUNTRY

9. SIGNATURE AND DATE: Copy the statement below; use handwriting.
"I hereby agree to the conditions set forth in the *Information Bulletin* and affirm that I am the person whose name and address are given on this answer sheet."

SIGNED:
(WRITE YOUR NAME IN PENCIL AS IF SIGNING A LEGAL IDENTIFICATION DOCUMENT.)
DATE: _____ MO. DAY YEAR

CITY
COUNTRY

DO NOT MARK IN TH
TEST FORM:
SAMPLE

SIDE 2

TEST FORM

TEST BOOK SERIAL NUMBER

ROOM NUMBER | **SEAT NUMBER**

SEX
○ Male
○ Female

DATE OF BIRTH

MO. DAY YEAR

Choose only one answer for each question. Carefully and completely fill in the circle corresponding to the answer you choose so that the letter inside the circle cannot be seen. Completely erase any other marks you may have made.

CORRECT	WRONG	WRONG	WRONG	WRONG
Ⓐ Ⓑ ● Ⓓ	Ⓐ Ⓑ Ⓒ Ⓓ	Ⓐ Ⓑ Ⓒ Ⓓ	Ⓐ Ⓑ Ⓒ Ⓓ	Ⓐ Ⓑ ● Ⓓ

NAME (Print)

FAMILY NAME (SURNAME) GIVEN NAME MIDDLE NAME

REGISTRATION NUMBER

SIGNATURE

SECTION 1

(answer grid, questions 1–50, options A B C D)

SECTION 2

(answer grid, questions 1–40, options A B C D)

SECTION 3

(answer grid, questions 1–50, options A B C D)

SAMPLE

IF YOU DO NOT WANT THIS ANSWER SHEET TO BE SCORED

If you want to cancel your scores from this administration, complete A and B below. The scores will not be sent to you or your designated recipients, and they will be removed from your permanent record.

To cancel your scores from this test administration, you must:

A. fill in both circles here and B. sign your name below

○—○
○

ONCE A SCORE IS CANCELED, IT CANNOT BE REPORTED AT ANY TIME.

FOR ETS USE ONLY

1R	2R	3R	TCS
1CS	2CS	3CS	

L

TEST OF ENGLISH AS A FOREIGN LANGUAGE

TOEFL ANSWER SHEET   SIDE 1

I.N. 996948   72701 • 004170 • TF43M171e   KAJ03045   Q2058-1/1

3049060

DO NOT WRITE IN THIS SPACE

1. NAME: Copy your name from your admission ticket. Use one box for each letter. First print your family name (surname), then your given name, and then your middle name, if you have one. Leave one box blank between names. Below each box, fill in the circle that contains the same letter.

2. REGISTRATION NUMBER
Start here

3. INSTITUTION AND DEPARTMENT CODES: Give the code numbers of the institutions and departments to which you want your official score report sent. Be sure to fill in the corresponding circle below each box.

INSTITUTION CODE   DEPT. CODE

6. NUMBER OF TIMES YOU HAVE TAKEN TOEFL BEFORE TODAY

4. DO YOU PLAN TO STUDY FOR A DEGREE IN THE U.S.A. OR CANADA?
○ YES   ○ NO

5. REASON FOR TAKING TOEFL (FILL IN ONLY ONE CIRCLE.)

1. To enter a college or university as an undergraduate student.
2. To enter a college or university as a graduate student.
3. To enter a school other than a college or university.
4. To become licensed to practice my profession in the U.S.A. or Canada.
5. To demonstrate my proficiency in English to the company for which I work or expect to work.
6. Other than the above (please specify).

Use a No. 2 (H.B.) pencil only. Do not use ink. Be sure each mark is dark and completely fills the intended circle. Erase errors or stray marks completely.

EDUCATIONAL TESTING SERVICE, ETS and its logo, TOEFL and its logo, are registered trademarks of Educational Testing Service. The modernized ETS logo is a trademark of Educational Testing Service.

© Copyright © 2003 by Educational Testing Service, Princeton, NJ 08541-0001. All rights reserved. Printed in U.S.A.

9. SIGNATURE AND DATE: Copy the statement below; use handwriting.
"I hereby agree to the conditions set forth in the Information Bulletin and affirm that I am the person whose name and address are given on this answer sheet."

SIGNED: _____
(WRITE YOUR NAME IN PENCIL AS IF SIGNING A LEGAL IDENTIFICATION DOCUMENT)

DATE: ___ MO. ___ DAY ___ YEAR

7. TEST CENTER (Print.)
CENTER NUMBER
CITY
COUNTRY

8. PLEASE PRINT YOUR NAME AND MAILING ADDRESS
FAMILY NAME (SURNAME)   GIVEN NAME   MIDDLE NAME
STREET ADDRESS OR P. O. BOX NO.
CITY   STATE OR PROVINCE
POSTAL OR ZIP CODE   COUNTRY

DO NOT MARK IN T...

TEST FORM:

SAMPLE

SIDE 2

TEST FORM

TEST BOOK SERIAL NUMBER

ROOM NUMBER   **SEAT NUMBER**

SEX ○ Male   ○ Female   **DATE OF BIRTH** MO. / DAY / YEAR

Choose only one answer for each question. Carefully and completely fill in the circle corresponding to the answer you choose so that the letter inside the circle cannot be seen. Completely erase any other marks you may have made.

CORRECT	WRONG	WRONG	WRONG	WRONG
Ⓐ Ⓑ ● Ⓓ	Ⓐ Ⓑ ⊘ Ⓓ	Ⓐ Ⓑ ⊗ Ⓓ	Ⓐ Ⓑ Ⓒ Ⓓ	Ⓐ Ⓑ Ⓒ Ⓓ

NAME (Print)
FAMILY NAME (SURNAME)   GIVEN NAME   MIDDLE NAME

REGISTRATION NUMBER   **SIGNATURE**

SECTION 1

1 Ⓐ Ⓑ Ⓒ Ⓓ	18 Ⓐ Ⓑ Ⓒ Ⓓ	35 Ⓐ Ⓑ Ⓒ Ⓓ
2 Ⓐ Ⓑ Ⓒ Ⓓ	19 Ⓐ Ⓑ Ⓒ Ⓓ	36 Ⓐ Ⓑ Ⓒ Ⓓ
3 Ⓐ Ⓑ Ⓒ Ⓓ	20 Ⓐ Ⓑ Ⓒ Ⓓ	37 Ⓐ Ⓑ Ⓒ Ⓓ
4 Ⓐ Ⓑ Ⓒ Ⓓ	21 Ⓐ Ⓑ Ⓒ Ⓓ	38 Ⓐ Ⓑ Ⓒ Ⓓ
5 Ⓐ Ⓑ Ⓒ Ⓓ	22 Ⓐ Ⓑ Ⓒ Ⓓ	39 Ⓐ Ⓑ Ⓒ Ⓓ
6 Ⓐ Ⓑ Ⓒ Ⓓ	23 Ⓐ Ⓑ Ⓒ Ⓓ	40 Ⓐ Ⓑ Ⓒ Ⓓ
7 Ⓐ Ⓑ Ⓒ Ⓓ	24 Ⓐ Ⓑ Ⓒ Ⓓ	41 Ⓐ Ⓑ Ⓒ Ⓓ
8 Ⓐ Ⓑ Ⓒ Ⓓ	25 Ⓐ Ⓑ Ⓒ Ⓓ	42 Ⓐ Ⓑ Ⓒ Ⓓ
9 Ⓐ Ⓑ Ⓒ Ⓓ	26 Ⓐ Ⓑ Ⓒ Ⓓ	43 Ⓐ Ⓑ Ⓒ Ⓓ
10 Ⓐ Ⓑ Ⓒ Ⓓ	27 Ⓐ Ⓑ Ⓒ Ⓓ	44 Ⓐ Ⓑ Ⓒ Ⓓ
11 Ⓐ Ⓑ Ⓒ Ⓓ	28 Ⓐ Ⓑ Ⓒ Ⓓ	45 Ⓐ Ⓑ Ⓒ Ⓓ
12 Ⓐ Ⓑ Ⓒ Ⓓ	29 Ⓐ Ⓑ Ⓒ Ⓓ	46 Ⓐ Ⓑ Ⓒ Ⓓ
13 Ⓐ Ⓑ Ⓒ Ⓓ	30 Ⓐ Ⓑ Ⓒ Ⓓ	47 Ⓐ Ⓑ Ⓒ Ⓓ
14 Ⓐ Ⓑ Ⓒ Ⓓ	31 Ⓐ Ⓑ Ⓒ Ⓓ	48 Ⓐ Ⓑ Ⓒ Ⓓ
15 Ⓐ Ⓑ Ⓒ Ⓓ	32 Ⓐ Ⓑ Ⓒ Ⓓ	49 Ⓐ Ⓑ Ⓒ Ⓓ
16 Ⓐ Ⓑ Ⓒ Ⓓ	33 Ⓐ Ⓑ Ⓒ Ⓓ	50 Ⓐ Ⓑ Ⓒ Ⓓ
17 Ⓐ Ⓑ Ⓒ Ⓓ	34 Ⓐ Ⓑ Ⓒ Ⓓ	

SECTION 2

1 Ⓐ Ⓑ Ⓒ Ⓓ	15 Ⓐ Ⓑ Ⓒ Ⓓ	29 Ⓐ Ⓑ Ⓒ Ⓓ
2 Ⓐ Ⓑ Ⓒ Ⓓ	16 Ⓐ Ⓑ Ⓒ Ⓓ	30 Ⓐ Ⓑ Ⓒ Ⓓ
3 Ⓐ Ⓑ Ⓒ Ⓓ	17 Ⓐ Ⓑ Ⓒ Ⓓ	31 Ⓐ Ⓑ Ⓒ Ⓓ
4 Ⓐ Ⓑ Ⓒ Ⓓ	18 Ⓐ Ⓑ Ⓒ Ⓓ	32 Ⓐ Ⓑ Ⓒ Ⓓ
5 Ⓐ Ⓑ Ⓒ Ⓓ	19 Ⓐ Ⓑ Ⓒ Ⓓ	33 Ⓐ Ⓑ Ⓒ Ⓓ
6 Ⓐ Ⓑ Ⓒ Ⓓ	20 Ⓐ Ⓑ Ⓒ Ⓓ	34 Ⓐ Ⓑ Ⓒ Ⓓ
7 Ⓐ Ⓑ Ⓒ Ⓓ	21 Ⓐ Ⓑ Ⓒ Ⓓ	35 Ⓐ Ⓑ Ⓒ Ⓓ
8 Ⓐ Ⓑ Ⓒ Ⓓ	22 Ⓐ Ⓑ Ⓒ Ⓓ	36 Ⓐ Ⓑ Ⓒ Ⓓ
9 Ⓐ Ⓑ Ⓒ Ⓓ	23 Ⓐ Ⓑ Ⓒ Ⓓ	37 Ⓐ Ⓑ Ⓒ Ⓓ
10 Ⓐ Ⓑ Ⓒ Ⓓ	24 Ⓐ Ⓑ Ⓒ Ⓓ	38 Ⓐ Ⓑ Ⓒ Ⓓ
11 Ⓐ Ⓑ Ⓒ Ⓓ	25 Ⓐ Ⓑ Ⓒ Ⓓ	39 Ⓐ Ⓑ Ⓒ Ⓓ
12 Ⓐ Ⓑ Ⓒ Ⓓ	26 Ⓐ Ⓑ Ⓒ Ⓓ	40 Ⓐ Ⓑ Ⓒ Ⓓ
13 Ⓐ Ⓑ Ⓒ Ⓓ	27 Ⓐ Ⓑ Ⓒ Ⓓ	
14 Ⓐ Ⓑ Ⓒ Ⓓ	28 Ⓐ Ⓑ Ⓒ Ⓓ	

SECTION 3

1 Ⓐ Ⓑ Ⓒ Ⓓ	31 Ⓐ Ⓑ Ⓒ Ⓓ
2 Ⓐ Ⓑ Ⓒ Ⓓ	32 Ⓐ Ⓑ Ⓒ Ⓓ
3 Ⓐ Ⓑ Ⓒ Ⓓ	33 Ⓐ Ⓑ Ⓒ Ⓓ
4 Ⓐ Ⓑ Ⓒ Ⓓ	34 Ⓐ Ⓑ Ⓒ Ⓓ
5 Ⓐ Ⓑ Ⓒ Ⓓ	35 Ⓐ Ⓑ Ⓒ Ⓓ
6 Ⓐ Ⓑ Ⓒ Ⓓ	36 Ⓐ Ⓑ Ⓒ Ⓓ
7 Ⓐ Ⓑ Ⓒ Ⓓ	37 Ⓐ Ⓑ Ⓒ Ⓓ
8 Ⓐ Ⓑ Ⓒ Ⓓ	38 Ⓐ Ⓑ Ⓒ Ⓓ
9 Ⓐ Ⓑ Ⓒ Ⓓ	39 Ⓐ Ⓑ Ⓒ Ⓓ
10 Ⓐ Ⓑ Ⓒ Ⓓ	40 Ⓐ Ⓑ Ⓒ Ⓓ
11 Ⓐ Ⓑ Ⓒ Ⓓ	41 Ⓐ Ⓑ Ⓒ Ⓓ
12 Ⓐ Ⓑ Ⓒ Ⓓ	42 Ⓐ Ⓑ Ⓒ Ⓓ
13 Ⓐ Ⓑ Ⓒ Ⓓ	43 Ⓐ Ⓑ Ⓒ Ⓓ
14 Ⓐ Ⓑ Ⓒ Ⓓ	44 Ⓐ Ⓑ Ⓒ Ⓓ
15 Ⓐ Ⓑ Ⓒ Ⓓ	45 Ⓐ Ⓑ Ⓒ Ⓓ
16 Ⓐ Ⓑ Ⓒ Ⓓ	46 Ⓐ Ⓑ Ⓒ Ⓓ
17 Ⓐ Ⓑ Ⓒ Ⓓ	47 Ⓐ Ⓑ Ⓒ Ⓓ
18 Ⓐ Ⓑ Ⓒ Ⓓ	48 Ⓐ Ⓑ Ⓒ Ⓓ
19 Ⓐ Ⓑ Ⓒ Ⓓ	49 Ⓐ Ⓑ Ⓒ Ⓓ
20 Ⓐ Ⓑ Ⓒ Ⓓ	50 Ⓐ Ⓑ Ⓒ Ⓓ
21 Ⓐ Ⓑ Ⓒ Ⓓ	
22 Ⓐ Ⓑ Ⓒ Ⓓ	
23 Ⓐ Ⓑ Ⓒ Ⓓ	
24 Ⓐ Ⓑ Ⓒ Ⓓ	
25 Ⓐ Ⓑ Ⓒ Ⓓ	
26 Ⓐ Ⓑ Ⓒ Ⓓ	
27 Ⓐ Ⓑ Ⓒ Ⓓ	
28 Ⓐ Ⓑ Ⓒ Ⓓ	
29 Ⓐ Ⓑ Ⓒ Ⓓ	
30 Ⓐ Ⓑ Ⓒ Ⓓ	

SAMPLE

IF YOU DO **NOT** WANT THIS ANSWER SHEET TO BE SCORED

If you want to cancel your scores from this administration, complete A and B below. The scores will not be sent to you or your designated recipients, and they will be removed from your permanent record.

To cancel your scores from this test administration, you must:

A. fill in both circles here   and   B. sign your name below

○—○ _____

ONCE A SCORE IS CANCELED, IT CANNOT BE REPORTED AT ANY TIME.

1R	2R	3R	TCS
1CS	2CS	3CS	
		FOR ETS USE ONLY	M

L
I.N. 996948   72701 • 004170 • TF43M171e   KAJ03045   Q2058-1/1

3049060

DO NOT WRITE IN THIS SPACE

TEST OF ENGLISH AS A FOREIGN LANGUAGE

1. NAME: Copy your name from your admission ticket. Use one box for each letter. First print your family name (surname), then your given name, and then your middle name, if you have one. Leave one box blank between names. Below each box, fill in the circle that contains the same letter.

Use a No. 2 (H.B.) pencil only. Do not use ink. Be sure each mark is dark and completely fills the intended circle. Erase errors or stray marks completely.

2. REGISTRATION NUMBER
Start here

3. INSTITUTION AND DEPARTMENT CODES: Give the code numbers of the institutions and departments to which you want your official score report sent. Be sure to fill in the corresponding circle below each box.

INSTITUTION CODE   DEPT. CODE

6. NUMBER OF TIMES YOU HAVE TAKEN TOEFL BEFORE TODAY
(0) (1) (2) (3) (4+)

5. REASON FOR TAKING TOEFL (FILL IN ONLY ONE CIRCLE.)

1. To enter a college or university as an undergraduate student.
2. To enter a college or university as a graduate student.
3. To enter a school other than a college or university.
4. To become licensed to practice my profession in the U.S.A. or Canada.
5. To demonstrate my proficiency in English to the company for which I work or expect to work.
6. Other than the above (please specify).

4. DO YOU PLAN TO STUDY FOR A DEGREE IN THE U.S.A. OR CANADA?
○ YES   ○ NO

© Copyright © 2003 by Educational Testing Service, Princeton, NJ 08541-0001. All rights reserved. Printed in U.S.A. ⓔⓣⓢ

EDUCATIONAL TESTING SERVICE, ETS and its logo, TOEFL and its logo, TOEFL and its logo, are registered trademarks of Educational Testing Service. The modernized ETS logo is a trademark of Educational Testing Service.

9. SIGNATURE AND DATE: Copy the statement below; use handwriting.
"I hereby agree to the conditions set forth in the *Information Bulletin* and affirm that I am the person whose name and address are given on this answer sheet."

SIGNED: _____

DATE: ___ / ___ / ___
MO.   DAY   YEAR

(WRITE YOUR NAME IN PENCIL AS IF SIGNING A LEGAL IDENTIFICATION DOCUMENT.)

7. TEST CENTER (Print.)
CENTER NUMBER
CITY
COUNTRY

8. PLEASE PRINT YOUR NAME AND MAILING ADDRESS
FAMILY NAME (SURNAME)
GIVEN NAME
MIDDLE NAME
STREET ADDRESS OR P. O. BOX NO.
CITY
STATE OR PROVINCE
POSTAL OR ZIP CODE
COUNTRY

DO NOT MARK IN TH...
SAMPLE
TEST FORM:

SIDE 2

TEST FORM

TEST BOOK SERIAL NUMBER

ROOM NUMBER | SEAT NUMBER

SEX
○ Male
○ Female

DATE OF BIRTH
/ /
MO. DAY YEAR

Choose only one answer for each question. Carefully and completely fill in the circle corresponding to the answer you choose so that the letter inside the circle cannot be seen. Completely erase any other marks you may have made.

NAME (Print)

FAMILY NAME (SURNAME) | GIVEN NAME | MIDDLE NAME

REGISTRATION NUMBER

SIGNATURE

CORRECT	WRONG	WRONG	WRONG	WRONG
Ⓐ Ⓑ ● Ⓓ	Ⓐ Ⓑ Ⓒ̸ Ⓓ	Ⓐ Ⓑ Ⓧ Ⓓ	Ⓐ Ⓑ Ⓒ̷ Ⓓ	Ⓐ Ⓑ ⊙ Ⓓ

SECTION 1

SECTION 2

SECTION 3

IF YOU DO NOT WANT THIS ANSWER SHEET TO BE SCORED

If you want to cancel your scores from this administration, complete A and B below. The scores will not be sent to you or your designated recipients, and they will be removed from your permanent record.

To cancel your scores from this test administration, you must:

A. fill in both circles here

and   B. sign your name below

○—○

ONCE A SCORE IS CANCELED, IT CANNOT BE REPORTED AT ANY TIME.

FOR ETS USE ONLY

1R	2R	3R		TCS
1CS	2CS	3CS		

L

REGISTRATION NUMBER

Start here

TEST CENTER NUMBER

TOPIC

Ⓐ
Ⓑ
Ⓒ

Test of Written English (TWE)

Answer Sheet

SIDE 3

TEST DATE

Begin your essay here. If you need more space, use the other side.

SAMPLE

ADDITIONAL SPACE IS AVAILABLE ON THE REVERSE SIDE.

CHW02010   Q2035-3

3049060

DO NOT WRITE IN THIS SPACE

Continuation of essay

_____

_____

_____

_____

_____

_____

_____

_____

_____

_____

_____

_____

_____

_____

_____

_____

_____

_____

_____

_____

_____

_____

_____

_____

SAMPLE

_____

THE AREA BELOW IS FOR ETS USE ONLY. DO NOT MARK.

	READER NO.		0 1 2 3 4 5 6 7 8 9			A B C D E F G H I J K L M
1			0 1 2 3 4 5 6 7 8 9	1		N O P Q R S T U V W X Y Z
			0 1 2 3 4 5 6 7 8 9			
2	READER NO.		0 1 2 3 4 5 6 7 8 9	2		A B C D E F G H I J K L M
			0 1 2 3 4 5 6 7 8 9			N O P Q R S T U V W X Y Z
			0 1 2 3 4 5 6 7 8 9			
3	READER NO.		0 1 2 3 4 5 6 7 8 9	3		A B C D E F G H I J K L M
			0 1 2 3 4 5 6 7 8 9			N O P Q R S T U V W X Y Z
			0 1 2 3 4 5 6 7 8 9			

372

TEST OF ENGLISH AS A FOREIGN LANGUAGE

TOEFL ANSWER SHEET

I.N. 996948

72701 • 004170 • TF43M171e   KAJ03045   Q2058-1/1

3049060

DO NOT WRITE IN THIS SPACE

1. NAME: Copy your name from your admission ticket. Use one box for each letter. First print your family name (surname), then your given name, and then your middle name, if you have one. Leave one box blank between names. Below each box, fill in the circle that contains the same letter.

Use a No. 2 (H-B.) pencil only. Do not use ink. Be sure each mark is dark and completely fills the intended circle. Erase errors or stray marks completely.

2. REGISTRATION NUMBER
Start here

3. INSTITUTION AND DEPARTMENT CODES: Give the code numbers of the institutions and departments to which you want your official score report sent. Be sure to fill in the corresponding circle below each box.

INSTITUTION CODE   DEPT. CODE

4. DO YOU PLAN TO STUDY FOR A DEGREE IN THE U.S.A. OR CANADA?
○ YES
○ NO

5. REASON FOR TAKING TOEFL (FILL IN ONLY ONE CIRCLE.)

1. To enter a college or university as an undergraduate student
2. To enter a college or university as a graduate student.
3. To enter a school other than a college or university.
4. To become licensed to practice my profession in the U.S.A. or Canada.
5. To demonstrate my proficiency in English to the company for which I work or expect to work.
6. Other than the above (please specify).

6. NUMBER OF TIMES YOU HAVE TAKEN TOEFL BEFORE TODAY
0 1 2 3 4+

EDUCATIONAL TESTING SERVICE, ETS and its logo, TOEFL and its logo, are registered trademarks of Educational Testing Service. The modernized ETS logo is a trademark of Educational Testing Service.

® Copyright © 2003 by Educational Testing Service, Princeton, NJ 08541-0001. All rights reserved. Printed in U.S.A. ETS

7. TEST CENTER (Print.)

CENTER NUMBER

8. PLEASE PRINT YOUR NAME AND MAILING ADDRESS

FAMILY NAME (SURNAME)   GIVEN NAME   MIDDLE NAME

STREET ADDRESS OR P. O. BOX NO.

CITY   STATE OR PROVINCE

POSTAL OR ZIP CODE   COUNTRY

9. SIGNATURE AND DATE: Copy the statement below; use handwriting.

"I hereby agree to the conditions set forth in the *Information Bulletin* and affirm that I am the person whose name and address are given on this answer sheet."

DATE: MO. DAY YEAR

SIGNED:
(WRITE YOUR NAME IN PENCIL AS IF SIGNING A LEGAL IDENTIFICATION DOCUMENT)

DO NOT MARK IN TH...

TEST FORM:

SAMPLE

TEST FORM

Choose only one answer for each question. Carefully and completely fill in the circle corresponding to the answer you choose so that the letter inside the circle cannot be seen. Completely erase any other marks you may have made.

CORRECT	WRONG	WRONG	WRONG	WRONG
Ⓐ Ⓑ ● Ⓓ	Ⓐ Ⓑ Ⓒ̸ Ⓓ	Ⓐ Ⓑ Ⓧ Ⓓ	Ⓐ Ⓑ Ⓒ Ⓓ	Ⓐ Ⓑ Ⓒ Ⓓ

TEST BOOK SERIAL NUMBER

ROOM NUMBER   **SEAT NUMBER**

NAME (Print)

FAMILY NAME (SURNAME)   GIVEN NAME   MIDDLE NAME

SEX ○ Male ○ Female   **DATE OF BIRTH**   MO.   DAY   YEAR

REGISTRATION NUMBER   **SIGNATURE**

SECTION 1
1 Ⓐ Ⓑ Ⓒ Ⓓ
2 Ⓐ Ⓑ Ⓒ Ⓓ
3 Ⓐ Ⓑ Ⓒ Ⓓ
4 Ⓐ Ⓑ Ⓒ Ⓓ
5 Ⓐ Ⓑ Ⓒ Ⓓ
6 Ⓐ Ⓑ Ⓒ Ⓓ
7 Ⓐ Ⓑ Ⓒ Ⓓ
8 Ⓐ Ⓑ Ⓒ Ⓓ
9 Ⓐ Ⓑ Ⓒ Ⓓ
10 Ⓐ Ⓑ Ⓒ Ⓓ
11 Ⓐ Ⓑ Ⓒ Ⓓ
12 Ⓐ Ⓑ Ⓒ Ⓓ
13 Ⓐ Ⓑ Ⓒ Ⓓ
14 Ⓐ Ⓑ Ⓒ Ⓓ
15 Ⓐ Ⓑ Ⓒ Ⓓ
16 Ⓐ Ⓑ Ⓒ Ⓓ
17 Ⓐ Ⓑ Ⓒ Ⓓ
18 Ⓐ Ⓑ Ⓒ Ⓓ
19 Ⓐ Ⓑ Ⓒ Ⓓ
20 Ⓐ Ⓑ Ⓒ Ⓓ
21 Ⓐ Ⓑ Ⓒ Ⓓ
22 Ⓐ Ⓑ Ⓒ Ⓓ
23 Ⓐ Ⓑ Ⓒ Ⓓ
24 Ⓐ Ⓑ Ⓒ Ⓓ
25 Ⓐ Ⓑ Ⓒ Ⓓ
26 Ⓐ Ⓑ Ⓒ Ⓓ
27 Ⓐ Ⓑ Ⓒ Ⓓ
28 Ⓐ Ⓑ Ⓒ Ⓓ
29 Ⓐ Ⓑ Ⓒ Ⓓ
30 Ⓐ Ⓑ Ⓒ Ⓓ
31 Ⓐ Ⓑ Ⓒ Ⓓ
32 Ⓐ Ⓑ Ⓒ Ⓓ
33 Ⓐ Ⓑ Ⓒ Ⓓ
34 Ⓐ Ⓑ Ⓒ Ⓓ
35 Ⓐ Ⓑ Ⓒ Ⓓ
36 Ⓐ Ⓑ Ⓒ Ⓓ
37 Ⓐ Ⓑ Ⓒ Ⓓ
38 Ⓐ Ⓑ Ⓒ Ⓓ
39 Ⓐ Ⓑ Ⓒ Ⓓ
40 Ⓐ Ⓑ Ⓒ Ⓓ
41 Ⓐ Ⓑ Ⓒ Ⓓ
42 Ⓐ Ⓑ Ⓒ Ⓓ
43 Ⓐ Ⓑ Ⓒ Ⓓ
44 Ⓐ Ⓑ Ⓒ Ⓓ
45 Ⓐ Ⓑ Ⓒ Ⓓ
46 Ⓐ Ⓑ Ⓒ Ⓓ
47 Ⓐ Ⓑ Ⓒ Ⓓ
48 Ⓐ Ⓑ Ⓒ Ⓓ
49 Ⓐ Ⓑ Ⓒ Ⓓ
50 Ⓐ Ⓑ Ⓒ Ⓓ

SECTION 2
1 Ⓐ Ⓑ Ⓒ Ⓓ
2 Ⓐ Ⓑ Ⓒ Ⓓ
3 Ⓐ Ⓑ Ⓒ Ⓓ
4 Ⓐ Ⓑ Ⓒ Ⓓ
5 Ⓐ Ⓑ Ⓒ Ⓓ
6 Ⓐ Ⓑ Ⓒ Ⓓ
7 Ⓐ Ⓑ Ⓒ Ⓓ
8 Ⓐ Ⓑ Ⓒ Ⓓ
9 Ⓐ Ⓑ Ⓒ Ⓓ
10 Ⓐ Ⓑ Ⓒ Ⓓ
11 Ⓐ Ⓑ Ⓒ Ⓓ
12 Ⓐ Ⓑ Ⓒ Ⓓ
13 Ⓐ Ⓑ Ⓒ Ⓓ
14 Ⓐ Ⓑ Ⓒ Ⓓ
15 Ⓐ Ⓑ Ⓒ Ⓓ
16 Ⓐ Ⓑ Ⓒ Ⓓ
17 Ⓐ Ⓑ Ⓒ Ⓓ
18 Ⓐ Ⓑ Ⓒ Ⓓ
19 Ⓐ Ⓑ Ⓒ Ⓓ
20 Ⓐ Ⓑ Ⓒ Ⓓ
21 Ⓐ Ⓑ Ⓒ Ⓓ
22 Ⓐ Ⓑ Ⓒ Ⓓ
23 Ⓐ Ⓑ Ⓒ Ⓓ
24 Ⓐ Ⓑ Ⓒ Ⓓ
25 Ⓐ Ⓑ Ⓒ Ⓓ
26 Ⓐ Ⓑ Ⓒ Ⓓ
27 Ⓐ Ⓑ Ⓒ Ⓓ
28 Ⓐ Ⓑ Ⓒ Ⓓ
29 Ⓐ Ⓑ Ⓒ Ⓓ
30 Ⓐ Ⓑ Ⓒ Ⓓ
31 Ⓐ Ⓑ Ⓒ Ⓓ
32 Ⓐ Ⓑ Ⓒ Ⓓ
33 Ⓐ Ⓑ Ⓒ Ⓓ
34 Ⓐ Ⓑ Ⓒ Ⓓ
35 Ⓐ Ⓑ Ⓒ Ⓓ
36 Ⓐ Ⓑ Ⓒ Ⓓ
37 Ⓐ Ⓑ Ⓒ Ⓓ
38 Ⓐ Ⓑ Ⓒ Ⓓ
39 Ⓐ Ⓑ Ⓒ Ⓓ
40 Ⓐ Ⓑ Ⓒ Ⓓ

SECTION 3
1 Ⓐ Ⓑ Ⓒ Ⓓ   31 Ⓐ Ⓑ Ⓒ Ⓓ
2 Ⓐ Ⓑ Ⓒ Ⓓ   32 Ⓐ Ⓑ Ⓒ Ⓓ
3 Ⓐ Ⓑ Ⓒ Ⓓ   33 Ⓐ Ⓑ Ⓒ Ⓓ
4 Ⓐ Ⓑ Ⓒ Ⓓ   34 Ⓐ Ⓑ Ⓒ Ⓓ
5 Ⓐ Ⓑ Ⓒ Ⓓ   35 Ⓐ Ⓑ Ⓒ Ⓓ
6 Ⓐ Ⓑ Ⓒ Ⓓ   36 Ⓐ Ⓑ Ⓒ Ⓓ
7 Ⓐ Ⓑ Ⓒ Ⓓ   37 Ⓐ Ⓑ Ⓒ Ⓓ
8 Ⓐ Ⓑ Ⓒ Ⓓ   38 Ⓐ Ⓑ Ⓒ Ⓓ
9 Ⓐ Ⓑ Ⓒ Ⓓ   39 Ⓐ Ⓑ Ⓒ Ⓓ
10 Ⓐ Ⓑ Ⓒ Ⓓ   40 Ⓐ Ⓑ Ⓒ Ⓓ
11 Ⓐ Ⓑ Ⓒ Ⓓ   41 Ⓐ Ⓑ Ⓒ Ⓓ
12 Ⓐ Ⓑ Ⓒ Ⓓ   42 Ⓐ Ⓑ Ⓒ Ⓓ
13 Ⓐ Ⓑ Ⓒ Ⓓ   43 Ⓐ Ⓑ Ⓒ Ⓓ
14 Ⓐ Ⓑ Ⓒ Ⓓ   44 Ⓐ Ⓑ Ⓒ Ⓓ
15 Ⓐ Ⓑ Ⓒ Ⓓ   45 Ⓐ Ⓑ Ⓒ Ⓓ
16 Ⓐ Ⓑ Ⓒ Ⓓ   46 Ⓐ Ⓑ Ⓒ Ⓓ
17 Ⓐ Ⓑ Ⓒ Ⓓ   47 Ⓐ Ⓑ Ⓒ Ⓓ
18 Ⓐ Ⓑ Ⓒ Ⓓ   48 Ⓐ Ⓑ Ⓒ Ⓓ
19 Ⓐ Ⓑ Ⓒ Ⓓ   49 Ⓐ Ⓑ Ⓒ Ⓓ
20 Ⓐ Ⓑ Ⓒ Ⓓ   50 Ⓐ Ⓑ Ⓒ Ⓓ
21 Ⓐ Ⓑ Ⓒ Ⓓ
22 Ⓐ Ⓑ Ⓒ Ⓓ
23 Ⓐ Ⓑ Ⓒ Ⓓ
24 Ⓐ Ⓑ Ⓒ Ⓓ
25 Ⓐ Ⓑ Ⓒ Ⓓ
26 Ⓐ Ⓑ Ⓒ Ⓓ
27 Ⓐ Ⓑ Ⓒ Ⓓ
28 Ⓐ Ⓑ Ⓒ Ⓓ
29 Ⓐ Ⓑ Ⓒ Ⓓ
30 Ⓐ Ⓑ Ⓒ Ⓓ

SAMPLE

IF YOU DO **NOT** WANT THIS ANSWER SHEET TO BE SCORED

If you want to cancel your scores from this administration, complete A and B below. The scores will not be sent to you or your designated recipients, and they will be removed from your permanent record.

To cancel your scores from this test administration, you must:

A. fill in both circles here   and   B. sign your name below

○ — ○ _____

ONCE A SCORE IS CANCELED, IT CANNOT BE REPORTED AT ANY TIME.

1R	2R	3R	TCS
1CS	2CS	3CS	
		FOR ETS USE ONLY	M

REGISTRATION NUMBER

TEST CENTER NUMBER

TOPIC

Test of Written English (TWE)

Answer Sheet

SIDE 3

Start here

(A) (K) (U) (0) (0) (0)
(B) (L) (V) (1) (1) (1)
(C) (M) (W) (2) (2) (2)
(D) (N) (X) (3) (3) (3)
(E) (O) (Y) (4) (4) (4)
(F) (P) (Z) (5) (5) (5)
(G) (Q) (6) (6) (6)
(H) (R) (7) (7) (7)
(I) (S) (8) (8) (8)
(J) (T) (9) (9) (9)

(A)

(B)

(C)

TEST DATE

Begin your essay here. If you need more space, use the other side.

SAMPLE

ADDITIONAL SPACE IS AVAILABLE ON THE REVERSE SIDE.

Q2035-3

CHW02010

3049060

DO NOT WRITE IN THIS SPACE

Continuation of essay

SAMPLE

THE AREA BELOW IS FOR ETS USE ONLY. DO NOT MARK.

1 READER NO.

2 READER NO.

3 READER NO.

TEST OF ENGLISH AS A FOREIGN LANGUAGE

TOEFL ANSWER SHEET   SIDE 1

I.N. 996948   72701 • 004170 • TF43M171e   KAJ03045   Q2058-1/1

3049060

DO NOT WRITE IN THIS SPACE

1. NAME: Copy your name from your admission ticket. Use one box for each letter. First print your family name (surname), then your given name, and then your middle name, if you have one. Leave one box blank between names. Below each box, fill in the circle that contains the same letter.

Use a No. 2 (H.B.) pencil only. Do not use ink. Be sure each mark is dark and completely fills the intended circle. Erase errors or stray marks completely.

2. REGISTRATION NUMBER
Start here

3. INSTITUTION AND DEPARTMENT CODES: Give the code numbers of the institutions and departments to which you want your official score report sent. Be sure to fill in the corresponding circle below each box.

INSTITUTION CODE — DEPT. CODE

4. DO YOU PLAN TO STUDY FOR A DEGREE IN THE U.S.A. OR CANADA?
○ YES
○ NO

5. REASON FOR TAKING TOEFL (FILL IN ONLY ONE CIRCLE.)

○ 1. To enter a college or university as an undergraduate student.
○ 2. To enter a college or university as a graduate student.
○ 3. To enter a school other than a college or university.
○ 4. To become licensed to practice my profession in the U.S.A. or Canada.
○ 5. To demonstrate my proficiency in English to the company for which I work or expect to work.
○ 6. Other than the above (please specify).

6. NUMBER OF TIMES YOU HAVE TAKEN TOEFL BEFORE TODAY
○ 0   ① 1   ② 2   ③ 3   ④ 4+

© Copyright © 2003 by Educational Testing Service, Princeton, NJ 08541-0001. All rights reserved. Printed in U.S.A. (ETS)

EDUCATIONAL TESTING SERVICE, ETS and its logo, TOEFL and its logo, are registered trademarks of Educational Testing Service. The modernized ETS logo is a trademark of Educational Testing Service.

9. SIGNATURE AND DATE: Copy the statement below; use handwriting.
"I hereby agree to the conditions set forth in the *Information Bulletin* and affirm that I am the person whose name and address are given on this answer sheet."

SIGNED: _____
(WRITE YOUR NAME IN PENCIL AS IF SIGNING A LEGAL IDENTIFICATION DOCUMENT)

DATE: ___ / ___ / ___
MO. DAY YEAR

7. TEST CENTER (Print.)
CENTER NUMBER

8. PLEASE PRINT YOUR NAME AND MAILING ADDRESS
FAMILY NAME (SURNAME)   GIVEN NAME   MIDDLE NAME
STREET ADDRESS OR P. O. BOX NO.
CITY   STATE OR PROVINCE
POSTAL OR ZIP CODE   COUNTRY

CITY
COUNTRY

DO NOT MARK IN THIS
TEST FORM:

SAMPLE

TEST FORM

TEST BOOK SERIAL NUMBER

ROOM NUMBER   SEAT NUMBER

SEX
○ Male
○ Female

DATE OF BIRTH
/ /
MO. DAY YEAR

Choose only one answer for each question. Carefully and completely fill in the circle corresponding to the answer you choose so that the letter inside the circle cannot be seen. Completely erase any other marks you may have made.

NAME (Print) _____
FAMILY NAME (SURNAME)   GIVEN NAME   MIDDLE NAME

REGISTRATION NUMBER

SIGNATURE

CORRECT	WRONG	WRONG	WRONG	WRONG	WRONG

SECTION 1

SECTION 2

SECTION 3

SAMPLE

IF YOU DO NOT WANT THIS ANSWER SHEET TO BE SCORED

If you want to cancel your scores from this administration, complete A and B below. The scores will not be sent to you or your designated recipients, and they will be removed from your permanent record.

To cancel your scores from this test administration, you must:

A. fill in both circles here   and   B. sign your name below

ONCE A SCORE IS CANCELED, IT CANNOT BE REPORTED AT ANY TIME.

FOR ETS USE ONLY

1R	2R	3R	TCS
1CS	2CS	3CS	

L

378

REGISTRATION NUMBER

↓ Start here

0	0	0	0	0	0	0
1	1	1	1	1	1	1
2	2	2	2	2	2	2
3	3	3	3	3	3	3
4	4	4	4	4	4	4
5	5	5	5	5	5	5
6	6	6	6	6	6	6
7	7	7	7	7	7	7
8	8	8	8	8	8	8
9	9	9	9	9	9	9

TEST CENTER NUMBER

A	K	U	0	0	0
B	L	V	1	1	1
C	M	W	2	2	2
D	N	X	3	3	3
E	O	Y	4	4	4
F	P	Z	5	5	5
G	Q		6	6	6
H	R		7	7	7
I	S		8	8	8
J	T		9	9	9

TOPIC

Ⓐ

Ⓑ

Ⓒ

TEST DATE

Begin your essay here. If you need more space, use the other side.

SAMPLE

ADDITIONAL SPACE IS AVAILABLE ON THE REVERSE SIDE.

CHW020l0 Q2035-3

Continuation of essay

SAMPLE

THE AREA BELOW IS FOR ETS USE ONLY. DO NOT MARK.

1 READER NO.		0 1 2 3 4 5 6 7 8 9 0 1 2 3 4 5 6 7 8 9 0 1 2 3 4 5 6 7 8 9	1		A B C D E F G H I J K L M N O P Q R S T U V W X Y Z
2 READER NO.		0 1 2 3 4 5 6 7 8 9 0 1 2 3 4 5 6 7 8 9 0 1 2 3 4 5 6 7 8 9	2		A B C D E F G H I J K L M N O P Q R S T U V W X Y Z
3 READER NO.		0 1 2 3 4 5 6 7 8 9 0 1 2 3 4 5 6 7 8 9 0 1 2 3 4 5 6 7 8 9	3		A B C D E F G H I J K L M N O P Q R S T U V W X Y Z

RECORDING SCRIPT

LISTENING COMPREHENSION DIAGNOSTIC PRE-TEST

Part A, p. 3

1. (man) How was the concert last night?
   (woman) It was wonderful.
   (narrator) WHAT DOES THE WOMAN MEAN?

2. (woman) How much will it cost to mail this package to New York?
   (man) Two dollars.
   (narrator) WHERE DOES THIS CONVERSATION PROBABLY TAKE PLACE?

3. (woman) How old is your daughter now?
   (man) She's just a year and a half.
   (narrator) WHAT DOES THE MAN MEAN?

4. (man) Is Paul on the basketball team?
   (woman) But he's not tall enough.
   (narrator) WHAT DOES THE WOMAN IMPLY ABOUT PAUL?

5. (man) I think this seminar's going to be really great!
   (woman) Me, too.
   (narrator) WHAT DOES THE WOMAN MEAN?

6. (woman) Are you going to the meeting this afternoon?
   (man) Where is it?
   (narrator) WHAT DOES THE MAN WANT TO KNOW?

7. (man) I don't feel like cooking.
   (woman) Let's go out to dinner, then.
   (narrator) WHAT DOES THE WOMAN SUGGEST?

8. (man) Are you going to call Joe?
   (woman) I phoned him already.
   (narrator) WHAT DOES THE WOMAN MEAN?

9. (woman) How did you win that game?
   (man) Actually, I was very lucky!
   (narrator) WHAT DOES THE MAN MEAN?

10. (woman) Why don't we take your car to the movies instead of mine?
    (man) But mine's not very clean.
    (narrator) WHAT DOES THE MAN SAY ABOUT THE CAR?

11. (man) When will the plane be landing?
    (woman) The plane will be landing in just a few minutes, so you'll need to fasten your seat belt.
    (narrator) WHO IS THE WOMAN MOST LIKELY TO BE?

12. (woman) Where is your desk located?
    (man) Right in the middle of the office.
    (narrator) WHAT DOES THE MAN MEAN?

13. (man) I don't know how to play golf, but I'd really like to learn.
    (woman) Why not take a few lessons?
    (narrator) WHAT DOES THE WOMAN SUGGEST TO THE MAN?

14. (woman) Is it time to leave yet?
    (man) Not for a while.
    (narrator) WHAT DOES THE MAN MEAN?

15. (man) Can I turn in the homework next week?
    (woman) No, it's due tomorrow.
    (narrator) WHAT DOES THE WOMAN MEAN?

16. (woman) The trees are really beautiful at this time of year.
    (man) I'll say!
    (narrator) WHAT DOES THE MAN MEAN?

17. (man) Can you show me where I can try these clothes on?
    (woman) The fitting rooms are at the back of the store.
    (narrator) WHERE DOES THE WOMAN MOST LIKELY WORK?

18. (man) Are you on your way out now?
    (woman) I need to buy some groceries.
    (narrator) WHAT DOES THE WOMAN IMPLY?

19. (man) Stan got the highest grade on the exam.
    (woman) Of course he did. He's not exactly dumb.
    (narrator) WHAT DOES THE WOMAN SAY ABOUT STAN?

20. (woman) I've been studying for five hours straight!
    (man) Why not take a break for a bit?
    (narrator) WHAT DOES THE MAN SUGGEST?

21. (woman) Is Sharon ready to go?
    (man) She's busy packing her suitcase.
    (narrator) WHAT DOES THE MAN SAY ABOUT SHARON?

22. (man) It's too bad our team lost the game.
    (woman) You can say that again!
    (narrator) WHAT DOES THE WOMAN MEAN?

23. (man) How's Bob feeling after the accident?
    (woman) He's a bit better, but he's still not very strong.
    (narrator) WHAT DOES THE WOMAN SAY ABOUT BOB?

24. (woman) Is there something wrong with the car?
    (man) The engine doesn't sound good.
    (narrator) WHAT DOES THE MAN MEAN?

25. (man) How much time will we have at this art museum?
    (woman) We'll stop here for two hours, and then you should be back on the bus at three o'clock.
    (narrator) WHO IS THE WOMAN MOST LIKELY TO BE?

26. (woman) This apartment is a mess.
    (man) Let's clean it up quickly.
    (narrator) WHAT DOES THE MAN SUGGEST?

27. (man) Why is Alec so happy?
    (woman) He just got a huge bonus check.
    (narrator) WHAT DOES THE WOMAN SAY ABOUT ALEC?

28. (man) Let's go shopping today.
    (woman) Okay, but I don't want to go to a store that's far away.
    (narrator) WHAT DOES THE WOMAN MEAN?

29. (woman) How could you tell that Alice was angry?
    (man) When she left, she slammed the door.
    (narrator) WHAT DOES THE MAN MEAN?

30. (man) Do you have any plans for Saturday?
    (woman) We're going for a hike in the woods. Do you want to go?
    (narrator) WHAT IS THE WOMAN PLANNING TO DO?

Part B, p. 6

Questions 31 through 34. Listen to two students discussing how to get to school.

(woman) Do you know where I can get a bicycle? It doesn't have to be a new bicycle, but it does have to be rather cheap.
(man) Why do you need a bicycle?
(woman) I just found a great apartment, but it's a little bit far from school. I really want to take this apartment, but I have to find some transportation. A bicycle would be great!
(man) How far away from school is the apartment?
(woman) Just a little over two miles, so I definitely could walk if I had to. But it would save so much time if I had a bicycle. My problem is that I can't afford a really new, expensive bicycle.
(man) Well, you happen to be in luck today. I have a friend who wants to sell his old bicycle because he just bought a new one, and I think you can get it cheap. Do you want to go see the bicycle?
(woman) Thanks. That sounds great. Let's go there now.

31. WHAT DOES THE WOMAN WANT TO GET?
32. APPROXIMATELY HOW FAR AWAY FROM SCHOOL IS THE WOMAN'S APARTMENT?
33. WHY IS THE MAN'S FRIEND SELLING HIS OLD BICYCLE?
34. WHAT WILL THE MAN AND WOMAN PROBABLY DO NEXT?

Questions 35 through 38. Listen to a conversation about a camping trip.

(woman) What are those?
(man) They're some pictures of the camping trip that some friends and I took last weekend. Would you like to see them?
(woman) Thanks. I would.
(man) These photos show the tent that we stayed in.
(woman) How many of you stayed in that tent? It looks awfully small.
(man) There were four of us.
(woman) Four of you? In that small tent? Wasn't it awfully crowded?
(man) It was a little crowded, but it was fun anyway.
(woman) And whatever are you doing in these pictures? It looks like you're just standing in a river with big boots on.
(man) Well, we were trying to fish.
(woman) Did you catch a lot of fish?
(man) No, not a lot. . . .
(woman) Well, did you catch a few fish?
(man) No, not a few . . . actually we didn't catch any . . . but it was still a great way to spend a day.

35. WHAT ARE THE MAN AND WOMAN DOING?
36. WHAT DOES THE WOMAN SAY ABOUT THE TENT?
37. WHAT WAS THE MAN DOING WHEN HE WAS WEARING THE BOOTS?
38. HOW MANY FISH DID THE MAN CATCH?

Part C, p. 7

Questions 39 through 42. Listen as a chemistry professor begins a lecture.

(man) Before I start today's lecture, I'd like to make sure that you know everything you need to know about the exam that we're having on Friday. The exam will cover the first three chapters in the chemistry textbook plus any additional information from the class lectures, so be sure to study your class notes in addition to the three chapters in the text. The exam will be mostly multiple choice—you'll have fifty multiple-choice questions—and two short written essay answers. You'll have an hour and a half for the exam; you'll need about an hour for the fifty multiple-choice questions and about thirty minutes for the two essays. Any questions about the exam? Okay, then. Let's get on with the lecture.

39. WHAT INFORMATION IS COVERED ON THE EXAM?
40. WHAT TYPES OF QUESTIONS ARE INCLUDED ON THE EXAM?
41. HOW MUCH TIME WILL THE STUDENTS HAVE FOR THE EXAM?
42. WHAT WILL THE STUDENTS PROBABLY DO NEXT?

Questions 43 through 46. Listen as a tour guide describes Alcatraz.

(woman)   As the boat continues on out to Alcatraz Island, let me tell you a little bit about what we're going to see.

As you can clearly see from here, Alcatraz is a rocky island out in the middle of San Francisco Bay. The name Alcatraz comes from the Spanish word for "pelican," which is a type of bird. When a Spanish explorer discovered the island in 1775, there were many, many pelicans living on the island, and no people.

The first prison was built on Alcatraz in 1848, and Alcatraz remained in use as a prison until 1963. During that time, 39 men tried to escape from the island by swimming across the bay. Of the 39 men who tried to escape, 24 were recaptured, 10 died, and 5 were never heard from.

Since 1972, Alcatraz has been open to the public for tours. In a moment, you'll be able to walk through the empty prison cell blocks and get an idea of what prison life was like here in the past.

43. WHERE DOES THIS TALK TAKE PLACE?
44. WHAT IS A PELICAN?
45. HOW MANY MEN TRIED TO ESCAPE FROM ALCATRAZ?
46. WHAT IS TRUE ABOUT ALCATRAZ TODAY?

Questions 47 through 50. Listen to a talk about a new type of plant.

(woman)   Today I'd like to discuss something new that botanists may be bringing us in the near future: plants that produce plastic. I'm not talking about artificial plants made from plastic. I'm talking about living, growing plants that produce a plastic-like substance.

The natural plastic from these plants has at least one major advantage over the artificial plastic that's so common today. This new plastic from plants biodegrades quickly, which means that it is much better for the environment. Today's artificial plastic biodegrades very slowly. When people finish with plastic products and throw them away, the plastic remains intact for years. These unused plastic products are covering the Earth and causing quite a problem. Perhaps the new, natural plastics from plants can help to solve that problem.

47. WHAT TYPE OF PLANTS IS THE WOMAN DISCUSSING?
48. WHAT IS THE MAJOR ADVANTAGE OF THE NEW NATURAL PLASTIC?
49. WHAT IS THE PROBLEM WITH TODAY'S ARTIFICIAL PLASTIC?
50. THIS LECTURE MIGHT BE GIVEN IN WHICH COURSE?

LISTENING PART A

TOEFL EXERCISE 1, p. 13

1. (man)   How was the dance last night?
   (woman)   We had such a good time.
   (narrator) WHAT DOES THE WOMAN MEAN?

2. (man)   Are you ready to leave?
   (woman)   I need about thirty minutes.
   (narrator) WHAT DOES THE WOMAN MEAN?

3. (woman)   I'm really having trouble in psychology class.
   (man)   You should talk with the teacher.
   (narrator) WHAT DOES THE MAN MEAN?

4. (man)   Have you found a job yet?
   (woman)   I actually started my new job yesterday.
   (narrator) WHAT DOES THE WOMAN MEAN?

5. (man)   Do you know why Stan wanted to talk to me?
   (woman)   He needs to find someone to share an apartment.
   (narrator) WHAT DOES THE WOMAN SAY ABOUT STAN?

6. (woman)   When are you taking your vacation?
   (man)   In the fall.
   (narrator) WHAT DOES THE MAN MEAN?

7. (man)   Did you enjoy the book?
   (woman)   It was quite pleasant to read.
   (narrator) WHAT DOES THE WOMAN MEAN?

8. (woman) Why were you so late?
   (man) Traffic was very heavy.
   (narrator) WHAT DOES THE MAN MEAN?

9. (woman) Do you want to go to the game with us tonight?
   (man) Sorry, I can't. I have to finish the report for history class.
   (narrator) WHAT DOES THE MAN MEAN?

10. (man) Does Steve work for you?
    (woman) No, Steve manages his own business.
    (narrator) WHAT DOES THE WOMAN SAY ABOUT STEVE?

TOEFL EXERCISE 2, p. 15

1. (woman) Why were you so late getting here?
   (man) But I wasn't late!
   (narrator) WHAT DOES THE MAN MEAN?

2. (man) Did you bring the book with you?
   (woman) Oh, I'm sorry. I didn't remember to bring it.
   (narrator) WHAT DOES THE WOMAN MEAN?

3. (man) Is the baby awake yet?
   (woman) No, she's not.
   (narrator) WHAT DOES THE WOMAN SAY ABOUT THE BABY?

4. (woman) Are you going on the trip by yourself?
   (man) No, I'm traveling with a large group of people.
   (narrator) WHAT DOES THE MAN MEAN?

5. (man) Do you have time to go to the park for a while?
   (woman) Sure. I'm not very busy.
   (narrator) WHAT DOES THE WOMAN MEAN?

6. (woman) Why is it all wet in here?
   (man) The rain got in because the windows weren't closed.
   (narrator) WHAT DOES THE MAN MEAN?

7. (man) I think you should throw that plant out. It looks dead.
   (woman) But I'm sure it's not dead!
   (narrator) WHAT DOES THE WOMAN MEAN?

8. (woman) That apple looks good.
   (man) It may look good, but it's not. It's not sweet at all.
   (narrator) WHAT DOES THE MAN SAY ABOUT THE APPLE?

9. (man) I don't think we should go out to dinner tonight. We can't afford it.
   (woman) No problem. I've found a restaurant that's not very expensive.
   (narrator) WHAT DOES THE WOMAN SAY ABOUT THE RESTAURANT?

10. (woman) Look at this rock by the side of the path. It's beautiful. Do you think I should take it with me?
    (man) It's too big. You can't take it with you.
    (narrator) WHAT DOES THE MAN IMPLY?

TOEFL REVIEW EXERCISE (Skills 1–2), p. 16

1. (man) What did you think of the exam?
   (woman) I thought it was quite simple!
   (narrator) WHAT DOES THE WOMAN MEAN?

2. (woman) Will you be finished soon?
   (man) Sorry. I don't work very quickly.
   (narrator) WHAT DOES THE MAN MEAN?

3. (man) How did your mother and father feel when you got home so late?
   (woman) They were very angry.
   (narrator) WHAT DOES THE WOMAN MEAN?

4. (woman) I hear that you got a new car.
   (man) I got a car, but it's not really new.
   (narrator) WHAT DOES THE MAN MEAN?

5. (man) Is it time for my appointment yet?
   (woman) Please have a seat.
   (narrator) WHAT DOES THE WOMAN ASK THE MAN TO DO?

6. (woman) How was your football game this afternoon?
   (man) I'm not too happy. We didn't win.
   (narrator) WHAT DOES THE MAN MEAN?

7. (woman) Are you going to pay the rent today?
   (man) Oh, I did that the day before yesterday.
   (narrator) WHAT DOES THE MAN MEAN?

8. (man) Can Barry go camping with us this weekend?
   (woman) Oh, I don't think he's old enough.
   (narrator) WHAT DOES THE WOMAN MEAN?

9. (woman) Let's go to the movies right now.
   (man) Sorry, I can't now. I have to finish the laundry.
   (narrator) WHAT DOES THE MAN MEAN?

10. (woman) The weather here is always so wet.
    (man) Yes, and I really don't like humid weather.
    (narrator) WHAT DOES THE MAN MEAN?

TOEFL EXERCISE 3, p. 18

1. (man) I'd like to work out this afternoon.
   (woman) Let's go to the gym for a while.
   (narrator) WHAT DOES THE WOMAN SUGGEST?

2. (woman) I can't finish the work today. I'm too tired.
   (man) Why not finish it tomorrow?
   (narrator) WHAT DOES THE MAN SUGGEST?

3. (man)   It's rather cool in here.
   (woman)   Let's turn on the heat.
   (narrator) WHAT DOES THE WOMAN
              SUGGEST?

4. (woman)   My old car has broken down again.
   (man)   Why don't you get a new one?
   (narrator) WHAT DOES THE MAN SUGGEST?

5. (man)   We've got so many books here. I
              can't find the one I want.
   (woman)   Let's organize them on the shelves.
   (narrator) WHAT DOES THE WOMAN
              SUGGEST?

6. (woman)   These clothes are too small for me.
   (man)   Why not let your sister have them?
   (narrator) WHAT DOES THE MAN SUGGEST
              TO THE WOMAN?

7. (man)   It's too late to leave tonight.
   (woman)   Let's put off the trip until tomorrow.
   (narrator) WHAT DOES THE WOMAN
              SUGGEST?

8. (woman)   I really need to get going on this
              term paper.
   (man)   Why not plan on staying in the
              library all day?
   (narrator) WHAT DOES THE MAN SUGGEST
              TO THE WOMAN?

9. (man)   There's a really funny program
              coming on television now.
   (woman)   Let's watch it then.
   (narrator) WHAT DOES THE WOMAN
              SUGGEST?

10. (man)   It's unbelievable, but I've actually
              got a little extra money now.
   (woman)   Why not put it in the bank?
   (narrator) WHAT DOES THE WOMAN
              SUGGEST TO THE MAN?

TOEFL REVIEW EXERCISE (Skills 1–3), p. 18

1. (man)   It seems that Bob's not home often.
   (woman)   That's because he travels a lot for his
              job.
   (narrator) WHAT DOES THE WOMAN SAY
              ABOUT BOB?

2. (woman)   It's time to wash the car.
   (man)   Not now!
   (narrator) WHAT DOES THE MAN MEAN?

3. (man)   The apartment where I'm living is
              just too noisy.
   (woman)   Why not move to a new apartment?
   (narrator) WHAT DOES THE WOMAN
              SUGGEST?

4. (woman)   Alan, why were you late for work
              this morning?
   (man)   I overslept.
   (narrator) WHAT HAPPENED TO ALAN?

5. (woman)   It's a little difficult to get to know
              Betty.
   (man)   She's not a very talkative person.
   (narrator) WHAT DOES THE MAN SAY
              ABOUT BETTY?

6. (man)   I'm rather thirsty. What about you?
   (woman)   Let's make some lemonade.
   (narrator) WHAT DOES THE WOMAN
              SUGGEST?

7. (woman)   Can you tell me about the
              assignment for tonight?
   (man)   Call me up later, and I can tell you
              about it.
   (narrator) WHAT DOES THE MAN WANT
              THE WOMAN TO DO?

8. (man)   My hair has gotten way too long.
   (woman)   Why don't you get it cut this
              afternoon?
   (narrator) WHAT DOES THE WOMAN
              SUGGEST TO THE MAN?

9. (man)   Do you think Tim was telling the
              truth?
   (woman)   I'm not sure I believe him.
   (narrator) WHAT DOES THE WOMAN SAY
              ABOUT TIM?

10. (woman)   What time is the break today?
   (man)   It's at the regular hour.
   (narrator) WHAT DOES THE MAN MEAN?

TOEFL EXERCISE 4, p. 21

1. (man)   Did the package from your family
              arrive?
   (woman)   Yes, and I already opened it.
   (narrator) WHAT DOES THE WOMAN MEAN?

2. (woman)   How's your report coming along?
   (man)   It was finished this morning.
   (narrator) WHAT DOES THE MAN IMPLY?

3. (man)   Why aren't the children in bed now?
   (woman)   Their parents let them stay up.
   (narrator) WHAT DOES THE WOMAN MEAN?

4. (woman)   Why aren't you inside the house?
   (man)   I lost the key to the front door.
   (narrator) WHAT DOES THE MAN MEAN?

5. (woman)   Where are the flowers that I just
              picked?
   (man)   I put them on the dining room table.
   (narrator) WHAT DOES THE MAN MEAN?

6. (man)   Martha, what's the matter? You look
              upset.
   (woman)   I just noticed that my purse was
              stolen.
   (narrator) WHAT DOES THE WOMAN MEAN?

7. (woman)   Would you like to pick up one of my pet snakes?
   (man)   No, thanks. They frighten me more than a little.
   (narrator) WHAT DOES THE MAN MEAN?

8. (man)   Did you get the project done, as I asked?
   (woman)   I followed your directions to the letter.
   (narrator) WHAT DOES THE WOMAN MEAN?

9. (woman)   Do we have time to play some tennis now?
   (man)   No, it's time to cook supper.
   (narrator) WHAT DOES THE MAN MEAN?

10. (man)   Why aren't we having the exam tomorrow?
   (woman)   The date of the exam has changed.
   (narrator) WHAT DOES THE WOMAN IMPLY?

TOEFL REVIEW EXERCISE (Skills 1–4), p. 22

1. (man)   Do you want to go out in the sailboat today?
   (woman)   Oh, it's too windy.
   (narrator) WHAT DOES THE WOMAN MEAN?

2. (man)   I have a bad headache.
   (woman)   Why don't you take some aspirin?
   (narrator) WHAT DOES THE WOMAN SUGGEST TO THE MAN?

3. (woman)   When is the park open?
   (man)   It's open from sunrise to sunset each day.
   (narrator) WHAT DOES THE MAN MEAN?

4. (man)   Did Steve pay for his part of the meal?
   (woman)   Yes, he handed me five dollars.
   (narrator) WHAT DOES THE WOMAN MEAN?

5. (woman)   Did you do well on the math problem?
   (man)   In fact, I was completely incorrect.
   (narrator) WHAT DOES THE MAN MEAN?

6. (woman)   Is the washing machine still broken?
   (man)   No, I fixed it this morning.
   (narrator) WHAT DOES THE MAN MEAN?

7. (man)   I couldn't get registered in the algebra course that I wanted.
   (woman)   Why don't you take it next semester?
   (narrator) WHAT DOES THE WOMAN SUGGEST?

8. (woman)   You don't want me to walk in the kitchen now?
   (man)   No, I just washed the floor, and it's still wet.
   (narrator) WHAT DOES THE MAN SAY ABOUT THE FLOOR?

9. (man)   Is there enough food for everyone at the party?
   (woman)   You can relax. Everyone has enough to eat.
   (narrator) WHAT DOES THE WOMAN MEAN?

10. (woman)   Did everyone know about the meeting?
   (man)   Yes, I informed everyone.
   (narrator) WHAT DOES THE MAN MEAN?

TOEFL EXERCISE 5, p. 24

1. (man)   Do you want to go into the water?
   (woman)   No, thanks. I prefer to lie here on the sand.
   (narrator) WHERE DOES THIS CONVERSATION PROBABLY TAKE PLACE?

2. (woman)   What's the assignment for tomorrow's class?
   (man)   You should read Chapter 5 and answer the questions at the end of the chapter.
   (narrator) WHO IS THE MAN MOST LIKELY TO BE?

3. (man)   Can you tell me how long I can keep these books?
   (woman)   You can check them out for two weeks.
   (narrator) WHERE DOES THIS CONVERSATION PROBABLY TAKE PLACE?

4. (woman)   Are there many problems with my teeth? I've tried to brush regularly.
   (man)   I see one tooth that needs to be filled.
   (narrator) WHO IS THE MAN MOST LIKELY TO BE?

5. (woman)   The seat belt light is flashing.
   (man)   Yes, I think we're going to land soon.
   (narrator) WHERE DOES THIS CONVERSATION PROBABLY TAKE PLACE?

6. (man)   The wedding is actually tomorrow.
   (woman)   I can't believe that tomorrow's our wedding day.
   (narrator) WHO IS THE WOMAN MOST LIKELY TO BE?

7. (man)   Should we fill up the tank?
   (woman)   Yes, and put some air in the tires.
   (narrator) WHERE DOES THIS CONVERSATION PROBABLY TAKE PLACE?

8. (woman)   Are you going to the gym to work out this morning?
   (man)   Yes, to the gym in the morning and to team practice in the afternoon.
   (narrator) WHO IS THE MAN MOST LIKELY TO BE?

9. *(woman)* Can I help you?
   (man) Yes, I'd like to pick up some shirts I left to be cleaned.
   (narrator) WHERE DOES THIS CONVERSATION PROBABLY TAKE PLACE?

10. *(man)* I'm not sure which day I want to leave on this trip.
    (woman) When you decide on the date of the trip, come back to the office and you can make reservations and purchase the tickets.
    (narrator) WHO IS THE WOMAN MOST LIKELY TO BE?

TOEFL REVIEW EXERCISE (Skills 1–5), p. 25

1. *(woman)* It's quite cool in here, don't you think?
   (man) Let's close the window.
   (narrator) WHAT DOES THE MAN SUGGEST?

2. *(man)* Did the flight get in at two o'clock?
   (woman) It arrived right on schedule.
   (narrator) WHAT DOES THE WOMAN MEAN?

3. *(woman)* Are you ready to go home yet?
   (man) I'd like to swim a few more laps first.
   (narrator) WHERE DOES THIS CONVERSATION PROBABLY TAKE PLACE?

4. *(man)* Does Ralph like the new sofa?
   (woman) He's not too pleased with it.
   (narrator) WHAT DOES THE WOMAN SAY ABOUT RALPH?

5. *(woman)* Why did you yell so loud?
   (man) I'm sorry. It was a big mistake.
   (narrator) WHAT DOES THE MAN MEAN?

6. *(man)* When are the school fees due?
   (woman) The school fees must be paid tomorrow.
   (narrator) WHAT DOES THE WOMAN MEAN?

7. *(man)* What happened to Tony?
   (woman) Someone ran into him and hurt him during a football game.
   (narrator) WHAT DOES THE WOMAN SAY ABOUT TONY?

8. *(woman)* Why were you standing at the back of the room during the lecture?
   (man) There were no empty seats.
   (narrator) WHAT DOES THE MAN MEAN?

9. *(man)* This soup tastes awfully boring.
   (woman) Let's put some more spices in it.
   (narrator) WHAT DOES THE WOMAN SUGGEST?

10. *(woman)* I'm here for an appointment with the dean at three o'clock.
    (man) Please take a seat, and she'll be with you in a moment.
    (narrator) WHO IS THE MAN MOST LIKELY TO BE?

TOEFL EXERCISE 6, p. 27

1. *(man)* I think we should visit Sam in the hospital.
   (woman) Me, too.
   (narrator) WHAT DOES THE WOMAN MEAN?

2. *(man)* The news really surprised me.
   (woman) You can say that again.
   (narrator) WHAT DOES THE WOMAN MEAN?

3. *(woman)* I think it would be nice to have a pet.
   (man) So do I.
   (narrator) WHAT DOES THE MAN MEAN?

4. *(woman)* That movie was so boring.
   (man) I'll say!
   (narrator) WHAT DOES THE MAN MEAN?

5. *(man)* I'm so glad those three classes are over.
   (woman) You can say that again!
   (narrator) WHAT DOES THE WOMAN MEAN?

6. *(woman)* I prefer playing sports rather than watching sports.
   (man) Me, too.
   (narrator) WHAT DOES THE MAN MEAN?

7. *(man)* The coffee is really strong.
   (woman) I'll say!
   (narrator) WHAT DOES THE WOMAN MEAN?

8. *(woman)* I thought the math exam was almost impossible.
   (man) Me, too.
   (narrator) WHAT DOES THE MAN MEAN?

9. *(man)* I think we should go out for dinner tonight.
   (woman) So do I!
   (narrator) WHAT DOES THE WOMAN MEAN?

10. *(woman)* The new teacher certainly made history interesting.
    (man) You can say that again!
    (narrator) WHAT DOES THE MAN MEAN?

TOEFL REVIEW EXERCISE (Skills 1–6), p. 28

1. *(woman)* The apple pie sure looks good.
   (man) Let's have some of it.
   (narrator) WHAT DOES THE MAN SUGGEST?

2. *(man)* How much time is left on the test?
   (woman) You have about thirty minutes.
   (narrator) WHAT DOES THE WOMAN MEAN?

3. *(man)* I think we should pay the bills tonight.
   (woman) So do I.
   (narrator) WHAT DOES THE WOMAN MEAN?

4. *(woman)* Are you going to plant the new rose bushes today?
   (man) Yes, after I weed the tomato plants and cut the bushes around the yard.
   (narrator) WHO IS THE MAN MOST LIKELY TO BE?

5. *(woman)* Did Karla pass the statistics exam?
   (man) Not exactly.
   (narrator) WHAT DOES THE MAN SAY ABOUT KARLA?

6. *(man)* What can I get for you?
   (woman) A sandwich and fries to go, please.
   (narrator) WHERE DOES THIS CONVERSATION PROBABLY TAKE PLACE?

7. *(woman)* Doesn't the lake look beautiful from here?
   (man) Let's go down for a swim.
   (narrator) WHAT DOES THE MAN SUGGEST?

8. *(man)* Do you think Peter answered your questions honestly?
   (woman) I'm sure he expressed his true feelings.
   (narrator) WHAT DOES THE WOMAN SAY ABOUT PETER?

9. *(woman)* A cold drink would taste good now.
   (man) I'll say!
   (narrator) WHAT DOES THE MAN MEAN?

10. *(woman)* Do you think the lawn should be watered?
    (man) It hasn't been watered in weeks.
    (narrator) WHAT DOES THE MAN IMPLY?

LISTENING PART B

EXERCISE 8, p. 34

1. The first part of Conversation 1 is:

   (woman) Did you understand the assignment the professor gave us today? I'm not sure that I did.
   (man) He said to read Chapter 6, didn't he?

   (narrator) WHAT IS THE TOPIC OF CONVERSATION 1?

2. The first part of Conversation 2 is:

   (woman) Did you hear what happened to Greg?
   (man) I heard he got stung by a bee.
   (woman) Well, he did get stung, but it wasn't by a bee. It was a hornet that stung him while he was out walking in the park.

(narrator) WHAT IS THE TOPIC OF CONVERSATION 2?

3. The first part of Conversation 3 is:

   (man) Can you tell me about the university shuttle bus system? This is such a large campus, and I have classes all over campus. I need to take the shuttle bus from one class to another, or I'll never make it on time.
   (woman) What do you need to know?

   (narrator) WHAT IS THE TOPIC OF CONVERSATION 3?

EXERCISE 9, p. 36

Conversation 1

Questions 1 through 4. Listen as two students discuss what a professor said in a recent class.

   (woman) Did you understand the assignment the professor gave us today? I'm not sure that I did.
   (man) He said to read Chapter 6, didn't he?
   (woman) Yes, he said to read Chapter 6. Then I think he also said something about answering the questions at the end of the chapter.
   (man) He said to answer the questions, too? I didn't hear that part of the assignment.
   (woman) I think he did, but I'm not sure. Maybe we should go ask one of the other students what the assignment is, just to be safe.
   (man) I think we should!

1. WHAT ARE THE MAN AND WOMAN DISCUSSING?
2. HOW MUCH ARE THEY SUPPOSED TO READ?
3. WHAT PART OF THE ASSIGNMENT IS UNCLEAR?
4. WHAT WILL THEY PROBABLY DO NEXT?

Conversation 2

Questions 5 through 8. Listen as two people describe something that happened to a friend.

   (woman) Did you hear what happened to Greg?
   (man) I heard he got stung by a bee.
   (woman) Well, he did get stung, but it wasn't by a bee. It was a hornet that stung him while he was out walking in the park.
   (man) If it was a hornet, then Greg probably came very close to the hornet's nest. I understand that hornets usually only attack if they're trying to protect the nest where the eggs are waiting to hatch.

(woman)　So hornets are only dangerous if you come close to their nests?

(man)　Yes, so Greg probably came close to a hornet's nest while he was out on his walk in the park.

(woman)　Then we should find out where Greg was walking and <u>not</u> go walking there.

5. WHAT HAPPENED TO GREG?
6. WHY DO HORNETS ATTACK?
7. WHAT DID GREG PROBABLY COME CLOSE TO?
8. WHAT IS THE WOMAN'S ADVICE?

Conversation 3

Questions 9 through 12. Listen to two students on a university campus.

(man)　Can you tell me about the university shuttle bus system? This is such a large campus, and I have classes all over campus. I need to take the shuttle bus from one class to another, or I'll never make it on time.

(woman)　What do you need to know? I think it's a really great system.

(man)　First of all, where does it go?

(woman)　The university shuttle bus system goes all over campus. It doesn't leave the campus; if you want to travel off-campus, you'll need to take the city bus system. But the university shuttle bus system will get you from one class to the next very efficiently.

(man)　And how much does it cost?

(woman)　It's free, can you believe it? So you don't have to pay a cent to get all around the university campus.

(man)　That's really great. And how do I catch the shuttle bus?

(woman)　Just look for one of the bright yellow shuttle bus signs, and go stand next to it. You can see the yellow shuttle bus signs all over campus. A shuttle bus will come along approximately every five minutes, so you shouldn't have to wait long.

(man)　That all sounds good. Thanks for your help.

(woman)　No problem.

9. WHAT ARE THE MAN AND WOMAN DISCUSSING?
10. WHAT AREA DOES THE UNIVERSITY SHUTTLE BUS COVER?
11. HOW MUCH DOES THE SHUTTLE BUS COST?
12. WHAT COLOR ARE THE SHUTTLE BUS SIGNS?

TOEFL EXERCISE (Skills 7–9), p. 37

Conversation 1

Questions 1 through 4. Listen as a man asks for directions.

(man)　Can you tell me where the post office is? I need to mail a package.

(woman)　Oh, that's easy. It's very close by.

(man)　Where is it exactly?

(woman)　You go down the street for one block and then turn right. You'll see it right there.

(man)　Do you know what time the post office closes?

(woman)　I'm pretty sure that it's open until five.

(man)　Oh, that's great. It's only four o'clock now, so I should be able to get there and get this package mailed today. Thanks for your help.

(woman)　No problem!

1. WHAT ARE THE MAN AND WOMAN DISCUSSING?
2. HOW FAR AWAY IS THE POST OFFICE?
3. HOW MUCH LONGER IS THE POST OFFICE OPEN TODAY?
4. WHAT WILL THE MAN PROBABLY DO NEXT?

Conversation 2

Questions 5 through 8. Listen as a man and woman discuss some interesting information that the woman just learned.

(woman)　Did you read this magazine article? The information in it is unbelievable.

(man)　What's the article about?

(woman)　It's about paper, specifically about how much paper Americans use up each year.

(man)　Why are you so interested in paper?

(woman)　It's not paper that I'm interested in; it's trees. Because Americans use so much paper, many trees have to be cut down.

(man)　According to the article, how much paper do Americans use?

(woman)　About 50 million tons of paper a year, can you believe it?

(man)　That's probably a lot of trees, isn't it?

(woman)　You bet it is; 850 million trees a year.

(man)　I can't believe we really <u>need</u> to use so much paper.

(woman)　Neither can I. I'm sure we could reduce the amount of paper we use if we wanted to.

5. WHERE DID THE WOMAN LEARN THE INFORMATION?
6. WHAT IS THE TOPIC OF THE CONVERSATION?

7. APPROXIMATELY HOW MUCH PAPER DO AMERICANS USE IN ONE YEAR?
8. WHAT DOES THE WOMAN WANT PEOPLE TO DO?

Conversation 3

Questions 9 through 12. Listen as two students discuss a problem with one of their classes.

(man)   Can you believe how much reading we have for our American literature class?

(woman)   When I signed up for a literature class, I knew that there would be lots of reading, but I never expected this much.

(man)   Yes, and I thought that since it was a class on American novels, we would just be reading some novels.

(woman)   What a surprise. Not only do we have to read a bunch of novels, we also have to read the textbook, which gives information about the authors and their novels. And we also have to find journal articles in the library, which have commentary about the novels.

(man)   So we have three things to read: the novels themselves, the textbook, and journal articles.

(woman)   That's right. And there's a lot to read from each of the three.

(man)   Well, I'm heading for the library right now to get started on all that reading. What about you?

(woman)   I'm on my way back to the dorm, but I'll be doing the same thing that you are, spending the rest of the afternoon with my books.

9. WHAT PROBLEM ARE THE MAN AND WOMAN DISCUSSING?
10. WHICH CLASS ARE THE MAN AND WOMAN DISCUSSING?
11. WHAT DO THE MAN AND WOMAN NOT HAVE TO READ FOR THE CLASS?
12. WHAT ARE THE MAN AND WOMAN BOTH GOING TO DO NEXT?

LISTENING PART C

EXERCISE 11, p. 42

1. The first part of Talk 1 is:

(man)   One of the most deadly plants in the world is poison hemlock. This plant grows in many parts of the world. It is quite dangerous to humans; people can die if they eat it.

(narrator)   WHAT IS THE TOPIC OF TALK 1?

2. The first part of Talk 2 is:

(woman)   Today we're going to see something that most of you have probably never seen before: a frog-jumping contest. This frog-jumping contest is part of the Calaveras County Fair, in Calaveras County, California.

(narrator)   WHAT IS THE TOPIC OF TALK 2?

3. The first part of Talk 3 is:

(man)   Hello. I'm Mr. Teale, the head librarian, and I'd like to explain to you about checking out books from this library.

(narrator)   WHAT IS THE TOPIC OF TALK 3?

EXERCISE 12, p. 44

Talk 1

Questions 1 through 4. Listen to a lecture by a biology professor.

(man)   One of the most deadly plants in the world is poison hemlock. This plant grows in many parts of the world. It is quite dangerous to humans; people can die if they eat it.

One thing that makes poison hemlock really dangerous is that it looks like some plants that people normally eat. Hemlock belongs to the same family of plants as the carrot. The leaves of the plant look very much like parsley, and its roots look like carrots. People have died when they've made a mistake and have eaten poison hemlock when they thought that they were eating either parsley or carrots.

1. WHAT IS THE TOPIC OF THE TALK?
2. WHERE IS HEMLOCK FOUND?
3. WHAT IS TRUE ABOUT HEMLOCK?
4. WHAT CAN HAPPEN TO SOMEONE WHO EATS HEMLOCK?

Talk 2

Questions 5 through 8. Listen as a tour guide describes what some tourists are going to see.

(woman)   Today we're going to see something that most of you have probably never seen before: a frog-jumping contest. This frog-jumping contest is part of the Calaveras County Fair, in Calaveras County, California.

In this frog-jumping contest, about 2,000 frogs and their owners participate, and more than 40,000 people usually come to watch. The frog owners encourage their frogs to jump by yelling, screaming, jumping, singing, talking, blowing, any way they can. To win the contest, a frog needs to jump three times in a row.

This contest is based on a story by Mark Twain; it's called "The Celebrated Jumping Frog of Calaveras County." Twain published the story in 1865. Sixty-three years later, in 1928, the people of Calaveras County decided to hold a contest just like the one that Twain had described a number of years earlier.

5. WHAT TYPE OF CONTEST IS IT?
6. APPROXIMATELY HOW MANY FROGS PARTICIPATE EACH YEAR?
7. HOW MANY TIMES DOES A FROG NEED TO JUMP TO WIN?
8. WHAT IS TRUE ABOUT THE FROG-JUMPING CONTEST?

Talk 3

Questions 9 through 12. Listen to a talk given to a group of new university students.

(man)   Hello. I'm Mr. Teale, the head librarian, and I'd like to explain to you about checking out books from this library. Students with ID cards can check out books, and the books may be kept for up to two weeks. The process for checking the books out is really quite simple because of the computerized check-out system.

When you find a book in the library that you would like to check out, just bring it here to the circulation desk. The circulation desk is the desk where you check materials out from the library. All you need when you come to the circulation desk is the book or books that you want to check out and your student ID card.

At the circulation desk, the clerk will take the book and the ID card and run them through the computerized scanner. A form is printed quickly by the computer, and you need to sign the form. That's all there is to it. Just remember to bring your ID card when you come to the library, to sign the form at the circulation desk, and to return the books within two weeks, and you won't have any problems here at the library.

9. WHO IS GIVING THIS TALK?
10. WHAT IS THE CIRCULATION DESK?
11. WHAT DO THE STUDENTS NEED TO TAKE BOOKS FROM THE LIBRARY?
12. HOW LONG MAY STUDENTS KEEP THE BOOKS?

TOEFL EXERCISE (Skills 10–12), p. 45

Talk 1

Questions 1 through 4. Listen to a description of the Ringling Museum.

(man)   In a few minutes, we'll be arriving at the Ringling Museum, in Sarasota, Florida. This museum was built by John Ringling and his wife, Mabel. John Ringling became famous as one of the Ringling Brothers, who formed the Ringling Brothers Circus.

We'll be visiting two areas: the Museum of Art and the Circus Gallery. The Museum of Art contains some excellent baroque paintings, including some by Rubens. The Circus Gallery contains items from circuses of years past, including a 100-year-old circus parade wagon.

Enjoy your visit to the Ringling Museum. I'll see you back at the bus in three hours.

1. WHO IS PROBABLY TALKING?
2. WHY DID JOHN RINGLING BECOME FAMOUS?
3. WHAT IS INCLUDED IN THE CIRCUS GALLERY?
4. WHAT SHOULD THE PEOPLE DO IN THREE HOURS?

Talk 2

Questions 5 through 8. Listen to a lecture by a business professor.

(woman)   Henry Ford's Model T automobile is a great example of the benefits of mass production. Henry Ford introduced the Model T in 1908. These first Model T cars weren't mass produced. They were sold for a price of $850 each. The Model T cars were very popular, and many people wanted to own them. To meet this high demand, Henry Ford designed the first major assembly line. With this assembly line, cars could be produced more quickly, efficiently, and cheaply. Using the assembly-line method of production, the company was able to produce 1,000 identical cars a day. The price of the Model T dropped from $850 to $440 per car by 1914. The price dropped even further, to $290 per car, by 1924. This example clearly demonstrates the effect that mass production can have on prices.

5. WHAT IS THE MODEL T?
6. WHEN WAS THE MODEL T INTRODUCED?
7. WHAT WAS NOT TRUE ABOUT ASSEMBLY-LINE PRODUCTION BY FORD?
8. WHAT HAPPENED TO THE PRICE OF THE MODEL T OVER TIME?

Talk 3

Questions 9 through 12. Listen to a talk by a university graduate student advisor.

(woman)   Hello, I'm Ms. Barker, the graduate advisor in the Psychology Department. You should all be new graduate students in this department. Because I'm your advisor, we'll be seeing a lot of each other during your studies.

Today, I'd like to explain a choice that you have to make about your program in psychology. You must decide how you want to finish your program. At the end of this program you must do one of two things: either you must write a thesis, or you must take comprehensive exams. Let me tell you a little bit about each of them. A thesis is a long research paper, perhaps one or two hundred pages long; it's an in-depth study of one area from your graduate studies. Comprehensive exams are exams that cover all of the material in your graduate program. Basically, you must decide if you want to cover one area in depth in your program, so you would write a thesis, or if you'd like a more general program, so you would take comprehensive exams. You don't need to decide today about the thesis or comprehensive exams. You have six months to think about it.

9. WHO IS MS. BARKER TALKING TO?
10. WHAT CHOICE DO THE STUDENTS HAVE TO MAKE?
11. WHAT ARE COMPREHENSIVE EXAMS?
12. WHEN DO THE STUDENTS NEED TO MAKE THE DECISION?

LISTENING COMPREHENSION POST-TEST

Part A, p. 47

1. (man)   When is your art class?
   (woman)   It begins tonight.
   (narrator) WHAT DOES THE WOMAN MEAN?

2. (woman)   I'd like a cup of coffee, please.
   (man)   Would you like me to bring that with the dessert?
   (narrator) WHO IS THE MAN MOST LIKELY TO BE?

3. (woman)   Have you seen Ellen?
   (man)   She drove to the shopping center.
   (narrator) WHAT DOES THE MAN SAY ABOUT ELLEN?

4. (man)   Why are you so upset with Bill?
   (woman)   Because he didn't tell me the truth.
   (narrator) WHAT DOES THE WOMAN SAY ABOUT BILL?

5. (woman)   These prices are really good.
   (man)   I'll say!
   (narrator) WHAT DOES THE MAN MEAN?

6. (woman)   I'm sorry. I didn't hear what you said.
   (man)   Please pay better attention.
   (narrator) WHAT DOES THE MAN WANT THE WOMAN TO DO?

7. (man)   Look how hard it's raining.
   (woman)   Let's stay inside today.
   (narrator) WHAT DOES THE WOMAN SUGGEST?

8. (woman)   Who made the decision?
   (man)   The decision was made by the judge.
   (narrator) WHAT DOES THE MAN MEAN?

9. (man)   Did you finish that long chemistry problem?
   (woman)   No, I was unable to solve it.
   (narrator) WHAT DOES THE WOMAN MEAN?

10. (woman)   How about if we stay here tonight and watch television?
    (man)   But I don't want to stay home.
    (narrator) WHAT DOES THE MAN WANT TO DO?

11. (man)   Can you tell me when the term paper for this course is due?
    (woman)   In the last week of the semester.
    (narrator) WHERE DOES THIS CONVERSATION PROBABLY TAKE PLACE?

12. (man)   Where's Hank?
    (woman)   He's in the pool.
    (narrator) WHAT DOES THE WOMAN IMPLY ABOUT HANK?

13. (woman)   I'm always so tired during the day.
    (man)   Why don't you get a little more sleep at night?
    (narrator) WHAT DOES THE MAN SUGGEST?

14. (man)   Have you read the chapter for today?
    (woman)   I tried, but it wasn't easy to get through.
    (narrator) WHAT DOES THE WOMAN MEAN?

15. (woman)   Are you having much success with your garden?
    (man)   No, there are too many rocks in the soil.
    (narrator) WHAT DOES THE MAN MEAN?

16. (man)   This weather is incredibly beautiful!
    (woman)   You can say that again!
    (narrator) WHAT DOES THE WOMAN MEAN?

17. (woman)   Have you figured out the problem with my car?
    (man)   Yes, the engine needs to be tuned up.
    (narrator) WHO IS THE MAN MOST LIKELY TO BE?

18. (man)   I hope you enjoyed your lunch.
    (woman)   That sandwich was really tasty.
    (narrator) WHAT DOES THE WOMAN MEAN?

19. (woman)   Is Marie feeling better now?
    (man)   Yes, she's finally feeling quite healthy.
    (narrator) WHAT DOES THE MAN IMPLY ABOUT MARIE?

20. (man)   I'm really having problems in this psychology class.
    (woman)   Why don't you see your professor during her office hours?
    (narrator) WHAT DOES THE WOMAN SUGGEST TO THE MAN?

21. (woman)   Why are you saving your money?
    (man)   I'd like to buy a house at the beach.
    (narrator) WHAT DOES THE MAN MEAN?

22. (woman)   I think Sally really said some mean things.
    (man)   So do I!
    (narrator) WHAT DOES THE MAN MEAN?

23. (woman)   Can you turn the stereo up? I can't really hear it.
    (man)   The music is a little soft.
    (narrator) WHAT DOES THE MAN MEAN?

24. (man)   What happened when you gave Larry the present?
    (woman)   He thanked me over and over.
    (narrator) WHAT DOES THE WOMAN SAY ABOUT LARRY?

25. (woman)   Can I help you?
    (man)   I'd like to check in, please. I need a single room for one night.
    (narrator) WHERE DOES THIS CONVERSATION PROBABLY TAKE PLACE?

26. (man)   I really like these photos of my hometown.
    (woman)   Why don't you put them up on the wall?
    (narrator) WHAT DOES THE WOMAN SUGGEST?

27. (man)   Does Carl know about the meeting?
    (woman)   I'll have to let him know about it.
    (narrator) WHAT DOES THE WOMAN MEAN?

28. (woman)   Why was your textbook cheaper than mine?
    (man)   Mine wasn't new.
    (narrator) WHAT DOES THE MAN MEAN?

29. (woman)   What did the teacher just say? I didn't hear it.
    (man)   She announced that she would be giving an exam soon.
    (narrator) WHAT DOES THE MAN MEAN?

30. (man)   How often does the government conduct a census?
    (woman)   Once each decade.
    (narrator) WHAT DOES THE WOMAN MEAN?

Part B, p. 49

Questions 31 through 34. Listen as two friends discuss a meeting of the ski club.

(woman)   Hi, Jack.
(man)   Hi, Wanda. Where are you rushing to?
(woman)   I'm heading for a meeting of the ski club. It starts at three o'clock.
(man)   The ski club?
(woman)   Yes, the ski club. Do you want to come along?
(man)   What does the ski club do?
(woman)   Well, you get to know other people who enjoy skiing, listen to lectures and presentations on skiing techniques and equipment, and— best of all—plan skiing trips. Doesn't that sound good?
(man)   It does sound great, but I don't exactly know how to ski very well.
(woman)   That doesn't matter. You don't have to know how to ski. You just have to want to learn how to ski.
(man)   That sounds like my kind of club. I guess I'll come along with you and try it.
(woman)   We've got to hurry. It's almost three o'clock.

31. WHAT TIME DOES THE MEETING BEGIN?
32. WHAT DO PEOPLE DO AT SKI CLUB MEETINGS?
33. WHAT PROBLEM DOES THE MAN HAVE?
34. WHAT WILL THE MAN PROBABLY DO NEXT?

Questions 35 through 38. Listen as a man and woman discuss a new type of fast-food packaging.

(man)   I was reading an article in the paper about a new type of fast-food packaging. It's really great!

(woman)   What's so great about this packaging for fast food?

(man)   What's great is that the packaging is edible.

(woman)   Edible?

(man)   That's right. With this new packaging, you can go to a fast-food restaurant, order a burger and fries, and then eat the wrappings that the burger and fries came in.

(woman)   So, you'd be eating paper?

(man)   (laughs) Oh, no. The wrappers sort of look and feel like paper, but they're really made from things like soybeans, corn, flour.

(woman)   It sounds like the wrappers might be even better for you than the fast food!

35. WHERE DID THE MAN LEARN ABOUT THE NEW FAST-FOOD PACKAGING?
36. WHAT IS INTERESTING ABOUT THE NEW FAST-FOOD PACKAGING?
37. WHAT IS USED TO MAKE THE FAST-FOOD PACKAGING?
38. WHAT DOES THE WOMAN THINK ABOUT THE NEW FAST-FOOD PACKAGING?

Part C, p. 51

Questions 39 through 42. Listen to a guide on a bus tour.

(man)   I'm sure you all enjoyed that trip along the Grand Canyon and the Colorado River. It's quite amazing, isn't it?

The next stop on our tour is the Petrified Forest. This is a huge desert forest that is not exactly made of trees. You see, the trees are so old that they've fallen and have turned to stone. They look just like fallen logs, but they're no longer made of wood. Instead they are made of beautifully colored stone, such as jasper, agate, carnelian, and onyx. It's unbelievable to see all of these fallen trees from a distance and then up close see that they're really stone and not wood.

When we arrive at the Petrified Forest, please be sure to keep in mind that it's against the law to take any petrified wood out of the forest with you. You may think about picking up just a tiny little piece, but please don't do it.

39. WHERE HAVE THEY JUST BEEN?
40. WHERE ARE THEY HEADING NOW?
41. WHAT HAS HAPPENED TO THE WOOD?
42. WHAT DOES THE MAN ASK THEM NOT TO DO?

Questions 43 through 46. Listen to a talk by a university student advisor.

(woman)   You're all seniors now, and you should all be graduating in June, at the end of this school year. But now, at the beginning of your senior year, you have a couple of things to remember in order to graduate in June.

First of all, you need to fill out a request-to-graduate form. You should fill this form out and turn it in to your advisor. You need to do this by December if you want to graduate in June.

The second thing you need to do is to order your cap and gown. During the graduation ceremony at this university, all the graduating seniors wear the same blue and gold cap and gown. You'll also need to place your order for your cap and gown by the end of December.

So remember the two important things if you want to graduate in June. Fill out the request-to-graduate form, and order your cap and gown. Don't forget, now!

43. WHAT IS THE WOMAN MAINLY DISCUSSING?
44. WHAT MUST THE STUDENTS DO WITH THE REQUEST-TO-GRADUATE FORM?
45. WHAT MUST THE STUDENTS ORDER?
46. WHEN MUST THE STUDENTS PLACE THEIR ORDERS?

Questions 47 through 50. Listen to a talk by a man who works with animals.

(man)   Today dogs are being trained in a variety of ways. One way that dogs are being trained involves "smell." For example, dogs are being trained to use their sense of smell to find missing persons, hidden drugs, or explosives such as dynamite.

Dog trainers have found that almost all types of dogs have equally good senses of smell. Even though different types of dogs have equivalent senses of smell, they aren't equally good at different tasks. However, certain types of dogs are better at certain tasks because of other characteristics they have. For example, beagles are small and friendly, so they're often used at crowded airports to smell for illegal food products in luggage. German shepherds have quick reactions, so they're often used to smell for explosives such as dynamite. Golden retrievers work well in the cold, so they're often used to find people lost in the snow.

47. WHAT IS THE TOPIC OF THE PASSAGE?
48. WHAT IS TRUE ABOUT THE VARIOUS TYPES OF DOGS?
49. WHY ARE GERMAN SHEPHERDS USED TO FIND EXPLOSIVES?
50. WHAT ARE SOME DOGS TRAINED TO FIND?

COMPLETE TEST ONE:
Listening Comprehension

Part A, p. 246

1. *(man)* When is your trip?
   (woman) I'll be leaving in a few days.
   (narrator) WHAT DOES THE WOMAN MEAN?

2. *(woman)* When should I pay the rent for the apartment?
   (man) Rent should be paid to me on the first of each month.
   (narrator) WHO IS THE MAN MOST LIKELY TO BE?

3. *(man)* Did you hear how Rob did on the math exam?
   (woman) Yes. He got the top grade.
   (narrator) WHAT DOES THE WOMAN SAY ABOUT ROB?

4. *(man)* Where's Mike? He should be in his seat now.
   (woman) He's absent today.
   (narrator) WHAT DOES THE WOMAN SAY ABOUT MIKE?

5. *(woman)* That rain storm really did some damage.
   (man) I'll say!
   (narrator) WHAT DOES THE MAN MEAN?

6. *(man)* Peter really lost his temper.
   (woman) At least he apologized.
   (narrator) WHAT DOES THE WOMAN SAY ABOUT PETER?

7. *(woman)* I've run out of bread.
   (man) Let's go to the market and get some more.
   (narrator) WHAT DOES THE MAN SUGGEST?

8. *(man)* Have you been to the post office yet?
   (woman) Yes, and I mailed all the letters.
   (narrator) WHAT DOES THE WOMAN MEAN?

9. *(woman)* There's no problem if you want to borrow the book.
   (man) Thanks. I'll return it in a couple of days.
   (narrator) WHAT DOES THE MAN MEAN?

10. *(woman)* Is that chair comfortable?
    (man) The seat is too hard.
    (narrator) WHAT DOES THE MAN MEAN?

11. *(man)* Oh, no. Our team is losing.
    (woman) Not for long. They've got the ball, and they're going to score.
    (narrator) WHERE DOES THIS CONVERSATION PROBABLY TAKE PLACE?

12. *(woman)* Susan has a nicer car than most people.
    (man) That's because she's richer than most people.
    (narrator) WHAT DOES THE MAN SAY ABOUT SUSAN?

13. *(woman)* These physics problems are too hard.
    (man) Why not get some help?
    (narrator) WHAT DOES THE MAN SUGGEST TO THE WOMAN?

14. *(woman)* Did you find an apartment?
    (man) Yes, and it's close to the university.
    (narrator) WHAT DOES THE MAN MEAN?

15. *(woman)* Do you think Bonnie enjoyed her surprise party?
    (man) She was certainly smiling the whole time.
    (narrator) WHAT DOES THE MAN SAY ABOUT BONNIE?

16. *(man)* Traffic is unusually heavy today.
    (woman) You can say that again!
    (narrator) WHAT DOES THE WOMAN MEAN?

17. *(woman)* Is there a problem, officer?
    (man) You were driving much faster than the speed limit. May I see your driver's license?
    (narrator) WHO IS THE MAN MOST LIKELY TO BE?

18. *(woman)* Oh, no. I spilled some coffee on my homework paper.
    (man) Now you're going to have to rewrite it.
    (narrator) WHAT DOES THE MAN SAY THAT THE WOMAN SHOULD DO?

19. (woman)   Are you going swimming today?
    (man)   The water's not warm enough for me.
    (narrator) WHAT DOES THE MAN MEAN?

20. (woman)   This store is closed today.
    (man)   Then, let's go to another one.
    (narrator) WHAT DOES THE MAN SUGGEST?

21. (man)   Does the university have a modern theater?
    (woman)   A new theater is being built.
    (narrator) WHAT DOES THE WOMAN MEAN?

22. (man)   I think we should leave tomorrow instead of today.
    (woman)   So do I.
    (narrator) WHAT DOES THE WOMAN MEAN?

23. (man)   Why was your homework grade so low?
    (woman)   I didn't do the assignment carefully.
    (narrator) WHAT DOES THE WOMAN IMPLY?

24. (woman)   Did you have a nice weekend?
    (man)   It was peaceful, and that's what I needed.
    (narrator) WHAT DOES THE MAN MEAN?

25. (woman)   Should we take our seats now?
    (man)   That's a good idea. I think the orchestra is about to begin.
    (narrator) WHERE DOES THIS CONVERSATION PROBABLY TAKE PLACE?

26. (woman)   I overslept again this morning.
    (man)   Why don't you set your alarm to wake you up?
    (narrator) WHAT DOES THE MAN SUGGEST?

27. (man)   What do I need to bring to the test?
    (woman)   You'll need some extra pencils and paper.
    (narrator) WHAT DOES THE WOMAN MEAN?

28. (man)   Is the baby still sick?
    (woman)   His temperature is still high.
    (narrator) WHAT DOES THE WOMAN MEAN?

29. (man)   Alex didn't go on the trip with the others.
    (woman)   I gave him the opportunity to go, but he decided not to.
    (narrator) WHAT DOES THE WOMAN MEAN?

30. (woman)   I can't believe Anna's reaction.
    (man)   She sometimes acts like a child.
    (narrator) WHAT DOES THE MAN SAY ABOUT ANNA?

Part B, p. 248

Questions 31 through 34. Listen as a man and woman discuss a chance they have to see some whales up close.

(man)   You're going on the boat trip this afternoon?
(woman)   Yes, I am, and I can't wait. I've never been up close to a whale before. Do you think we'll see many whales today?
(man)   We should. This is the best time of the year to see some whales.
(woman)   Why is winter the best time of the year to see whales?
(man)   At this time of year, the whales are heading south from Alaska to warmer water for the winter. Then they'll return to Alaska before summer.
(woman)   How long is the boat trip, do you know?
(man)   The boat leaves at one o'clock and returns at about three o'clock.
(woman)   Only a two-hour trip?
(man)   Yes, the whales travel pretty close to shore, so we don't need to go out very far in the ocean to see them.
(woman)   I guess two hours is probably enough. I've never actually been out on the ocean in a boat, and I'm not really sure I'll like it.

31. WHAT KIND OF TRIP ARE THE MAN AND WOMAN DISCUSSING?
32. WHAT SEASON IS IT?
33. WHAT ARE THE WHALES DOING NOW?
34. HOW LONG IS THE BOAT TRIP?

Questions 35 through 38. Listen as one student gives some advice to another student.

(woman)   I see that there are two ways to register for classes at this university: mail-in registration and walk-through registration.
(man)   That's right. Either you can mail in your registration materials, or you can start at the administration building on registration day and walk from office to office completing your registration.
(woman)   Which type of registration is better, do you think?
(man)   No question about it, the mail-in registration is far easier. It's very efficient, and it takes almost no time. You just write the courses that you want on the registration form, mail it in, and you'll receive your course schedule in the mail. If you go to walk-through registration, you'll probably spend many hours standing in a number of long, long lines.

(woman)   That does <u>not</u> sound good to me. It's the mail-in registration for me!

35. WHAT ARE THE MAN AND WOMAN DISCUSSING?
36. HOW DOES THE MAN DESCRIBE MAIL-IN REGISTRATION?
37. HOW DOES THE MAN DESCRIBE WALK-THROUGH REGISTRATION?
38. WHAT DOES THE WOMAN DECIDE TO DO?

Part C, p. 250

Questions 39 through 42. Listen to a description of an apartment.

(man)   The next apartment that I'd like to show you is one of the larger apartments that we have for rent. This is a three-bedroom apartment. As you can see, one of the bedrooms is larger, and two of the bedrooms are smaller.

The kitchen area is large. Because of those windows, it's also very sunny. The stove and refrigerator that you see there are included in the rent. The living room isn't very large, but it does have a fireplace and some nice built-in bookshelves.

This apartment is unfurnished, so you'll need furniture. If you have your own furniture already, that's great. If you don't have any furniture of your own, I can show you where you can rent some.

Do you have any questions?

39. WHO IS PROBABLY TALKING?
40. HOW MANY BEDROOMS ARE THERE IN THE APARTMENT?
41. WHAT IS TRUE ABOUT THE KITCHEN?
42. WHAT IS TRUE ABOUT THE APARTMENT'S FURNITURE?

Questions 43 through 46. Listen to a talk by a history professor.

(woman)   In the last class, we talked about the development of the railroad system in the United States. Today, we're going to talk about the development of the subway. I'm going to start with the New York City subway because this was the first subway system in the United States.

The New York City subway took quite some time to get started. Beginning in 1870, several private business groups tried to start subway systems in New York City, but these groups were unsuccessful.

Finally, in 1900, a former mayor of the city set up the Interborough Rapid Transit Company, or IRT. This company got the present-day system started. Four years later, in 1904, the first leg of the subway opened. On the first day of operations in 1904, more than 110,000 people went for a ride on the new subway.

43. WHAT WAS THE TOPIC OF THE PREVIOUS CLASS?
44. WHAT IS THE TOPIC OF TODAY'S LECTURE?
45. WHAT IS THE LECTURER'S POINT ABOUT THE NEW YORK CITY SUBWAY?
46. WHEN DID THE FIRST LEG OF THE SUBWAY OPEN?

Questions 47 through 50. Listen to a lecture by a university professor.

(man)   When scientists are studying animals in the wild, they often want to follow the animals' movements.

One way that scientists have often tracked wild animals in the past has been with radio transmitters. A radio collar could be attached to an animal, and the animal could be tracked on a radio receiver. The major problem has been that radio signals weren't very reliable. They could come and go as animals traveled too far.

Now scientists are using a new way to track animals in the wild. This new way of tracking animals uses satellites. Transmitters are attached to animals in the wild, and the transmitters send signals into the atmosphere every few hours. Weather satellites circling the Earth receive the signals from the animals, and scientists get the information from the satellites.

47. WHAT IS THE TOPIC OF THE TALK?
48. HOW DID SCIENTISTS FOLLOW ANIMALS IN THE PAST?
49. WHAT IS THE NEW WAY OF FOLLOWING ANIMALS?
50. IN WHICH COURSE WOULD THIS TALK PROBABLY BE GIVEN?

COMPLETE TEST TWO:
Listening Comprehension

Part A, p. 270

1. (man)   I need to see the math professor.
   (woman)   Let's go to her office now.
   (narrator)   WHAT DOES THE WOMAN SUGGEST?

2. (woman)   Will you be at the meeting by four
               o'clock?
   (man)   No, I'll be there a bit later.
   (narrator) WHAT DOES THE MAN MEAN?

3. (man)   Did you get the material very
               quickly?
   (woman)   No, the material didn't come at all
               quickly.
   (narrator) WHAT DOES THE WOMAN SAY
               ABOUT THE MATERIAL?

4. (man)   It was really hard to find a place to
               park this morning.
   (woman)   You can say that again!
   (narrator) WHAT DOES THE WOMAN MEAN?

5. (woman)   You picked up your exam already?
   (man)   Yes, the professor put the graded
               exams in the office. You can get
               yours there.
   (narrator) WHAT DOES THE MAN MEAN?

6. (man)   Where are you going now? Are you
               heading to the library to study?
   (woman)   Well, my necklace broke, and I want
               to get it fixed first. Then I'll start
               studying.
   (narrator) WHO IS THE WOMAN MOST
               LIKELY GOING TO SEE NOW?

7. (man)   Sorry, I can't play tennis this
               afternoon. I need to do some
               shopping then.
   (woman)   Why not go shopping now, and then
               we can play tennis later?
   (narrator) WHAT DOES THE WOMAN
               SUGGEST?

8. (man)   Have you been to the new restaurant
               down the street?
   (woman)   Yes, I have. The food there is quite
               tasty.
   (narrator) WHAT DOES THE WOMAN SAY
               ABOUT THE FOOD?

9. (woman)   Is the paper due this Friday?
   (man)   No, the due date was changed by the
               professor.
   (narrator) WHAT DOES THE MAN MEAN?

10. (man)   I think we'll be able to finish all
               these problems before class.
    (woman)   Me, too!
    (narrator) WHAT DOES THE WOMAN MEAN?

11. (man)   Do you want to meet at eight o'clock
               tomorrow morning?
    (woman)   Not that early, please.
    (narrator) WHAT DOES THE WOMAN MEAN?

12. (woman)   What did the doctor say?
    (man)   He told me to take some medicine
               and get some rest. I'm going to get
               this prescription filled now.
    (narrator) WHERE IS THE MAN MOST
               LIKELY GOING?

13. (man)   Could you see what the professor
               wrote on the board at the end of the
               lecture?
    (woman)   No, I couldn't. The writing was too
               tiny.
    (narrator) WHAT DOES THE WOMAN MEAN?

14. (woman)   Is your answer correct? I have a
               different answer to this problem.
    (man)   I'm not quite sure of my answer.
    (narrator) WHAT DOES THE MAN MEAN?

15. (man)   What should we do about the
               assignment? I just don't understand
               it.
    (woman)   Let's ask someone else for help.
    (narrator) WHAT DOES THE WOMAN
               SUGGEST?

16. (woman)   I think that article on the front page
               of the school paper was so unfair!
    (man)   So do I!
    (narrator) WHAT DOES THE MAN MEAN?

17. (woman)   My car is having problems. Can you
               recommend a place where I can get
               it fixed?
    (man)   You should see Mark at the service
               station on the corner. He's really
               good at fixing cars.
    (narrator) WHO IS MARK MOST LIKELY TO
               BE?

18. (man)   Where are you going this evening?
    (woman)   I'll be at the business club meeting.
               The club president invited me to
               give a speech at the meeting.
    (narrator) WHAT HAPPENED TO THE
               WOMAN?

19. (man)   Did you like the apartment you saw
               yesterday?
    (woman)   Not really. I don't want to be so far
               from campus.
    (narrator) WHAT DOES THE WOMAN MEAN?

20. (woman)   Do you want to drive to the game?
    (man)   Why not walk instead? It's not very
               far.
    (narrator) WHAT DOES THE MAN SUGGEST?

21. (woman)   It was really cold in the classroom
               today.
    (man)   It was, wasn't it? Did you see that
               the window wasn't shut completely?
    (narrator) WHAT DOES THE MAN MEAN?

22. (woman)   You didn't get an A on your paper?
    (man)   No, I didn't. I made one very large
               error.
    (narrator) WHAT DOES THE MAN MEAN?

23. (woman)   Did you read the fax from the office
               yet?
    (man)   I saw that the fax arrived, but I
               haven't had time to look at it yet.
    (narrator) WHAT DOES THE MAN MEAN?

24. (woman) Where are you heading now?
    (man) I need to get reservations for my flight home.
    (narrator) WHERE IS THE MAN MOST LIKELY GOING?

25. (man) What did you think of the presentation we just saw?
    (woman) There were lots of good ideas, but they weren't very organized.
    (narrator) WHAT DOES THE WOMAN MEAN?

26. (woman) I could hardly pay attention to the lecture this morning. It was so boring.
    (man) I'll say!
    (narrator) WHAT DOES THE MAN MEAN?

27. (woman) You're going on a cruise? How lucky. How long is the cruise?
    (man) It's a seven-day cruise.
    (narrator) WHAT IS THE MAN GOING TO DO?

28. (man) Do you want to go and get something to drink?
    (woman) Let's get something hot. It's so cold, and maybe a hot drink will warm us up.
    (narrator) WHAT DOES THE WOMAN SUGGEST?

29. (woman) How was your French class?
    (man) Not very good. I was called on three times, and I didn't know any of the answers to the questions.
    (narrator) WHAT HAPPENED TO THE MAN?

30. (woman) Should we get tickets at the front or the back of the auditorium?
    (man) As close to the front as possible. I like to watch the dancers' movements up close.
    (narrator) WHERE ARE THE MAN AND WOMAN MOST LIKELY GOING?

Part B, p. 272

Questions 31 through 34. Listen to a conversation between two students. The conversation is about an exam.

    (man) Are you ready for the exam tomorrow?
    (woman) Tomorrow? I thought the exam was next week.
    (man) No, it's tomorrow. The teacher said today that the exam was on Wednesday, and that's tomorrow. Today is Tuesday, and the exam is tomorrow, on Wednesday.
    (woman) Yes, but when she said Wednesday, I thought she meant Wednesday of next week, not tomorrow. Are you sure it's tomorrow?

    (man) Absolutely! The syllabus even lists the dates of the exams, and the syllabus lists an exam on the 13th. That's tomorrow.
    (woman) Oh, my goodness. Have I got a problem! The exam is tomorrow, and I haven't begun preparing for it yet.
    (man) Then you'd better get started as soon as you can.
    (woman) No kidding. I'll go and get started studying now and keep on studying as late as I can.
    (man) I hope you'll be able to cover all the material. There certainly is an awful lot of it on the exam.
    (woman) I know there is. I don't think I'm going to be getting much sleep tonight.

31. WHAT PROBLEM DOES THE WOMAN HAVE?
32. ON WHAT DAY IS THE EXAM BEING GIVEN?
33. WHAT IS TODAY'S DATE?
34. WHAT IS THE WOMAN MOST LIKELY GOING TO DO?

Questions 35 through 38. Listen to a conversation between two students. The conversation is about the school dormitories.

    (man) Are you living in one of the school dormitories, or are you living off campus?
    (woman) Me? I'm living in one of the school dorms. I think it's easier to live in the dorm than to live off campus in an apartment or house while I'm in school.
    (man) Me, too. I live in one of the dorms, too. I live in Baker Hall.
    (woman) In Baker Hall? Isn't that one of the newer dorms?
    (man) Yes, it is. I prefer living in one of the newer dorms. Everything is more up-to-date.
    (woman) I don't live in one of the newer dorms. I'm staying in one of the older dorms.
    (man) You like the older dorms? You think they're better than the newer dorms?
    (woman) What I like about the older dorms is that they're much closer to the center of campus. The newer dorms are on campus, but they're farther away from the center of campus. I like being so close to the center of campus. That's why I'm in one of the older dorms.
    (man) Well, it would be nice to be a little closer to the center of campus, but I prefer the newer dorms, even though they're farther away from the center of campus than the older dorms.

35. WHERE IS THE MAN LIVING?
36. WHERE IS THE WOMAN LIVING?
37. WHY DOES THE MAN PREFER HIS DORM?
38. WHY DOES THE WOMAN PREFER HER DORM?

Part C, p. 274

Questions 39 through 42. Listen to a lecture by a professor in a zoology course. The lecture is on the octopus.

(man)   In previous lectures, I've been talking about different invertebrates. Today, we'll be talking about another of the invertebrates, the octopus. If you remember from the last lecture, when we discussed vertebrates and invertebrates, we said that a vertebrate is an animal with a backbone and an invertebrate is the opposite, an animal without a backbone. An octopus, the sea animal with eight long tentacles, is, of course, an invertebrate because it doesn't have a backbone.

The interesting point that I'd like you to note about the octopus is related to its brain. You might be surprised to learn that an octopus actually has a rather large brain; in fact, it has one of the largest brains of all the invertebrates.

A large part of the brain of an octopus deals with eyesight. The octopus has really excellent eyesight; the octopus is able to see quite well. It is because such a large part of its rather large brain deals with eyesight that the octopus is able to see so clearly.

39. WHAT WAS DISCUSSED IN EARLIER LECTURES?
40. WHAT IS TRUE ABOUT AN OCTOPUS?
41. WHAT IS TRUE ABOUT THE BRAIN OF AN OCTOPUS?
42. WHAT IS TRUE ABOUT THE ABILITY OF AN OCTOPUS TO SEE?

Questions 43 through 46. Listen as an advisor talks to a group of new students. The talk is on meeting deadlines.

(woman)   All of you will be starting your university studies next week. Before you start your studies, I'd like you to think about the importance of meeting deadlines. It's necessary for you to meet deadlines if you want to be successful students, and I can give you some ideas for how to meet deadlines.

In your university studies, you'll have many deadlines. You'll often take three, four, or five courses at the same time, and each course will have deadlines.

The most important first step in dealing with deadlines is for you to have a clear idea of when important deadlines are. To do this, you need to be organized. You should each get a large calendar. Then take the class syllabus for each class, and write the important deadlines for each class together on the one calendar. For example, you should write down the dates when assignments or papers are due, the dates of presentations, and the dates of exams. If you put all of the deadlines for all of your classes together on one calendar, then you can clearly see when you'll be very busy in the coming semester.

43. WHAT DOES THE ADVISOR SAY IS IMPORTANT?
44. WHAT DOES THE ADVISOR SUGGEST?
45. WHAT SHOULD MOST LIKELY <u>NOT</u> BE ON THE CALENDAR?
46. WHY SHOULD STUDENTS CREATE CALENDARS?

Questions 47 through 50. Listen to a talk by a professor in a literature course. In the talk, the professor is explaining an assignment.

(woman)   Now, I'm going to explain the next assignment for this course. The assignment is to study a poem and present the poem to the rest of the class.

This is a group assignment; this means that you'll complete this assignment in groups of three. I've already assigned each of you to a group, and I've already assigned a poem to each group. The names of the group members and the poems that have been assigned to each group are on the wall next to the door of the classroom. You should check the list before you leave class today. You should note who the other members of your group are and which poem your group will be studying. Tonight you should read your poem. Then, tomorrow in class, you'll have the time to meet with your group members to discuss your poem and begin planning your presentations.

The presentations will be on Friday. Each group presentation should be no longer than ten minutes. Eight groups will be giving presentations on Friday, so we should easily be able to finish eight presentations in the hour-and-a-half class on Friday.

Is the assignment clear to you? Find out who's in your group and which poem you'll be studying as you leave class today, read your poem tonight so that you'll be ready to discuss it tomorrow in class with your group, and then have your ten-minute group presentations ready for Friday.

That's all for today. See you tomorrow.

47. HOW WILL EACH STUDENT COMPLETE THE ASSIGNMENT?
48. HOW HAVE THE GROUPS BEEN SELECTED?
49. HOW MANY PRESENTATIONS WILL BE GIVEN ON FRIDAY?
50. WHAT WILL THE STUDENTS DO TOMORROW?

COMPLETE TEST THREE:
Listening Comprehension

Part A, p. 294

1. (man) I can't go skating. I don't know how.
   (woman) But it's so easy to learn.
   (narrator) WHAT DOES THE WOMAN SAY ABOUT SKATING?

2. (woman) What did you think of that literature class?
   (man) It wasn't exactly interesting.
   (narrator) WHAT DOES THE MAN SAY ABOUT THE CLASS?

3. (woman) The flight we wanted is full.
   (man) Let's take the train instead.
   (narrator) WHAT DOES THE MAN SUGGEST?

4. (man) Do we need to fix supper for the children?
   (woman) I already gave them their supper.
   (narrator) WHAT DOES THE WOMAN SAY ABOUT THE CHILDREN?

5. (woman) Did Sally go home over the holidays?
   (man) No, she remained on campus instead.
   (narrator) WHAT DOES THE MAN SAY ABOUT SALLY?

6. (man) What should I do for this sore throat and cough?
   (woman) I'm going to prescribe some medication, and then you should return to my office next week.
   (narrator) WHO IS THE WOMAN MOST LIKELY TO BE?

7. (woman) Are you going to buy that stereo system?
   (man) I don't think so. It's not cheap.
   (narrator) WHAT DOES THE MAN IMPLY?

8. (man) I just can't play that song very well.
   (woman) Try it over again from the beginning.
   (narrator) WHAT DOES THE WOMAN WANT THE MAN TO DO?

9. (man) I have the papers that you need.
   (woman) Could you please send them to me as soon as possible?
   (narrator) WHAT DOES THE WOMAN WANT THE MAN TO DO?

10. (woman) It's difficult to work and go to school at the same time.
    (man) You can say that again!
    (narrator) WHAT DOES THE MAN MEAN?

11. (woman) How much of your hair would you like me to cut?
    (man) Please take a little off the top and sides.
    (narrator) WHERE DOES THIS CONVERSATION PROBABLY TAKE PLACE?

12. (man) Eve, you look so cheerful today.
    (woman) I'm happy that it's not raining.
    (narrator) WHY DOES EVE LOOK CHEERFUL?

13. (woman) Can I just estimate my expenses?
    (man) No, your expenses must be listed precisely.
    (narrator) WHAT DOES THE MAN MEAN?

14. (man) Robin's new car certainly looks impressive.
    (woman) I'll say!
    (narrator) WHAT DOES THE WOMAN MEAN?

15. (woman) Have you noticed Wanda's desk?
    (man) Yes. It's always so messy.
    (narrator) WHAT DOES THE MAN MEAN?

16. (man) I need help finding these statistics for my report.
    (woman) Did you look in the reference section? That's where they should be.
    (narrator) WHO IS THE WOMAN MOST LIKELY TO BE?

17. (woman) I'm not very good with these new computer programs.
    (man) Why don't you take a computer class?
    (narrator) WHAT DOES THE MAN SUGGEST?

18. (woman) Could you get tickets for the concert?
    (man) I tried, but the ticket agency doesn't have any more tickets to sell.
    (narrator) WHAT DOES THE MAN MEAN?

19. (man)   What did Lou want to know?
    (woman)   He asked why I dropped out of school.
    (narrator)   WHAT DOES THE WOMAN SAY ABOUT LOU?

20. (man)   Were you able to get the package mailed?
    (woman)   I scarcely got to the post office before it closed.
    (narrator)   WHAT DOES THE WOMAN IMPLY?

21. (woman)   I can't believe you didn't apply for the position at the bank. Only this morning two new people were hired.
    (man)   I think I missed the boat.
    (narrator)   WHAT DOES THE MAN MEAN?

22. (man)   Do you think the lecture's going to start soon? If it doesn't, we're going to be here all day.
    (woman)   Your guess is as good as mine.
    (narrator)   WHAT DOES THE WOMAN MEAN?

23. (woman)   You're going to take five courses next semester? Don't you know a full program is only four?
    (man)   It's not unheard of, and I'm sure I can handle it.
    (narrator)   WHAT DOES THE MAN IMPLY?

24. (man)   A new family has just moved into the apartment across the hall.
    (woman)   Perhaps we should call on them a bit later.
    (narrator)   WHAT DOES THE WOMAN MEAN?

25. (woman)   I saw that the police officer stopped you. Did he give you a ticket?
    (man)   If he'd given me a ticket, I'd be a little unhappier.
    (narrator)   WHAT DOES THE MAN MEAN?

26. (man)   Do you mean to say you want to go dancing tonight after running in the race today?
    (woman)   You've hit the nail right on the head!
    (narrator)   WHAT DOES THE WOMAN SAY ABOUT THE MAN?

27. (woman)   I heard that you won the scholarship from the Music Department. Congratulations!
    (man)   No one was more surprised than I was.
    (narrator)   WHAT DOES THE MAN MEAN?

28. (woman)   The history exam's tomorrow, and I think it's going to be pretty hard.
    (man)   Oh, I guess I'll have to brush up on a few dates before then.
    (narrator)   WHAT DOES THE MAN MEAN?

29. (man)   What do you think of this suit? Does it look right for the wedding?
    (woman)   So you have decided to go!
    (narrator)   WHAT HAD THE WOMAN ASSUMED ABOUT THE MAN?

30. (woman)   What happened to you? You don't look so good.
    (man)   Well, I went skiing for the first time, and I wish I hadn't tried to learn how to ski on the steepest slope.
    (narrator)   WHAT DOES THE MAN IMPLY?

Part B, p. 296

Questions 31 through 34. Listen as two friends discuss an arts and crafts fair.

  (woman)   How would you like to go down to the park this afternoon?
  (man)   To the park? What's going on there? Would we just be walking around, or sitting and relaxing, or what?
  (woman)   There's a wonderful arts and crafts fair going on, so the park's going to be pretty crowded. We won't be able to relax, but we should see a great arts and crafts fair.
  (man)   An arts and crafts fair?
  (woman)   Yes, an arts and crafts fair. It's an annual event here, and it's really popular. Artists from around the area bring a lot of their artwork and crafts and display them in the park. You can just walk around and look at the crafts if you want, or you certainly can buy things that you like, or you can just "people watch."
  (man)   Oh, I don't know much about arts and crafts. What kinds of things will there be?
  (woman)   Oh, all kinds. Paintings, pottery, jewelry, woodworking, leather goods. All kinds.
  (man)   Which kind do you prefer?
  (woman)   I like all of it, but I guess I'll probably spend most of my time looking at jewelry. There are always handmade silver items and lots of interesting stones.
  (man)   Do you think you'll just be looking? Or are you going to take your wallet with you to the park?
  (woman)   Oh, I always start out just looking, but in the end I'm sure I'll need my wallet.

31. WHERE DOES THE ARTS AND CRAFTS FAIR TAKE PLACE?
32. HOW OFTEN DOES THIS ARTS AND CRAFTS FAIR TAKE PLACE?
33. WHAT WOULD PROBABLY NOT BE FOUND AT THE ARTS AND CRAFTS FAIR?
34. WHAT DOES THE WOMAN IMPLY THAT SHE'LL DO?

Questions 35 through 38. Listen as two students discuss a course.

(woman) Hi, Joe. I understand that you took Introduction to Physics last semester. Can you tell me about the course?

(man) Sure. The lecture or the lab?

(woman) You mean, there are both a lecture and a lab in this course?

(man) Actually, there are three lectures each week and one lab.

(woman) Do I have to take both the lecture and the lab? The lecture doesn't sound too bad to me, but I know I don't want to spend my time in the lab.

(man) Well, you're going to have to spend some time in the lab if you want to take physics. It's required that you take the two of them together in the same semester.

(woman) When do the lectures and lab sessions meet?

(man) The lectures are three times a week, on Monday, Wednesday, and Friday mornings for one hour each day. Then you must also take the lab, on either Tuesday or Thursday afternoon, from one o'clock to five o'clock.

(woman) For four hours? Does it really take four hours each week to complete the physics lab?

(man) (laughs) Oh, it usually takes more than four hours, and then you have to go home and write the lab report.

(woman) There's a lab report every week?

(man) Yes, indeed, usually about ten pages' worth.

(woman) A ten-page lab report every week in addition to more than four hours in the lab?

(man) Oh, and don't forget the lectures and all the reading assignments and exams.

(woman) This does not sound like a fun course to me.

(man) Interesting, maybe. But fun, no. And a lot of work, definitely.

35. WHY DOES THE WOMAN WANT TO TALK TO JOE?
36. HOW MANY LECTURES ARE THERE EACH WEEK?
37. HOW MANY HOURS IS THE LAB EACH WEEK?
38. HOW DOES THE MAN DESCRIBE THE COURSE?

Part C, p. 298

Questions 39 through 42. Listen as a professor discusses a term paper assignment.

(woman) That's the end of today's lecture. However, before you leave, I'd like to make sure that everything is clear about the term papers that you're working on. The term papers should be almost finished now. I hope you've been working hard on them for the last two months. I can assure you that it's quite clear to me when students try to do all the work on their term papers at the last moment.

There are two important things that I'm very strict about: (1) the due date and (2) the length of the paper.

The term papers are due next Tuesday, by five o'clock, without fail. I see some unhappy faces out there, but the deadline is absolute. You've had the assignment for two months, so I see no need to extend the deadline. I will not accept any papers after five o'clock Tuesday. And needless to say, you will receive a failing grade if the paper isn't turned in on time.

As far as the length is concerned, the papers should be ten to twelve pages long. This means that the papers should not be shorter than ten pages and should not be longer than twelve pages. Don't think that you can improve your grade on the term paper by turning in twenty or thirty pages.

Please be very careful about the length of your paper, and be sure to get it in on time.

39. WHEN DOES THE TALK TAKE PLACE?
40. HOW LONG SHOULD THE STUDENTS HAVE BEEN WORKING ON THEIR TERM PAPERS?
41. WHAT TIME ARE THE PAPERS DUE?
42. WHAT NUMBER OF PAGES IS NOT ACCEPTABLE?

Questions 43 through 46. Listen to a description of the job of smoke jumper.

(man) The Forest Service is the government agency that has the difficult job of fighting forest fires. One major problem in fighting forest fires is that forest fires often burn in areas where there're no roads, or inadequate roads, so it can be quite difficult to get workers and equipment into the area to fight the fire. A very specialized job has developed within the Forest Service as a result, and that job is the job of smoke jumper.

A smoke jumper is a firefighter who parachutes, or jumps, into an area where there's a forest fire. It's necessary to use smoke jumpers to fight a fire when the fire occurs in an area without roads. If there're no roads, the only way to get firefighters into an area quickly is for them to parachute in.

After the smoke jumpers parachute into an area around a forest fire, they work on the ground to fight the fire. They may spend several days fighting the fire, and they often have to work long hours without adequate heavy equipment to battle the fire. Then, when that work is done, the only way to get out is to walk. After days of fighting a fire, they may have to walk for hours and hours to get to the nearest road.

43. WHAT DO SMOKE JUMPERS DO?
44. HOW DO SMOKE JUMPERS GET TO FIRES?
45. WHEN MUST SMOKE JUMPERS BE USED TO FIGHT A FOREST FIRE?
46. WHAT DO THE SMOKE JUMPERS HAVE TO DO IMMEDIATELY AFTER THE FIRE IS OUT?

Questions 47 through 50. Listen to a lecture by a university professor.

(woman)   Everyone please take a seat because the lecture is about to start. The topic for today is glaciers, those huge blocks of ice that are found in the northernmost and southernmost parts of our world. Glaciers can be thousands and thousands of years old, and scientists are able to learn a lot by studying these ancient glaciers.

The first thing that scientists can determine when studying a glacier is its age. In fact, it's very easy for scientists to learn exactly how old a particular glacier is from the number of layers in the glacier. Scientists drill into the ice, and then they just count the layers in the glacier, and from this they can determine the glacier's age.

In addition to learning the ages of glaciers, scientists have also been able to learn a lot about the Earth's past by studying glaciers. For example, something that you might not have thought about is that glaciers can be used to determine a tremendous amount about volcanoes in the past. Sometimes, there's some volcanic dust in one layer of a glacier. By measuring where the volcanic dust occurs in the glacier and how much dust exists, scientists can determine how many years ago a volcano erupted on Earth and get an approximate idea of the strength of the volcano.

That's all for today. For the next class, you should read the next chapter in the textbook.

47. IN WHICH COURSE WOULD THIS LECTURE MOST PROBABLY BE GIVEN?
48. HOW DO SCIENTISTS DETERMINE THE AGE OF GLACIERS?
49. WHAT HAVE SCIENTISTS FOUND WITHIN GLACIERS?
50. WHAT SHOULD THE STUDENTS DO FOR THE NEXT CLASS?

APPENDIX A, p. 321

EXERCISE A1

1. The new lamp does not work.
2. There were holes in the road.
3. Sue leaped with joy.
4. I'm worried about being robbed.
5. This culture's lore is amazing.
6. He had an unbelievable leer on his face.
7. The boy was standing on the rail.
8. Sally is attracted by the lure of city life.
9. There is a row of low buildings.
10. The lane was filled with rain.
11. My friend lent me the money for rent.
12. There's no room for the loom.
13. They need to get rid of the lice.
14. We raced to the lake.
15. There are several robes on the rack.

EXERCISE A2

1. Tom tries to cheat at cards.
2. We need a sheaf of paper.
3. The gel is on the shelf.
4. I'm going to chop the tomatoes.
5. The chest was full of junk.
6. Jill suddenly felt a chill.
7. Sue hit her shin on a chair.
8. The jam is in a jar.
9. Tom choked on a chunk of food.
10. The ship is offshore.
11. Chet bought a cheap jeep.
12. It was only a joke; it was all in jest.
13. I've had my share of chips.
14. I need to jot a note on a sheet of paper.
15. It was a chore to shear the sheep.

EXERCISE A3

1. Pam placed a pan under the fan.
2. The pile of trash has a vile smell.
3. Sometimes he's a pest, but he's my best pal.
4. The veal was a good buy.
5. Chet took his pet to the vet.
6. We have a great view of the vast area.
7. The van had to veer to avoid being hit.
8. The pew was made of fine pine.
9. Vera could feel the veil on her face.
10. Frank had a fat file filled with documents.
11. The ban on bets is the bane of her existence.
12. The pace of the race was too fast for all but a few.
13. We tried to bail with a pail, but we failed.
14. Suddenly a bat flew past her face.
15. The berry pie was the very best.

EXERCISE A4

1. He took a seat on the movie set.
2. I feel bad because I fell.
3. Peter picked a peck of peppers.
4. The teen was out until ten.
5. He has a pit bull for a pet.
6. I made a bet that my team would beat the other.
7. We got rid of the red chair.
8. Dave is dead because of his bad deed.
9. It's neat that she can knit.
10. The dean heard the din in the den.

EXERCISE A5

1. There's too much water in the dam.
2. Lee offered a lame excuse for his actions.
3. The fish took a bite of the bait.
4. The pane was edged in pine.
5. You might look under the mat.
6. Kate was playing with the kite.
7. It was her fate to be involved in the fight.
8. He tried in vain to stop the blood flowing from his vein.
9. I hate the height that the hat gives you.
10. The man works in the main mine.

EXERCISE A6

1. The sun will come out soon.
2. The pole was in the pool.
3. The oil boom was a boon for the town.
4. He can't find the boot, but he's looking.
5. He coped with being cooped up.
6. I am not in the mood to play in the mud.
7. The root caused a rut in the road.
8. They roam the room looking for rum.
9. The nun who was known arrived at noon.
10. The dumb idea to add a dome to the building is doomed.

EXERCISE A7

1. Tom told a tall tale about the team.
2. Mae enjoyed the sun's rays as she lay on the sand.
3. It's really rare for Ron to get so riled.
4. We want to get rid of the pests who are making a din.
5. I leaned on the rail of the ferry as it crossed the lake.
6. Mike read in bed and jotted down a few notes.
7. I'm going to vie for first place in the race.
8. I had to bail my friend out of jail when he failed to pay the fine.
9. You need to heed the dean's advice and respect the ban on beer.
10. Please sit in the closest seat and set the box on the mat in the rear of the room.
11. Pete peered out the window, where he had a view of a few boats on the bay.
12. The fans let out a roar when the ball hit the bat.
13. At the shore, he picked up some seashells and watched the ships pass by.
14. The crowd booed and jeered at the terrible joke.
15. Steve had a plate of raw vegetables and chips in his lap. When the plate landed on the floor, he had a really sheepish grin on his face.